TIGER HEAD, SNAKE TAILS

CHINA TODAY, HOW IT GOT THERE AND WHY IT HAS TO CHANGE

JONATHAN FENBY

**SIMON &
SCHUSTER**

London · New York · Sydney · Toronto · New Delhi

A CBS COMPANY

First published in Great Britain by Simon & Schuster UK Ltd, 2012
This paperback edition published in 2013
A CBS COMPANY

1 3 5 7 9 10 8 6 4 2

Simon & Schuster UK Ltd
1st Floor
222 Gray's Inn Road
London WC1X 8HB

www.simonandschuster.co.uk

Simon & Schuster Australia, Sydney
Simon & Schuster India, New Delhi

A CIP catalogue record for this book
is available from the British Library

ISBN: 978-1-84739-411-8
Ebook ISBN: 978-1-4711-2832-5

Typeset in the UK by M Rules
Printed and bound by CPI Group (UK) Ltd, Croydon, CR0 4YY

With love once again
to Renée,
without whom . . .

CONTENTS

A NOTE ON NAMES

In Chinese names the surname comes first followed by the given name: so Hu Jintao was President Hu and Wen Jiabao was Prime Minister Wen. I have used the *pinyin* system of transliteration (for example, Mao Zedong) except for those names better known by the older system (such as Chiang Kai-shek) and for Taiwanese names, for which the older system is commonly used.

PREFACE

I should preface this book by saying what it is not intended to be. It is not written primarily for China experts, though I hope that they may find interest in its analysis and conclusions. Nor is it intended to compete with the stream of fine works of recent years on subjects ranging from the Communist Party to village life, from women factory workers to the Great Famine under Mao Zedong. Nor is it another polemic arguing that China will either rule the globe or implode. My aim, rather, is to provide a one-stop account of where the fastest-growing major nation stands and what that will mean both for China and the world in which it looms so large.

With a wholesale change in the Chinese leadership starting in the autumn of 2012 this seems an apposite time at which to take stock – three decades after China began to amaze the world, just as Napoleon (nearly two centuries earlier) apparently predicted it would. It is dangerous to identify any country as unique, but China has an excellent claim to that status. And there is, to my knowledge, no single book bringing together the political, economic, social, regional and demographic elements which constitute that uniqueness. Only by linking them can one hope to get an idea of what this nation is and where it is heading. Everything connects with everything else everywhere, but nowhere more so than in China because of the nature of the system. So identifying and pulling together the strands is vital to understanding what determines the evolution of this massive state that now has such a huge global influence.

I have been observing China for some seventeen years from both outside and within – first as editor of the *South China Morning Post* and, most recently, as head of the China team at Trusted Sources, the emerging markets research service, with the help of my valued colleagues. This book is based on my experience and analysis during that time of its

TIGER HEAD, SNAKE TAILS

political, economic and social developments, from changes in the Politburo to the situation in agriculture, from currency policy to social conditions.

Sweeping judgements on China, positive or negative, make for snappy headlines and striking book titles, but they rarely accord with reality. The more I delve into China, the more convinced I am that the essential element in seeking to understand the country is to try to grasp the complexity behind its apparently unified state, culture and behaviour patterns claimed from antiquity. The Great Wall was never quite what it seemed and was a poor defence against those determined to challenge Chinese certainties. So it is today with the apparent monolith that seems destined to eat everybody else's breakfast, lunch and dinner. This book's title is an adaptation of a Chinese phrase with various shades of meaning, from which I have chosen the one that best suits my purpose. It is meant to suggest that one has to take into account not just the China that hits the headlines, or the top-line economic statistics or the straight-line projections to a future that may or not come to pass, but also a host of down-to-earth factors which actually determine how the country functions and where it is going. That is what this book seeks to do.

Jonathan Fenby, 2013

KEY ECONOMIC CHARTS
AND CURRENCY RATES

GDP 1970–2010

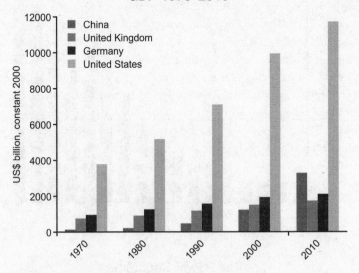

China's Real GDP 1978–2012

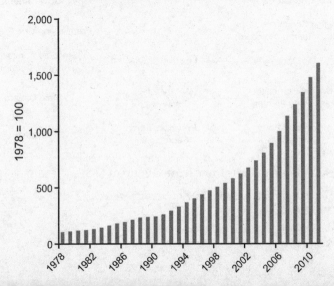

China's Trade 1996–2012

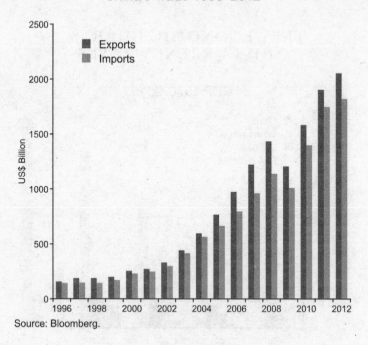

Source: Bloomberg.

The Power Structure

Communist Party	Government
Standing Committee of the Political Bureau (Politburo)	Premier and Vice Premiers
Politburo ———— Leading Groups	Standing Committee of State Council
Central Committee and Party Plenum / Military Affairs Commission	State Council
Provincial Party Congresses / Provincial Party Secretaries	Ministries

These and other charts from Trusted Sources (TS).

The exchange rates at the time of writing were:
£1 = 9.8 yuan
$1 = 6.2 yuan
€1 = 8.4 yuan

1

NEVER BEFORE

China's explosive rise arouses shock and awe, a catalogue of material achievements garlanded with superlatives as the Middle Kingdom wrenched itself from more than a century of decline to become the great global game-changer of our time, pulling more people out of poverty in a shorter space of time than ever before in human history.

Since the launch of market reform in 1978, indelibly linked to the doughty survivor Deng Xiaoping, the world's most populous nation has regained its status and pride and is forecast to house the largest economy on earth by 2016. But, spectacular as the progress of the last three-and-a-half decades has been, the last major state ruled by a Communist Party faces a huge set of challenges to its political, economic and social system that its leaders are ill-adapted to deal with. The regime that has presided over the nation's material renaissance is now confronted with problems that reach beyond its mindset. The impressive tiger head has to deal with an array of writhing snake tails, and the outcome is of vital importance not simply for itself but for the world at large.

At first sight, the People's Republic of China (PRC) may seem the inevitable winner of the twenty-first century. It is the world's biggest manufacturer, exporter and builder of infrastructure. It is the largest maker of steel and the biggest user of energy, with demand surging by 220 per cent since the start of this century compared with a global increase of 20 per cent. As the international economy faltered in 2011, the cry went up 'Will China save the world?' Emerging from a summit to try to rescue the euro-zone, President Sarkozy of France immediately telephoned Beijing to seek help, which was not forthcoming.

China's trade surplus in 2012 hit $231 billion, 50 per cent up on 2011. If they were nation states, six of its thirty-one provinces, municipalities and regions would rank among the world's thirty-two largest countries in terms of purchasing power. Shanghai is on a par with Saudi Arabia, Shandong and Jiangsu each the equivalents of Switzerland. The country's size and huge population (five of its provinces have more inhabitants than do Western Europe's five most populous nations) mean that it does everything on a massive scale that breeds shock and awe. The taste of its rulers for the gigantic dates back to the great edifices put up by the First Emperor, Qin Shi Huangdi (who ruled from 221–210 BC).

This is not simply a matter of material progress. Growth is also designed to deliver a political message. Qin was asserting himself as the unifying ruler after centuries of civil war. Mao put more than a million people to work on the expansion of Tiananmen Square until it was bigger than Red Square in Moscow, and had the Great Hall of the People built with a meeting space capable of accommodating 10,000 people to show that the People's Republic would not be dwarfed by the other great Communist power. Today, enormous infrastructure projects drive home the twin messages that China is back as a major global player and that its Communist Party (CCP), which has held power since 1949, is the only organization capable of achieving the growth the country needs, by developing the world's longest high-speed train network on earth, the longest sea bridge (across Jiaozhou Bay in Shandong), and Beijing Capital International Airport, the second-busiest on the planet with a terminal that ranks as the world's third-largest building. The economy and politics, both domestic and external, are inextricably linked. When things go well, that benefits both. When there are problems, both suffer.

Growth and modernization have transformed society and demographics. Average annual per capita income soared from 528 yuan at the start of the economic-reform process in the early 1980s to 19,100 in urban areas and 5,900 in the countryside at the end of the first decade of the twenty-first century. The aim is to double that between 2012 and 2020. Rising wealth, however unevenly distributed, has spawned materialism – as epitomized by the young woman on a television dating show who said it was better to 'cry in the back of a BMW than laugh on the back of a bicycle'. In the mid-1960s, as Mao – hailed as China's Great Helmsman – prepared to launch the Cultural Revolution, 18 per cent of the population lived in cities and the proportion was still just 21 per cent in the early 1980s; today more than half the Chinese are urban dwellers. The PRC is forecast to have 219 cities with more than a million inhabitants by 2025 (compared to 35 in Europe) and two dozen of those centres will house more than five million people. The plan is to increase the urban population to 70 per cent of the total by 2035 – one billion people.

Air travel, multi-lane highways and high-speed trains have overcome the natural barriers of distance, mountains and deserts. China has shared to the full in the revolution of modern communications despite the censors. Its demography has changed dramatically. Infant mortality has fallen by a factor of six since the 1960s but the birth rate is one-third of what it was in 1964, while the slice of the population aged over sixty-five has doubled to 9 per cent.[1]

The People's Republic plays a pivotal role in the global supply chain, assembling goods for foreign firms at prices they could not achieve at home. It has the largest monetary reserves of any country, topping $3.2 trillion. Its cheap labour, cheap capital, productivity and sheer competitiveness have exported price deflation to the globe while its voracious appetite for raw materials laps up oil from Africa, the Middle East and Latin America, iron ore from Brazil, coal and more ore from Australia, timber from Russia, energy from Canada and key metals from wherever they are mined. It was the prime force behind the 'super-cycle' in hard commodities at the start of this century. It accounts for between 37 and 45 per cent of global demand for nickel, tin, lead, zinc, aluminium and lead, and for 38 per cent of copper consumption, leading a consultancy to reckon that its requirements in twenty-five years' time will amount to more than all the copper mined in the world today. Chinese demand for metal has incentivized thieves in British cities to make off with drain covers to sell as scrap; I was once advised that my train to Edinburgh was running slow because copper track cabling had been stripped off by 'criminals who are sending it to China'.[2]

The size of the PRC's demand affects global markets in a way never seen before, depressing world prices when the government supplies industry from its substantial reserves to cushion the effect of high prices. When it starts buying to replenish those reserves, miners can smile again. At a time of slow growth in the West and Japan the PRC has thus become the determinant of demand-driven price levels for the materials needed for industry and construction globally. Forecasting Chinese demand is a preoccupation of commodity traders. Materials China wants enjoy sudden surges in demand – its building boom trebled the price of sludge from beaches in Africa and Australia used for pigments in paint in six months in 2010. As if this was not enough, mainland demand for imported commodities is the main influence on bulk-cargo shipping rates; at a peak of buying in 2008 the rush to bring in raw materials from Australia, Latin America and elsewhere sent the daily cost for using the largest bulk ships to an unprecedented $234,000 a day, affecting the cost of moving cargoes anywhere in the world.

In other ways, too, China has joined the world with a vengeance. The PRC lends more than the World Bank to developing nations. It is the largest emitter of CO_2 gases. Greenpeace estimates that its power plants produce enough toxic ash to fill one Olympic-size swimming pool every two-and-a-half minutes. Sixty-five million Chinese travel abroad each year. Mainlanders make up the biggest proportion of foreign students in the US and contribute significantly to the revenue of British universities. The Chinese are such assiduous shoppers that some shops in Paris limit the number of goods they are permitted to buy. Stores in London and Paris have installed Chinese-bank cash distributors. Chinese taste for Clarks shoes has turned the small town where the brand used to be made into a Mecca for visitors to England, even though the footwear is made elsewhere.

The flow goes the other way too. Western singers from Beyoncé to Bob Dylan play sell-out concerts and 2011 saw the first Chinese-language adaptation of a Western musical, *Mamma Mia!* China's demand underpins the price of European luxury goods, fine French claret and advanced German machinery. But it is China that manufactures 65 per cent of the world's toy exports and supplies between 40 and 50 per cent of garments worn in America and Europe including uniforms for the US Olympic team in 2012. It has three of the nine biggest banks in the world by capitalization. Its largest insurance company is worth some $130 billion and its second $66 billion. Its spectacular recovery from a short downturn in 2008–2009 made it the main hope for global growth in the second decade of this century as it boosted its quarterly growth rate from 6.1 per cent to 8.5 and then on into double digits.

However, that triumphal story comes with more than its fair share of negatives and reservations, which will run through this book. On taking up the country's top job, General Secretary of the Communist Party, the new leader, Xi Jinping, spoke of how the Chinese people 'yearn for better education, stable jobs, more satisfactory income, greater social security, improved medical and healthcare'. The dramatic fall of the rising political star Bo Xilai earlier in the year showed the cracks in the regime's unity and the Party Congress that installed Xi in November 2012 demonstrated the strength of conservatism. The environment remains in crisis. Social tension is rising. Xi and his predecessor, Hu Jintao, have both warned of the corrosive effect of corruption.

Even the core of China's renaissance, its economy, is open to serious question. Hu acknowledged 'problems of imbalance, lack of coordination and unsustainability in development' while the outgoing Prime Minister, Wen Jiabao, called the economy unstable, unsustainable, unbalanced and uncoordinated. By 2012, the official expansion figure had slowed from double digits to 7.5 per cent. This was still impressive by Western or Japanese standards, but there was a clear requirement to rebalance the model to boost consumption, reduce reliance on investment and exports, and move up the value chain. China needs structural reforms to land ownership, the labour system, the financial sector, and water and energy pricing. State-owned enterprises are too powerful; private enterprise is too squeezed and exposed. But such changes would involve significant political cost while cutting growth and increasing inflation short-term. So the inclination has been to put them off in the hope that the PRC can continue to grow without taking the risks of reform. That is likely to be a vain and dangerous hope as pressures rise on all sides.[3]

The World Economic Forum ranks China twenty-seventh in terms of competitiveness. For ease of doing business the World Bank puts the PRC at 79 out of 183 countries. The annual index of economic freedom drawn up by the Heritage Foundation and the *Wall Street Journal* places China at 135 of 179 nations. A survey by the Harvard Business Review in 2013 placed only three Chinese chief executives among the top 100 worldwide in terms of achieving growth for their firms.

The imbalances are evident and, this being China, big-scale. The tiger's head of China's renaissance faces the world, but the snake tails of problems closer to the ground are ever present. The premium put on crude GDP numbers has led to a forest of distortions, particularly because growth is the main determinant in promotion for officials. Ironically for a nation run by a Communist party – and counter-intuitively for a state with a population the size of China's – capital has benefited more than labour from the expansion of recent decades as the increase in personal income has lagged behind that of the general economy. Low state-set interest rates have favoured public sector companies and penalized households. Wide spreads between deposit and lending rates mean that savers pay to strengthen the balance sheets of the big state banks. Fixed-asset investment in infrastructure and construction is too high relative to the rest of the economy, accounting for more than half the growth recorded in 2010 and equivalent to 70 per cent of GDP – twice the scale reached in Japan at the height of its construction boom in the 1980s. The credit unleashed to restore growth in 2009–10 will lead to a mountain of bad debts, increasing by 60 per cent the ratio of debt to national output in five years. Private firms have to depend on 'shadow banking', which rose by 33 per cent in 2012.

Chinese productivity has advanced rapidly but is still far below that of the US and has to grow fast to absorb rising costs and face competition from even-cheaper manufacturing nations. Artificially low, subsidized rates for water and energy result in large-scale waste of two resources of which China is short. Excess capacity is rife, at around 28 per cent in steel, 33 per cent in aluminium and 22 per cent in cement. Though exports of Chinese cars hit the million mark in 2012 (from only 22,000 ten years earlier), vehicle makers are likely to have 20 per cent too much plant by the middle of this decade, according to the KPMG service firm. The 26.4-mile bridge across Jiaozhou Bay in Shandong is not due to reach capacity traffic till 2028. Headlong expansion in hotels means only 60 per cent occupancy, at big chains.[4]

The currency has been kept controversially undervalued. State monopolies and oligopolies abound. Corruption infests the system; 146,000 CCP members were sanctioned for graft in 2010 and a survey of international business people by Transparency International put China among the nations perceived to be the most corrupt. Business is shot through with favours. Though less of a casino than it once was, the stock market does not reflect the real economy. Credit is regulated administratively with loan quotas set by the central authorities. Implementation of government decisions is spotty. The PRC has an adequate legal framework to protect intellectual property from piracy; the trouble is that it is not put into practice.

The falling number of births and greater lifespan of the population threaten the 'demographic dividend' of a young workforce that has helped to underpin growth – so will the PRC grow old before it grows rich? Ecological degradation is widespread and extremely serious; China grapples with major problems of air and land pollution, water shortages and desertification. But environmental offices are part of local governments that have an interest in polluting factories or do not want to impose restrictions which would hurt the growth figures they report. Those same local governments are often deeply in debt and depend for their revenue on selling state-owned land grabbed from farmers: in just one decade they have displaced 40 million people from their homes.

There are estimated to be some 180,000 popular protests a year on matters ranging from official malfeasance and land grabs to fuel prices and lead poisoning. Wealth disparities yawn. Forty per cent of privately held national wealth is estimated to be in the hands of 1 per cent of the population. Thirteen per cent of Chinese live on less than $1.5 a day. More than 200 million Chinese are still what the United Nations defines as relatively poor and more than 20 million live in absolute poverty. At the other end of the wealth scale, nearly one million people are reported to have personal wealth exceeding 10 million yuan (making them dollar millionaires). 271 were ranked as dollar billionaires in 2011, though concealed wealth may make the real number considerably higher. The way that families of the powerful can do very well indeed was shown by an investigation by Bloomberg in the summer of 2012 that reported relatives of the coming leader Xi Jinping had substantial investments in firms with assets of $376 million. A similar exercise by the *New York Times* later that year reported that relatives of outgoing Premier, Wen Jiabao, had built up assets of $2.7 billion (£1.67 billion) – the Foreign Ministry accused the newspaper of 'blackening China's name' from ulterior motives.

Regulation is poor. Scandals erupt regularly about food containing dangerous additives or just plain nasty stuff. Health problems are pervasive; government spending on medical services accounts for only 2.7 per cent of GDP (compared to 16 per cent in the US and 8.4 per cent in the UK). The incidence of breast cancer is increasing by 6 per cent a year, 50 per cent above the global average. Two hundred thousand people are estimated to suffer from syphilis. A national survey in 2010 reported that 40 per cent of Chinese aged between thirty-five and forty-four had periodontal gum disease and that 80 per cent had bleeding gums. Some 92 million Chinese suffer diabetes, 27 per cent of the world total. The number of reported deaths from AIDS rose from 7,743 in 2010 to 14,000 in the first ten months of 2011, many of them from contaminated blood. The increase in life expectancy since 1981 has actually been lower than in countries starting from the same base such as Mexico, Malaysia and Columbia. Material growth has fractured the 'iron rice-bowl' of Maoist cradle-to-grave (albeit poor-quality) protection and people are worried: a national survey published in Communist Party media reports that 73.5 per cent of respondents feel 'vulnerable'.

The political system is stuck in a one-party straitjacket under a leadership that claims to be the fount of all wisdom in the line of imperial dynasties of the past. Official lies often trump awkward truths. The historical record is distorted. Foreign relations are scratchy and ill thought-out. The People's Republic that gained control of the mainland of China in 1949 still insists on its right to recover the 'renegade province' of Taiwan off the east coast by force if necessary and has more than 1,000 missiles pointing across the ninety-mile Taiwan Strait. Chinese army and police impose control over Tibet and the vast Muslim territory of Xinjiang on the border with Central Asia; in Tibet some patrol with fire extinguishers after a wave of self-immolation by Buddhist monks protesting at Chinese rule.

As throughout its history, China is ruled by man – now in the form of the Communist Party, to which the Justice Ministry ordered judges in 2012 to swear a loyalty oath. When as high a figure as the Prime Minister spoke of the need for political and legal reform he was slapped down by the Party and the censor told websites not to report his remarks to CNN. Deaths in custody from beating or neglect are shuffled under the carpet – a newspaper in the city of Hangzhou published a list of unnatural fatalities of people in jail that included 'death from sleeping in an improper position', 'death from picking at acne' and 'death from face-washing'. A manual on how to deal with troublemakers advises taking care to ensure that no blood is left on their faces or visible wounds on their bodies and that there were no witnesses in the vicinity. Lawlessness often begins with the law enforcement agencies themselves.

Those who express disagreement with the regime are ruthlessly persecuted. The dissident who went on to win the Nobel Peace Prize of 2010 was sent to jail for eleven years for advocating democracy. Human-rights lawyers disappear for weeks or months and are told to say nothing about their experiences in custody, but still some do speak and report having been tortured. A teacher who campaigned on behalf of the parents of children buried alive by shoddy school buildings in the 2008 earthquake in Sichuan was sent for a year of 'reform through labour' without trial. Petitioners who follow the traditional route of going to Beijing to seek justice from the central authorities after being oppressed by local officials may find themselves locked up by thuggish private-security men in 'black jails' before being shipped back home; these establishments are run as private businesses and charge the authorities 150–300 yuan a day per detainee, of which there are estimated to be 10,000 a year.

Safety scandals affect everything from unregulated coal mines to untrained airline pilots. The museum in the Forbidden City in Beijing, which in peak periods has 80,000 visitors a day, has been hit by a string of snafus. These range from the breakage of a 1,000-year-old plate, the loss of 100 ancient books and the failure to eradicate termites in the woodwork to allegations that it has sold Song dynasty letters and the theft of valuable old powder-compacts loaned by a Hong Kong collector – not to mention a critical report from a UNESCO World Heritage committee and an accusation of ticket-receipt tax evasion. When reports spread that a renovated section closed to the public was to become an elite club with a 1-million yuan membership fee, the museum denied the story as 'pure nonsense'; then photographs circulated on the Internet of the club's opening ceremony.[5]

This is symptomatic of the trust deficit that runs through mainland China. As goes a saying: you can believe something only when the authorities deny it. The initial official reaction to the first crash of a high-speed train, in July 2011 – which killed at least thirty-nine people and raised serious questions about the breakneck pace of expansion – reeked of a cover-up: there was widespread suspicion that the reported death toll was set in order to avoid the more thorough investigations applied to disasters resulting in forty or more fatalities. An editorial in the main Communist Party newspaper, *People's Daily*, warned of a 'crisis of faith' between officials and citizens which could affect 'the development, harmony and stability of society'. A collection of the blunt comments made by Premier Zhu Rongji in the 1990s about China's problems became an instant bestseller when it appeared in 2011 – here was a man who had spoken the truth about substandard construction, bankers who were 'accomplices' in crime and a regime that might owe its people an apology.

One major question addressed by this book is how the constraints of the system can cope with a fast-changing and increasingly multifaceted society. So far the CCP has managed to maintain itself in monopoly power by delivering material progress: it has used this to legitimize its rule, using economic growth for a political purpose to reinforce the regime. But keeping this up is a challenge that grows steadily more difficult each year, breeding complexities and contradictions that may be insoluble – particularly for a leadership so wedded to the political status quo at a time when society is mutating so broadly and so fast.

For the first time, China has evolved a middle class and is developing a commuter society in places like the belt between Shanghai and Suzhou or the outlying suburbs of Beijing. Many of the country's most successful people, as well as those seeking to ascend the ladder, lead complex lives in which they balance individual achievement and aspiration with the confines of the political straitjacket, the absence of an objective legal system and the difficulty of knowing who or what to believe. Those who game the system and have the right web of contacts enjoy enormous mobility and may move cash abroad to safer domains. But, at the same time, heredity is asserting itself as a group of 'princelings' – children and grandchildren of the First Generation of Communist leaders such as Xi Jinping – take on leadership in politics and business and use their connections to amass power and money.

'Red capitalists' prosper from their inside track and – however dynamic they may be in their business activities – oppose political change that could undermine their privileged position. Some see the dangers in this as China's new elite chooses not to advocate the kind of gradual power-sharing that enabled the British aristocracy to survive for so long. Comparisons can be drawn with the way in which closed-in elites, pervasive corruption and strong power groups undermined dynasties. 'When the eunuchs are running the country then the dynasty is nearing its end,' one member of a top family remarked to Jamil Anderlini of the *Financial Times* in 2011.[6]

The appeal of the status quo is nonetheless enormous to those who benefit most from it. Newspapers write of 3,000 families controlling assets of 1.7 trillion yuan, meaning that their average riches amount to the equivalent of £54 million or $82 million each. A poll published by *People's Forum* magazine in 2010 found that 91 per cent of those questioned thought that 'the newly rich have benefited from networking with government officials' and that 69 per cent of participants had a bad impression of rich families. One study for Credit Suisse put undeclared 'grey income' at ten trillion yuan, or 30 per cent of GDP. If you are wealthy people assume you must be corrupt, a leading property developer lamented. Will those who have gained so much be ready to cede at least some of their advantages or, as seems likely, is the People's Republic set for conflict between those who have a great deal and the far larger number of people who feel they do not have enough?[7]

In short, this is far from the finely ordered society imagined by some admirers in the West. The men at the summit of power are aware of at least some of the problems they face. Hu Jintao proclaimed the need to build a 'harmonious society' in which people are more equal and to fight 'power abuse'. Both he and his successor, Xi Jinping, have been critical of the Party for being too distant from the people and too bureaucratized and corrupt. The CCP issues instructions against the 'marriage of power and money' and recognizes that it needs to rejuvenate itself and improve the quality of its cadres. But it continues to concentrate power for itself in a pyramid system that grants supreme authority without election to the elite – like Hu before him, Xi is not only the General Secretary of the monopoly party but also State President and Chair of the Military Commission that runs the armed forces. Change is stifled by the choking effect of a regime intent above all on self-preservation.

The PRC's surge of the last three decades and its emergence on to the world scene has had a greater impact than any other development since the end of the Cold War, creating a set of unique circumstances for our time and straining the international system in the process – as the Chairman of a major Chinese bank puts it: 'You can't keep a big fish in a washbasin.'

When China overtakes the United States, the world's biggest economy will no longer belong to the most domestically prosperous nation on earth or to a democracy. The PRC's rise has become a commonplace of world affairs with attendant fears of lost jobs and markets invaded by the seemingly unstoppable wave of Chinese goods – a theme of the 2012 US presidential contest. Ministries round the globe flounder as they try to reconcile economic partnership and profound differences in values. Washington seeks to forge a working relationship while hedging its bets in case something goes horribly wrong. Consumers internationally have become used to cheap Chinese goods that have kept down inflation while the US has relied on low-interest loans from the PRC to lower the cost of borrowing and help to fund the federal deficit. For many governments the platitude of 'constructive engagement' hides a desire not to have to make a choice where China is concerned; to profit from its economic growth while avoiding confrontation over human rights or Tibet. One may sympathize with them given the novelty of the situation provoked by China's rise but their ambiguity is, by its nature, a frailty.

The global commentariat is sharply divided. Sinomania and Sinophobia go hand in hand. For some, China is a welcome corrective to US leadership; for others it is a ruthless mercantilist power set on global domination, a twenty-first-century equivalent of imperial Germany. For some, it has evolved a new economic, social and political system that will see off Western democracy; for others, it is the latest exercise in mass tyranny founded on repression, unfair business practices, an undervalued currency and rampant counterfeiting and copying of foreign products. For some, the rise of the PRC means that it is bound to become top global dog; for others, it is heading for perdition amid exploding bubbles and an unsustainable system.

At a time of government blockages in the West, the supposed efficiency of the 'Chinese model' holds considerable appeal to those admirers of China who see its leaders making 'rational decisions that balance the needs of all citizens over the long term', as the *Economist* put it. The financial woes of the United States and European Union since 2008 have given the PRC added lustre. The political scientists Francis Fukuyama and Nancy Birdsell believe that China can 'avoid the delays of a messy democratic process' because the bureaucracy at its upper levels 'is capable of managing and coordinating sophisticated policies'. For financier George Soros, China has 'not only a more vigorous economy, but actually a better-functioning government than the United States'. The author and *New York Times* columnist Thomas Friedman has argued that a one-party autocracy 'led by a reasonably enlightened group of people, as China is today [...] can also have great advantages. That one party can just impose the politically difficult but critically important policies needed to move a society forward in the twenty-first century.' The Chinese economist David Daokui Li, who frequently appears at international gatherings, argues that his country's economic emergence 'is showcasing a new model of economic growth and interaction between China and the rest of the world'. Others claim that the PRC is run by a singularly enlightened meritocracy that puts Western democracies to shame.

On a trip to the PRC in 2010 the historian Niall Ferguson, who has argued that the twenty-first century belongs to China, found that the refrain of 'We are the masters now' kept running through his brain. He imagined President Obama seeing a thought bubble with those words over the head of Hu Jintao when they met. Stephen Roach of Morgan Stanley argues that 'Unlike the West, where the very concept of strategy has become an oxymoron, China has embraced a transitional framework aimed at resolving its sustainability constraints. Moreover, unlike the West, which is trapped in a dysfunctional political quagmire, China has both the commitment and the wherewithal to deliver on that strategy.' The title of a book published in 2009 by the British writer Martin Jacques was unequivocal – *When China Rules the World*.

There is an equally convinced troop on the other side who adduce a range of reasons why China will not rise to global domination. Indeed, having made a trip round China in 2011 during which he was struck by the extent of the country's property bubble and the size of its bank loans, Professor Ferguson came to wonder whether China was premature in 'gloating at our misfortunes' and might be heading for a collapse of its own. The eminent historian Roderick MacFarquhar argues with impeccable logic that China is sitting on a political and social San Andreas Fault that must someday open. The esteemed political scientist Minxin Pei sees China in a 'trapped transition' while the commentator Fareed

Zakaria of *Time* magazine regards it as ideologically and operationally ill-prepared for the new era it is entering. While Henry Kissinger makes plain in his book *On China* that he rates the Chinese as partners worthy of him, at a debate in 2011 he noted that 'they will have a huge demographic problem [...] so one shouldn't project a straight line in which China emerges as totally dominant.'

When it comes to the economy, some regard China's economic rise as an unstoppable factor of global existence. As he forecast 12 per cent growth for 2010, Jim O'Neill, then the chief economist at Goldman Sachs, threw an arm in the air in the victory sign of champion sprinter Usain Bolt and added 'and then the sky's the limit'. Arvind Subramanian, former IMF official and Senior Fellow at the Peterson Institute in the US, sees the world 'living in the shadow of China's economic dominance' with the PRC using its muscle to force the US to withdraw its naval forces from the Asian side of the Pacific Ocean.

For pessimists China bears ominous similarities with the seemingly all-conquering Japan of the 1980s, which then suffered the bursting of its asset bubble leading to the 'lost decades' starting in the 1990s. At best, for those pessimists, it will find itself in the 'middle-income trap' whereby growth stalls and the country lags far behind the United States. Critics point to the misallocation of capital and the growth of non-performing bank loans, and to corruption and infrastructure projects that will never earn an economic return. In the title of one of his books the American writer Gordon Chang has been forecasting *The Coming Collapse of China* for more than a decade. The prominent hedge-fund manager Jim Chanos insists that the PRC is on 'a treadmill to Hell'. The British commentator Will Hutton posits that the weak institutional framework and the lack of Enlightenment values will halt progress. For economist Nouriel Roubini, who forecast the sub-prime crash, the PRC is on a dangerous economic-growth path that can lead it only to trouble some time between 2013 and 2015 as the outcome of 'immense over-capacity and a staggering non-performing loan problem'. Another sceptical economist, Edward Chancellor, portrays the country as caught in a classic constellation of bubbles. A poll of global investors by Bloomberg in 2011 reported that 40–45 per cent expected a financial crisis in China; only 7 per cent thought the PRC could escape turmoil.

Another survey by the same service in the autumn of 2011 found 59 per cent of those replying expecting that the PRC's annual growth would drop to below 5 per cent by 2016 – 12 per cent expected that to happen within a year.[8]

While Wen Jiabao claimed that, thanks to socialism, China is able 'to make decisions efficiently, organize effectively and concentrate resources to accomplish large undertakings', Hu Jintao warned that the CCP is 'now faced with many new developments, problems and challenges'. At a conference in Beijing at the end of 2010 the audience rose to its feet to applaud a professor who insisted on the perils that lay ahead should the system not be thoroughly reformed. China's best-known international artist, Ai Weiwei, who was arrested for 'economic crimes' in 2011, has compared his nation to 'a runner sprinting very fast – but it has a heart condition.' Prominent academic Yu Yongding warns of the threat from rising social tensions, pollution, lack of public services and reliance on exports and property development to fuel growth. The pattern, he says, 'has now almost exhausted its potential and without painful structural adjustments the momentum of economic growth could suddenly be lost.' Professor Zhang Weiying of Peking University notes how rarely China hits its targets; he argues that stimulus spending cannot buy development and calls the central planners 'a bunch of smart people doing something really stupid'.

What are we to make of such diversity of opinion? Simply that China is an extremely complex, multifaceted nation. There is no single reality but, since the PRC holds such a central place in discussions of the future of the world, commentators feel a need to hold forth as if there was. Though many of the aforementioned opinions make sense in their own terms, the weakness of most sweeping verdicts is that they ignore facts that point in the opposite direction, or take a Western view of today's China, or have highly elastic timeframes that render them virtually meaningless. Be it positive or negative, the hedgehogs, in Isaiah Berlin's classification of those who held One Big Idea, make the running as soothsayers. Better to approach China as would Berlin's foxes, who know many things, and try to get the measure of a country that is as unique as it is varied, and whose rise since the 1980s is sui generis. Or, to take the title of this book, one has to observe the many snake tails below the great head of the tiger.

That said, China faces the world with a unique set of new factors. Never before has a country in which up to 300 million people do not have access to clean drinking water competed so strongly with far richer nations and become a global provider of everything from consumer staples to huge steel units for the new San Francisco–Oakland Bay Bridge. PRC construction firms signed contracts worth $134 billion in 2010 – fifty times the figure for twenty years earlier – and fifty-four of them figure on the list of the top 225 international engineering contractors, the most for any nation. Their work ranges from a vast resort complex in the Bahamas to a bridge crossing the Danube – even (despite protests) the construction by Chinese stoneworkers of sculptor Lei Yixin's Martin Luther King, Jr. Memorial in Washington.[9]

Never before has a state whose concerns are primarily domestic housed three of the seven most valuable companies on the planet or built up a treasure chest of foreign exchange that could buy the whole of Italy or all the sovereign debt of Portugal, Ireland, Greece and Spain (as of 2011), plus Google, Apple, IBM and Microsoft plus all the real estate in Manhattan and Washington, DC plus the world's fifty most valuable sports franchises. Never before has a mismatch between the size of a country's population and its relative lack of natural resources had such an effect on global commodity prices and shipping rates. Never before has the world's superpower been so dependent on funding and cheap imports from a state whose nominal per capita wealth is equivalent to that of Angola, creating a completely new monetary-political relationship: 'How do you get tough on your banker?' as US Secretary of State Hillary Clinton summed up Washington's dilemma. Yet, on the other side of the Pacific, the PRC finds itself stuck with a huge stockpile of dollar-denominated securities it would prefer to be without but cannot dispose of.

Never before has a nation come back from such a long history of revolts, invasions, repression and natural disasters to awe the world. Never before, for that matter, has China been so involved with the rest of the globe: though less isolated than is often supposed, the great imperial dynasties were essentially inward-looking, content to focus on their vast domains. Never before have so many people in a single country been so focused on simultaneous material advancement. Never before has a leader who defines his goal as being simply to achieve 'moderate prosperity' for his state been selected as the most powerful figure on earth, as was Hu Jintao by *Forbes* magazine in the US in 2011. Never before has a country whose ruling party aims to apply 'socialism with Chinese characteristics' and to follow the path of 'scientific socialism' pursued such a red-blooded approach to market competition and crude economic growth. Never before has such a globally vital nation been so attacked for cheating in so much of what it does.

Never before has such a state possessed the ultimate weapon of mass destruction, the world's largest army and a permanent seat at the top of the major global forum. Never before has technology enabled manufacturers and traders deep in China to communicate instantly with the world or hackers to pose a security threat to foreign nations. Never before has an avowedly left-wing regime been so stingy in healthcare, education, welfare and pensions – and urged others to reduce their social spending.

In short, by leading the Communists to victory in 1949, Mao Zedong changed his country; by steering the People's Republic on a new path, Deng Xiaoping changed the world. This book will set out what that means for China and for the global community with which it is so intimately entwined, leading to the conclusion that, unless the new leadership which took office at the end of 2012 undertakes major reforms, the PRC will face a growing array of challenges that will mean that the past is no longer a reliable guide to an increasingly uncertain future.

2

A NATION ON SPEED

In the late eighteenth and early nineteenth centuries the empire of China's Middle Kingdom is estimated to have accounted for one-third of global wealth. The People's Republic has not yet reached that level but it is engaged in a headlong race to make up for lost time, capable of producing more in two weeks now than it did in a whole year in the 1970s. Though Mao and Deng ruled into old age, the image of China as a gerontocracy is no longer true. Hu Jintao and Wen Jiabao joined the CCP Central Committee when they were forty; the new leaders, Xi Jinping and Li Keqiang, did so in their early forties. Top leaders retire after passing their 69th birthday and their successors are in their fifties. In the State Council, 85 per cent of ministers were appointed in 2007 or afterwards. More than a dozen bosses of major state companies are aged under fifty-five and 57 per cent of those in charge in 2011 had been appointed since 2007. China's ultra-rich are younger than their Western counterparts, averaging thirty-nine years of age.

Everything moves at high velocity, often fuelled by money, as epitomized by the breakneck late-night races round Beijing's ring roads by rich young people in supercharged sports cars. In ten years the PRC's rudimentary telephone system has adopted the most modern technology, with 930 million mobile handsets and 538 million Internet users, 300 million social media registrations, 80 social networks and 2,000 online coupon sites; the PRC is, unsurprisingly, the world's largest market for personal computers. The backwardness of retailing outside the main cities means that e-commerce turnover is likely to overtake that of the US by 2015, with the number of online shoppers set to vault from 145 million in 2010 to 348 million in 2014. Robin Li, the forty-two-year-old co-founder of China's biggest search engine, Baidu, has a fortune estimated at more than 60 billion yuan. At the end of 2012, China's Lenovo became the world's biggest maker of computers.

In 2000 the PRC produced 2 million cars; ten years later it was the world's biggest automobile market, with 18 million new vehicles sold in 2010. The state grid is set to spend 500 billion yuan on ultra-high-voltage transmission systems using technology not applied anywhere else. The number of insurance premiums taken out by Chinese soared by 32 per cent in 2010 alone. Suning, the biggest retailer of electronics goods, which started with a single shop in Nanjing in 1996, has 1,300 outlets with plans to add 300 more. The rickshaws that have re-appeared in cities are, naturally, pulled by electric bicycles.

The government's latest Five Year Plan, covering 2011–15, aims to move the country up the value chain and away from the low-cost manufacturing of the last three decades through increased spending on research and development (R&D) and getting into advanced industrial sectors. China intends to have a 174-seat airliner flying by 2015–16 – it has already signed a preliminary agreement with the low-cost airline Ryanair. The number of nuclear-power stations is set to rise from the present 13 to 70 by 2020 and then to more than 120. The PRC is the world's biggest manufacturer of solar panels and sells wind farms round the globe.[1]

The recovery of Hong Kong in 1997 gave China a prime international financial centre (like Macau, the former British colony had its status guaranteed for fifty years as a Special Administrative Region (SAR) of the PRC). A genomics institute based in Hong Kong and the city of Shenzhen across the border is on its way to becoming the biggest DNA-sequencing laboratory on earth. The National University of Defense Technology has built a computer, the Tianhe-1A, with a speed of 2.5 petaflops enabling it to make 2.5 quadrillion calculations a second; this was, for a time, the fastest computer on earth. In terms of the number of scientific papers published per country, China ranks second and is expected to exceed the United States by 2020, according to the Royal Society in London. The number of patent applications has risen from 50,000 to 300,000 a year since 2000 (again placing China second only to the USA), boosted by government incentives and company bonuses for employees who file them. A Chinese astronaut has walked in space. After the launch of an unmanned craft from the Gobi desert in 2011, Chinese astronauts docked their craft with the space laboratory in mid-2012 as part of a plan to set up a space station and land somebody on the moon by 2020 – it was revealed at the end of 2012 that tests were being conducted to see if vegetables could be grown there to meet China's rising food demand. The government is spending 1 billion yuan on a scheme to use silver iodine, dry ice and liquid nitrogen fired from planes to manipulate the weather. Technology is even enrolled to maintain tradition – people away from home at the time of the spring-time Qingming grave-sweeping ceremony can now go through the ritual at an online 3D virtual memorial hall.

As China has sped away from the uniformity of the first three decades of Communist rule it has become a deeply materialistic society with a wide array of consumer goods. In place of Mao suits, people can choose the clothes they want to buy. They are free to travel round the country and abroad. Diets have become more varied. Alcohol consumption is forecast to rise by a third between 2009 and 2014; drinking of the strong, sorghum-based liquor *baijiu* increased by 50 per cent in the last three years and a survey found that half the 56 per cent of men who regularly consume it can be classed as binge drinkers. For many, what you own defines who you are – whether that is a top-range Italian sports car or the company headquarters being built by a steel trader in the north-east who explained, as he showed me the plans, that it was modelled on a Dutch royal palace 'only bigger'. A pharmaceutical firm in the same region houses its boardroom and corporate museum in rooms replicating the Palace of Versailles. The village of Huaxi in Jiangsu, said to be the richest in the land, has put up a 328-metre skyscraper costing 3 billion yuan; the building is topped by a figure of an ox made from a ton of gold.[2]

Many of the country's rich people are self-made, drawing their fortunes from a wide range of businesses, from manufacturing and mining to home appliances and IT. Top of the *Hunrun Rich List* for 2011 was Liang Wengen, founder and President of the Sany heavy-machinery group, whose fortune rose by 89 per cent in 2010 to 70 billion yuan, or more than $10 billion. In 2012, this place was taken by Zong Qinghou, head of the Wahaha soft-drinks group. Though hit by a slowing economy and falling property prices in 2012, the fortunes of the 100 or so dollar billionaires was up 40 per cent on 2010 and 1,000 per cent on the start of the century. The biggest concentration of millionaires – 7,000 of them – is not in Beijing and Shanghai but in Ordos in Inner Mongolia, situated on the edge of a huge coal field and dubbed 'China's Dubai'.[3]

Being mega-rich does not necessarily provide a path to longevity or happiness. A Chinese publication has reported that more than fifty billionaires have died of unnatural causes since 2003; of these seventeen committed suicide, fifteen were murdered and fourteen were executed. In all, thirty had either been sentenced to jail or death or put under investigation for corruption in the last decade, including the head of Gome, China's biggest electric retailer, who was in 2008 listed as the country's richest man.[4]

Some beneficiaries of material progress are unashamed practitioners of conspicuous consumption as they follow the dictum attributed to Deng Xiaoping (though there is no record of him having said it): to get rich is glorious. During a visit to the Hermès shop in Paris the wife of a Shanxi-province coalmine owner asked to be shown the most expensive handbag and then ordered two dozen. In the eastern city of Wenzhou a wedding motorcade can consist of ten Bentleys, eight Rolls-Royces, four Ferraris and four Lamborghinis while the local Gucci store offers an alligator purse that retails at 270,000 yuan.[5] A tycoon decided that a replica of a French château he had built outside Beijing was not grand enough, so he added an extra wing.

At the Hôtel Crillon in Paris the granddaughter of a Mao-era minister, Chen Yuan, was the belle of the debutantes' ball wearing an Oscar de la Renta gown and a diamond necklace. Her boyfriend, the grandson of another Mao-era 'immortal', Bo Yibo, is known for his taste for Ferraris. Shanghai and Tianjin have polo clubs; entry to the one in Tianjin is by invitation only and costs from 200,000 yuan for individuals to 10 million if you have a team. Golf has become a 60-billion-yuan business and its popularity among the newly rich has resulted in 600 courses being opened across China in contravention of a central-government ban. Sales of luxury goods in China are put at $15 billion a year.

Business is conducted without frills. A successful entrepreneur laughed as he told me that, to cut deals in the construction business at the basic level, all one required was an ability to drink a lot, smoke and gamble. (A recruitment advertisement from a company making security equipment backed up his first point when it specifically stated that 'candidates with good drinking ability will be prioritized'.) 'It's all a matter of money,' he went on, and illustrated his point with the story of a friend of his who had fallen for a waitress in a restaurant in the ancient city of Xi'an. The woman's employer kept her from him, so he bought the establishment outright and she was now his mistress. The businessman ended our chat by asking if I would like to be photographed with the Prime Minister – he could arrange it for 800,000 yuan.[6]

Growing upscale consumer demand has boosted the price of everything from the latest computer gadgets to third-class art. To increase its appeal to rich clients, an estate agency in Nanjing obliged its sales agents to buy Armani suits to wear at work. Villas in gated communities outside Beijing fetch 40 million yuan. One bathroom-equipment firm offers a $6,400 toilet with a heated footrest, temperature-controlled seat and built-in music system, access to Skype and the means to play video games and read e-books. Top-of-the range limousines have internal software for share trading, instant-message exchange, poker games and access to China's version of Facebook, Renren. The Geely company's GE model car, which bears an extraordinary resemblance to a Rolls-Royce, comes with a single throne seat at the back. Hainan Island off the southern coast, which is being developed to create 'China's Hawaii', has experienced a massive property boom, while local companies sell high-priced yachts, business jets, Ferraris and Bentleys; the island has nearly 100 golf courses, an array of luxury resort hotels and spas with pools in which one can be gently nibbled by exotic fish. In 2011 it hosted a luxury fair that raised an estimated 10 billion yuan.

Plastic surgery is booming everywhere from smart surgeries in Shanghai to small establishments in towns far up the Yangtze. As middle-class diets grow more varied the demand for biological food steadily increases – a pig farm with 30,000 animals in central China proclaims its pork to be 'non-toxic', meaning that no artificial feeds are used. In place of the spectre of famine, more than 15 per cent of the Chinese are reckoned to be overweight, according to the recent book *Fat China*. In part this is simply because people consume a lot more than they did under Mao, and exercise is rare. But diet also counts: spoilt 'little emperors', single male children, are allowed by their parents to gorge on junk foods, which has led to an upsurge in obesity among the young; 'a fat child is almost like having a BMW, it's a display of your wealth,' as Paul French, author of *Fat China*, remarks. Sales of slimming products and use of liposuction are rising steadily and the American Weight Watchers group opened up in the PRC in 2010.[7]

The juxtaposition of old and new is part of everyday life for most people. In Chengdu, the capital of Sichuan, a huge white statue of Chairman Mao stands with one arm outstretched at the end of a broad avenue lined with European fashion outlets, the celebrity City Hotel and smart restaurants. In a Daoist temple in Guangzhou, capital of Guangdong province, a young woman in a trim black trouser suit genuflects in front of an altar of a fearsome deity while conducting an animated conversation on her mobile telephone. The abbot at the martial-arts centre at the Shaolin temple in Henan province travels in a luxury car and the robe he wears, donated to him by a brocade firm, contains gold thread said to be worth £5,000.

Upmarket demand means that price differences are enormous. A bottle of the local beer costs 4 yuan in the neighbourhood restaurant where I often eat in Beijing, but in the bar of a smart hotel across town patrons are happy to pay 58 yuan for exactly the same drink. For young people, owning an apartment is the sign of having arrived in life; unlike their parents, who lived through hard times, they have never known a prolonged downturn. In such a world the urge is to be on the upward material escalator. As a young female dating-show contestant put it: 'I would choose a luxury house over a boyfriend who always makes me happy without hesitation. And my boyfriend has to have a monthly salary of 200,000 yuan.' Elsewhere, 70 per cent of her female peers told pollsters that they would not marry a man who did not own a flat, hold a good, stable job and have substantial savings. When a Guangdong newspaper asked primary school pupils what they wanted to be when they grew up, a six-year-old girl said, 'When I grow up, I want to be an official.' 'What kind official?' the journalist asked. 'A corrupt official,' came the reply, 'because corrupt officials have a lot of good stuff.'[8]

As the material society marched on, advertising on national television rose by 18 per cent in 2010 to top 10 billion yuan for the first time. Gossip columns reveal celebrity 'love cheats' and serve up a diet of 'hunks' and 'unnaturally well-endowed' models. Job-hopping is endemic among young professionals and brings increased salaries – according to the recruitment consultancy DDI, annual staff turnover averages 18.5 per cent at Chinese private firms, 10 per cent at state enterprises and 25 per cent at foreign firms. Young women in Shanghai take pride in having none of their income left at the end of each month. In 2010 the first Chinese-made 'chick flick' appeared; entitled *Go Lala Go*, it was poor stuff but still earned 124 million yuan at the box office.

Eighty per cent of young people at college want to join the Communist Party, according to an Education Ministry poll in 2011, and 40 per cent of the 1.2 million new members in 2010 were students. However, it is a safe bet that ideological attraction is not the spur; rather membership is seen as a useful career card. One young woman with little faith in the regime explained that she kept up her CCP Youth

League membership because it would aid her in job hunting. Party membership is a particular help in landing civil-service posts or employment in state-owned enterprises.

Wealth and political influence often run hand in hand since the CCP recognized 'advanced productive forces' – that is, business people – at the start of this century. Seventy members of China's legislature, the National People's Congress (NPC), have assets totalling 493 billion yuan ($75 billion) between them. They include Zong Qinghou of Wahaha, with a personal fortune equivalent to $12 billion, while Richard Li, China's previous richest man, was put in the upper house of the legislature in 2013.

Social conditions have altered beyond all recognition from the drab days of Mao. Though political control remains strong, and the one-child policy still affects most couples, people live freer lives. Despite censorship, they have access to a much-enhanced and more varied flow of information. Most remain trapped below, but upward mobility is there for those with skills, determination or an ability to work the system. University education has expanded hugely. This is reflected at the top: in 1982 none of the Politburo had gone to college; in 2007, twenty-three of its twenty-five members had degrees. Though the sacred texts cleave to old ideology, the class struggle has been abandoned. Though only a third of those who study abroad return to the mainland, those who do bring with them experience of the world unknown to their parents. Despite the march of materialism, this officially atheist nation is undergoing a religious boom – between 60 and 80 million people are estimated to go to Christian churches on Sundays while Buddhism thrives and folk religions have revived.

Gender equality is state policy, in keeping with Mao's observation that women hold up half the sky. Sexual harassment has been a crime since 2005. But the definition is vague and there is no shortage of oppression of women. A survey of ten factories in four regions reported that 20 per cent of female staff said they had been the victims of sexual harassment. Until the Hunan provincial government was exposed to public ridicule it required women civil servants to have 'symmetrical breasts'. An electronic-goods company in Nanchang ranks female employees by their looks, graduating pay accordingly.

The Railways Ministry, whose head had eighteen mistresses, laid down that female attendants on high-speed trains must be aged under twenty-eight with a fair complexion and 'a shapely figure that conforms to selection standards'.

Still, the condition of women has been greatly improved, particularly by education and earning power; half the enrolments at universities are now female. Women constitute 46 per cent of the labour force and contribute on average half of household incomes compared to 20 per cent at the start of economic reform. The young women who make up the bulk of migrant workers in factories in Guangdong earn three times as much as they would have in 2000 and it is estimated that three-quarters of female graduates aspire to management positions, compared to half their US counterparts.

Politically the PRC is a place for men. In keeping with China's imperial centuries, during which only two women exercised authority equivalent to their male counterparts, the Communist Party's Politburo has contained only a few women throughout its six decades in power, and none has sat in its top Standing Committee (even if Mao's last wife wielded great influence during the Cultural Revolution). Only 20 per cent of CCP members, thirteen of the 200-strong Central Committee, three of the State Council ministers and a single provincial boss are female. Eight per cent of company directors are women – half the UK number and a third of the total in the US. Still, women head several big firms and constitute half the world's self-made female billionaires, operating in everything from property and underground shopping centres to paper and packaging. Five figured in the *Financial Times*' list of the top 50 global business women in 2011.[9]

Zhang Yin, head of the Nine Dragons paper company, was ranked as the country's richest person in 2006 and then as the world's wealthiest self-made woman in 2010. Dong Mingzhu, the 'Iron Lady' who presides over the Gree electrical-appliance group – which makes 34 million air conditioners a year and has annual sales of 60 billion yuan – is almost a caricature of a driven executive, known for rarely smiling at staff and issuing such proclamations as, 'I never make mistakes and am always correct' and 'Femininity in the business world is the equivalent of admitting women are weak'. Widowed in her twenties, she likes reading

Jane Eyre and *Gone with the Wind,* and lamented to an American interviewer that most Chinese women just wanted to be 'endearing little birds'. 'Where Sister Dong walks, no grass grows', it is said.[10]

Zhang Xin runs the big Soho property company with her husband. As a young child, she was sent to the countryside during the Cultural Revolution with her mother, who had been a translator at the Foreign Languages Bureau. They subsequently moved to Hong Kong and at the age of fourteen Zhang began working in small factories. Five years later she had built up sufficient savings to fly to Britain, where she won university scholarships and went into investment banking (which she says she hated), then returned to the PRC, met her husband at a property firm, got married and set up Soho, which has developed more than 25 million square feet of real estate and expanded in defiance of bearish forecasts of a market crash. Her stake in Soho was valued in 2010 at around 14 billion yuan, making her as rich as Oprah Winfrey.

As women have grown richer, they have become increasingly important personal consumers. The female savings rate has halved since 2006, according to a survey in *Women of China* magazine. Women buy twice as many luxury goods as do men, whose comparable spending is concentrated on 'man bags', in which to carry their accoutrements and cash, and on grooming products, including hair dye. In 2010 the average female luxury consumer spent 22 per cent more than in the previous year. A third of the Maserati cars sold in China are bought by women, compared with 5 per cent in the US and 2 per cent in Europe. Chinese women also drink more whisky than do their Western counterparts.

It is reckoned that more than 90 per cent of mainland officials investigated for corruption in recent years have kept mistresses just as their predecessors maintained concubines. One provincial vice-governor was reported to have forty-six. An Association of Mistresses staged 'mistresses festivals' to mark International Women's Day in March 2011 and has an online forum where members exchange tips on how to handle wealthy elderly men and how much money to expect (not less than 200,000 yuan a month, one blogger advised). Meishan city in Sichuan felt it necessary to issue an edict to its bureaucrats to stay faithful to their spouses. The authorities in Guangdong offer courses to warn young women of the dangers of acquiring sugar daddies.

A poll by *China Youth Daily* found that 60 per cent of respondents, most of them aged under thirty, said they knew a woman who wanted to marry or rely on a rich and powerful man as a way of fulfilling personal ambitions. 'Several years ago, I thought I could realize my dream, through my own efforts, but that was so naive,' a twenty-eight-year-old woman working for a big company in Shanghai said. 'Cruel reality showed me that those who were born into rich families can rely on parents, and those who were born into average families, like me, can only count on a wealthy man.' As a university professor commented: 'On the one hand, men who have attained a higher social status want more than one woman. On the other, young girls see a chance to exchange their youth and beauty for a better life even if it means hurting someone else's marriage.' One joke says that so long as officials have so many dalliances the luxury-goods market and upmarket real estate will remain buoyant on the back of all the gifts and accommodation.

Deng Xiaoping said that it was natural for some people to get rich faster than others; the problem today is that those who have become wealthy are getting even wealthier faster than those below them on the income scale. An academic study published in 2012 showed the Gini coefficient, which measures wealth disparities, standing at 0.61 for China compared to 0.45 for the US and 0.38 for Japan (the higher the number, the greater the inequality). That is well above the level generally taken as pointing to social unrest.

Though the percentage of the population living in absolute poverty by international standards has dropped greatly, a reclassification of the poverty level at the end of 2011 to net annual earnings of 2,300 yuan meant that more than 100 million people were classified as being poor and qualify for livelihood subsidies. If the United Nations standard of $1.25 a day was applied, the number would rise to 250 million. The top 10 per cent of households earn an average of 139,000 yuan a year while the bottom 10 per cent take in 5,350 yuan, according to a 2010 study; the same study also reported that much of the earnings of the rich is concealed from the authorities, meaning that the official wealth-disparity figure is a significant underestimate. China Merchants Bank, the biggest private-sector financial institution in China, has found that 45 per cent of deposits and 67 per cent of managed assets at its 500 branches are held by 1.5 per cent of clients. The economist Victor Shih puts the wealth of the top 1 per cent of the population at anywhere from $2 trillion to $5 trillion.[11]

Inequalities abound in the public and private sectors. Ninety per cent of China's 18,000 hospitals are run by the state but they depend on selling expensive branded medicines for much of their revenue. People queue through the night for access to desks issuing tickets to see a doctor, sometimes only to find that those tickets have been snapped up by scalpers selling them on at a price. It was only in 2009 that a programme for a decent health service was launched, and this will not come into full effect for years. Much state education is also poor; the Education Ministry says that 54.6 million people are illiterate. Meanwhile the pension system is a black hole.[12]

China officially has no slums. However, it does have plenty of broken-down shacks lacking modern amenities; and shantytowns, built for workers by state-owned enterprises in the old days of cradle-to-grave 'iron rice-bowl' welfare provision but abandoned since the outset of economic reform. For all the economic progress, 600 million people still do not have a bank account. In this supposedly Communist state the share of public housing for the poor fell from 17 per cent of total construction in 1999 to 5 per cent in the second half of the first decade of the twenty-first century.

In this nation on speed, companies adapt at a blinding pace to changes in global demand – copies of the wedding dress worn by Kate Middleton for her marriage to Prince William in 2011 were on sale on a Chinese website within hours of the ceremony in Westminster Abbey. (Ultra-cheap rip-offs of her sapphire-and-diamond engagement ring had already been sold worldwide.) The PRC's farmers switch swiftly between crops as prices rise and fall. Armies of pig traders hurry round the country with their trucks tracking overnight movements in the cost of the country's favourite meat. An advertisement in the back of a taxi in the north-eastern city of Shenyang offers 'instant one-stop worldwide company-formation service', using various Hong Kong banks, with 'no verification of funding required, no registration of business sector'. When the government launched a programme to encourage the solar industry, entrepreneurs with no experience piled in, and some went spectacularly bust. As liquidity bubbles inflate in anything from choice tea to postage stamps, speculators dodge and weave in search of quick profits.

Runaway growth breeds a sense of impermanence as the new is laid sometimes uneasily on old foundations. While big urban centres power ahead with spectacular volumes of construction, the countryside and smaller towns are full of half-completed buildings, as if the people who started them didn't have time to finish, had moved on to something else or had simply run out of money. Small towns and villages develop in a haphazard way; a drive through them can take you abruptly from a metalled road to a rutted track, from modern residences to tumbledown shacks. Beyond their centres many cities have grown so fast that there has not been time to create an integrated urban structure. In Wuhan, 'China's Chicago', with a population of nine million on the middle Yangtze, swamps and fields lie between the huge, ultra-modern high-speed train station and the urban development along the river. Chongqing, in the south-west, is often described as China's biggest city; in fact it is a sprawling metropolis of which 70 per cent is forest or farmland.

China has 'ghost cities' of apartments in which nobody lives and cavernous shopping malls where very few goods are actually bought. But the building goes on amid recurrent warnings of a property bust that has not yet materialized. Except during peak holiday periods, airports in smaller cities and the lavish high-speed train stations are half-empty. Out in the provinces, four- or six-lane highways often have few vehicles on them. China's motto might be 'Build and they will come – but build now'. Capital is available from the state and it has often been spent without any real measure of the likely financial return.

In line with the speed needed by China to keep its economic machine upright in the short term, companies are out to ratchet up productivity even further as they face rising wages, thin profit margins and competition from even-lower-cost nations. Foxconn, the biggest assembler of IT equipment, announced plans in 2011 to boost the number of robots at its plants from 10,000 to a million – the size of its current workforce on the mainland. So far China's drive to stay ultra-competitive has worked. At the start of the century's second decade, the minimum wage rose by 20 per cent a year, input costs were boosted by rising commodity prices and the yuan appreciated in value (though not by as much as foreign critics of the PRC's currency policy would have liked). But the price of Chinese imports into the US increased by only 2.8 per cent in a year and, in the summer of 2011, overall exports were 20 per cent up on the same period of the previous year, boosting the trade surplus to $31 billion a month, the highest figure for two years. Throw a challenge at the PRC and it will be surmounted, it seems.

For those on the left who have for so long been waiting for America's terminal decline, China's rise is manna; if capitalism beat Communism in the shape of the Soviet Union, the rise of a non-American model offers solace from a state led by what its President calls 'a great, glorious and correct Marxist political party'. For those on the right, the PRC is akin to a vast apolitical corporation that has seen the light after some rocky years and is now showing that capitalism can work in all its primitive, freewheeling glory, with a business-friendly political machine, a minimal welfare state and patchy regulation. What, from both sides, is there not to love about China?

All the more so because of the country's size and population of 1.37 billion – 1.339 billion of them on the mainland – around 20 per cent of the people on earth. The political and social constraints, flaws and challenges that will run through this book are all too easy to overlook when one is overwhelmed by the sheer scale of China and the effects of growth since the 1980s – even more so if one is overawed by the official version of the country's history. Half a billion people have been pulled out of extreme poverty by economic reforms. The number of migrant workers who have added to the global labour force in the last three decades is put officially at 211 million. Forty million small and medium-sized enterprises (SMEs) employing 160 million people have sprouted across the country.

Eighty million Chinese belong to the Communist Party – 20 million people apply to join annually and the CCP runs 2,000 schools to ensure that cadres are told how to align remnant Marxism with the market. The People's Liberation Army (PLA) has 2.28 million active troops (compared to 1.58 million for the US) plus 1.5 million paramilitaries and

800,000 reserves. The Agricultural Bank counts 320 million customers and 440,000 staff.

Chinese smoke 38 per cent of the cigarettes consumed globally; more than a million people die each year from smoking-related illnesses but the government is loath to crack down seriously because it gains 9 per cent of its annual fiscal revenue from the state monopoly and tobacco taxes. An estimated 35 million Chinese are learning to play the piano. Since pork is the preferred meat, the PRC contains 55 per cent – or 500 million – of the world's pigs; the average urban resident eats the equivalent of one pig a year. It is also home to the world's biggest fish processor. China produces 6 billion condoms a year and state media report 13 million abortions annually. Cinemas, many of them equipped to show 3D films, open at the average rate of three a day, with the industry forecasting 40 per cent annual growth to put China on a par with the US by 2020; Hengdian studios in Zhejiang province is the biggest open-air lot on earth. The former Portuguese colony of Macau, having returned to Chinese sovereignty in 1999, has raced ahead of Las Vegas in its gaming turnover, which tripled between 2008 and 2011.

The size of the population in the municipality of Chongqing – 32 million – is greater than that of Peru, Malaysia or Iraq. A plaque at the West Lake restaurant in Changsha, capital of Hunan, proclaims this to be the biggest eating house in the world, with 5,000 seats and 1,000 staff, including 300 chefs. The top television talent show attracts audiences of 400 million. There are 3.3 million retail outlets across the country. The leading online commerce site, Taobao, has 370 million users and registers as many as 48,000 trades a minute. Newspaper circulations total 50 billion a year.

Tailbacks on the road between Beijing and Inner Mongolia, which is used by 70,000 vehicles a day (three times the planned capacity), stretch for 75 to 100 miles and involve thousands of trucks carrying coal to the capital. The death toll on China's roads is officially put at 65,000 a year, but may well be considerably higher. There are also half a million cases of drunk-driving annually – when, in 2011, drunk-driving was made a criminal offence, 7,000 police armed with teargas were deployed in Beijing to catch offenders. A book on the teachings of Confucius sold 10 million copies. The National Museum in Beijing, the largest on earth, contains a million cultural relics in nearly 200,000 square metres of floor space. The capital is estimated to have more than a million dogs and 200,000 stray cats. At 6 to 7 million, the number of blind people in the PRC is greater than the total population of Denmark or Finland. Annually China carries out more executions (1,718) than any other nation; 68 crimes are punishable by death, increasingly by means of lethal injection rather than the old practice of shooting (for which the dead person's family might incur a charge for the bullet).

China, a unitary state inhabited overwhelmingly by people of the Han race, is a continent rather than a country. It is the third-largest nation on earth (some way smaller than Russia but only a little behind Canada) and borders a dozen other countries. Its mainland stretches 3,400 miles from north to south and 3,100 miles from east to west, with 2,700 miles of coast from north-east to south-west. Its longest river, the Yangtze, runs for 4,000 miles from the Himalayas to the sea beside Shanghai. The Yellow River, cradle of Han civilization, whose floods have earned it the name of 'China's Sorrow', flows through nine provinces on its 3,400-mile course to the coast south-east of Beijing.

The legacy of the tectonic crash that raised the Himalayas 35 million years ago and the geographical size of today's China combine to breed diversity, with terrain ranging from the paddy fields of the south to the vast stony deserts in the north and far west, from the wheat belt of the centre-north to some of the highest mountains on earth, including Everest. It houses an unequalled variety of flora and fauna: China contains 30,000 species of plants (compared to 17,000 in all North America). Climate conditions vary enormously. Yunnan in the deep south-west is semitropical. The Pearl River Delta is cloyingly humid and the 'three furnaces' of Nanjing, Wuhan and Chongqing along the Yangtze are searingly hot in the summer. In the north, in the words of an early-twentieth-century book on China that remain as true today as then, 'in winter it is cold as death itself, and great hurricanes of northerly winds sweep over the country chilling man and beast till they cannot move. There is but little spring, and by May the winter cold is exchanged only for a burning dry heat which sends the thermometer above one hundred degrees.'

Droughts and floods alternate. Nature is not kind. Three of the ten costliest (in terms of deaths and financial loss) natural disasters since 1995 have been in the PRC. The Sichuan earthquake of 2008 killed at least 68,000 people and the 250,000 death toll of the Tangshan earthquake in northern China in 1976, as Mao lay dying, made it the worst of the twentieth century. On a lesser but still murderous scale, more than 1,000 people died or were missing in floods and landslides in central China in the early summer of 2011. In 2009 severe cold weather brought southern China to a halt and caused damage of 100 billion yuan. The cost of natural disasters in 2010, when China suffered 178 earthquakes of a magnitude of 5 or above, was put at 534 billion yuan.

China's variety makes it home to an array of rare species, and, of course, to the panda, which the World Wildlife Fund has adopted for use as a symbol. Beijing regularly loans the animals out to foreign zoos in a diplomatic exercise that has led critics to brand those who are beguiled by the PRC's hospitality and favours as 'panda huggers'. But the panda policy in the animals' home province of Sichuan took questionable forms before recent efforts to ensure their preservation, the results of which remain to be seen. Economic growth has eliminated or put at extreme risk endangered species, especially those prized for their supposed restorative properties. For 800 yuan per plate, specialist restaurants serve 'mountain-cat meat' – the flesh of tigers – while bears kept in 'crush cages' have their gall extracted to be sold to traditional medical suppliers. For all the outcry that such practices arouse, demand and tradition keep the trade flourishing. If nature is not kind in China, the country's people can be brutal towards wild places and the animals that live there. There is, in general, little time to stop and consider the effects. Like the bicycle riders who no longer dominate the streets of China's cities, keeping up the velocity of forward movement is the prime concern – all the way from the top leadership to those far below who aspire to get on to the escalator of material improvement in this meganation on speed.

3

RIDING THE RAIL

The speed of development has brought a great jumble of old and new, rich and poor. The high-speed train station at Changsha is a temple to modernity with its seven dedicated platforms, huge marble-floored concourse and airy skylight ceiling. But when I passed through in 2010 a man in faded jeans and a torn T-shirt was poking through an enormous mound of fetid rubbish piled up at the entrance to the car park, which is itself vast and was almost entirely empty. The exit barrier did not work. Outside we drove past a muddle of half-finished buildings and crumbling hovels – and, sat on the pavement, a four-poster bed on which a pile of vegetables had been deposited.[1]

There were more piles of rubbish below a sign reading 'Caves Maître Vin' (complete with circumflex) and then the road narrowed to two lanes as it passed a sprawling wholesale market selling wood, coal and every kind of metal goods. A huddle of small factories in the process of being demolished led to a four-lane highway (soon to be expanded to eight) with signs, in English, warning 'Rear End Colusion (*sic*) Keep Space' and hoardings advertising a housing estate, adorned with a depiction of a stagecoach driven by a man in a top hat. At the toll booth a soldier wearing camouflage uniform and helmet with a rifle held in front of him watched the vehicles pass through.

The town of Zhuzhou is an industrial sprawl, with its factories belching smoke and new tower blocks covered in green netting sprouting along the main roads, a Kentucky Fried Chicken outlet and a small sex shop nestled between a bank and a clothes shop. A smaller road with a cracked surface led into what was, in the 1920s, the heartland of the Communist Party in this part of China and later became the scene of savage fighting between landlords and peasants that may have awakened the taste for violence in the province's most famous son, Mao Zedong.

The county town of Lining, a centre for ceramics, had seen better days. The road here was lined with tumbledown structures, heaps of bricks for buildings that were never erected, stagnant ponds and disused workshops. Suddenly, around a corner, a clump of new residential blocks appeared, with a filling station offering bottles of 'C'est bon' water with our petrol. But on closer examination the white tiles of the new buildings' facades had become discoloured by rusting fasteners and pipes below them. Dongbao village was more upbeat, with its 'Sunlight Resort' round a little lake. Posters by the roadside extolled the virtues of birth control. Then we turned off along a dirt track and, for no particular reason, stopped briefly at a small pig farm with two satellite-television dishes on the ground by the door. The farm was run by a woman whose adult family members had gone off to work in the city, leaving her to look after a gaggle of small children as well as the pigs. Her house was made of compacted clay; it was twenty-five years old but could have been there for centuries. On one wall of the otherwise bare bedroom were photographs of the film star Jet Li torn from a magazine and an advertisement for Starlight City entertainment centre.

Trucks lumbered by, sending up clouds of dust from the red earth. By a dried-up riverbed opposite a paddy field tended by an elderly man in a white singlet and knee-length trousers was another of the myriad haphazard piles of garbage dotting China. This dump contained chunks of wood, stones, bricks, roof tiles, plastic bags, processed-food wrappings and a single discarded glove. A chicken strutted round looking for pickings. We drove on behind a truck loaded with steel bars for one of the many tentacles of the high-speed train network that epitomizes better than anything else China's rush to move ahead, its adoption of foreign technology, the power politics of development, the taste for immense infrastructure projects, the corner-cutting and the consequent dangers.

At the end of the track, in a hollow below verdant hills, 300 migrant workers from Sichuan were digging tunnels for the high-speed track that will one day cover 1,200 miles from the city of Kunming in the far south-west to Shanghai on the east coast. Nearby, a makeshift cement plant had been built on a slope to supply more than thirty tunnels and bridges being constructed for the line in this county alone. The supervisor wore a T-shirt with the English invitation 'We can have a picnic – all can come'.

The tunnel workers, organized by a contracting firm from Fujian, would be in the area for a year completing their tasks. They were living in prefabricated cream-and-blue dormitories that moved with them from project to project. Their earnings were equivalent to what they would earn in a factory in a coastal manufacturing region, but with little here on which to spend their cash most of it was being remitted back to their home villages to pump up rural incomes or being added to savings. The workers employed the time-honoured technique of inserting dynamite into holes drilled into the rock then retreating to a safe distance as it explodes, but their foreman was also using satellite tracking to ensure that the tunnel followed a straight line. The heavy lifting was done by machines – Swedish and Japanese, plus one from China's own Sany group. Groups of workers sat around playing cards or chatting by the stream running down the hillside, which was clogged with debris and refuse – plastic bottles, discarded playing cards, empty noodle and cigarette packets, drinks cans, paper, sacks, gloves, bricks and plastic eating utensils.

The air was filled with dust. Piles of steel girders lay by the opening in the hill. A short, smiling, bespectacled quality controller from the railway authority walked round making notes on a clipboard while men in yellow hardhats and gloves welded the struts of the tunnel. An elderly man in a faded army uniform watered a grass slope with a hose: as the foreman explained, they were contractually obliged to leave the area as they found it – besides the tunnel, of course.

Below, sat in the sun, were the family of foresters who had the lease on the land where the railway was to run – the father with swept-back hair and a grey suit; his brother in a blue tracksuit. The mother was drying chilli peppers in big wicker baskets. Boxer shorts and Y-fronts hung on a washing line alongside a designer top with its brand name, Hengis, picked out in spangles. The family collected site refuse to sell off for recycling; several sacks already stood filled with empty drinks cans. The tunnel manager told me they had been well compensated and would probably move to a nearby town soon. Their home had a rock floor. A refrigerator stood in one corner of the main room and photographs of Mao and other early Communist leaders were pasted to the bedroom wall. On the floor were carrier bags decorated with images of film stars and the cartoon character Hello Kitty.

China's railways lagged behind its economic development for much of the first decade of this century. They carried a quarter of global freight and passenger traffic on 6 per cent of the world's lines. Single tracks meant long delays. During the boom year of 2007 it was quicker and cheaper to bring coal from Australia by sea than to carry it by rail from the fields in Shanxi in the north to the power stations and factories on the south-eastern coast.

Then came the high-speed programme, forming a major element in the government stimulus package launched to pull the country out of the economic dip of 2008 as the global financial crisis hit demand for exports and domestic measures to fight inflation proved too effective. The programme had been in the making for several years but now became the icon of China's ability to quickly do things that would take far longer – or would not be done at all – in the West; it was rammed through by a combination of political will, mobilization of state-investment funds and the evolution of what is known as 'indigenous re-innovation'.

This latter element demonstrated perfectly what is involved for countries and companies offering their technology to get into the huge market on the China mainland. When the State Council decided, in 2004, to lay plans to develop the railway system it invited submissions from European, Japanese and Canadian manufacturers who would work in joint ventures with Chinese firms. The first bids submitted by companies such as Siemens, Alstom, Kawasaki and Bombardier were turned down – and reconsidered only when they included offers of more technology to be shared with their mainland partners. The dedicated high-speed network went into operation in 2008 between Beijing and the port city of Tianjin; at the end of 2009 the first long-distance line opened, covering 600 miles between Guangzhou in the south and Wuhan in the Middle Yangtze region with a stop at Changsha.

The station in Guangzhou is like an airport terminal, light, airy and very clean, with marble floors and fifty platforms. There are green and brown armchairs in the waiting section for first-class passengers. Free bottles of water are handed out by attendants in blue uniforms. The eight-coach train has speedometers in each carriage and people take photographs when the needle goes past 200kph. Though fares are high, the passengers are a social mix: business people alongside workers, the apparently affluent alongside the apparently ordinary.

The track burrows through mountains, woods and bamboo forests that once separated Guangdong from the rest of China, following the route into Hunan taken by the National Revolutionary Army in 1926 when it marched out of the south under Chiang Kai-shek to establish its government in Nanjing. There are poor villages and small industrial clusters on either side of the track. Then comes Hengyang, where the Chinese fought a gallant rearguard action against the Japanese in 1944, and Changsha, where Chiang had his teeth fixed at an American hospital before moving on to take the three Yangtze cities now grouped in Wuhan. It is here that the high-speed line ends for now, in another vast station built outside the city at the heart of a new development zone. In time, it is due to run all the way to Beijing.

By the end of the first decade of this century the domestic joint-venture partners had not only absorbed sufficient foreign technology to enable them to complete most of the job themselves, but had also started signing contracts to build and supply high-speed links elsewhere: first in Saudi Arabia, then between Ankara and Istanbul, followed by a 600-mile double-track line in Kazakhstan. They are now also bidding for work in Brazil, Iran, Russia, Algeria and the USA (if plans materialize there) as well as to create a line through Laos and Thailand to Singapore and a rail link across the Darien Gap in Colombia between the Atlantic and Pacific coasts as an alternative to the Panama Canal. China sold 228 trains to Malaysia and signed an agreement with General Electric to produce rolling stock for potential US high-speed lines. When Prime Minister Wen Jiabao visited Britain in 2011 there was much talk about his country doing the work on a link between London and Birmingham. In a nice twist, PRC railway firms filed international patents to protect their 'indigenous re-innovation' techniques.

Chinese managers insist that they introduced genuine innovations, but the trains on the Beijing–Shanghai line which began operating in 2011 are very similar to those made by one of the joint-venture partners, Kawasaki of Japan, whose executives told the *Wall Street Journal* that there had just been a few tweaks to the external paint scheme and interior trims and a beefed-up propulsion system for the highest speeds. 'How are you supposed to fight rivals when they have your technology and their cost base is so much lower?' one Japanese manager asked the newspaper.

Investment in the emblematic railway system increased by more than 70 per cent in the two years of the initial stimulus programme and the Five-Year Plan for 2011–15 earmarked 2.8 trillion yuan to develop the system further to take total lines from 56,000 to 74,000 miles, half of it double-track and 60 per cent electrified.

Long an adjunct of the army, the Railways Ministry ran like an autonomous fiefdom – with two million employees, its own 70,000-strong police force and a courts system employing 7,000 staff, including judges who are retired train conductors with no legal training. Expertise in rail matters was not a prerequisite for its senior figures; for a time it was headed by a senior cadre who had been Deng Xiaoping's bridge partner and who subsequently went on to run the Communist Party's Propaganda Department. The Ministry acted as both operator and regulator and laid down rigorous rules for staff; in addition to the appearance requirements already cited, the regulations stipulate that female attendants on high-speed trains must be able to speak English (a qualification not apparent on several trips I have taken), weigh less than 60 kilos and be between five feet five inches and five feet seven inches tall (height is used elsewhere as a benchmark in China – for example, there is a rule that children under four feet tall get free admission to historic sites).

Spending on railway infrastructure nearly tripled between 2004 and 2007 with 95 per cent coming from the state. The Five-Year Plan covering the period from 2005 to 2010 provided for spending of more than one trillion yuan on railway development to match the massive building of highways since the 1990s. The broad need to bring the different areas of China closer together made a major expansion of the rail network an obvious target for the boom in state spending decided in 2008 to combat the downturn in the economy. The two big state construction companies, China Railway Group and China Railway Construction, as well as makers of rolling stocks and station facilities were assured of huge orders as China set out to show once more that it could do anything it wished to faster than anywhere else on earth, drawing on government funding without worrying too much about the financial return on capital.

The man in charge of this, Railway Minister Liu Zhijun, was an autocratic figure in his late fifties who ran his department very much on his own terms. He held Cabinet rank and did not answer to the supposedly integrated Ministry of Transport. A native of Wuhan, he insisted that the first long-distance dedicated line should be built between there and Guangzhou instead of in northern China. His brother, said to be a member of the 'Wuhan railway mafia', was convicted of embezzling 40 million yuan and received a suspended death sentence for arranging the murder of a man who had crossed him.

The expansion in the 2008 infrastructure-stimulus programme of the fast passenger network from 7,200 to 10,000 miles was not enough for Liu, who presided over the laying of almost double the scheduled amount – including the completion of the 820-mile route between Beijing and Shanghai – in only three years at a cost of 240 billion yuan. Speeds were increased as high as 300kph, 50 per cent above the 200kph ceiling laid down by foreign technology suppliers. Fares rose and luxury VIP carriages were introduced, with special seats at the front of the train to maximize the thrill of speed. Stations as big as airports sprouted, with marble halls and huge vaulted glass roofs. The minister became known as 'Great-Leap Liu' in keeping with his motto of 'Seize the opportunity; build more railways, and build them fast.' What he said went: 'It was difficult for the law to curb him,' a transport expert commented. Despite the accelerated development of the track and the trains, drivers received just ten days' training – compared to six months or more given in Europe and Japan. When safety concerns were raised (for instance about speeds or the quality of concrete used on the track bedding), the Ministry said it had found 68,634 problems and solved 98 per cent of them in short order.

Then, in February 2011 Liu hit the buffers. He was dismissed after being accused of having skimmed off up to 1 billion yuan in bribes and to have worked in collusion with a ring of contractors. With him went his lieutenant, Zhang Shugang, the engineering pioneer of the new technology. The National Audit Office disclosed that sixteen construction firms had submitted 1,297 fake invoices worth 324 million yuan in connection with work on Beijing–Shanghai line, that bidding for contracts had been rigged and 189 million yuan stolen. It was found that borrowing by the Ministry had rocketed from 670 billion yuan in 2008 to 1.98 trillion yuan two-and-a-half years later. The Communist Party newspaper, *People's Daily*, lamented 'an extremely large waste for the nation'. The State Information Office ordered media not to 'hype' the case and to make no mention of Liu's eighteen mistresses. In May 2012, the Communist Discipline Commission announced that Liu had been expelled from the Party for 'serious disciplinary violations' and leading 'a corrupt life' by taking big bribes and colluding with the Chairwoman of an investment company to funnel contracts her way. His gains were confiscated and he was handed over to the judicial authorities for prosecution. In a sign of the changed atmosphere, informed sources said the Ministry's police were being merged with the regular force and its law courts with the general judicial system.

Liu's fall was not simply a matter of ambition and graft run wild. His independence had become unbearable for the central government. As we will see, high-level anticorruption cases usually involve a political element: accusations of graft are used to unseat powerful figures who fall foul of the leadership. In Liu's case, he was not only doing his own thing but also had links with the group of politicians from Shanghai whom Hu Jintao was seeking to marginalize.

His successor, Sheng Guangzu, who had established his credentials for cleaning out stables during a major investigation into smuggling and corruption at the turn of the century, called a safety review and said the emphasis would shift from 'leapfrog development' to 'sustainable development'. Speeds were cut; the trains on the Beijing–Shanghai route ran without the carriage speedometers that were a feature of the Guangzhou–Wuhan line. Fares were reduced and first-class compartments were replaced with more egalitarian seating. People buying tickets were required to give their real names and the number they could buy was limited in order to fight scalping (which had caused discontent during the peak Chinese New Year holiday in 2011). A choice of trains at various velocities was also introduced on some runs, as customer satisfaction took priority over devotion to technology. At the end of 2011, ten officials in northern China were sacked for fraud involving railway bridges built with gravel and garbage in the place of cement.

Then, at night in late July 2011, came the crash. One high-speed train had lost power outside the eastern city of Wenzhou and another ran into the back of it. As well as the 39 reported fatalities some 200 people were injured. The initial explanation given was that a freak bolt of lightning had disabled the electronic system that should have warned the oncoming train. But similar power losses had been recorded on the track between Beijing and Shanghai and the lightning-bolt story soon dissolved as evidence pointed to a software fault in the signalling system.

The State Information Office told print and online media to keep stories off front pages. 'Do not report the accident too frequently,' it instructed. 'Report moving stories about people donating blood or taxi drivers not taking fares from victims. Do not investigate the cause of the accident [. . .] from now on use the headline "Great Love in the Face of Great Tragedy". On television, provide the relevant information but be careful of the music used.' There was great public anger at what appeared to be an official attempt at a cover-up that included blaming the weather rather than a mechanical fault, trying to bury the carriage in which most people died and offering the families of victims quick compensation deals on condition that they kept quiet.

One independent-minded newspaper, the *Economic Observer*, defied the censors to publish an eight-page special report entitled 'No Miracles in Wenzhou', with a commentary in the form of a letter to a two-year-old survivor whose parents died in the accident. This included such statements as 'there were two completely different images of China: one blossoming in the midst of the people, the other hidden in official-dom', and 'if every fact we seek becomes a secret, we'll never know the truth. If we keep giving up halfway in our pursuit of dignity, we will never be treated with dignity.' The popular tabloid *Beijing News* ran a page querying the way in which the disaster had been handled. Even *People's Daily* was moved to observe that 'China needs development, but not "blood-smeared GDP".'[2]

Wen Jiabao, who usually makes a point of hurrying to comfort disaster victims, did not arrive in Wenzhou for several days after the crash. He said he had been unable to visit beforehand because he had been bedridden with illness; however, website posts showed the Premier receiving a Japanese delegation a few days earlier. He pledged a greater focus on safety and more accountability. Three officials were sacked. The Chairman of a signalling company that had worked on the line died of a heart attack while being visited by a government inspection team. Then, in October, an investigation by the *Wall Street Journal* found that local engineers had not fully understood the Japanese components used in the signalling system; Hitachi had apparently sold parts with the inner workings concealed from the Chinese purchaser for fear that the technology might be stolen. An online poll reported that 97 per cent of respondents said they were unhappy with the handling of the disaster. It then transpired that one of the men appointed to replace the sacked officials had himself been held responsible and demoted after a major rail disaster in 2008. The initial inquiry commission was dominated by the Railway Ministry and had to be reconstituted to bring in independent outsiders.[3]

In mid-August the State Council announced that new railway projects would be suspended during an examination. There were further reductions in speed and longer intervals between trains. *Caixin* magazine reported fractures in axles on high-speed trains. The Ministry disclosed that there had been 168 glitches in the high-speed network in the single month of July 2011, 106 of which had stemmed from problems with rolling stock. In the summer of 2012, official media reported that more than twenty high-speed lines had substandard components holding together concrete sections of tunnels – the Chinese companies involved had charged a 30 percent mark-up by claiming that the parts they provided were made in Germany. But the ministry announced in July 2012 that spending would resume with 450 billion yuan – equivalent to $65 billion – to be disbursed in the second half of 2012.

The shock of the crash, of the minister's disgrace and of the media revelations was all the greater because of the way in which Liu's great project represented the tenacity of the People's Republic to succeed – and even more quickly than was reasonable. Trust in the authorities went down another notch. But pulling back was difficult: so much is based on the thesis that the scope and scale of China's achievements mean it can simply succeed if it wants to.

4

MEGA-CHINA

Though China has been until very recently a predominantly rural nation, its cities always had an awesome dimension to them, impressing foreign visitors and assuring the population that the rulers were capable of great things. The First Emperor laid out his capital of Chang'an near present-day Xi'an to face the four points of the compass with eight surrounding sets of buildings like stars: broad avenues, canals, nine markets, raftered houses, orchards, quarters for dignitaries adorned with silk and a hunting park with rhinoceroses, exotic birds and horses from Central Asia. When it served as capital for the late Han dynasty it was the biggest city on earth, with fifteen miles of walls. The other early capital, Luoyang, had walls ten metres high, twelve gates and two huge palaces connected by overhead walkways; at its peak around 50 AD it contained 500,000 people. Marco Polo was stunned by the richness of Hangzhou, capital of the Southern Song in the thirteenth century, and the Ming emperor Yongle made sure that the 250-acre Forbidden City, with its palaces containing 9,000 rooms set round courtyards behind towering walls, demonstrated the power of the dynasty when he moved the capital there from Nanjing in the early fifteenth century. Closer to the present, Mao Zedong tore down Beijing's city walls, had factories built close to the middle of the city and set about his spectacular expansion of Tiananmen Square.

China's capital, with a population of 20 million, has been transformed by an avalanche of buildings that – to the dismay of those who loved the old city with its rabbit-warren *hutong* alleyways of single-storey homes – has flattened most traditional dwellings and put up a mass of tower blocks where prices for a family flat spiral up to 5 million yuan or more and those for the smart upper-middle-class fetch twice as much.

Owning and modernizing a *hutong* house is now a badge of success costing anything between 50,000 and 120,000 yuan per square metre. A businessman who invited me to visit his greatly refurbished alley home was visibly pleased when I marvelled at the lavish array of fashionable furniture, both ancient and modern, the thick wall hangings, the electronic gear and the basement karaoke room.

An ever-expanding network of ring-roads reaches out into what was once farmland, producing a circular pattern characteristic of Chinese cities. The 2008 Olympics were the spur for development of the capital's infrastructure, including a network of urban railway lines that have turned once outlying villages into commuter-dormitory towns. In the woods beside the motorway to the airport, villas in gated communities go for 20 million yuan. At the time of the Games there was a huge drive to clean up the environment, with mass tree-planting and efforts to reduce air pollution. But in 2011 the World Health Organization (WHO) ranked Beijing as the tenth-dirtiest capital city on earth, and put it twenty-sixth out of thirty mainland cities for the cleanliness of its air. Clear visibility is often 100 yards.

Beijing is seeking to cope with its massive traffic jams by limiting the number of new cars or the days on which people may drive. The pressure for housing in the city is such that any available space is pressed into service. This includes the air-raid shelters built during the Cold War and now used for accommodation – or, as is the case at Renmin University, as a cavernous shopping complex (with instructions for action should bombers strike still on the walls). The authorities have taken measures to increase the obstacles to migrant workers acquiring property in the capital; in the summer of 2011, independent schools that had been set up to give tens of thousands of migrant children the education the city does not provide were declared unsafe and some were demolished, though protests led to a relaxation.

Half an hour away by high-speed train the municipality of Tianjin, with 12 million inhabitants, is engaged in a hectic programme to expand its port, highways, subways, train lines, residential and financial districts – one of which is modelled on Manhattan – development zones, parks and a planned eco-city. There remain parts of Tianjin dating from the European colonial era, including an Austro-Hungarian section by the river and an Italian square with villas built in Mediterranean style. Leafy streets run through the old British concession and a local man has built a museum and restaurant in the style of the Spanish architect Gaudi. But the highway to the port is clogged with lorries and lined with new apartments and a couple of power stations belching smoke towards them. Together with other cities in the region, Beijing and Tianjin will be at the centre of a new development zone designed to balance the growth of the last three decades in southern China and around Shanghai, but the effect on the environment, especially given dwindling water resources, threatens to add to the nation's challenges.

Shanghai, where 23 million people live, has constructed the equivalent of 334 Empire State Buildings in fourteen years. In the mid-1990s, when I first visited the once swampy area of Pudong, across the Huangpu River from the monumental colonial-era buildings on the Bund, the plans laid out by the authorities seemed like dreams; now they have become reality, with skyscrapers reaching 400 metres into the air, hotels perched above the smog clouds and an ultra-modern business district where every global financial group has to have an office. Nor is progress simply a matter of concrete, steel and glass: in 2010, Shanghai's schools were ranked number one in the world in reading, maths and science by the Organization for Economic Co-operation and Development (OECD). The local Shenhua soccer club shelled out major sums for ageing stars from European teams, Nicolas Anelka and Didier Drogba (though this has brought little success on the field, and both have since announced their departures). The city has even woken up to its history turning buildings from the foreign concession era into smart restaurants, hotels, clubs and luxury fashion outlets. The surrounding Yangtze River Delta is a major manufacturing hub, a centre of property development and home to high-tech firms in cities such as Suzhou and Wuxi, linked to Shanghai by fast trains and motorways.[1]

China spends up to $400 billion a year on buildings, putting up 28 billion square feet of new residential property annually. It is forecast to account for 40 per cent of global construction in the next ten years.

What that means is shown in Wuhan. In 2011 more than 5,700 construction projects were under way there. The city's position on the major waterway in the middle of the mainland has always made it important. It housed the country's first iron works in the late nineteenth century and a flourishing foreign concession with fine buildings along the riverside Bund; one still bears the name of the National City Bank of New York and another of the Banque de l'Indochine. Wuhan was briefly the capital of the left-wing Nationalist Republic in the 1920s and then Chiang Kai-shek's stopping place as he retreated from the Japanese in 1938. Under Mao, a mile-long double-deck road and rail bridge was built across the Yangtze to show off China's engineering prowess – it is now a favourite spot for suicides. At age 73, Mao sought to show that he was still a life force with a famous swim in the river during the Cultural Revolution, though the city descended into anarchy with fifty Red Guard factions fighting among themselves and with the army.

Today, Wuhan is key in the programme to develop the Yangtze freight channel to central and Western China. Barges ply up and down in the morning passing big floating cranes while fishermen cast nets and ferries chug by. A new bridge is being built across the Yangtze and a huge wholesale-trading centre is under construction. As well as the high-speed rail link with Guangzhou, and eventually with Beijing, Wuhan will spend 500 billion yuan on airports, a financial and a cultural district and a promenade with a tower twice as high again as the Empire State Building.

On the outskirts a new river port is being built by a six-lane highway surrounded by logistics parks. Around them are acres of unoccupied flats. The spending far exceeds the city's revenue and as I walked through the acres of empty apartment blocks in 2010 I could only wonder whether they would become a string of white elephants. But a local man reassured me: 'The government is on our side; the people will come.'

As an example of the Chinese urban-development engine, consider the enormous growth in municipal railway systems in places like Wuhan, which plans to build 225 kilometres of track at a cost of 300 billion yuan in the time it will take New York City to complete three kilometres of its Second Avenue subway. These projects are being constructed or expanded in no fewer than twenty-eight cities with eight more awaiting approval from Beijing; it is likely that, in all, more than 170 mass-transit systems will be built in China by 2030, compared to fifty in the whole of Europe. The spending will total at least 2.64 trillion yuan over ten years. The projects will spur demand for steel and other construction materials, produce work for civil-engineering firms, create employment for migrant labourers and use building machinery; as well as spawning orders for rolling-stock manufacturers as the effects are felt far beyond the basic purpose of moving city residents around and reducing traffic jams.[2]

The urbanization drive goes hand in hand with the ambitions of regions that spent centuries in the boondocks of China, cut off from the mainstream by mountains, deserts and history. They now aim for double-digit annual growth. For example, Anhui, traditionally a poor province that exported migrant labour to more prosperous parts of the country, received 460 billion yuan in investment in 2009. The Gree air-conditioner company runs a 730,000-square-metre plant in its capital, Hefei, producing 6 million units annually. The city hall sports two thirty-storey curved towers that face a water garden dubbed Swan Lake.

*

On the other side of the country, Chongqing, China's biggest municipality, reports directly to the central government in Beijing rather
than to the surrounding province of Sichuan. It covers 31,800 square
miles with a population of 32 million, only a third of whom live in
urban areas – 70 per cent of its territory is occupied by forests and
farms, which are major producers of rice and fruit. It used to be
described by journalists as 'the biggest city you've never heard of'; that
is less true since it became a major industrial hub and the base of
China's most flamboyant politician, Bo Xilai, before he crashed to
disgrace in 2012.

Located above the Three Gorges of the Yangtze at the junction of the
Yangtze and Jialing rivers, Chongqing traces its heritage back to the
quasi-legendary state of Ba in the eleventh century BC. It is a place
long known for its terrible overcast climate (it was said that when the
sun came out the dogs barked in alarm), dirt and unfriendly people.
Chiang Kai-shek moved the headquarters of the Nationalist regime
there during the Second World War after being driven by the Japanese
from the capital of Nanjing and then from Wuhan. The Generalissimo's
gloomy home in the wooded mountains outside the city has been
turned into a museum to commemorate the Chinese people's resistance to the Japanese in which, against the historical record, the
Communists claim the leading role. However, when I visited in 2011
there was hardly a trace of the Red forces. The buildings were filled with
photographs of the ruler chased out of the mainland in 1949 and his
glamorous American-educated wife, who acted as the regime's
spokesperson to the West. She was somewhat improbably nominal commander of the air force and occupied her own villa in the mountain
woods. In the city is a museum devoted to 'Vinegar Joe' Stilwell, the
American general sent to be Chiang's Chief of Staff, who feuded inces-
santly with the Nationalist leader from 1942 until he was recalled in
1944 and who had a higher opinion of the Communist army than of
the Nationalists. Visitors can also drive out to visit 'Happy Valley' in the
hills where the Nationalist secret police, abetted by American advisers,
ran a torture-and-execution camp.

At the end of 1949, back in Chongqing, as the Communists advanced
across China, Chiang tried to rally a last stand. But the People's

Liberation Army (PLA) closed in and the Nationalist leader had to flee
to the provincial capital of Chengdu before going on to the safety of
Taiwan; the political commissar of the PLA unit that took Chongqing
was Sichuan native Deng Xiaoping, who then became CCP First
Secretary in south-west China. Under Mao, Chongqing was developed as
an inland military centre in case of war with the US or the USSR. During
the Cultural Revolution an estimated 1,700 people died when Red
Guards attacked the authorities and then dissolved into factions which
fought one another with arms taken from local weapons factories. The
city contains what is thought to be the only cemetery in the whole country dedicated to Red Guards. The municipal government decided in
2009 to preserve the last resting place of 531 people; they are commemorated by pillars and obelisks, topped with an emblem of a torch,
carvings of Maoist slogans and the number 815, signifying the Red
Guard 'August 15' faction – that being the date in 1966 on which they
were formed. The cemetery is now in great disrepair, its gravestones covered by undergrowth and its rusting gate locked.

Today, Chongqing is key to the development programme for western
China that will counterbalance the focus on the coastal regions which
has marked the PRC's economy since the 1980s. It is an important
centre for steel and houses Asia's biggest aluminium plant. The main
state oil company is planning a big refinery at the end of a pipeline connected with Burma. There are coal, gas and mineral reserves nearby.

The municipality is planning expansion of 12.5 per cent a year of its
GDP up to 2015, well above the central government's national target of
7 per cent. The development of the Yangtze as a waterborne freight
channel means that containers can be loaded at Chongqing's modernized port and taken to the sea at Shanghai. A map in the City
Development Office shows railway links reaching to Russia and then to
Germany and the North Sea port of Rotterdam, which avoids the long
journey down the Yangtze – and the time taken to get by sea to Western
markets – and thus halves the distance Chongqing's products must
travel to reach European consumers.

More than a score of major foreign manufacturing companies have
set up in Chongqing, investing $6.3 billion there in 2010, along with an

army of smaller enterprises. Its high-tech parks are planned to turn out 100 million laptops a year. The municipal government receives input from an advisory board of leading foreign business executives. In 2011 Henry Kissinger paid a visit during which he extolled the progress that had been made. Work has started on a cloud-computing centre stretching over 2 million square metres and costing 40 billion yuan. Ford has a large joint-venture plant. The city is the biggest producer of motorcycles in China. Looking abroad, Chongqing firms have bought a machine-tools business in Yorkshire and farmland in South America.

Migrant workers from Sichuan are being encouraged by the municipal authorities to find jobs in Chongqing, close to their homes, rather than travelling all the way to plants in the south-east. Wages are lower than they are in Guangdong but so is the cost of living and people may go home to their villages during their time off. Officials point to the 66 per cent increase in earnings of urban residents since 2005 to just over 10,000 yuan while property prices have remained relatively subdued at less than a quarter of the average in Beijing. There has been heavy investment in public housing – one project accommodates 18,000 people. There are to be 20 satellite towns with 300,000 inhabitants as the municipal authorities proclaim their aim of promoting 'Liveable Chongqing' and 'Accessible Chongqing'. Police have been told to help citizens, not to harass them, and 500,000 surveillance cameras are being installed in the streets and buildings.

The city centre still has winding streets lined with fruit and vegetable stalls and with washing lines hanging between tenements. A stretch of old buildings by the Yangtze has been turned into a shopping and food complex specializing in Sichuan hotpot. 'Bangbang' porters, numbering 100,000 in all, carry loads on bamboo poles on their shoulders up and down the steep slopes above the rivers, just as they have for centuries, earning around 20 yuan a day. But many of the older structures are being torn down to make way for tower blocks and industrial sites. There are more cranes at work here than there are in Shanghai or Beijing, and more cement mixers, more construction crews. On an average day, upwards of 100,000 square metres of floor space is laid down as the local economy expands by 10 million yuan every twenty-four hours. Forty blocks line one stretch of an eight-lane highway leading to an industrial park housing automobile makers flanked by showrooms displaying American, Japanese and European luxury limousines. Down below, on a bend where the two rivers meet, stands a green, boat-shaped, 3,000-seat German-designed opera house. There is a Circus World with 1,500 seats and, of course, a financial district together with a large university, an art plaza, a convention and exhibition centre, museums, and libraries. An 'Eye' Ferris wheel offers a panoramic view when the cloud and fog do not intervene. From the outside, the local-government offices resemble a luxury hotel.

All the activity has ensured that the city is far from the pleasant metropolis the authorities say they are aiming to create. Its position in a bowl of mountains has always been a disadvantage as regards the weather. Industrial development has compounded that. The growth will continue despite the fall of Bo Xilai whose career and family history epitomised the vagaries of China under Communist rule. Bo is the son of a First Generation Communist leader, Bo Yibo, Finance Minister under Mao who was savagely purged and tortured during the Cultural Revolution; like so many other young people, his son was sent down to work in the countryside (though there are also reports that he served as a Red Guard previously and joined in the attacks on his father). The younger Bo bounced back to become Mayor of the port city of Dalian, Governor of the north-eastern province of Liaoning and then Commerce Minister in 2003 after the country's entry into the World Trade Organization (WTO).

His appointment as Party Secretary of Chongqing four years later was seen by some observers as a demotion, given that he might have aspired to advancement in Beijing. But he grasped the opportunity offered by the municipality: promising to make a reality of the 'Go West' programme, which had been talked about for more than fifteen years, he took a highly unusual high profile for a Chinese politician, deploying populist campaigning in a manner that constrasted sharply with the buttoned-up style of his peers. He wore smartly tailored suits, was media-savvy and sent his son to the expensive English school Harrow, followed by Oxford and Harvard, where he was known for his flamboyant lifestyle and courted the granddaughter of another Mao-era figure, the economist Chen Yuan.

As well as his drive for economic expansion Bo burnished his reputation with a major crusade against some of the city's powerful underworld bosses, who had for years operated more or less freely with the complicity of local officials. The crusade was implemented by a take-no-prisoners police chief, Wang Lijun, who had worked with Bo since the 1990s. In 2009 more than 3,000 people, including fourteen high-ranking civil servants and policemen, were arrested on an array of charges. Thirteen were given death sentences at the end of a mass trial in the huge new courthouse; among them was a former senior police officer, who sat dejectedly as he was found guilty of taking 16 million yuan in bribes from criminals. His sister-in-law, who was said to maintain luxury villas for sixteen young male lovers, was sentenced to eighteen years' imprisonment for bribing officials and operating illegal casinos.

A number of complications and loose ends remained, however. Police were alleged to have tortured some defendants to get them to confess. A controversial defence lawyer was arrested and received an eighteen-month jail sentence for 'coaching his client to make false claims of torture'; a retired forestry worker was sentenced to a year of 're-education through labour' when he alleged in a website post that Bo had given his underlings excrement for delivery to the lawyer (who sent it back).

There were suggestions that the anti-crime crusades had simply increased the influence of other gangs that were not targeted. There was an unmistakable political backdrop because Bo's predecessor in Chongqing, Wang Yang, belongs to another group in the leadership: his reputation could only suffer from his failure to fight organized crime during his time in the mega-metropolis.

Dapper, articulate and media-savvy, Bo, the princeling, was clearly hoping to be elevated to the CCP's top body, the Standing Committee of the Politburo, when the party held its five-year Congress at the end of 2012. Chongqing was his launching pad to the very top. A book called *The Chongqing Model*, written by three academics, saw the municipality as a model for state-led expansion and extolled Bo's anti-mafia campaign as the way to save China from counter-revolutions. Bo attracted fresh attention when he launched a populist campaign to get people to sing patriotic 'Red songs' and sent officials to work with the peasants in

Cultural Revolution style – as we will see, this was a political manoeuvre rather than the sign of a Maoist renaissance. His word appeared to be law and a personality cult grew up around him among officials anxious to ingratiate themselves with the boss. When it became known that Bo was fond of them, ginkgo trees were imported from other provinces and planted in place of the traditional banyans. *China Economic Weekly* reported that anywhere from thirty to fifty trucks carrying ginkgos made their way to Chongqing every day in spring 2011. The main source of the trees, Guangxi, had none left. No matter that these narrow trees gave less shelter than the banyans; when asked about this, officials said the banyans cut off sunlight.

The Mayor, Huang Qifan, sought to turn Chongqing into a world centre for small financial transactions while officials experimented with reforms of pensions and the residence registration system. Bo seemed to be on his way to the top of the political tree. Then disaster struck. The princeling had out-reached himself in a regime which puts a premium on obedience to the centre. His enemies were waiting. They got their chance when the police chief, Wang, tried to defect to the United States, setting off a train of events that ended with Bo disgraced, his wife sentenced for murder and Wang in prison for fifteen years. The drama, which will be told in Chapter Eight, brought down the rock star of Chinese politics, but it did not mean an end to the Chongqing story. A trusted Party figure went in to steady the ship, Bo's associates were dealt with, foreign investors were reassured – and the biggest story on earth rolled on.

The move inland epitomized by the growth of Chongqing and Wuhan raises questions about the future of the Pearl River Delta, which led the economic revolution launched by Deng Xiaoping in the late 1970s. The Delta, which now contains 120 million people, registered 16 per cent annual growth in the 1980s and attracted half the foreign investment into the PRC – benefiting from its proximity to Hong Kong, whose entrepreneurs moved jobs and expertise across the border. Today its economy is almost as big as that of Indonesia and is said to produce 5 per cent of all the goods manufactured worldwide. Its people are among the wealthiest in the country. The influx of migrant workers means that

Guangdong, which covers most of the Delta, is China's most heavily populated province, with 104 million inhabitants.

Natives of the Guangdong and Guangxi provinces and Hong Kong speak Cantonese, which emerged from the Old Chinese language predating Mandarin; their population has, over the centuries, been increased by the influx of tens of millions of *Hakka* (visitors) moving from northern and central China in a series of emigrations as foreigners invaded their own homelands. Cantonese have traditionally been among the most outward-looking inhabitants of China. Cut off from the rest of the country by mountains on its northern border with Hunan, and protected by a maze of waterways, the region was outside Beijing's effective control for long stretches of imperial history. It has been home to merchants and Triads and the Taiping rebels, who marched from Guangxi to conquer Nanjing in the early 1850s and there established their Heavenly Empire – fighting the Qing dynasty across China in a fourteen-year rebellion that is estimated to have taken about 20 million lives.

Canton, now Guangzhou, was the only port authorized for foreign trade under the Qing Empire, shipping out porcelain, tea and art to meet the eighteenth-century European taste for *Chinoiserie* and then becoming the scene of the First Opium War, of 1839–42, when the British brought in narcotics from India to make money and redress the balance of trade. The region saw a series of revolts against the late empire led by 'the Father of the Republic', Sun Yat-sen. Sun was born in a Delta village in 1866 and got his further education and converted to Christianity in Hong Kong before pursuing a peripatetic career as a revolutionary, which led to him becoming the first President of the Chinese Republic for a few months in 1912.

During the warlord era of national division that followed, Canton housed one of twentieth-century China's truly progressive regional governments before it was ousted in a struggle with Sun, who wanted the city as a base from which to lead a military expedition to reunite the country. In 1926, a year after Sun's death, the National Revolutionary Army of his Kuomintang Party did stage the promised march north (under the leadership of Chiang Kai-shek) to establish the Nationalist Republic in Nanjing, which ruled China, with considerable difficulty, until 1949.

In the 1930s the province showed its autonomist tendencies once more under a warlord who acted independently of Nanjing before being overcome by Chiang's familiar mixture of bribery and military threats. It was occupied by the Japanese in the Second World War and taken by the PLA in the later stages of the civil war in 1949. Three decades later the province's commercial past, trading experience and position next to Hong Kong made it the natural spearhead for the market-led economic reforms launched by Deng Xiaoping.

Today Guangzhou is China's third most heavily populated urban centre, the heart of a web of manufacturing centres being brought together by an urban railway network that will connect 40 million people. The city has developed ultra-modern docks running down the river as well as the usual array of tower blocks, highways, a planned eco-city and the high-speed train station from which the journey to Wuhan takes three hours instead of the previous ten. An International Biotech Island is planned in the Pearl River. At nearly 440 metres tall and with 70 high-speed lifts, the slender, stylish Guangzhou International Finance Centre, the work of British architect Chris Wilkinson, is the ninth-tallest structure in the world – the dome at St Paul's cathedral would fit into the atrium at the hotel occupying its 39 top floors. The city's granite-and-glass opera house stands beside a 103-storey tinted-glass tower and a large library in a brick building meant to look like an open book. Designed on 'intergalactic' lines by the Iraqi architect Zaha Hadid, the opera house was described in the *New York Times* as 'the most alluring opera house built anywhere in the world in decades'. But, just a year after it opened, big cracks appeared in walls and ceilings, glass panels fell from windows and rain seeped into the structure – all because of shoddy construction work. It also lacks a permanent opera company.

There are some traces of the colonial and Nationalist-era past in Guangzhou. An island in the Pearl River contains a few villas and terraces from the era of the British concession and the Whampoa Military Academy – which formed the Nationalists' Revolutionary Army with both Chiang Kai-shek and Mao's future lieutenant, Zhou Enlai, as instructors – has been rebuilt as a historic monument after being bombed by the Japanese. As well as local delicacies, such as water beetles, the Cantonese still eat animals that are protected elsewhere. The market's range has been cleaned up somewhat but the place remains full of 'exotic' small beasts whose consumption is supposed to increase longevity or sex drive or confer general wellbeing. Thus it seemed quite normal when, as my wife and I returned to our hotel one night, a man on the back of a passing truck tossed a writhing sack full of snakes on to the pavement.

East of Guangzhou, Zengcheng city – and in particular its district of Xintang – turns out 200 million pairs of blue jeans a year, a number that by some estimates accounts for half the emblematic trousers sold in the USA. The Conshing Group's factory employs 3,000 workers on a 32-hectare site making jeans sold by the Polo, Lee, Guess and Abercrombie & Fitch brands. Margins for the manufacturers are as low as 1 yuan per pair. A third of Zengcheng's 1.5 million residents come from Sichuan, 1,500 miles away. There is a yawning gap between most of them and the rich factory owners and others who have profited from the city's growth, supporting five-star hotels, luxury cars and upscale restaurants offering French vintages to accompany the delicacies for which Guangdong is celebrated. On leaving a Xintang hotel after a ten-course banquet a visiting journalist from Hong Kong was warned against carrying bags, even plastic ones, because motorcycle riders were known to snatch them in the street.

Shenzhen, a fishing village in the 1970s, became a spearhead of development as the first Special Economic Zone (SEZ) in 1980 – China's first McDonald's outlet opened there in 1990. It now houses more than 10 million people. A portrait of an avuncular Deng, who used the city as the launching pad for the 'socialist market economy', beams out from a wall by a roundabout, testimony to the changes his policies wrought in this symbolic centre of China's growth. The city contains 6,000 firms involved in making cellular telephones, which between them employ 1 million people, and has become a global assembly line with 24 -hour customs clearance to Hong Kong. It houses biotech companies and Tencent QQ, China's biggest Internet firm by market capitalization (in 2011 QQ had more than 700 million users), with the largest instant-messaging service on earth, a vast array of online games and a virtual currency. Shenzhen's Hua Qiang North Road market is the world's biggest sales centre for counterfeit mobile-telephone handsets and iPhones; production runs to an estimated 255 million units a year, though activity has dropped as the authorities have moved to protect domestic brands and the copiers have started making smartphones of their own.

Seventy per cent of the people in Shenzhen are migrant workers, mostly in their late teens or early twenties; many of these are young women doing mind-numbingly repetitive assembly-line work with very long hours and minimal breaks, living in Spartan conditions behind high walls and wire fences. They face discriminatory hiring practices and are presented with 'take it or leave it' contracts that skirt round tougher labour legislation introduced in recent years – in some cases agreements are written in English and not understood.

Western human-rights and labour groups depict such people as an oppressed underclass toiling in what amounts to slavery. There is, indeed, a parallel with the role of slavery in the New World; like the plantations, the huge plants that supply the world with goods could not function without them. Their labour underpins the emergence of the entrepreneurial middle class and provides the muscle for construction projects across the country as China pushes its urbanization. They form the human bridge between the cities and the countryside, with remittances from their wages keeping many villages financially afloat. They are the potential mass drivers of the increase in consumption the government wants to see. Unlike slaves, they have gone to work voluntarily far from home, but they remain second-class citizens not because of their working conditions (though these are often at the bottom of the labour pile) but on account of the *hukou* registration system under which all Chinese are tied to their place of origin, regardless of where they live and work, and have no rights to health, education or welfare elsewhere.

Many of the big plants are organized in military style in order to instil discipline on the assembly line. Migrants work eleven-hour days with one or two days off each fortnight. They live in company dormitories or small apartments and eat in company canteens during short meal breaks, paying for both accommodation and food with their wages. They are liable to be fined if they spend more than five minutes in the toilet. Managers patrol the line urging them to work faster and pay is docked for illness. Though the law limits overtime to thirty-six hours a week migrants on assembly lines often put in far more to boost wages to 1,500-plus yuan a month. Samsung Electronics of South Korea has been accused of 'inhumane' working conditions and hiring children at its plants in China – and acknowledged abuses late in 2012. Apple, Motorola and Microsoft have also been criticised.

Oppressive and extreme though these conditions are, at least some of those on the assembly lines in Shenzhen seem to view themselves as risk-takers who have thrown off the shackles of rural life. They work very large amounts of overtime not simply because the employers demand it but also because they want to maximize their earnings both to save and to be able to send remittances back to their villages to keep relatives there afloat. They are cut off from the locals not only by the factory fences but also by the fact that most do not speak Cantonese, and as such develop and depend on friendships – indeed the crowds of young women streaming out of the big plants are rather akin to girls leaving a vast school, with groups from different provinces sticking together.

Their earnings many times exceed what they could make back in their home villages. The big factories are modern and safety conditions have generally been improved – when chemicals affected the fingers of workers at a supplier for Apple, they were given compensation of 80,000 yuan or more and the case was reported on state television as an example of benevolent management. The second generation of migrants is, in general, more individualist and less pliant to heavy-handed management methods than their parents were. Some grew up in manufacturing centres and so know nothing of farming or the countryside. Others who left backward regions of Sichuan or Anhui as teenagers sense that they are undertaking the journey of a lifetime, and want a degree of respect in return. With a labour shortage of 2 million people in Guangdong, they are aware of their worth as inland cities – notably Chongqing – compete for their services. Most of these young people far from home have no desire to return to their villages. They see more opportunity to set up small businesses in urban centres than in the rural hinterland. Research by the Harvard sociologist Martin Whyte shows an overwhelming desire to get on in life – and one may extrapolate a corresponding anger when they see themselves as being held back by discrimination, procedural obstacles and oppressive employers and local authorities.

Hu Jintao has warned of the potential danger to stability this slice of 16 per cent of the population represents while a government think tank noted that if they were not absorbed into society 'many conflicts will accumulate'. However, relaxing the registration system is a sensitive political matter because the cost of giving migrants access to urban services is not an expenditure that cash-strapped local authorities want to undertake. Beijing has reacted sternly to occasional press suggestions for reform, firing editors and deleting such postings from websites.

Migrants in Guangdong have begun to stage strikes. One in 2010, by nearly 2,000 young workers at a Honda vehicle-parts factory, lasted for two weeks while others hit a dozen other foreign-owned car plants and Japanese factories making electronics goods and glass. The main issue was pay but there were also calls for greater shop-floor representation. Stoppages spread to Chinese factories up the east coast, though reports in state media focused only on those at plants connected with foreign enterprises.

In the summer of 2011 employees at a watch plant in Guangdong stopped work to protest at long working hours. Four thousand staff at a factory owned by a South Korean company producing handbags for upmarket brands such as DKNY, Burberry and Coach went on strike for three days. Their protest was against the 'harsh environment' in which they had to work: this constituted having to stand up for twelve hours a day and being forbidden to drink water or use toilets except during set breaks every four hours; their monthly wages ran up to 1,900 yuan. 'The Korean management treats us [as] less than human beings,' one worker told the *South China Morning Post*. 'The male managers walk into female toilets any time they please; we can't contain our anger any more.' That winter, thousands of staff at Guangdong factories making sports shoes, women's underwear and other products went on strike as wages were cut in response to falling demand for exports. In the town of Huangjiang, 8,000 workers took to the streets, clashing with police.

The names of many of the electronic-manufacturing services (EMS) companies that employ the migrant workers of Guangdong are unfamiliar to the international public that buys the goods they put together under famous brand names. The IT hardware firm Foxconn, which is owned by Hon Hai Precision Industry of Taiwan and turns out computers, mobile telephones, video consoles and other equipment for multinational corporations (including Apple, Dell, Hewlett-Packard, Nokia and Sony), is the biggest employer with 1 million staff in the province; another 200,000 are employed by Foxconn elsewhere. Its revenue grew by an annual 30 per cent in seven years of the first decade of the twenty-first century to reach $85 billion; in recognition of the problems in maintaining such growth the company slashed annual targets from 2011, yet they were set even then at 15 per cent. It employs 400,000 in Shenzhen alone. Its main site in the city comprises fifteen different units, with restaurants, shops, banks, medical facilities and its own fire brigade. A former manager compares the enterprise to 'an occupation army'.[3]

Dressed in regulation company sports shirts, cotton trousers and plastic slippers, employees at Foxconn and other mass assembly lines have their working routine minutely choreographed in order to maximize production. Some start their shifts with company songs intended to motivate them. Interns taken on from vocational schools have told of working fourteen hours a day, standing up, for 500 yuan a month. The next logical stage in the production process will be more automation with large-scale introduction of robots; as wages rise, robots will become more cost-effective – and can of course work round the clock without meal or toilet breaks. When Foxconn announced its plan to install 1 million robots by 2014 it said the decision was driven by its 'desire to move workers from more routine tasks to more value-added propositions in manufacturing, innovation and other areas that are equally important to the success of our operations'. But one can only wonder how many of the million-plus migrants it employs will be needed for 'value-added propositions' and whether China will start to feel the effects of domestic outsourcing – to robots.

Fourteen Foxconn workers committed suicide in 2010, jumping to their deaths from the factory roofs. The nature of their work was no doubt the most significant motivation, but other factors were also relevant: loneliness, the loss of their social context by being removed from the inland villages where they grew up and uncertainty about how to manage the new world in which they found themselves. 'At seventeen or eighteen, we don't know how to handle the boss, handle money and how to speak,' as one former assembly-line worker who is now in a corporate-responsibility programme at Fuji Xerox in Shenzhen told the *Financial Times* in 2011. In response to the deaths Foxconn installed yellow nets around the tops of the buildings on its main production campus, appointed counsellors, set up staff-support groups and established a 'care centre' with a computerized database to log and track workers who expressed personal distress. Wages were also increased. Another big Pearl River Delta employer, Flexitronics, with a township of 52,000 workers in the Guangdong city of Zhuhai has begun 'big brother, big sister' mentoring and says staff turnover fell by 20 per cent in 2010.

Foxconn's tango-dancing commander, Tai-Ming Gou, has been Chairman since it was set up in 1974 to make plastic television-tuner knobs in Taiwan. Born in 1950 to a couple from Shanxi who had fled across the Strait in 1949, 'Terry' Gou moved operations to the mainland as costs in Taiwan rose in the mid-1980s. When in Shenzhen, he works from a spare, concrete-floored office with a worn carpet; he sleeps there in a bed with a green mosquito net. He calls the suicides 'wrenching', but insists the company is not a sweatshop. In 2013, Foxconn said trade union elections would be instituted at its PRC plants.[4]

Still, China has no shortage of exploitative factory owners and managers. An undercover investigation into the Sturdy Products factory in Shenzhen, which supplies the big Mattel toy group, found that children as young as fourteen were employed there. Staff had to sign a 'voluntary' agreement to do overtime of up to 120 hours a month. They were fined for failing to reach quotas, and shouted at on the assembly line by managers. Dangerous chemicals caused illnesses. In May 2011 a forty-five-year-old female worker jumped to her death at the plant, which makes *Toy Story* and *Cars* toys for Disney and Barbie dolls as well as supplying the *Thomas the Tank Engine*, Matchbox and Fisher Price ranges.[5]

In Beijing, the city's Labour Office reported in the spring of 2011 that it had dealt with 14,361 cases involving 39,200 migrants who had not been paid wages owed to them; one property-development firm had withheld cash for fourteen months. In factories migrants may be rejected for employment on arbitrary grounds: for being too short or being aged over thirty, or simply for being from a region with a bad reputation for diligence. The pressure to produce as quickly as possible is such that even when safety standards are posted they may be ignored in the rush to maximize output – particularly in smaller plants.

Dotting the country are workshops where migrants work in stifling conditions in the summer and freezing temperatures in winter. Fatal fires, in which employees burn to death while locked inside dormitories, have become less common, but incidents of workplace malpractice are nonetheless frequent and certainly many of them go unreported. As an editorial on the state news agency Xinhua noted: 'If they are left in the state they are in now in the near future, their increasing discontent with their working and living conditions will quite probably turn them into a source of social instability.'

Such visceral confrontations seem far away from the manicured headquarters of the big communications-technology provider Huawei, down the road from Foxconn. Half the company's 30,000 staff in Shenzen (out of 90,000 worldwide) are engaged in research and development; 70 per cent have a master's degree and their average age in 2011 was thirty-one. The main campus could be in California; it houses 3,000 of the employees, who have a supermarket, a hairdressing salon and a swimming pool. There is a 100-room training centre complete with a Muslim prayer space with an arrow pointing to Mecca. Employees used to have to sing revolutionary songs; now they undergo a lengthy training programme designed to nurture the 'wolf spirit' said to drive the firm.

Huawei says its equipment serves one-third of the world's population and is used by twenty-four of the top thirty global telecommunications operators. In 2010 it reported sales of $28 billion, only $2 billion lower than those of the industry leader, Ericsson, and ahead of its main Chinese rival, ZTE, also based in Shenzhen. Huawei has twenty research-and-development centres round the globe, including a $150-million unit being set up in India. It has evolved the world's first 100G technology for long-distance wireless transmission of large amounts of data, and has launched a smartphone that gives users access to cloud computing. Though it trails the likes of Nokia and Samsung, Huawei is among the world's ten leading brands of handsets and aims to become the top supplier by 2015 by switching from supplying mobile operators to selling under its own name. In 2011 it bid to provide mobile-telephone connections in the London Underground railway system for the 2012 Olympics. Its data centre contains 2,000 servers; security inside is tight, with staff forbidden to carry mobile telephones and everybody required to wear 'foot gloves' – grey for men, black for women. The 11,000-square-metre logistics centre handles material from 1,000 global suppliers, including equipment worth $2 billion from the USA in 2010.

However, the company's efforts to expand through acquisitions in the West, particularly in the United States, have been blocked by suspicions that it is controlled by the army where its founder, Ren Zhengfei, was once an engineer and that its services may be compromised as a result. Huawei denies this and hired a former chief information officer for the British government to oversee its cyber security. It says Ren's holding has dropped below 2 per cent of its share capital, which is mainly owned by the staff as a whole. But the allegations are used persistently by politicians and lobbyists wishing to block its acquisitions abroad; its equipment was banned for a time in India on national-security grounds. Lack of full disclosure by its directors has added to the fears of Huawei as a stalking horse for the Chinese state and its military and security arms. As we will see in Chapter Nine, this is a burden bred by the system within which they operate that dogs a number of PRC companies as they seek to remain Chinese while becoming international.

Driving from Guangzhou to Hong Kong via Shenzhen, it is hard to know where one city stops and another starts. The whole region is a succession of cities with low-rise manufacturing plants and residential complexes linked by multi-lane highways and dotted with airports. Many of the factories are monotonously dreary collections of anonymous buildings that could be making anything. Near Shenzhen lies a cluster of entertainment parks. Splendid China reproduces the country's main historical and natural beauty spots; Window on the World does the same for the globe as a whole, with 118 miniature scenic spots – from the Eiffel Tower and the Taj Mahal to Niagara Falls. As so often happens in this region, a grey cloud of smog blotted out the sun when I visited.

There is more serious pollution in villages, where ponds and streams are clogged with rubbish and rivers are full of chemical pollution. There are occasional stretches of green countryside but not too many; this is, after all, the workshop of the world – signs over the highway from Guangzhou to Shenzhen extol the role of road safety in advancing 'a prosperous economic future'. Between them Dongguan (China's third-biggest exporting centre), Jiangmen (a thriving port), Foshan (the Delta's third-largest city), Zhongshan (birthplace of Sun Yat-sen), and Zhuhai (another of the first SEZs, on the border with Macau and home to Flexitronics with its 52,000 staff making Microsoft components), have a population of 20 million. An extraordinary range of goods is made here as well as the IT equipment that pours out of the likes of Foxconn – furniture, appliances of all kinds, plastic and metal products, tools, toys, electrical and electronic appliances, building materials, textiles, ceramics, motorcycles, garments and textiles, stainless-steel products, toilet paper, packaging and synthetic fibres. The cities house electronics parks, software developers and biotechnology enterprises, large oil - and natural-gas- storage reservoirs as well as one of the first golf courses built to cater to the new rich. Grown here are rice, sugar, bananas, fruit and flowers for domestic and foreign markets. These places are the native homes of many millions of Chinese living abroad; Cantonese is the lingua franca of many Chinatowns from Sydney to London.

The question is whether Guangdong can sustain the momentum of the last three decades by going up the value chain. The rate at which residents of Shenzhen start new businesses has fallen to less than half that in 2004, according to a study by the local Academy of Sciences and the Chinese University of Hong Kong. Budding entrepreneurs face scarcity of land, rising wages as the union federation pushes collective bargaining as never before, and a tighter legal framework than was in place in the early boom years. Outside investors have become more careful.

With migrants preferring to stay close to home in places like Chongqing, Guangdong is experiencing labour gaps – so must pay workers more and offer inducements, such as waived school fees for 3 million children of migrants. The number of firms from Hong Kong with operations in Guangdong has dropped from 56,000 to 40,000 since 2009. As costs rise and export markets tighten, their representative association says, 'some will be forced out of business; some will be sold; and some will be relocated to remoter parts of the country or even overseas.' A survey in 2010 reported that more than one-third of the former colony's 80,000 firms operating in the Pearl River Delta area plan to shift part or all of their production capacities. Operating margins at Foxconn have dropped from 4–5 per cent to 1–2 per cent in ten years. Rising sales meant the company could absorb that but, if demand in rich countries continues to drop at a time when costs per employee in Guangdong are rising by 30 per cent a year, the firm will be under heavy pressure. Its parent company, Hon Hai, missed its profit targets for three consecutive quarters in 2010–11. As well as its one-million robots programme, Foxconn is considering the transfer of 300,000 jobs to the middle of China. Guangdong will retain a role but, as one local observer puts it, it will no longer be *the* place to manufacture.[6]

There has been talk of political and legal reform – especially in Shenzhen, where competitive elections for municipal posts have been mooted and the authorities have experimented in delegating a few aspects of administration to non-governmental organizations (NGOs), a few of which are allowed to operate without official patrons, and providing better service for migrant workers. Still, these initiatives have been few and far between – and have been carefully monitored. The provincial authority has called for public opinion to make itself heard and for a relaxation of media controls. But Wang Yang, the Guangdong CCP Secretary, says what he wants from the media is good news. The regional Nanfang publishing group, which owns eight newspapers, including China's bestselling serious weekly and is a leading exponent of investigative journalism and a voice for reform, is constantly operating on the margins of what is allowed while a local editor said he had been told that greater openness was designed to help the government 'rather than cause trouble' and 'must not go beyond limits'.[7]

Activists anxious to get behind the curtain of official opacity have tried to use an open-governance law passed in 2008 but have had limited success. Yang Jianchang, a member of that city's local congress, received an avalanche of complaints about the local authorities when he opened a personal office for citizens to contact; he had some success but he had been threatened and physically attacked. In 2010 the national legislature passed a law banning such personal offices. The following year Guangdong announced that it was putting its provincial budget online but the figures for only four departments appeared and meant little: 'openness is no new breakthrough', a local newspaper commented.

Wang Yang, a Hu Jintao protégé who was moved there from Chongqing in 2007, has said that his main aim is to improve wellbeing among the province's inhabitants to create a 'Happy Guangdong'. He was quoted by a local newspaper as acknowledging that 'long-term development on all fronts will be hampered if we don't pay attention to outstanding [social] problems.' He emerged in 2011–12 as a leading advocate of reform but failed to get a seat on the Standing Committee of the Politburo, despite his ability to get rid of local rivals, ousting the previous power elite in the province amid accusations of corruption and reports of its links with the Triad underworld.

Growing prosperity has certainly bred corruption: a report by the Chinese Academy of Social Sciences (CASS) found that 1,640 people fled abroad from Guangdong between 1998 and 2004 with 155 billion yuan in illegal cash between them – four times as many as from the second-ranked province, Fujian. Chen Shaoji, former provincial Police Chief and leading political adviser to the Guangdong government, was sentenced to death for having taken 30 million yuan in bribes. The Mayor of Shenzhen, Xun Zongheng, was sentenced to death with a two-year grace period for accepting 33 million yuan in bribes; he was said to have spent 20 million in bribes to get the job in the first place. Chinese media connected him with China's one-time richest man, Huang Guangyu, Chairman of Gome, the country's biggest electrical-goods retail chain, who was himself sentenced to fourteen years in jail for bribery and insider trading. The Mayor of Zhongshan, Li Qihong, who was also Director of the city's Party Organization Department with over-sight on appointments, was ousted on charges that she, her husband and their children had illicitly amassed assets of more than 2 billion yuan.

Such purges are a familiar element in the political landscape of the

PRC. What will count more for Guangdong will be its ability to adapt to changing economic circumstances in which the sheer size of output and the labour force will no longer be enough to ensure competitiveness. This makes the province that led the way in the 1980s a touchstone of China's future, but that future will also be determined by a myriad of small enterprises which work away from the mega-cities and their huge firms like Foxconn – for, despite the power of the tiger's head, this is a nation with a multiplicity of snakes' tails down on the ground.

THE MOTLEY NATION

Unlike Chongqing, Guangzhou, Beijing and Shanghai, Yiwu is neither a major seaport nor a traditional urban centre, but lies on a plain with small mountains visible through the pollution haze in Zhejiang province in the east of China. There are no visible attractions here, nothing historic or beautiful – not even a theme park celebrating some recently rediscovered ancient hero. There is only one reason for visiting this place: to buy Chinese products. The twice-yearly Canton Fair is China's biggest trade exhibition, held in a million-square-metre hall and registering turnover of $23 billion a year; it has achieved a degree of international prominence and perpetuates the name by which Guangzhou was once known to foreigners. Yiwu, which bills itself as 'China's city of small commodities', is much less known, but has come to play a core role in the global commercial supply chain.

It reflects a characteristic of China, being a centre comprising many small elements – simultaneously huge and fragmented. The main trading complex at Yiwu consists of 90 buildings covering 600,000 square metres. Inside are 8,000 individual shops, most of which are crammed into small units run by one or two people. They sell anything you could want that the People's Republic makes, short of heavy machinery. This being China, the local authorities plan further expansion so that the trading centres will offer 20,000 product ranges, drawing in goods from abroad as well as from China. If they achieve their aim to sell imports from fifty countries to domestic buyers or for re-export, Yiwu will be confirmed as the global trading capital.

In the main complex, one floor sells nothing but small electrical appliances. Walk on and you pass shop windows displaying kitchen utensils, knives, vacuum cleaners, refrigerators, bathroom equipment, cockroach traps, superglue, prayer beads, artificial flowers, shoes, clothing and accessories of all kinds, jewellery, scarves, garden gnomes, and LED displays flashing out 'Merry Christmas', 'BAR!' 'NAILS' or 'PIZZA'. There is a floor devoted to beads and cheap fashion accessories. Another is lined with shop after shop offering electrical plugs and batteries. Then there are the souvenirs made to order for other places – artefacts for antique shops in the Middle East and badges for cities round the world, not to mention knick-knacks to commemorate the 2011 British Royal Wedding. Half the Christmas goods sold in Europe and America are traded here.

Profit margins are tiny. Orders are taken only in bulk. There are rip-offs of foreign brands, their names often a transmutation of the original into something that sounds like the Chinese pronunciation of it (as in Cadaier for Cartier). On the other side of the city lies a six-storey building covering 160,000 square metres devoted to furniture display and offering all styles of tables, chairs, beds, mock-European drawing-room suites, curtains, wall decorations and garden stuff. In addition Yiwu houses a huge timber yard, a jade market and a Buddhist Trade Centre.

Streets are dedicated to specific goods – one stretch for bedding, others for jewellery, laptops or packaged food.

Light manufacturing plants have moved in to be close to the wholesalers. They are involved in weaving, tobacco processing, printing, lace making and the production of 'seamless underwear', toys, waterproofs, 'sweetheart clothing', ribbons and 'stickiness products'. One company makes 30 per cent of China's socks; another turns out 4 million zippers a day.

Migrant workers, most of them from poorer neighbouring provinces, such as Jiangxi, mill around in four blocks of a street where employment agencies and companies post notices of jobs. Many sleep on the pavement at night. Local farmers who have been given subsidized accommodation in the city to free land for development move into cheaper accommodation and let out their new red-brick homes at a nice profit to traders; our taxi driver said the rent could reach 100,000 yuan a year. The population has risen to around 2 million.

At the start of Yiwu's growth its GDP was two-thirds of the provincial average; now it is double and still rising. Businesses radiate optimism: the Evergrowing Bank, Zhejiang Hopeful Transportation, the Perfect and Excellent Company. Property prices have soared as people from the province's manufacturing hub of Wenzhou have invested in the choicer part of the city. Glitzy car salerooms line the street to the new railway station: cars are forbidden to drive up the ramp leading to the station entrance because of the jams they would cause. Prostitution is concentrated on a few streets in the city centre; these are lined with karaoke parlours, bars, run-down single-storey houses outside which women smoke, wait and wave at us as we drive past, and 'hairdressing' salons with revolving barbers' poles outside offering much more than a short back and sides.

One main road in Yiwu is filled with Muslim restaurants; many shops and stalls have signs in Arabic. French logistics companies advertise their services to ship goods to Africa. There are speedy trains to Shanghai and the usual multi-lane highway, but, strangely, only four destinations are served from the modern airport outside town. To get to Yiwu from Sichuan province on the other side of China, I flew to the provincial capital of Hangzhou then travelled for ninety minutes on a night bus. On the way back out, on a Friday, I took a flight to Guangzhou. Having just missed an afternoon departure, I sat for a couple of hours in the smart airport terminal, at the café with a mother and daughter focused on their mobile telephones and a backpacking European couple who worked out if they could afford a pot of noodles. The gleaming hall was otherwise eerily empty, seemingly yet another example of the over-building that characterizes today's China. Then, suddenly, an avalanche of people arrived by car, taxi and bus to fill the plane. They had no time to waste waiting for the flight; they had business to conclude. There were passengers from Nigeria, Uganda, Palestine, the United States, Denmark, Colombia, Turkey, Central Asia and India, most of them lugging large suitcases filled with samples with which to solicit orders from buyers back home.

The city's people got into trading in the 1980s. In 2003, when the coming leader of China, Xi Jinping, was in charge of Zhejiang, the local government pushed the full-scale development of the new trading units, reaping big profits from the sale of land leases and revenue from its stake in the municipal holding company. Modern communications played their part, too. Buyers from New York or Nairobi need make only one visit to identify the products they want; thereafter they put in repeat orders via the Internet or by telephone. Consequently, despite its size and scope, Yiwu is a relatively empty place. Nobody stays when they have completed their business. 'What the hell is there to do here?' a jewellery buyer from Brooklyn asked me over breakfast in the Kingdom Hotel, where the talk among clients is of exchange rates, delivery schedules and rising Chinese wages. Just one thing: buy.

There are places like Yiwu strung across China: places that nobody abroad (besides those involved in doing business there) has ever heard of but that have become vital hubs of the country's development as it grew into the world's biggest manufacturer and exporter and contributed a quarter of global growth this century. Such places are far from Beijing and Shanghai, where foreigners most usually visit. Some can trace their current line of business back to the past; but many, like Yiwu, seem to have grown largely by accident from an initiative by a few people who, once started, were not going to stop. The decisive spurt of growth in the 1980s came from private enterprises built up from the ground by individuals and families. As we will see, that model was altered in the 1990s by the reform of the big state-owned enterprises (SOEs), which were given priority while the small players were squeezed. The same process was at work in the stimulus programme launched at the end of 2008, under which most bank credit and orders for big-ticket projects – such as high-speed trains – went to SOEs. The result has been that, overall, the state sector is profitable, but thanks largely to the preferential treatment it receives.

Still, small-scale enterprise continues to play a key role in the economy, with individual outfits often grouped together in clusters to supply one another or each contribute a single element to a finished product. Big contracts given to a single company are split up between a myriad of subcontractors down to individual workers.

This division of labour is replicated in the financial system. Alongside the four state giants, the PRC contains more than 3,500 banking institutions. Corporate bonds, 'informal' loans between individuals and companies on the 'shadow-banking system' and funding from family savings are a frequent source of finance, with interest rates varying from 10 to 20 per cent a year for tried and trusted borrowers with solid collateral to far more in the overnight 'gambling' market. Official figures in 2011 reported that 3,366 financial institutions outside the formal banking system had extended loans worth 287.5 billion yuan – the true total is higher since the statistics do not capture all lending. A crackdown at the end of the year revealed hundreds of unregulated electronic equity and futures exchanges. In 2012, funding for local government projects came mainly from corporate bond issues and private trusts outside the formal bank sector.

Such fragmentation is endemic in China and has given the economy a vibrancy that reaches far beyond the big state-run enterprises (SOEs). While the 121 largest firms operating under the State-Owned Assets Supervision and Administrative Commission (SASAC) tower over the economic landscape, China has another 114,400 state companies at central and local levels. Though chain stores have spread across the PRC in the past decade, the country's biggest retailers command less than 6 per cent of the market each. The number of car makers has reached around

100, even if some work for only part of the year. Big real-estate firms have expanded as a result of the property boom that began in the late 1990s but the largest developer, China Vanke, accounts for only 3 to 4 per cent of the market. One of the rare commodities of which China has an abundance, the rare earths used in mobile telephones, wind farms, hybrid cars and fluorescent light bulbs, is a patchwork of small open pits mined by families across Jiangsu, Guangdong, Guanxi and Inner Mongolia. The government has tried to bring the industry under control but the snake tails keep twitching in search of cash.[1]

Products ranging from beer to motorcycles are regionalized. Half the country's road-haulage firms are reckoned to have only one truck. Revenue from the 100 biggest food groups contributes only 8 per cent to the industry's total turnover. The thirty biggest skincare brands enjoy market share of just 1 to 2 per cent. China has nearly half a million food producers, 80 per cent of which have less than ten employees. Most farms are small, worked on leases from the local authorities to rural households that prevent the development of big agro-food businesses on the US, European or Brazilian model. They are far from the centre of political and economic power. As the ancient Confucian *Book of Odes* put it:

> We get up at sunrise
> At sunset we rest.
> We dig wells and drink.
> We till the fields and eat.
> What is the might of the emperor to us?[2]

Outside the city centres with their gleaming towers and traffic jams lie kilometres of urban markets with myriad small outlets specializing in household appliances, scrap metal, vehicle parts, pipes, steel bars, textiles, wood and anything else that can be traded. In Chongqing's Machine Town more than 1,000 small shops trade on the ground floor of two-storey yellow-painted terraced houses, selling tools, metal goods, wire, saws, tubes, cables and wheels made by factories and workshops clustered round them. In Wuhan the central wholesale market, at both street level and in a matching underground space, is a huge jumble of stalls selling everything under the sun organized by product, and the surrounding streets are a constant gridlock of cars, trucks, carts and men carrying sacks of goods on poles over their shoulders. 'If you spent five seconds in each shop, you'd need three months to visit them all,' a local restaurant owner says. The Zhongguancun high-technology area in Beijing groups 184 listed firms. It grew out of a market for electronic goods located close to universities; companies operating there early on were often spun off from academic institutes in a market-led development that was not centrally planned. There is now an administrative committee for the district but it has no powers over land use or taxation, though it can issue *hukou* permits to talented people it wants to attract.

Shanxi province has long been dotted with small coalmines and there are reckoned to be 750 steel markets through the country with 150,000 independent steel traders, some tiny but others controlling big stockpiles. One such entrepreneur I met in the north-east said, as he went through an elaborate tea-pouring ceremony in his office, that he was open to an investment of 'a billion' – he did not specify whether he was talking yuan or dollars. The central government has been trying to consolidate the steel industry since 1995, but has run into opposition from provincial and county administrations, owners and workers; attempts to rationalize two outdated mills in 2009 ended with an official being kidnapped in one case and the manager being beaten to death by workers in the other – the men were apparently led by thugs hired by the local authorities to stop the consolidation plan.

When divided by its population of 1.34 billion people the soar-away statistics produced by mainland China give a different view of the country, reducing it to everyday proportions. Though the nominal GDP of $5.78 trillion in 2010 meant that the PRC moved ahead of Japan to become the world's second-biggest economy, the mainland stands at 98 out of 181 nations in the World Bank's ranking of GDP per capita and at 58 out of 110 countries in the Legatum Institute's table of global wealth and wellbeing. If the economy progresses as forecast, wealth per inhabitant in 2016 will still only be equivalent to $13,700 compared to $57,300 for the US or $48,000 for Germany.

Only eight mainland companies figured in the top 100 global companies by size in a listing by the *Financial Times* in 2011, compared to ten from the UK and thirty-seven from the US. The number of Internet users may be the highest on earth but at 34 per cent penetration is less than half of the 78 per cent recorded in North America. Mainland China overtook the UK in its number of millionaires in 2009 but, in terms of population, Britain is 20 times ahead. China accounts for just 5 per cent of global wealth, compared to 31.5 per cent for the US and 13.4 per cent for Japan. While the mainland is the world's biggest car market, ownership works out at 6 per cent of the population compared to 75 per cent in the United States. The low cost of goods means that, though the Chinese smoke a lot, the revenue and profits of its state-monopoly cigarette firms are less than that of Philip Morris alone. The high absolute number of executions falls below that of Singapore and Iran in per capita terms.

The distribution of wealth is highly uneven in regional terms as well as between individuals. In 2010 national GDP per capita averaged 29,762 yuan. Inhabitants of Shanghai and Beijing had officially declared incomes averaging more than 70,000 yuan but 21 other provinces or regions registered less than 30,000 yuan, 11 of them less than 20,000. The figure for Shanghai was almost five times that of the Guizhou region. Striking as they are, such comparisons do not tell the full story, since it is estimated that wealthy Chinese hide up to one-third of their wealth. No wonder that the mainland is referred to as '*fu guo qiong min*' – rich country, poor people.

Back in Zhejiang, the coastal city of Wenzhou in the south-east grew in the 1980s into the icon for private enterprise and today has the fourth-highest per capita income in the country. It built itself into a major centre for small- to medium-sized manufacturers concentrating on textile goods, spectacles, leisurewear, shoes, watches and cigarette lighters – 80 per cent of global production of the latter in the mid-2000s. In 2011, its western suburb of Lucheng was the scene of the high-speed train disaster.

The population has risen to 9 million if two satellite towns and six counties are counted. The number of firms, many of them very small, operating in and around the city has been put at 400,000. Ninety per cent are private, their expansion backed by an informal banking system of loans that ignores the framework of the big state. Its business people have fanned out across China to sell their goods in around 200 cities as well as reaching 131 countries and territories, according to the Chamber of Commerce. Many of the 45,000 Chinese who have moved into the area around Prato in Italy to make leather goods from low-cost materials imported from the PRC hail from Wenzhou.[3]

The smart cars, shops, restaurants and upscale homes all attest to the city's prosperity. Local entrepreneurs have invested in airports in the province as well as coalmines in faraway Shanxi province – inhabitants of one village in the Wenzhou area have stakes in 200 mines while others have bought into mineral reserves even further away in northern China; one local said that his 15-million-yuan investment in a mine in Xinjiang was now worth 400 million. The head of a local computer firm told *China Daily* that he owned thirty properties across China, and estimated that Wenzhou residents have an average of 1.2 properties each in Shanghai.

A centre of early Western missionary activity, Wenzhou has a strong Christian community that is closely interlocked with its commercial world. Its 'boss Christian' priests preach in offices and hold networking lunches with business people as well as offer migrant workers food and soap to induce them to convert. The city's main leisurewear firm, Metersbonwe, has 3,000 shops across China and ventured into Hollywood product-placement by arranging for the protagonist of the *Transformers* film to wear one of its T-shirts. Founded by Zhou Chengjia, who started out by combining the roles of tailor by night and salesman by day, it outsources production to smaller companies and has enjoyed annual sales growth of 30 per cent to reach more than 10 billion yuan a year.[4]

For all their success, Wenzhou's manufacturers face growing competition domestically and a tougher future with exports as they have to pay double-digit salary increases to get workers; the province's minimum wage was raised in 2011 to 1,310 yuan a month, on a par with Shanghai's. The input prices of the materials they use, such as cotton, wool and fuel, have increased while foreign demand has risen more slowly than it did in the boom years. Buyers abroad take longer and longer to settle their bills, putting a strain on cash flow, and tighter credit squeezed firms in 2011. Some manufacturers have moved upmarket – a leading shoe company bought an Italian brand to give it access to higher-margin business. To retain and attract staff, workshops have improved their conditions – for example, by installing air conditioners.

Near the border with Fujian, the smaller city of Lishui has multiplied its GDP by twenty-five since 1978 by making everything from toys (using the wood from neighbouring forests) to eiderdowns, pens, soap and small electronic machines. It produces replicas of ancient swords and has workshops where armies of painters churn out European classical urban and rural scenes for mass sales on the other side of the world. To the north, Shaoxing, a historic city of 4 million people famous for its yellow rice wine, houses more than 40,000 textile-exporting companies operating in a main market with a floor area of 600,000 square metres; it has also achieved notoriety as a major centre for the origination of malicious spam messages. The Zhejiang town of Fenshui contains some 550 enterprises making and assembling every kind of pen; the local Communist Party secretary says it puts together 60 per cent of ballpoints sold in Europe and the United States. Some are made in factories employing several hundred staff but others are assembled by three generations of families in their homes, with the fastest workers producing 2,000 a day.

Three decades ago the people of Zhili, between the provincial capital of Hangzhou and Shanghai, worked in paddy fields. Today their town has grown into a city and is the world's biggest centre for the production of children's clothing. As in Wenzhou, private finance has been the investment driver: only one-fifth of funding came from formal banks. Most of the city's 5,000 separate firms work in clusters that are reckoned to operate in 80 per cent of China's textile industry. Under this process each provider specializes in the production of only part of a garment; the various components are put together at a central workshop. The city's output has trebled since the start of the century, but profits have risen by only 19 per cent; a survey found that the most successful plants were those founded by people with twelve or more years' education. The labour force is mainly made up of migrants who work, eat and sleep on the premises (safety regulations have been tightened in the wake of two deadly fires). As wages have risen, manufacturers have outsourced work to the poorer neighbouring province of Anhui.

Down the coast, opposite Taiwan in the province of Fujian, a man armed with a hammer, a pair of scissors and several sewing machines started making sports shoes in Jinjiang in the 1980s. The city is now home to 1,300 companies making sportswear. As manufacturing blossomed, global brands such as Nike, Adidas, Puma began to source production from there. Then local firms decided to launch their own products with their own outlets. One, ANTA, has more than 8,000 stores and is worth 25 billion yuan. Another, 361°, has a chain of similar size concentrating on working-class buyers in smaller Chinese cities. Jinjiang now accounts for one-fifth of global sports-shoe production and its county is the sixth richest in China.

The fragmentation of the People's Republic is most evident in the countryside that still contains more than half the population. Farms are generally small and run on sixty-year leases granted by local governments – all land remains in the ownership of the state.

Ninety per cent of China's 500 million pigs are raised on such small farms and in backyards; only half are killed in regulated slaughterhouses. More than 70 per cent of dairy enterprises have fewer than 100 cows – some only half a dozen. China's 300,000 sugar farmers produce half as much per hectare as their European counterparts.

Hundreds of millions of young people have deserted their homes in the rural hinterland to work in factories in places like Shenzhen. Many Chinese villages have been hollowed out to leave a population consisting mainly of grandparents and children. Deep in western China, officials bemoan the lack of active twenty- to forty-year-olds able to learn how to farm.

At the end of a rough road in the middle of Hebei province, beside a dried-up riverbed in which chickens search for food among discarded plastic shopping bags, I visited the stout, broad-faced, illiterate widow of a village teacher. In her home, in a small terrace of one-storey houses, she told me that she was one of only six adults left as permanent residents of her village; there were once 'hundreds'. During the week even the children are absent now, at school in a nearby town. She waved at the fields and said that she and the others were doing what they could to keep the crops growing but this was hard work for old people. However, she was not complaining given the improvements in rural life after decades during which (despite the official story of the peasants carrying the CCP to power) farmers were treated as second-class citizens whose main role was to provide food for cities.

She was born in 1945, before the Communists took power, and had lived through land reform, anti-rightist campaigns, the Great Leap Forward of the late 1950s and the ensuing famine that killed tens of millions, followed by the ten-year anarchy of the Cultural Revolution unleashed by Mao in 1966. That often violent upheaval was, she told me, 'a bad time' – adding that life was often difficult in the old days. But the portrait of the Great Helmsman was still pasted on her wall. When I pointed to it a smile creased her weather-beaten face. 'Things have got a lot better since then. Everything has changed for the better, so much better.'

On her bed was a thick green and crimson blanket embroidered with the English word 'Best' in its centre and 'Love, Love, Love' round its border. In one corner of the room a television set was showing a police drama. A neighbour stopped by to offer for sale some mushrooms he had picked on the hillside above the village; they were medicinal, he explained.

'What are they good for?' I asked.

'Everything,' he replied. The price was high but he said he had no trouble making good money selling them. I did not buy. He shrugged, lit a cigarette and walked off singing tunelessly.

Along a four-lane road below the high ridge on which the Great Wall snakes against the sky, past a sign reading 'No illegal gold mining', a complex of two-storey Western-style homes is being built for local farmers who will leave their villages forever under the New Socialist Countryside programme. The programme is designed to improve living standards as the central government tries to reverse decades of rural backwardness. The houses have solar panels on red-tiled roofs and each contains half-a-dozen rooms, with modern bathrooms and kitchens.

In a nearby village, where a brickworks and a collection of small workshops provide employment, there is a familiar pattern of half-finished houses and a 'country-style' restaurant with oil leaking out of the ventilation pipe near the door. It charges 1 yuan for hire of a plate, a bowl, a glass and chopsticks wrapped in cling-film, with marking to say that they have all been disinfected. When we visited, lunch for five at a big table comprised pig knuckle, a mountain of crisp-fried shrimp, fish and aubergine, green melon, home-made tofu, sausage, soup, rice, beer, soft drinks and tea, all for 150 yuan – the price of three bottles of beer at the smart Beijing Hotel bar. We could not finish it all, so our driver took away enough for several more meals in plastic boxes. On the way out of the village, at the request of a businessman in our party, we stopped at its small supermarket, which offered a jumble of Chinese and foreign branded goods – flavoured milk drinks, Sunny orange juice, Rejoice shampoo, Great Wall red wine, 42-Degree rice alcohol, English-labelled cans of 'Mackerel in Tomato Sauce', Safeguard soap, Crest toothpaste.

Our companion wanted to buy exercise books and ballpoint pens for a school he helps to support for children from local villages. He has a plan to build a theme park in the area and is anxious to be seen as a benefactor. He took me to see the school, an ochre building on a small hill in a town that is enjoying something of a boom because its iron-ore deposits are much in demand. Dressed in a uniform of blue and white tracksuits with 'Sport' written in English on the back, the children greeted me with a chorus of, 'How are you? Welcome to our school!' in English.

'England is good,' one child said.

'China best!' added another with thumbs up.

6

THE GIANT HOTPOT

The smaller-scale China visited in the previous chapter belies the image of a vast country with more than a billion people marching in a single mass towards world domination. Beneath its unitary umbrella, China is a nation of many parts – as it always has been. Politically, the central organs of the Communist Party rule at national level; but below them lies a patchwork of local interests often rooted in the history of an empire which was more disparate than the occupants of the Dragon Throne would have liked to admit. Imposing order on any group as large as the Chinese was bound to be a task beyond even the Sons of Heaven or the holders of today's Marxist-Maoist-Market mandate.

The economic revolution of the 1980s involved a high degree of decentralization under which provinces and individuals were left to get on with the job in their own way so long as they delivered growth. In the late 1990s a State Council official in Beijing suggested to me that the newspaper I was then editing in Hong Kong might send somebody to report on a proposal by an east-coast city to privatize its transport system; when the journalist arrived he found that the privatization had already taken place and that relatives of senior officials were installed on the board. Deng Xiaoping's observation that it was inevitable that some people would get richer quicker than others enshrined the acceptance of division in place of the Maoist aspiration for uniformity. The extent of the wealth disparities we have seen between provinces, cities and individuals bears witness to how accurate the patriarch was, with average wealth in the three richest municipalities more than double that in twenty other provinces or regions and the minimum wage in the provinces of Sichuan, Hunan, Ningxia and Shaanxi up to 40 per cent lower than in Shanghai, Guangdong and Zhejiang.

There is not one China but a hundred, a thousand or a million, with the diverse terrain underlining differences augmented by the uneven distribution of the population. This hotpot of localities is organized in twenty-two provinces, five autonomous regions, four giant municipalities and the Special Administrative Regions (SAR) of Hong Kong and Macau. Below this superstructure lie 1,460 counties with 370 county-level cities, 270 of them with at least a million inhabitants, 41,000 towns and townships – and 623,669 villages. Provincial bosses make up the largest group in the CCP's Central Committee, which selects the Politburo. Three-quarters of the superior body have held senior regional posts on their way to the top. While Beijing retains the last word, the Communist history of guerrilla warfare and grassroots organization, together with the decentralization that marked the launch of economic reform in the 1980s, has bred a governing style of ad hoc administration on the ground, often dominated by powerful local figures, in what is known as 'proceeding from point to surface'.[1]

China has fifty-five officially recognized ethnic minorities numbering 110 million people. Though they have been increasingly assimilated and turned into tourist attractions, some maintain their special customs – including south-western tribes who practise matriarchy under which women chose their partners at will. While the overwhelming majority of the population is Han, great regional differences distinguish them; there are seven main linguistic groups and almost 300 local dialects. One survey suggested that only 60 per cent of the population is at home in the national language of *Putonghua*, or Mandarin. Some 90 million people speak the Wu tongue in Shanghai, Jiangsu and Zhejiang and more than 70 million speak Cantonese in Guangdong, Guangxi and Hong Kong.

Food is mild and subtle in Guangdong, salty in the north-east, flavoured with vinegar in Shandong, fiery in Sichuan, Yunnan and Hunan. At the Shanghai Expo in 2010 the government of Guizhou promoted the local delicacy of dog meat while banquets served in the car city of Changchun feature deer tail, bear paws and snow toad from the nearby mountains. In Shanghai, where nut-flavoured milk drinks are popular, dishes are often oily and the dumplings especially juicy. The south is a land of rice; the north of wheat – but the jovial boss of the state grain reserve in the north-eastern city of Shenyang insisted to me over a banquet he laid on, which included foie gras beside traditional Chinese dishes, that the best rice in the country comes from round there because of the quality of the soil. Regions promote local industries with fees on interlopers or by employing more direct methods to keep out competitors from elsewhere in the nation. In 2009 the authorities in Anhui ordered that car companies there must use only locally made steel, while regional administrations were urged to buy vehicles made in the province.

The divisions crop up on every side from top to bottom. The CCP and the government draw a national line between the two main population groups, urban and rural dwellers, through the *hukou* registration system. Rural people are not expected to be as clever or educated as urbanites; the definition of literacy is set at the ability to read 2,000 characters for those in cities but only 1,500 for those in the country.

Individualism finds its reflection in an unexpected field: sport. The PRC is not much good at team games. It failed to qualify for the Football World Cups of 2006 and 2010 and its high point to date has been winning the East Asian Championship in 2005. At the 2008 Olympics the PRC took more gold medals (fifty-one) than the US (thirty-six) but only five were won collectively and most of those by pairs. On the other hand, gymnast Li Ning marked the PRC's first appearance at an Olympics with six golds at the 1984 Games; more recently, tennis player Li Na won the French Open in 2011.

An old saying points to the varied strong points of different parts of the country: marry in Suzhou (in Jiangsu province in eastern China, famous for its canals and silk work – and supposedly has the most beautiful women in the country); live in Hangzhou (the capital of Zhejiang is traditionally extolled as a paradise on earth with its West Lake, pagodas and historic relics); eat in Guangzhou (where people are said to consume everything on four legs except for tables and chairs); and die in Liuzhou (a city in the Guizhou Zhuang autonomous region of the south-west where the sandalwood coffins are supposed to preserve corpses). Alternatively, take the joke about what would happen to an extra-terrestrial landing in the People's Republic: in Beijing it would be put in a museum; in Shanghai it would do tricks in a circus; in Guangzhou it would be cooked.

The tall inhabitants of Shandong are seen as tough, stubborn and single-minded, the best soldiers in the country. The smaller folk of Guangdong are mercenary. People in Shanghai are pushy in business but conservative in politics. Those from the province of Anhui are poor and full of money-making tricks. Fujianese are risk-takers – many early emigrants from the mainland came from the province and it is a principal conduit for the smuggling of people out of China by 'snakehead' gangs. Natives of Sichuan are hot-tempered. The inhabitants of Henan, the birthplace of Chinese civilization, are deceitful but hard-working. Beijingers are snobbish and look down on their compatriots; on my first visit to the capital from Hong Kong, in the mid-1990s, a newspaper editor wondered how I could bear to live among the mercenary Cantonese – 'almost as bad as the Shanghainese'.

Old beliefs, often locally rooted, persist as they have for centuries.

The Yellow Turban sect contributed to the fall of the Han Dynasty at the end of the second century AD and millenarian groups struggled against dynasties thereafter. In the nineteenth century China saw the emergence of both the quasi-Christian Taiping movement setting out to found a Heavenly Kingdom and overthrow the Qing dynasty and the Boxers, convinced of their ability to gain immunity from bullets by swallowing secret texts. There were reckoned to be more than 300 different secret societies when the Communists won power in 1949. Zhu De, head of the People's Liberation Army, saw the organizational structure of the Elder Brothers, which he joined, as a model that the Party should follow, but a mass campaign against cults was launched in the 1950s. This was not only to combat superstition but also because sects were seen as potential allies of the Nationalists and even of the Americans – and had economic influence the CCP wanted to eliminate.

A profusion of local gods are housed in temples and brought out for processions at festivals. In a village in central China I visited on the way back from the railway tunnelling project in Hunan, the Daoist temple contained four bright-red palanquins with ornate interiors used to carry local idols through the streets and country paths on religious occasions. A table in front of the altar was covered with a lurid pink-and-red cloth emblazoned with the English words 'Miss You'. The steward of the temple was unhappy when I and two colleagues walked round inside, but when we gave him 100 yuan he produced a receipt book in which to record the donation and left us alone. A few years ago when I visited the large temple in Chengdu, which was filled with lurid images of Daoist deities and devils, it was crammed to bursting point for a ceremony to mark the birthday of Laozi, the founder of the belief. Mothers cradling babies munched sweetcorn as devotees prostrated themselves on the paving stones or stroked the lucky figure of a ram with the other eleven animals of the Chinese zodiac incorporated. Old women burned gold paper on a brazier. In front of a wall, you turned three times with your eyes closed and then advanced to touch one of three signs for the future – promising a high official post, longevity or happiness respectively; you could have only one. A black-robed monk with a cigarette standing upright in a holder interpreted ancient texts while another holy man offered massage. The air was heavy with incense and the ringing of mobile telephones. Getting into a taxi outside, I was greeted by 'Colonel Bogey' blaring from the car radio; an antimacassar on the seat was embroidered with an image of Winnie the Pooh.

Despite the repeated campaigns against superstitions under the Nationalist and Communist regimes, *Feng shui* is still alive and well. Red is a fortunate colour. Four (*si*) is still a bad number, since it sounds like the Chinese for 'death', while eight (*ba*), sounding like 'prosperity', is highly valued – the Beijing Olympics opened at eight p.m. on the eighth day of the eighth month of 2008. Car-number plates with several eights are much sought after. Old postage stamps that are both red and contain the lucky number fetch prices well above their real value. The 328-metre tower in China's richest village of Huaxi in Jiangsu province contains statues representing the key traditional elements of metal, wood, water, fire and earth.

The emergence in the 1990s of the Falun Gong, with its classical deep breathing and meditation techniques, showed that 'heterodox' spiritual movements can still have a powerful pull, even if, after initially promoting it abroad as part of traditional Chinese culture, Beijing has cracked down forcefully on its practitioners since deciding in 1999 that it was a threat. The office set up to fight the Falun Gong warned in 2006 that 'organizations in the countryside that are vying with the party for people's hearts' constituted an ever greater threat to CCP rule. Sects and cults thrive in poor inland rural areas left behind by the progress of cities and the coast. They promise healing when health services are poor or non-existent. Many prophesy an apocalypse and promise salvation to those who adhere and donate. Reporting in 2006 on banned sects drawing on Christianity, Joseph Kahn of the *New York Times* listed the Three Grades of Servants, Eastern Lightning Shouters and the Spirit Church, the Disciplines Association and White Sun, the Holistic Church and the Crying Faction. Since this is China, they can grow big. The Three Grades of Servants in northern China, which is based on Christianity, said it had several million followers. Its founder claims to speak directly to God and predicts a Second Coming in which nonbelievers will perish – this was originally forecast for 1989 but the date has been shifted forward since then.

Eastern Lightning, another northern group, which may be the

biggest sect in the country, was set up in 1990 by a leader who claims to be the returned Christ. It recruits mainly from other religious groups by means of spying, kidnapping and brainwashing (according to two people quoted by Kahn). It gives members quotas of converts to fulfil and urges them to be quick about it since the female Jesus would wipe out non-believers before long. The struggle with other sects descended into murder; in one case the corpse of a man who had converted away from the Three Grades was found with his face sliced off, a calling card of the group. One of those questioned about the killing died in custody, officially 'of a sudden heart attack'. Another tried to kill herself by drinking rat poison. 'This is exactly what happens when the world is coming to an end,' she told Kahn.[2]

For Han purists, the 'real' China lies in the territory of the early empire, centred on Henan and Hebei and reaching out along the Yellow River to the First Emperor's capital beside the ancient city of Xi'an. This leaves out most of the country, including the south-eastern coastal regions of Guangdong and Fujian, where economic growth took off in the 1980s, and the wild south-western territories of Yunnan and Guangxi that have lived for centuries isolated from the imperial centre with big populations of ethnic minorities following indigenous traditions. Sichuan is a huge world to itself; lying in a semicircle of mountains, it is home to 10 per cent of the country's half-billion pigs and its people speak with an accent that outsiders find difficult to understand.

To the north, a great arc of territory runs round China from the north-east through Mongolia and Xinjiang to Tibet in the west. Though Beijing claims that all such lands form an integral part of the People's Republic, their histories, cultures and geographical position set them apart to varying degrees.

Adjoining North Korea and sweeping round to the border with Russia, where rivers and lakes are still frost-bound in May, the north-east – with its three provinces of Liaoning, Heilongjiang and Jilin containing 110 million people spread over 300,000 square miles – used to be known as Manchuria from its dominant ethnic group. The semi-nomadic Liao and Jurchen tribes from the region dominated northern China at the start of the second millennium, founding the Khitan and

Jin kingdoms. In 1127 the latter captured Kaifeng, capital of the Northern Song dynasty; this forced the rulers to flee and set up as the Southern Song in Hangzhou, where they presided over a great flowering of art and culture that epitomizes the divide between the harsh, warlike context of northern China and the more relaxed south.

The Jin dynasty lasted till 1234, when the Mongols defeated its army and its emperor committed suicide. In Manchuria itself, however, the descendants of the Jurchen endured in the Qing ('pure') regime based in Shenyang (previously known as Mukden), which bided its time to renew the assault on the land beyond the Great Wall. Their state was well-organized, with the whole population registered, taxed and divided into units denoted by coloured banners. In 1644 the fast-riding troops under their separate banners together with Chinese mercenaries rampaged south to overthrow the last Han dynasty, the Ming, which had called them to help against a rebellion. The Qing then held the throne until the end of empire in 1912.

The Manchu are often thought to have been 'sinicized' as they adopted Chinese rituals in public and ruled in the traditional fashion from the Forbidden City. However, they remained profoundly different. Their Han subjects were forced to shave the front of their foreheads and to wear pigtails as a sign of submission; and Manchu women did not follow the Chinese practice of having their feet broken and bound. The emperors carried out rites from their homeland inside their palaces, consulted shamans from the north-east and laid out food for the ravens from which they believed they were descended. They spoke their own language.

The Manchus never constituted more than 2 per cent of the population of China, which they saw as part of a wide sweep of their domains from Manchuria through Mongolia and Xinjiang to Tibet. They had long banned emigration from other parts of the nation to their homeland. When, at the end of the nineteenth century, the last major Qing figure, the Dowager Empress Cixi, had to choose between preserving the status of the Manchu elite and its regime and allowing reform, she plumped for the first. All of which gives the lie to the often held notion that the Han absorbed their nominal masters from foreign parts by their subtle statecraft and the power of their ancient civilization.

The rule of three great Manchu Qing emperors in the seventeenth and eighteenth centuries marked an apogee of China's power as their armies established control over the rebellious south of the country and staged military expeditions to Tibet, Xinjiang, Korea and Taiwan. Their ornately decorated palaces in Shenyang bear testimony to the scale of their rule, though they are dusty and empty these days. Their Mountain Resort for Avoiding the Heat at the city of Chengde, north of Beijing, is a collection of more than 100 palaces, pagodas and pavilions built in the eighteenth century to provide views of scenic landscape where one can glimpse the rising moon and setting sun reflected at the same time in a lake. A smaller replica of the Potala Palace in the Tibetan capital of Lhasa bears witness to the Qing view of their empire, not as a Chinese creation but as a multi-ethnic, multicultural realm.

However, the nineteenth century grew increasingly difficult for the rulers, who did not know how to cope with social, economic and political complications rising around them. They were also hamstrung by their need to cater to the reactionary and unscrupulous Manchu nobles of the Banner troops who had proved so decisive in routing the Ming two centuries earlier. After the mid-century shock of revolts by the Taiping and an army of perhaps a million bandits called the Nien, the foundation of a Muslim kingdom in Yunnan and the secession of Xinjiang under another Muslim ruler, the dynasty ebbed away. Foreign powers, led by Britain after the First Opium War of 1839–42, carved out trading concessions where their subjects were immune from Chinese law or control.

A punitive Anglo-French expedition in 1860 forced the court to flee Beijing to seek safety in Chengde. That episode saw the emergence of the dominant figure of late-nineteenth-century China, the Dowager Empress, Cixi, who imposed young male relatives on the throne and became the major political influence at court. Conservative and cautious, she was unwilling – or unable – to push the country on a path of modernization as it was further buffeted by disastrous defeat at the hands of the despised 'dwarf bandits' from Japan in 1894–95 and the punishment inflicted by another foreign military expedition that took Beijing after the court threw its lot in with the anti-Western Boxers in 1900.

China's decline from the heights it reached in the first half of the Qing era can be attributed to a number of factors. The country was in what is called a high-equilibrium trap: it could generally produce enough food to feed the population and so had no incentive to improve agriculture or to seek economic development. Its merchant class was marginalized and capital was generally unavailable for industrial and commercial development. It seemed to feel no need to continue its tradition of invention. Its coal was in the wrong place, far from the few factories. Its rulers grew more cautious and their finances increasingly strained, while links with the Han population became less amicable. Its statecraft, much vaunted by admirers such as Henry Kissinger, was, on closer examination, far from successful; it might posit elegant notions of using the barbarians to destroy one another but it could show very few results.[3]

The Manchus came to be reviled in China as their empire floundered. The original opposition from Ming loyalists widened into the alienation of Chinese gentry and revolutionaries. There was growing resentment from the urban Han elite, who disliked the way the court tried to solve its shortage of money by parcelling out railway concessions to foreigners in return for cash; the Han bourgeoisie wanted such fruits for themselves and there were confrontations in several cities. The failure of the Banner troops to deal with great revolts against the dynasty in the middle of the nineteenth century forced the court to turn to Han leaders in the province to take action with locally raised forces, and further lowered the esteem felt for the rulers.

Expelling the 'devil Qing' was a core aim of the huge Taiping revolt that ravaged China between 1850 and 1864. As revolutionary agitation against the failing dynasty rose in the late nineteenth and early twentieth centuries, an eighteen-year-old student, Tsou Jung, summed up the sentiment in the opening of his book, *The Revolutionary Army*, by calling on the Han to 'sweep away thousands of years of despotism, cast off thousands of years of slavishness, exterminate the five million bestial Manchus, wash away the humiliation of 260 years of repression and sorrow, cruelty and tyranny, turn the Chinese soil into a free land.'

Such feelings are not completely dead and still feed on the Han supremacism endemic in China. At a book-signing event in Shanghai in

2008 a clothing entrepreneur slapped a historian who had published an account of the Manchu Kangxi emperor that the attacker regarded as a whitewash – he accused the author of being the equivalent of a Holocaust-denier. He was sentenced to fifteen days in jail and given a small fine. The case quickly provoked major online storms as bloggers rallied to the assailant's defence, calling him 'a truly brave warrior' and denouncing the historian as a traitor to the Han. An opinion poll by *People's Daily* found 93 per cent support for the slapping.[4]

Four years after Cixi died in 1908, the mother of the last emperor, the six-year-old Puyi, signalled the end of the empire that stretched back more than two millennia when she announced his abdication following a revolt by the urban gentry and modern elements in the army. Manchuria had been opened to emigration from the rest of China under the late Qing and received a flood of new inhabitants, mainly from Shandong. It regained its prominence in the decade of war-lordism under its Old Marshal, Zhang Zuolin, a former bandit who became the country's most powerful militarist as he expanded his domain over northern China, occupied Beijing and ruled territories as big as Western Europe. Zhang built himself a grand palace in Shenyang with his personal bank alongside; it is now a finance centre where you can have your photograph taken standing beside a waxwork of Bill Gates.

The Japanese carved out major concessions in Manchuria, as did the Russians. They saw the territory's mineral reserves, forests and agricultural resources as ripe for development and a stepping-stone to dominate the weakening neighbour across the sea. At the centre of their expansion lay Japan's South Manchurian Railway, stretching for 700 miles and operating independently of the Chinese with its own guards, schools and hospitals and 13,600 staff. Japan also had its own military unit in Manchuria: the Kwantung Army, one of whose officers, Ishiwara Kanji, envisaged a state of affairs under which the Japanese would exercise political leadership and run large industries while the Chinese provided labour and operated small-scale enterprises, with the Manchurians confined to animal husbandry.[5]

When Zhang tried to resist the growing power of Tokyo he was killed by buccaneering officers from the Kwantung Army who blew up a bridge as his train passed underneath. His son, Zhang Xueliang, the 'Young Marshal', ensured the victory of the Nationalists under Chiang Kai-shek by siding with them against a group of northern warlords and became a major figure in the new regime. He was a play-boy who flew his own plane and was accompanied by secretaries with syringes to cater for his morphine addiction, but he also saw the need for reform.

However, finding the son even less pliant than his father, the Kwantung officers in Mukden seized the city in September 1931 and swiftly extended their control across the whole region. Two years later they set up the puppet empire of Manchukuo, headed by Puyi, which covered 300,000 square miles. One million Japanese moved in and a Japanese offi-cial controlled the regime. The army's 100,000 troops ran banks, the post office, railways, markets, gold, iron, coal and oil deposits, forests, avi-ation, slaughterhouses, opium dens and horse racing. Gambling houses and brothels proliferated.

The Young Marshal was sacked from his northern command after failing to prevent the Imperial Army from pushing south and taking Chengde, which was run by a particularly corrupt and incompetent warlord. He flew to Shanghai, where he underwent a cold-turkey cure for his drug addiction, after which he took an extended holiday in Europe; on his return he was put in charge of the Nationalist fight against the Communists, but kidnapped Chiang Kai-shek at Christmas 1936 to try to make him line up with Mao against the Japanese. Though the Nationalists did form a united front with the Communists, Zhang's coup soon fell apart and he was detained at Chiang's pleasure as the world's longest-serving political prisoner before his release in 1991 after being held in loose house arrest in Taiwan. He moved to Hawaii and died there in 2001, aged 100.

The last puppet emperor, meanwhile, had been taken prisoner by the advancing Soviet forces at the end of the Second World War, sent back to the People's Republic, re-educated in the ways of Communism and employed as a gardener in the Forbidden City – he was also allowed to travel north to visit the shrines of his Manchu ancestors.

Under the People's Republic, the land of the Manchus built on indus-trialization started by the Japanese. Gao Gang was the regional

Communist boss, tough, ambitious and very much in the popular image of north-eastern men as big, rough fellows who speak loudly and brawl their way through life and whatever business is at hand. He was reputed to have 100 mistresses; he fancied himself as the Great Helmsman's successor and accumulated political power until he made the mistake of trying to recruit Deng Xiaoping to his cause. Deng promptly told Mao, who unleashed other subordinates to cut the younger man down to size. Gao killed himself with an overdose of sleeping pills after being sent to prison, supposedly after having had sex twice that night – 'Can you imagine such lust?' Mao remarked, according to his doctor.[6]

As an industrial centre, the region became a key element in the Five-Year Plans adopted by the PRC on the Soviet model – this was the era when Mao's number two, Liu Shaoqi, could declare that 'the Soviet road is the road all humanity will take'. Giant state enterprises ran steel, cement and heavy-machinery factories while huge collective farms turned out food for the cities. But in the 1990s Beijing began to streamline state firms to make them more competitive and millions of workers were laid off, leading to unrest – though this did not escalate to become a full-scale revolt.

At the same time, Shenyang was shaken by a huge crime-and-corruption scandal conducted under what the state news agency Xinhua subsequently described as 'a strong protective umbrella'. It was headed by Liu Yong, a slight man with grey hair in a brush cut. He was a senior figure of the city's CCP cell, a member of the local legislature and managing director of a seemingly honest conglomerate. This did not stop him and his men attacking people who stood in their way, torturing and sometimes killing rivals; according to one account, they even disembowelled a fortune teller who told Liu Yong that his health was poor.

The whole affair unravelled after the city's Deputy Mayor was caught on videotape gambling with more money than he should have had in a casino in Macau. He had amassed some 30 million yuan in bribes, and his wife was known for cruising through Shenyang in a red American Lincoln limousine. Beijing sent in a top anti-graft investigator. The Mayor, who had been heralded by a US television station as one of the 'faces of a new era' in China for his efforts to modernize the city, was arrested; a police raid at his home found gold bars, cash and jewels. He was tried and told the court, 'My heart has always been with the Communist Party. When I was young I was a very good person. Now I am very bad. This is my tragedy.' He was given a suspended death sentence and died of cancer in prison in 2002. Dozens of other officials were prosecuted or forced to resign.

Liu tried to flee across the Russian border only to be caught. He attempted suicide but was revived and, under questioning, named officials who had colluded with him. He was put on trial and sentenced to death and a fine of 15 million yuan but he won a reprieve from the provincial High Court on the grounds that it 'could not remove the possibility that Liu's confession had been extracted through torture'. A second trial found him guilty of causing 'wilful bodily injury', leading a crime ring, property sabotage, illegal business operations, bribery, illegal possession of firearms, and interference with law enforcement. He was swiftly executed.

In the first decade of the twenty-first century, Shenyang received large grants from the central government to help it become a cleaner, more modern industrial centre. Foreign investors were courted. Hong Kong property developers moved in. The World Bank lent the city $121 million to restructure its tool-making companies. Today, there is building on all sides, an underground-railway line is being constructed and five ring roads are planned. A Shenyang–EU Economic Cooperation Zone has been opened; opposite stands an extraordinary development consisting of towers, domes and cupolas complete with echoes of the Taj Mahal and the US Congress. The air is still heavy with what seems to be smog but is, local officials insist, just low cloud.

The region as a whole is trying to reinvent itself as a modern industrial area. Its imperial past is relegated to a few museums. Though 10 million people are classified as being Manchu, fewer than 100 are reckoned to be able to speak the language of the Qing. Han immigration has changed the nature of the region's people and the old ways have gone for ever. 'My grandfather took me hunting and together we would catch foxes, eagles, rabbits,' an inhabitant of the last Manchu village – Sanjiazi, in Heilongjiang province – told reporter Verna Yu in 2011. 'But we haven't hunted for more than forty years and children these days don't even learn to ride horses any more.'[7]

The north-east is now a centre for the manufacture of high-speed trains and cars in Changchun, where Puyi had his palace when he headed the puppet Manchukuo regime. The port city of Dalian, where Bo Xilai began his ascent, is promoted as a hub of high-tech industry, including a $2.5 billion Intel semi-conductor wafer-fabrication plant; it is billed as a 'green city' but environmentalists warn of rising levels of water and air pollution and danger from petrochemical plants. The port of Yingkou in Liaoning has undergone a 16-billion-yuan development and is a major centre for containers, oil and chemicals. Harbin, home to a thriving Russian Jewish community before the Japanese installed their puppet regime, attracts crowds to an annual ice festival.

On the Siberian border, Russians fall over one another to sell timber, coal and metals to the Chinese while PRC companies rent large expanses of farmland in the sparsely populated territory across the frontier, where they also invest in iron-ore mines. Further south lies the boundary with North Korea. China has acquired the right to develop an island in the Yalu River, which marks the border, as a light-industry centre using North Korean labour together with another similar zone by the Sea of Japan. This has prompted a rash of property construction and a 20 to 30 per cent annual rise in real-estate prices in the frontier town of Dadong from which the PLA surged at the start of the Korean War in 1950 to drive through American lines until it was halted on the thirty-eighth parallel.

Earlier schemes for China to develop North Korea have come to nothing. A casino-and-tourism complex backed by Hong Kong investors was abandoned when mainland officials used it to gamble with purloined funds. Another development zone crashed when the Chinese entrepreneur picked by Pyongyang to run it was arrested by the PRC authorities, from whom he had apparently failed to get authorization, and was sent to prison for eighteen years for fraud and other offences. If North Korea ever changes and adopts a Chinese-style drive for growth, the former Manchuria will be ideally placed to benefit. But this is a big if, as two cities face one another across the Yalu River: Dadong is a typical bustling place with bright lights but Sinuiju, on the other side, is a dark enclave with low-watt bulbs and a pervasive drabness.

*

Next door, to the north-east, lies the Autonomous Region of Inner Mongolia, covering 460,000 square miles and containing 25 million people. Its Khans conquered China to found the Yuan dynasty that ruled from 1279 to 1368 under the successors to Genghis. A shadowy underground movement seeks unification with Mongolia to the north, but Inner Mongolia has been the most tranquil of China's non-Han regions. Protests in the summer of 2011, after a Han truck driver ran over and killed a Mongolian herder, were the most serious for two decades. Han migration to the region had begun before the Communist regime but has increased since, making the Mongols a decided minority in their own land. But strong economic development has also been at work.

The region is celebrated for its grasslands – one of which covers 70,000 square miles – a desert with moving dunes and sand that makes a musical sound when walked upon, and its lamb and hotpot dishes. But the balance of its economy has shifted dramatically from animal husbandry to coal. The number of sheep is falling steadily as mines cut into the grasslands to satisfy China's huge appetite for black gold.

The PRC is the world's biggest coal producer – and Inner Mongolia has its biggest coal fields – but the scale of demand and the difficulty of getting the fuel from the fields far inland to coastal areas mean that it is a net importer. The government plans to reduce dependence on coal for energy generation from the present 70 per cent to 63 per cent by 2015 through greater use of natural gas, nuclear power and renewable energy. But, for the near future, the focus will be on digging as much as possible out of the fields in the north of the country.

As a result, Inner Mongolia – which produces more than 600 million tons of coal a year, recorded 14.9 per cent growth in 2010. Ordos, its most flourishing city, has grown richer even faster. Once a herder centre for desert nomads with a mausoleum dedicated to Genghis Khan (though he was probably buried elsewhere), it sits on the edge of a coalfield containing one-sixth of China's reserves. It now enjoys annual growth rates of 25 per cent, and is spoken of as either 'the new Hong Kong' or 'China's Dubai'; its GDP rose from 82 billion yuan in 2006 to 264 billion in 2010.

The per-capita wealth of Ordos has overtaken that of the former British colony. In addition to its 7,000 yuan billionaires there are

100,000 yuan millionaires, some of them farmers who have been well paid for the right to mine on the land to which they hold leases. Property prices have soared amid an enormous construction boom. A 'ghost city' has been built but left unoccupied in expectation of future expansion; local-government revenues have risen nearly fourfold since 2006 so the authorities believe they can afford it – though by orthodox standards this is a real-estate mega-bubble. But there is no shortage of confidence: as well as its rich coals seams the region has other lucrative products – rare earths, natural gas and wool.

The tide of cash has led to the development of a major unlicensed credit industry estimated to be as large as 100 billion yuan; an entre-preneur who killed himself in 2011 left private debts of 1.2 billion yuan, according to local media. The easy money has bred an expectation of high profits – private equity managers seeking to arouse interest from the rich of Ordos must offer annual returns of at least 30 per cent. Approached to invest 5 million in a private equity fund that had the inside track on a manufacturer of high-speed railway equipment, the owner of a coalmine and property company reflected that, 'I'll just go with a "try it and see" attitude. Five million is not much. It's like playing a round of mah-jong.' When I suggested to a Chinese economist that we might evaluate the wealth of Ordos by counting the number of BMWs in the main streets, he laughed and said, 'Ferraris, rather.'[8]

To the north lies Mongolia itself, whose enormous reserves of coal, copper and just about anything else to be found underground mean that the PRC is anxious to buy all it can from its neighbour and to invest in its mines. The Mongolians are, however, leery of becoming entirely dependent on China, which is already much the biggest buyer of its exports. To limit PRC influence there is a madcap scheme for a railway to be built from the rich mining region of the South Gobi desert not south to the nearby border with China but on a far longer route to Russia. Biding its time, China has built transport links to the frontier and seems confident that it will get what it wants in the end.

To the west are the wild regions of Qinghai, Ningxia, and Gansu. The first is a barren, high-altitude area on the Tibetan plateau; it is China's largest province and contains its biggest lake, stretching over 2,300 square miles, but has only 5 million inhabitants in an area the size of

France and contributes less than 0.5 per cent to the country's GDP. Ningxia is a 25,000-square-mile autonomous region with deserts and a largely Muslim population lying at the northern end of the great loess plain of the Yellow River. Gansu is a more developed region of 25 million people bordering both Tibet and Mongolia, home to the Hui, one of the larger ethnic minorities; its capital city of Lanzhou was named as the world's most polluted city in the 1990s.

Further away are Tibet and Xinjiang. Both these huge and sparsely populated territories were taken by the PLA after the Communist victory in China proper, and both have proved difficult to bring into the fold. Tibetans, owing prime loyalty to the exiled Dalai Lama, have staged recurrent revolts, with monks to the fore, and remain resistant to the PRC's heavy expenditure on their very different land – and even more alienated by the immigration of Han Chinese. The largest rising, in 1959, led to the Dalai Lama and 80,000 Tibetans crossing to India, where he headed a government-in-exile as the leader of opposition to Chinese occupation of his homeland. During the Cultural Revolution hundreds of villagers rallied behind a young Buddhist nun who was said to be possessed by a deity linked to a mythical warrior king. They attacked, killed and mutilated county officials, PLA troops and local residents. The Nyemo Incident in 1969 has been portrayed as an outbreak of Tibetan resistance in favour of independence from Chinese rule, but a recent study has concluded that it was, rather, spurred by discord between rival groups. Interpreting Tibet is a fraught job, especially given the passion it arouses.

Another outburst of Tibetan anger in 1989 was suppressed under the aegis of the region's Party Secretary of the time, Hu Jintao. As he rose through the senior CCP ranks to the very top, he set policy on Tibet and it has been unyielding.

The region's history is complex, varying between periods when it was the home to its own empire whose warriors penetrated deep into China and times when it was invaded by imperial dynasties, followed by Anglo-Russian rivalry in the Great Game. The Ming (1368–1644) did not rule over Tibet and, in the nineteenth century, the scholar Wei Yuan wrote of it as lying outside lands administered directly by the Dragon Throne.

The extent of Qing control at that point varied until a punitive expedition in the dynasty's last years established a degree of authority, only for the fall of the Empire to lead to de facto independence from 1912 to 1950 when the PLA marched in. Today Beijing insists that the 470,000 square miles of what it dubs the Tibetan Autonomous Region and its 2.6 million people constitute an integral part of the People's Republic, and rejects the Dalai Lama's policy of seeking real autonomy without claiming complete independence.

The spiritual leader is far from an extremist, acknowledging that 'if China overnight adopted a democratic system, I might have some reservations... If central authority collapsed, there could be a chaotic situation, and that's in no one's interest.' Still, Zhang Qingli, the CCP Secretary for Tibet from 2006 to 2011, spoke of 'a fierce blood-and-fire battle with the Dalai clique, a life-and-death battle between us and the enemy' and described the spiritual leader as 'a wolf in monk's robes, a devil with a human face but the heart of a beast'.[9]

Beijing has lined up its own candidate for the high-ranking post of Panchen Lama, or Great Scholar. The Dalai Lama named somebody else for the position in 1995, but his choice, five-year-old Gedhun Choekyi, disappeared soon afterwards. Beijing designated another boy, Gyaltsen Norbu, who spends most of his time in Beijing but in 2011 went to study at the Labrang Monastery, which contains 1,000 monks, on the edge of the Tibetan plateau in Gansu province. When I visited it photographs of the Dalai Lama were tucked behind objects on altars. Monks there joined in protests in 2008 that followed riots in Lhasa; they recognize the Dalai Lama's choice for Panchen Lama rather than Beijing's. When Gyaltsen Norbu arrived, amid a heavy police presence, monks were told to welcome him – but they talked loudly among themselves during the ceremony to signal displeasure, and he soon left.

There is no doubting the investment the central government has poured into Tibet including the world's highest altitude railway complete with oxygen masks for passengers, which brings in Han four times a day on its 1,200-mile track. The region's economy grew by 12.2 per cent in 2010. Tibet has mineral deposits, including copper and gold, which, though hard to mine, could boost China's development plans. The central authorities make much of their efforts to encourage growth and improve living conditions, pledging to allocate 330 billion yuan to 226 projects by 2015. The region has become a big tourist destination for Chinese. Beijing says it will spend 3 billion yuan to achieve university enrolment of 30 per cent of young people in the region. State media regularly run reports of material progress being made on behalf of the Tibetans. In the spring of 2011 the State Council Information office instructed websites to post on the first page of their news sections an article about a seventy-five-year-old Professor, Yang Changlin, who 'for thirty-three years has shown concern and love for Tibetan college students in almost 10,000 cases'. At the end of 2011, the authorities announced a pension scheme for Tibetan monks plus payment of medical costs.

If the Tibetans do not show appropriate gratitude but prefer to continue in their antiquated way of life, so the argument goes, that just shows how impossible they are in the face of such benevolence. Foreigners who want to ingratiate themselves with the PRC know that one of the easiest ways is to poor-mouth the Dalai Lama, as in the reference to him by Rupert Murdoch (when the media tycoon was still dreaming of making big money in the Chinese market) as 'a very political old monk shuffling around in Gucci shoes'.

Yet, beyond the capital of Lhasa, where Tibetan and Han districts are segregated, the region remains largely backward and dependant on subsistence agriculture, though its huge mineral reserves under the Himalayas ensure that it will be a target for development. For all the money it has spent Beijing has failed to win the hearts and minds of the Tibetans, who complain, with justification, that they do not want to abandon their way of life and that the beneficiaries of the cash are mainly Han who have moved in as Beijing encourages immigration to shift the population balance. Officials point to new houses built with state funds but nomadic Tibetans have no desire to live in them.

The Tibetan issue is not confined to Tibet itself, since two-thirds of Tibetans live outside the Autonomous Region that covers only half the territory Tibetans claim as theirs. A dozen Tibetan monks and nuns set fire to themselves, mainly in the borderlands, in protest in 2011. One called out as he burned, 'We Tibetan people want freedom' and 'Let the Dalai Lama return to Tibet'; the Xinhua report stated blandly that 'it was unclear why he had burned himself'. The 2008 protests by monks inside Tibet led to fighting with police that spilled over into neigh-bouring areas. According to state media, thirty people died in all with 620 civilians and police injured – eighty critically so; Tibetan exile groups put the death toll at eighty. On her blog, the Tibetan Tsering Woeser, a main voice of resistance, records how any Tibetan who stands up to authority is persecuted, arrested, tortured and imprisoned. For Chinese who thought Mao had 'liberated' the region, she adds, '2008 has been a shock, a chance to discover a little of historical truth'. As she notes, the region's intellectuals are the main target of attack; a profes-sor of English was sentenced to fifteen years in jail for having 'betrayed state secrets' on his literary website. Since the 2008 protests, the security clampdown has been ubiquitous with monasteries ringed by police and security cameras. According to Tibetan sources, eighty monks and nuns set fire to themselves in 2011–12, mostly in adjoining provinces. This led to further tightening, the shooting of two protestors and enforced denunciations of the Dalai Lama, whom the *People's Daily* compared to the leader of the Waco, Texas, siege of 1993.

Tibetans are generally regarded by Han Chinese as backward and untrustworthy. Their culture is portrayed as no more than antiquated superstition and feudal serfdom marked by isolation, poverty and back-wardness. Party Secretary Zhang Qingli summed up the patronizing attitude when he said that 'the Communist Party is like the parent to the Tibetan people, and it is always considerate about what the children need'. Regular demonstrations abroad to 'Free Tibet' cut no ice with the leadership. When in 2008 pro-Tibet sympathizers interrupted the passage of the Olympic Torch in Europe and North America the gen-eral reaction on the mainland was that this was just an excuse to try to harm the People's Republic – 'I love China' slogans flourished in response. 'They're jealous of our success and want to spoil our Olympic party,' was a typical reaction in Beijing.

The Dalai Lama's decision to retire as head of the government-in-exile in 2011 produced a tougher public tone from his political successor, Lobsang Sangay, an American-trained lawyer who is married to a descendant of an ancient Tibetan king but who has never set foot in the territory. He got 55 per cent support among Tibetan exiles voting in 2011 after a US-style campaign that alienated some more traditional monks at the government-in-exile's seat in north India. 'There is no socialism in Tibet,' he said in his inaugural address. 'There is colonialism. Chinese rule in Tibet is clearly unjust and untenable.' When interviewed by the *Financial Times* he quoted Mao Zedong to the effect that 'wherever there is repression there is resistance'. But he also called for 'genuine autonomy' rather than full independence.[10]

Sangay said he was ready to negotiate with the Chinese authorities 'any time, anywhere' but a PRC spokesman said he headed 'a separatist political clique that betrays the motherland, with no legitimacy at all and absolutely no status to engage in dialogue with the representatives of the central government'. The heightened security clampdown continued, with media banned from the region. A new Party Secretary appointed for Tibet in 2011 to replace the hard-line Zhang Qingli after his normal five-year spell in the post stressed that 'the central task is economic development' but added that the foundation for progress must be 'ethnic unity'.[11]

The number of Tibetans jailed for political reasons is put by Tibetan organizations at more than 800. Escaped prisoners tell of torture and extreme hardship in detention. Beijing draws an explicit link with alleged foreign foes. Talk of independence (in fact, all the Dalai Lama has asked for is greater autonomy) is 'cooked up by old and new imperialists' as part of a 'Western aggressors' scheme to carve up the territory of China,' declared a White Paper issued by the Chinese government in the summer of 2011 to mark the sixtieth anniversary of the territory's incorporation into the PRC. 'Within six decades Tibet has achieved development that would normally call for a millennium,' it added. 'Under the leadership of the Communist Party of China and the Chinese government, the people of Tibet have created a miracle. Only by adhering to the leadership of the CCP, the path of socialism, the system of regional ethnic autonomy, and the development mode with Chinese characteristics and Tibet's regional features, can Tibet enjoy lasting prosperity and a bright future.'

After President Sarkozy of France met the Dalai Lama, Beijing put him in the doghouse for the usual two years. Premier Wen Jiabao made the link between acceptance of China's claim to Tibet and commerce plain when he hailed the former British Prime Minister, Gordon Brown, as 'an old friend' because 'the most unforgettable thing is that you tackled our last historical issue when you were in office, that is the UK admitting Tibet is an inalienable part of China. Since then, China and the UK have no historical issues and burdens to deal with, and the two sides can cooperate.' But then Brown's successor, David Cameron, met the Dalai Lama when he visited Britain in May 2012, and Wu Bangguo, the second ranking member of the Politburo, cancelled a trip to London. The Foreign Ministry in Beijing said that the UK had 'hurt the feelings of the Chinese people, meddled in China's affairs and harmed Chinese-British relations'.

Beijing's insistence on its right to decide what happens in Tibet was further underlined in its reaction to a statement in 2011 in which the Dalai Lama said that, when he was 'about 90', he would consult the high lamas of Tibetan Buddhism, the Tibetan public and others concerned to re-evaluate whether the practice of reincarnation should continue. The authorities ruled that such a decision was not his to make – rather, it was a matter for the religious affairs department of the Chinese government at provincial and central level, they insisted. 'The title of Dalai Lama is conferred by the central government and is illegal otherwise,' a spokesman for the atheist government 2,500 miles away said. The Dalai Lama did not back down. He called Beijing's announcement 'outrageous and disgraceful' and added that 'they are waiting for my death and will recognize a fifteenth Dalai Lama of their choice'. He was almost certainly correct. On a trip to Lhasa the same year, Vice-President Xi Jinping vowed to 'thoroughly fight against separatist activities by the Dalai clique by firmly relying on all ethnic groups [. . .] and completely smash any plot to destroy stability in Tibet and jeopardise national unity'. No compromise is possible. For Beijing, the fundamental unity of the nation is at stake and no politician in Beijing is going to take any risks by being seen as soft. The Tibetan impasse is set to continue with the danger of an explosion by young, militant Tibetans once the calming influence of the Dalai Lama disappears.[12]

Sharply different as their mainly Muslim culture and history are, Xinjiang and its Uighur population are in much the same boat as Tibet and its people. But they attract much less attention from the outside world. For one thing, Xinjiang lacks a Dalai Lama figure or the appeal of apparently peaceful Buddhist monks in their colourful robes who want only to be left alone to burn incense and chant sutras. As Woeser observes, compared to her people, 'the Uighurs do not arouse a shadow of sympathy'.

Rebiya Kadeer is a Uighur businesswoman who was lauded by the Chinese and did well out of her position but then fell foul of them and is now her people's highest-profile representative. She has written: 'Politicians and human-rights organizations from all over the world were active on behalf of Tibet. The conditions in the Uighur nation are much the same. But interest from abroad in the two, though literally we were next-door neighbours, sharing a common border and both under Chinese occupation, could not have been more dissimilar.' After years of building up her business as Beijing's favourite 'Mother of all Uighurs' with a seat at the National People's Congress, Kadeer rebelled. She opened up her seven-storey trade building to local small merchants and, departing from her set text, asked the national legislature: 'Is it our fault that the Chinese have occupied our land? That we live under such horrible conditions.' After that she was arrested as she prepared to fly to Washington to talk to members of Congress, jailed for six years and then expelled from the PRC. Three of her children were arrested or put under house surveillance.

Even given the variety of China's terrain and inhabitants it is hard to see this territory of 640,000 square miles (a sixth of the land areas of the PRC, three times the size of France), with 22 million people and more than 3,000 miles of borders with eight nations, as being Chinese – whatever Beijing says. Two thousand miles separate it from the national capital. The indigenous population is made up mainly of Turkic Uighur people; the census shows them accounting for 45 per cent of the population compared to 40 per cent for the Han. Uighur history is entwined with the Silk Road and its great trading centre of Kashgar is a Central Asian city – visiting it one Sunday I counted only a dozen identifiably Han faces in the crowds. Eighty per cent of the city's 600,000 inhabitants are Uighur.

A 'special economic zone' is being developed in Kashgar; computer-generated images show a leafy modern city in the desert and the local newspaper writes of the creation of 600,000 jobs. Uighurs complain about their traditional adobe houses being repossessed for development. Most of the old city has been bulldozed in the name of modernization. Uighurs and Han live in different areas. Provision of social security depends on recipients giving up Muslim traditions such as wearing veils. In 2012, students and officials were banned from religious activity during Ramadan.

Beijing says tight security is necessary because of a threat of Islamic fundamentalism seeping across the mountains from Afghanistan. There have been periodic bomb blasts and the state authorities intermittently announce the discovery of terrorist rings, which they say are backed by al-Qaeda and run by the separatist East Turkestan Islamic Movement (ETIM) – designated by the US as a terrorist group in 2002. In 2011 they alleged that the attackers had been trained in camps in Pakistan across the Pamir Mountains.

At the time of the 2008 Olympics, twenty-two security personnel were reported killed in four separate attacks. In 2010 the authorities blamed Uighur terrorists for a car bomb that killed seven policemen. The following summer, violence flared once more in Kashgar; state media said it began when two men wielding knives hijacked a lorry, killed its driver and drove it into a crowd. In the desert town of Hotan, famed for its jade, a group of Uighurs stormed a police station, stabbed the officer at the front desk to death and started fires with petrol bombs. At least twenty people lost their lives; the Uighur World Congress, based in Germany, said the Hotan attack occurred after the crowd got no response when it called for the release of young men picked up by the police. To restore calm ahead of an international trade convention, Beijing deployed its anti-terrorism unit, the Snow Leopards, to the region.

The region's capital city of Urumqi has been a major destination for migration from the rest of China. Riots in Urumqi in 2009 which were started by Uighurs and met with counter-action by Han residents of the city killed 200 people and injured 1,700, most of them immigrants resented by locals for taking jobs and benefiting from preferential treatment. Beijing fingered Rebiya Kadeer as a ringleader but produced no convincing evidence. Rather the violence was the result of growing ethnic and economic tension that boiled over, and the initial failure of the local police to act.

Since then the central government has adopted a somewhat more benign approach, replacing the hard-line Party chief who had been in the job for fifteen years with an official who has unveiled a doubling of investment to 200–250 billion yuan a year between 2011 and 2015 with 'pairing assistance' from nineteen provinces. Thirty-six projects were launched in 2012 to develop the region's coal reserves put at two trillion tons – 40 per cent of China's total. The steel and cement industries, housing and education are to be greatly expanded. A free-trade zone is being developed on the Alataw Pass on the border with Kazakhstan to boost trade with Central Asia that reached 30.17 billion yuan in 2010. Social workers have been sent in to slums in Urumqi. Job-creation schemes have been launched. Six airports are to be built along with 3,000 miles of railway track. Property prices in Urumqi have risen steadily. A senior Politburo member, Zhou Yongkang, has explicitly linked development and stability.

Major questions remain – among them the role of one of China's lesser-known but very powerful bodies, the quasi-military Xinjiang Production and Construction Corporation (XPCC), which was set up after the army took control of the region in 1949. It owns companies and farms across Xinjiang, runs hospitals, five universities, science academies, a police force and its own judicial system as well as engaging in construction projects in Pakistan, Africa and Latin America. Responsible for 2.7 million people and employing 1 million of them directly, it reports straight to Beijing rather than going through the region's authorities. 'Once you step on the land of Xinjiang, you have come to our company,' a senior executive remarked. 'We are everywhere here.'

The Hanization of Urumqi continues apace. Academics argue about whether Xinjiang constitutes 'internal colonialism'. But the evidence on the ground is inescapable. Only 1 per cent of the workforce in Xinjiang's booming energy industry is Uighur. In Urumqi, there are gated European-style villa complexes like those outside Beijing for the immigrants. As in Tibet, the incomers feel that the locals do not appreciate the progress they are bringing.

On the back of outbreaks of violence there are recurrent wild rumours of the danger from Uighurs – one talked of HIV-infected needles to inject Han residents in the street. The movement of people from the desperately poor regions in the south-west of the territory to Urumqi has exacerbated social tensions. As a Uighur professor told the journalist Mark O'Neill of the *South China Morning Post*, there is a fundamental issue – 'The Uighurs will not accept economic prosperity in exchange for giving up their freedom of culture, language and religion. As in Tibet, economic development means large-scale immigration of Han, and inequality and marginalization of local people.' In Hotan, Han residents are afraid to go to the bazaar after sunset and in Urumqi, a Western journalist was told by the hotel clerk: 'You'd better not go to the Uighur part of town at night.'[13]

7

ON THE EDGE

On the other side of the People's Republic from Tibet and Xinjiang lie three regions that have spent substantial periods of their modern histories outside the control of Beijing but whose recovery forms an essential element in the national reunification narrative. The smallest, Macau, on the eastern side of the Pearl River Delta neighbouring Guangdong, was the first European settlement in China. Portuguese traders obtained the right to carry on business from their ships followed by permission from the Chinese authorities to set up a settlement that dealt both in goods and Chinese slaves for the Portuguese empire until the traffic was banned by the King of Portugal in 1624. The traders were soon followed by the Jesuits; the right forearm of St Francis Xavier who was carrying out missionary work in the region was brought to one of their churches. Saint Paul's Cathedral, the biggest Christian church in Asia at the time, was finished in 1602 and burned down in 1835. Its façade remains perhaps the finest piece of European architecture in East Asia.

After the British had imposed themselves on China in the First Opium War, the Portuguese expanded on to neighbouring islands and extracted 'perpetual occupation and government of Macau' from the declining Qing. Lisbon retained sovereignty during the Nationalist Republic and, after coming under a Japanese protectorate in the Second World War, found its agreement with China denounced by the PRC. But China made no move to take over the colony, and, though there were serious riots during the Cultural Revolution, Macau went its own way. Lacking arable land, pastures or woods and with much manufacturing, it chose the path of gambling, which became the mainstay of its economy.

From 1962 to 2002 the casino industry was run by a company headed by Stanley Ho, from one of the region's leading business families. Ho, an elegant figure and fine ballroom dancer whose home in Hong Kong was equipped with an array of James Bond–like devices, denied accusations of involvement with organized crime, though there was little doubt that Macau was a particularly free-and-easy place run by Lisbon on a loose rein. There were allegations that Portuguese political parties syphoned off money. The vast majority of the population was Chinese but the centre of Macau and the adjoining island of Coloane was like a dash of Latin Europe transported to the South China Sea. Compared to Hong Kong, an hour's ferry ride across the bay, it was a sleepy place that felt no need to modernize in a rush, living at its own pace in one of the most densely populated territories in the world where elaborate Portuguese colonial edifices stood beside Chinese shanty towns. When I visited with my wife in 1995 from super-efficient Hong Kong, the hotel in a former military fort with fine-tiled walls had mislaid our reservation, the bed head teetered down over us, the washbasin was cracked, the swimming pool full of leaves. The food at breeze-block Fernando's restaurant on the beach at Coloane reached out to all corners of Portugal's one-time empire – chicken from Brazil, fish from Mozambique and wine from the home country.

In 1999, following Hong Kong's return to Chinese sovereignty, Macau, covering just 11.4 square miles and with a population of 552,000, became another administrative region of the People's Republic, its government praised by Beijing and its casinos prized by officials anxious to gamble with public funds or to use the casinos as a vehicle for money-laundering. The arrival of casino operators from Las Vegas gave the once sleepy place a major shot in the arm, building huge, flamboyant entertainment temples and boosting the gambling turnover to the highest on earth in the public spaces and in private VIP rooms for high rollers. Turnover hit $23.5 billion in 2010 and rose by 42 per cent in 2011, with more than 13 million visitors from the mainland providing much of the increase. Growth slowed in 2012, though, because of the size of the turnover and the cooling of the mainland economy. The anti-corruption drive by Beijing may also have a negative impact. The Ho family descended into squabbles over its inheritance that provided the Hong Kong media with a great soap opera. A quarter of Macau's workforce is employed in casinos or the hotel and restaurant business. Macau will continue to go its own way, unstable but enduring.

The return of Hong Kong from British colonial rule to Chinese sovereignty on 1 July 1997 was a highly symbolic and, for many, highly emotional moment. The handover had been prepared thirteen years earlier by Deng Xiaoping and Margaret Thatcher, but when it finally came it epitomized the rising of the new power in the East and the relative decline of the West. President Jiang Zemin beamed and the Prince of Wales sailed out of the harbour in the rain. The democratic reforms introduced by Chris Patten, the Last Governor, were dismantled as the Special Administrative Region (SAR) of Hong Kong came into being as part of the People's Republic. From being ruled by a democratic regime on the other side of the world, the city was now under the control of a Communist regime 1,200 miles to the north.

However, just as it had enjoyed a large degree of liberty as a colony short of being allowed to elect its government, so Hong Kong was given a special status under the PRC. The Sino-British Joint Declaration of 1984 followed by the Basic Law drawn up for the SAR guaranteed existing freedoms for fifty years. The Common Law would continue to rule. The financial and economic system would be perpetuated, Hong Kong residents were free to travel and move their money wherever they wished. Freedom of expression was safeguarded. The Hong Kong dollar remained pegged to the US currency not to the yuan. Many of the richer and middle-class citizens have a second foreign passport, an important factor giving them the confidence to stay after the handover knowing that, if things went wrong, they had a bolt-hole to move to.

When Britain acquired Hong Kong Island in perpetuity after defeating the Qing forces in 1841, Lord Palmerston, the Foreign Secretary at the time, was none too pleased. He would have preferred a port to what he dismissed as 'a barren island with hardly a house upon it'. But the Treaty of Nanjing in 1842 made Hong Kong British, with its deep water harbour and position at the mouth of the Pearl River leading to Canton. The Kowloon Peninsula across the bay from the island was added in 1860 and, in 1898, Britain took a ninety-nine-year lease on the New Territories stretching up to the frontier with China. Those territories were essential for the island which had no water or agriculture of its own. Though Mao had not sought to occupy this 'pimple on the backside of China', Deng's desire to regain territories lost during the 'century of humiliation' meant that the colonial era would end when the lease on the New Territories expired. The handover negotiations were tortuous but London had no alternative to obtaining the best deal it could for its former subjects. Though Mrs Thatcher was asked pointedly by a local journalist how she felt about handing its people over to Communist rule, and the Beijing massacre of protestors in 1989 caused deep concern (Hong Kongers had sent assistance to the students in Tiananmen Square), there was no way the British sovereign possessions could exist without the New Territories which China was intent on reclaiming – and no way that the Royal Navy was going to sail in to seek to repel the PLA in the event of a confrontation.

Indeed, British domination of Hong Kong had been waning since the

Japanese marched in at the end of 1941 to occupy the place until their own defeat in 1945. Before the Second World War, Hong Kong had taken second place among British footholds in East Asia. Strategically placed beside the rubber plantations of Malaysia, Singapore was the main base; and, for those who wanted to make fortunes in China, Shanghai was the obvious destination where the colony's great trading houses earned the cash that went back to buy estates in Scotland and the Home Counties. The easy Japanese victory diminished the status of the British and the local population adapted to occupation, some profiting from working with their fellow Asians. A short-lived attempt by some enlightened figures to move Hong Kong towards electoral democracy was side-tracked by the British establishment and, by the 1950s, it was business that dominated.[1]

The Communist victory on the mainland enhanced Hong Kong's position as refugees arrived mainly from Guangdong, Shanghai and other east coastal centres to found enterprises that would grow into some of the colony's biggest undertakings. When China embarked on its strong growth path in the 1980s, Hong Kong prospered even more, its port handling a flood of traded goods and its firms investing in Shenzhen and other Special Economic Zones across the border. Given the restricted amount of land in the colony (all of it bar the Church of England cathedral owned by the government and leased out at auctions), property became a major source of wealth. The sons and daughters of first generation immigrants from the mainland closed their parents' factories, moved production to low-wage, low-cost plants in China and built flats and commercial property on the old manufacturing sites.

While Hong Kong contained poor people, including 'cage dwellers' in tiny cramped quarters, the overall standard of living came to exceed that of the colonial power. The rich lived a high-octane existence, helped by a low flat rate of income tax, maintaining residences in Mayfair, buying the finest French wines, driving luxury limousines whose mileage was exceedingly low given the lack of distance to cover on the island, and buying luxury boats where they served lavish weekend meals with cheese flown in from France but never took out of Hong Kong waters for fear of being attacked by pirates.

With their businesses flourishing, their main concern was what would happen when the hold on the New Territories expired. Since the property market so central to prosperity operated on a leasehold basis, a clear answer was required as to the future of those leases. Once the British had raised the issue with Deng in 1982, the die was cast. China would take back Hong Kong, knowing that Macau was going to follow. It was then simply a matter of working out the details after Mrs Thatcher had visited Beijing, seen Deng (whose spittoon was said to have caused her some surprise) and concluded that agreement, meaning withdrawal was the only option.

The Sino-British Joint Declaration signed in 1984 set 1 July 1997 as the date for the transfer under Deng's formula of 'One Country, Two Systems' to maintain the colony's way of life for half a century. The barren island of the 1840s was now a huge prize, giving the PRC a modern city, a major financial centre, a place known for its efficiency, legal system and commercial skills, an image of what Chinese cities of the future might aspire to become. Though the political negotiations were between London (via its representatives in Hong Kong) and Beijing, the colony's Chinese tycoons, most children of refugees but some from South East Asia, were the key constituency with which the PRC authorities dealt.

After he expanded the effective franchise to bring in democracy during the final years of British rule, Patten was vilified by Beijing as a 'serpent' and 'the whore of the East' who would be 'condemned for a thousand generations'. He returned the compliment by wearing a tie emblazoned with dinosaurs at his only face-to-face meeting with Chinese negotiators in Beijing, but was not sure if they got the point. The Governor's populist touch, including his taste for the local pastries, went down well with the people of Hong Kong, but he was much disliked by the business community which feared that he would upset the stable handover and might jeopardize their lucrative mainland connections. On the other side of the globe, some old China hands in the Foreign Office in London, and British businesses working with China, added to the opposition to the Last Governor which contrasted with his popularity among the colony's inhabitants.[2]

For all the forebodings and alarms in the foreign media, the birth of the SAR was a peaceful event. A downpour made it hard to discern whether the drop on the Last Governor's cheek was a tear or the rain. As the Chinese flag was raised at the Convention Centre, PLA soldiers presented arms and China's President, Jiang Zemin, gave a grave smile while Anson Chan, head of the civil service as Chief Secretary, sat regally above the stage. (See photograph at the start of this chapter.) The PLA took over from the British forces at the Prince of Wales barracks by the harbour but the English sign on the side of the building was not removed. Letter boxes retained the British monarch's coat of arms. The Chinese emissaries remained discreet in their new headquarters on the hill overlooking Government House. Pro-democracy politicians were not arrested and, with one exception which was not repeated, the new authorities respected the status of the Court of Final Appeal set up to protect the rule of common law.

China's friends fretted about annoying Beijing. The owner of the newspaper I edited told me repeatedly to dismiss independent writers who were critical of the PRC and to stop calling 4 June a massacre – I replied that, if he wanted such changes, he should sack me and appoint somebody who would do his bidding. Some media tacked to the wind but others remained highly independent. *Apple Daily*, the second-bestselling Chinese-language paper, was as outspoken as ever under its proprietor, Jimmy Lai, who had called Li Peng, the former Chinese Premier, a 'turtle's egg', a particularly rude insult, and continued to run stories the mainland authorities would have preferred to have kept under the carpet. I experienced only one overt (as against in-house) case of PRC pressure, when an official at the Hong Kong and Macau Office in Beijing told us that negative opinion polls we ran on the low popularity of the first SAR Chief Executive, Tung Chee-hwa, were wrong and should be corrected; we took no notice. After my contract was not renewed in 1999, the staff writers disliked by the owner were indeed pushed out amid a hectic turnover of editors. For a time coverage of the PRC revived but then, in 2012, the paper's first mainland-born editor raised fresh concerns by decisions that seemed to show a desire to down-play negative news.

There was no doubt that the reforms Patten introduced would be swept away on 1 July: Beijing had signed up to preserve the Hong Kong way of life as it had existed in the 1980s, not a new democratized form brought in ten years later. That, for the Governor's critics, was enough to damn his initiatives. But there can be no doubt that his measures strengthened the self-confidence of the Hong Kong people and thus left an unquantifiable but indisputable legacy shown in episodes after the handover when popular pressure forced the Beijing-approved administration to give way on controversial security issues and contributed to the resignation of the well-meaning but ineffective Tung Chee-hwa.

Hong Kong's 426 square miles are full of contrasts and superlatives. It has some of the heaviest concentrations of population on the planet, both on the island near the shore in Causeway Bay and in the high-rise residential developments in the New Territories. But it also possesses extensive country parks where wild dogs and water buffalos roam. Its Central District is an acme for upmarket shopping but also houses thriving cheap markets. It contains some of the most expensive residential property on the planet – at our more modest level, the monthly rent for our flat when I edited the *South China Morning Post* from 1995–99 was equal to what one would have paid annually in London. Office space is the most expensive on earth. The economy owes a debt to the demand from mainlanders since access was eased for them but the SAR retains a high degree of economic independence as part of the global system in a way the PRC, with its controlled capital markets and currency, its state presence and its corruption, cannot match. The territory's freedoms, both material and in legal matters and such areas as freedom of expression, matter a great deal to its inhabitants and are part of its unique character even if only half the legislature is elected by popular vote and progress towards allowing citizens to pick their chief executive has been extremely slow.

The former colony registered 6.8 per cent growth in 2010, recovering faster than had been expected from a downturn the previous year caused by the global financial crisis. Exports – most them in fact re-exports of mainland products brought across the border or down the Pearl River from Guangdong – increased by 17.3 per cent in real terms and private consumption was up by 5.8 per cent on 2009 while infrastructure projects boosted investment by 8 per cent in 2010.

Epitomising the SAR's dependence on the mainland, its Li and Fung company is the world's biggest source of goods, from the PRC. The peg to the declining US dollar and the resulting lack of flexibility in using interest rates to fight inflation remain a downside but, overall, Hong Kong and its 7 million people, some 95 per cent of them Cantonese but including just about every nationality on earth, have come through most of the fourteen years since the handover in quite good shape.

There is, however, a constant tension between the habitual business-as-usual climate in the territory and its regular accolade as the world's freest economy with minimal government involvement (even if the government's ownership of land somewhat contradicts the plaudits of free market institutes) and the longer-term issue of the SAR's connection with the giant country of which it has become part. However much the avuncular Tung Chee-hwa urged his fellow citizens that they should 'become more Chinese' (he told me over lunch to do the same which I felt would be rather tricky), Hong Kong is a very different place from the PRC. Polls show that its people regard themselves as 'Hong Kong Chinese' with the place of origin coming first.

The rocky outcrop between the Pearl River Delta and the South China Sea became rich well before mainland cities grew and prospered. It has an effective, clean civil service and a multiplicity of global contacts. But it is now part of a state run on very different lines and depends for its continuing growth on the mainland. There is a scheme to link it administratively with Shenzhen, with which it is already umbilically connected economically. Beijing has the last word on the selection of its senior administrators, including the Chief Executive, first businessman Tung Chee-hwa, and then Donald Tsang Yam-kuen, a former Financial Secretary and British knight, a polished ballroom dancer and only practising Roman Catholic to hold a senior position in Communist China.

The One Country, Two Systems idea has endured, if in a fashion with which Beijing feels comfortable. Though they would like to see the SAR introduce more draconian public-security laws, the PRC authorities have shown an awareness of the negative results that would flow if they adopted a more heavy-handed approach or reneged on the undertaking to respect the Hong Kong way of life until 2047. It is the only place under China's rule where the killings in Beijing on 4 June 1989 are publicly commemorated, by a large crowd staging a candle-lit vigil in Victoria Park. The 2012 turnout to pay tribute to the dead was put at a record 180,000 by organizers and 85,000 by police – mainland censors blacked out any web postings on the event.

Still there is an underlying friction that surfaces regularly and seems to grow more acute as hopes for meaningful democratization recede. Polls report that the proportion of people who say they are proud to be part of China has fallen to 41 per cent from around 50 per cent in 2007–10. Economically, things are not as rosy as they appear from the bounding statistics. Inflation rose steadily in 2011, in part because of low interest rates caused by the dollar peg, while property prices were 70 per cent up on early 2009. Cartels predominate in key sectors such as property and retailing, and there is no legislation to encourage competition. Despite the territory's overall wealth, half its workers earn less than a quarter of the per capita GDP. It was only in 2010 that a minimum wage was introduced. A UN survey in 2009 ranked it as having the highest income inequality on earth; 20 per cent of the population lives below the poverty line.

By the time he left office on July 1, 2012, Donald Tsang's approval rating had fallen to 20 per cent from 57 per cent in 2005. In the summer of 2011 a huge crowd – 200,000-strong, according to the organizers – marched to demand democratic rights. But Tsang's successor in 2012, self-made millionaire surveyor Leung Chun-ying was selected by a committee of 1,200 people approved by Beijing. However, the process was notable for the way in which the original official candidate, prominent businessman Henry Tang Ying-yen, was displaced after a series of scandals and missteps and how Tsang was buffeted in his last months in office by revelations that he had accepted favours from tycoons and stayed in high-priced accommodations when travelling on official business. Leung promised to aim for higher growth and pursue social policies, looking for support in the run-up to the promised election of the Chief Executive by a popular vote in 2017. But he soon ran into trouble by seeming too keen to line up with the mainland. Though Leung has always refused to say if he is a member of the Communist Party, he has long been seen as being close to Beijing. The former colony will continue to edge towards the political freedoms its people richly deserve but its history and location mean it will remain under the watchful supervision of the authorities to the north, however international its vocation may be.

Just as Beijing regards its sovereignty over Tibet as nonnegotiable so it classes the recovery of Taiwan following that of Hong Kong and Macau among its 'core interests'. It reserves the right to use force to reclaim what it regards as a 'renegade province' which broke away from the motherland when Chiang Kai-shek led the Nationalists and their Republic of China (RoC) across the 99-mile Strait in 1949. The People's Liberation Army has more than 1,000 missiles pointing at the 22,000-square-mile island and the mainland insists that other states do not recognize the government in the capital of Taipei. 'Taiwan is part of the sacred territory of the People's Republic of China,' the PRC constitution declares. 'It is the lofty duty of the entire Chinese people, including our compatriots in Taiwan, to accomplish the great task of reunifying the motherland.'

No matter that most of the island's 23 million people show no desire to be reunited with the mainland, preferring their own democratic way of life. No matter that Taiwan was under Chinese sovereignty for only 231 years of its history stretching back for thousands of years. No matter that its indigenous people are not Chinese and that most of the present Han inhabitants came under the last dynasty or with Chiang. No matter, of course, that in the last two decades Taiwan has evolved a vibrant democracy that has seen peaceful transfers of power between parties unknown in the history of the mainland.

Taiwan's evolution, both political and economic, has been admirable by Western standards. But it finds itself in an extremely difficult position. As the Republic of China it has a political system of its own but does not constitute a state recognized by the world at large. Western nations that declare their adherence to the spread of democracy accord it second-class status for fear of alienating Beijing. George W. Bush's administration advised caution when the island's President sought democratic backing for moves towards declaring independence. Such minor advances as being allowed observer status at the annual meeting of the World Health Organization (WHO) as 'Chinese Taipei' are hailed as triumphs on the island. Diplomatic relations are cloaked in weasel words: the US is represented by an 'institute' in Taipei and there was a frisson at the annual celebration in London of the RoC's national holiday a couple of years ago when a speaker from the Liberal Democratic Party referred to his host as 'ambassador'.

Taiwan has its faults, to be sure. It has a long tradition of corruption and money politics inherited from the Chiang regime. Chen Shui-bian, its autonomist-minded President from 2000 to 2008, is serving a nineteen-year jail sentence for bribery along with his wife. Its free politics can be rumbustious – fist fights break out in the legislature, and are shown on mainland television as evidence of the dangers of democracy. Chen's eight years in power were often shambolic and the remnant machine of Chiang's Kuomintang lurks behind his successor, Ma Ying-jeou. But the treatment the RoC receives from advanced democracies is an ultra-realist demonstration of the power of the PRC with which the island and its people have to live.

Lying on the Tropic of Cancer, Taiwan is a place of great natural beauty despite the urban sprawl of its main cities and its industrial pollution. It has modern industrial complexes, the largest operating on the cluster principle of bringing suppliers together, and a landmark tower, the 101 (from the number of floors), in Taipei that was for a time the tallest structure in the world. Most of its population comprises descendants of Chinese who migrated across the Strait from the seventeenth century together with a small group from the earlier aboriginal inhabitants. Around 12 per cent of its people are from families who crossed with Chiang Kai-shek in 1949. Its five mountain ranges reach as high as 3,952 metres, looking down on the main plain where most people live. Its shape leads its people to call themselves 'the children of the sweet potato'. Strategically, it is part of an island chain stretching from Okinawa to the Philippines, a fact that displeases the Chinese navy, which sees it as an impediment to access to the wider Pacific.

Evidence of human settlement on the island dates back to aborigines, probably of Polynesian origin, who settled there 4,000 years ago. Their hostility to outsiders kept away Chinese who sought to cross the Strait. But, in 1544, a Portuguese ship sighted the island, the crew giving it the name of Formosa, or 'beautiful island' by which it was long known in the West. The Dutch set up a base in 1624 and brought in workers from the mainland who staged two revolts against the colonialists, which were brutally suppressed. The Spaniards followed two years later.

Then the Manchu victory over the Ming and the foundation of the Qing dynasty brought the island into the orbit of China. A Ming loyalist, Koxinga, launched an offensive against the new rulers from 1658 to 1689, but was beaten back to the east coast. Isolated there, and hearing that the Dutch garrison was weakly manned, he crossed the Strait with 900 ships and 25,000 men and forced the Europeans to cede the island, which he planned to make the springboard for a fresh offensive against the Qing. But he died at the age of thirty in 1662, possibly killing himself at his failure to unseat the Manchus. The dynasty forced coastal dwellers in Fujian and Guangdong to move ten miles back from the coast to create a quarantine zone, but did not invade. Koxinga's son, Cheng Ching, imposed a Chinese-style administration, trained mandarins and welcomed 50,000 migrants from the mainland. The island traded with Japan and smugglers plied across the Strait. However, after Cheng Ching joined with Ming diehards in southern China to revolt against the dynasty, the Qing launched a victorious fleet against the island that became a prefecture of Fujian.

Taiwan remained a wild and distant place. There was said to be a minor revolt every three years and a major one every five – one temporarily drove out the imperial officials. Piracy was common. The original inhabitants, some of whom had retreated deep into the inland mountains, clashed repeatedly with the Chinese migrants. Secret societies flourished. The climate was unhealthy, though abundant crops made the island a valuable source of food for the mainland.

Still the Chinese population kept rising given that the island offered better prospects to make money out of rice, sugar and camphor than the barren coastland of Fujian. Nineteenth-century censuses reported 2.5 million people of mainland origin. Officials made up for the hardships of a posting to Taiwan by extracting maximum 'squeeze'.

The island's reputation as a hazardous place was reinforced in 1842 when 197 of the survivors of two British ships wrecked off its shore were executed, apparently on orders from Beijing. Busy with the Opium War, London did nothing for the moment but the Treaty of Tianjin in 1858 opened four Taiwanese ports to foreign trade. Russia, the United States and France all showed interest and Britain mounted a punitive expedition when a mob attacked camphor traders. Tokyo did the same after Japanese castaways were beheaded by tribesmen in 1871. A military expedition landed and Japan warned that it wanted to take over the island, but Britain, fearing a foreign presence close to the sea routes to Hong Kong, put pressure on the imperial court to declare that it would maintain sovereignty and pay an indemnity to get the invaders to leave. There was a fresh foreign intervention by the French during a war they fought with the Qing in 1884–85, which ended in stalemate.

Despite such troubles, Taiwan became one of the most developed parts of China in the later nineteenth century under a modernizer, Liu Mingchuan, who built a road across the island and a forty-two-mile railway line, as well as setting up a telegraph, developing coalmines, forestry and shipping, and encouraging manufacturing. Taipei was the first city under China's rule with electric light. Liu faced revolts, waging more than forty campaigns against the 'savages' while seeking to combat graft and improve tax revenue collection. In 1887 his work was rewarded when the island became a fully fledged province of China with him as its first Governor. But he had aroused opposition among officials, whose corruption he attacked, landowners, whose holdings he sought to control, and merchants, who disliked his taxes. Like other modernizers of the time, Liu depended on support from the court and that was not forthcoming when he proposed to grant British investors a twenty-year coal and kerosene monopoly in return for developing a big mine. Beijing turned down the idea, and sacked him.

China's defeat in its 1894–95 war with Japan broke the link with the mainland for just over half a century. The Chinese Governor had declared a short-lived republic and then tried to get the British or French to take control rather than coming under Japanese rule. But, the treaty the Qing were obliged to sign made the island Tokyo's first formal colony. The new East Asian power landed an army which subdued the island, despite losing thousands of men to the diseases for which Taiwan was feared. Sixteen thousand Japanese civilians followed. Periodic insurgencies by the native population were ruthlessly repressed; in one Tokyo's troops were ordered to kill every living thing within a five-mile radius of a town where there had been a revolt. In 1930 a group of 300 aborigines killed more than 130 Japanese children and parents taking part in a field day at a school – the colonial government riposted with artillery and air attacks, and an estimated 800 people were killed, committed suicide or went missing; a film of the event which appeared in 2011 was a hit on the island but aroused controversy for its depiction of beheadings by aborigines. Still, the colonialists improved infrastructure, which had been allowed to deteriorate after Liu's efforts. They encouraged industrialization, introduced land reform to give farmers ownership rights, which boosted output, and promoted education – on Japanese lines.

Taiwan's fate was decided by others once more in 1945 when, after Japan's defeat in the Second World War, Nationalist troops arrived on American ships to reassert Chinese control. As the civil war turned against his regime on the mainland, Chiang Kai-shek identified the island as a bolt-hole protected by naval and air cover and free of Communists. To ensure that it would be the safe haven the Nationalists increasingly needed, there was harsh repression of the non-Chinese population, including the 'White Terror' massacre of anywhere from 10,000 to 30,000 civilians by the army after a popular revolt broke out in 1947. Martial law was declared. Nationalist carpet-baggers seized property and assets. The divide between the incoming Chinese and the previous residents widened and remained the island's main fault line when Chiang finally flew from Chengdu on 10 December 1949 as the PLA advanced through Sichuan.

The Generalissimo and his followers never gave up the claim that the Republic of China remained the legitimate ruler of the whole of their country – legislators sat in parliament in Taipei representing provinces they would never see again. They brought with them shiploads of booty from the mainland, including gold from the central bank and the treasures of the National Museum. Chiang blamed himself for having put too much faith in the treacherous Mao and saw the influence of international Communism behind Harry Truman's decision not to intervene to save his regime in 1949. In fact, the US President was sick and tired of the failures and corruption of the Nationalists – 'They're all thieves, every damn one of them,' he said later. But the outbreak of the Korean

War in 1950 and Mao's decision to commit the PLA to fight the Americans changed the strategic picture and made Taiwan a valued ally for Washington.[3]

Though the island was used as a jumping-off point for sabotage and spy missions against the mainland, and there were artillery battles over outlying islands, the US turned down periodic suggestions from the Generalissimo for an invasion. Chiang remained a dictator ruling under martial law, but Taiwan's economic progress, which included land reform and encouragement for manufacturing and was helped by American money and advice, stood in stark contrast to the state of the PRC. The adherence of the classically schooled 'Confucian Fascist' dictator to old values also meant that the island was, in many ways, more traditionally Chinese than the mainland where Mao was seeking to destroy the past.

That, however, was not enough to prevent Richard Nixon visiting Beijing in 1972 and recognizing 'One China' under a diplomatic formula which suited both sides. Full diplomatic relations were established under Jimmy Carter in 1979 after the RoC lost the permanent Security Council seat granted to it by Franklin Roosevelt as one of the 'Four Policemen' of the post-war world. Despite soothing noises from Washington, Taiwan was largely on its own. Governments which recognized it could expect hostility from the PRC or blandishments to switch to the mainland. Today the RoC has diplomatic relations with just two dozen countries, most of them small states in Central America, Africa and Oceania that benefit from its largesse, plus the Vatican. Though Taipei and Beijing have agreed formally to stop bidding for recognition, there are recurrent stories of one side or the other trying to win points by offers of assistance.[4]

After the Generalissimo's death at the age of eighty-seven in 1975, political liberalization set in under his son, Ching-kuo, as opposition groups headed by the Democratic Progressive Party (DPP) overcame restrictions and electoral fraud to win legislative seats, drawing on the resentment of many voters for the Kuomintang regime. Martial law was lifted in 1987. The following year Ching-kuo died and was succeeded by Lee Teng-hui, a Taiwan native who saw off a challenge from the Generalissimo's aged widow, Soong Meiling, and pushed ahead with further democratization.

Legislators who had crossed the Strait in 1949 were forced to resign in 1991. The opposition DPP made advances in local elections. A campaign was launched in favour of Taiwanese culture and restrictions of the use of non-Han languages in schools were lifted. But the Kuomintang remained in power, bolstered by corruption and 'money politics'.

Despite the political estrangement, Taiwanese investors were major participants in the mainland's economic development after 1989, as exemplified by companies such as Foxconn and by the hundreds of thousands of Taiwanese working in the Shanghai region. As Lee became increasingly identified with an autonomous Taiwan, Beijing riposted by stepping up its rhetoric. It staged war games in the Strait in 1995 and again in 1996 in an apparent effort to persuade voters not to back Lee in the first popular presidential election on the island in 1996. The policy backfired badly. The Clinton administration put on the biggest American military exercise in Asia since the Vietnam War, sending two aircraft-carrier groups into the area, though they did not enter the Strait itself. The war games stopped and Lee was elected to the presidency.

Four years later, however, a split in the Kuomintang allowed Chen Shui-ban of the DPP to win on a minority vote. Politics polarized between the KMT's 'Pan Blue' grouping, which continued to see Taiwan as part of China, albeit ruled separately from the PRC, and the DPP and its allies in the 'Pan Greens', who pursued the defence of 'Taiwanese identity' with formal independence as a potential goal. The Democrats set about disbanding the legacy of Chiang whom many of them thoroughly hated for his repression – when I was speaking to one Taiwanese diplomat he used to refer to the Generalissimo as 'Chiang Kai-shit'. The Nationalist leader's face was removed from stamps and banknotes and the many bronze statues of him were uprooted from public places. His corpse and that of his son, meanwhile, remained in caskets at their country home awaiting eventual burial back on the mainland in keeping with their claim never to have lost the mandate to rule China.

Chen's re-election in 2004 heightened tension with Beijing as the DPP asserted the island's separate identity from China and called for the enactment of a new constitution for a 'normal country'. But low voter turnout negated proposals for referendums on a bid to rejoin the UN and to strengthen the island's defences. Chen was also hamstrung by declining economic growth, lack of a legislative majority and the inefficiencies of his administration. Washington worried that he might go for all-out independence, provoking military action from the PRC that would force it into hostilities under the somewhat vague provisions of the Taiwan Relations Act. Passed to accompany the recognition of the PRC, this lays down that the US will 'consider any effort to determine the future of Taiwan by other than peaceful means [as] a threat to the peace and security of the Western Pacific area and of grave concern to the United States'.

In opposition, the Kuomintang reshaped itself to become more appealing to an electorate that had turned its back on the pursuit of reunification. Its new leader, the charismatic Ma Ying-jeou, won the 2008 presidential poll comfortably and also enjoyed a legislative majority as the DPP descended into infighting amid the corruption accusations that saw both Chen and his wife imprisoned. Beijing had already extended olive branches to its longtime foe, and Ma set out to cement economic relations that produced a cross-Strait economic cooperation agreement, signed in 2010 and going into effect in 2011–13. There was agreement that both Taipei and Beijing believed in 'One China', the difference being how they interpreted the term. The PRC is ready to accept the resulting ambiguities – while Beijing claims the island as China's territory, departure signs at mainland airports list Taiwan with international destinations.

For the Ma administration this was the only way ahead, tapping in to the growth of the PRC while retaining political autonomy. Critics worried that the rapprochement would hollow out the island's economy and that, sooner or later, Beijing would turn the screw and impose itself on a dependent island. In that scenario, Washington would be more concerned with its relations with the mainland than with defending the RoC. The Taiwan Relations Act requires the administration to 'provide Taiwan with arms of a defensive character' and to 'maintain the capacity of the United States to resist any resort to force or other forms of coercion that would jeopardize the security, or the social or economic system, of the people on Taiwan'. But supplies of the most advanced weapons have been repeatedly delayed in the face of strident complaints from Beijing.

As part of a $5.9 billion deal in the autumn of 2011, the Obama administration turned down Taiwan's request for sixty-six new F-16 planes, offering instead to 'retrofit' its existing jets with modernized technology. Beijing reacted angrily, with PLA hawks warning of a 'serious obstacle' to Sino-American relations. But, as after a previous deal in 2010, it seemed probable that any suspension of military contacts between the two powers would be limited in scope and duration while, following the conviction of a senior Taiwanese general for spying for the PRC, some American sources raised concerns that mainland espionage might get hold of advanced military technology if it was sold to Taipei.

The RoC has undoubted vulnerabilities as well as the possible economic hollowing out by its growing closeness to the mainland. Politically it is caught in an apparently irresolvable debate between autonomy and independence. Economically, dependence on exports exposes it to volatility stemming from the ups and downs of the main markets for its semiconductors, laptops and mobile telephones as was evident as the economy slowed down in 2011–12, as the West took fewer exports.

Still, the island has considerable achievements to its credit. Economically, it has switched from agriculture to industry and become a world leader in electronic goods, notably semiconductors. Its GDP ranks seventeenth among world economies with average 8 per cent annual growth over the last three decades, a rate which, as shown in the second chart at the end of this chapter, has outstripped that of the PRC in recent years. Its trade exceeds $600 billion with a trade surplus of $40 billion. The RoC has the fourth-largest foreign exchange reserves on earth. As well as the PRC, it has big investments in Indonesia, Malaysia, the Philippines, Thailand and Vietnam. Its airline and shipping firms span the globe and its Din Tai Fung chain of dumpling restaurants has outlets from Shanghai to the United States and Australia. It has vibrant media and popular culture.

With Ma's presidential victory in 2008 and re-election in 2012, it has achieved a democratic somersault, the one-time dictatorial party having ceded power at the polls, reformed and then won back office, all done with an absence of the violence that has traditionally marked administration changes in China. The President faced problems familiar to any

democratic leader as his economic and financial policies ran into opposition. He was accused of aloofness and poor communications. Free
trade negotiations with the US were hit by an outcry over his desire to
allow imports of American beef treated with the feed additive rac-
topamine. The DPP, for its part, moved beyond the leadership of those
who suffered under Chiang Kai-shek to try to become a more professional political movement as it approached the presidential election of
2012. This may be evidence that there is no incompatibility between
democracy and the Chinese. But some provisos are in order – Taiwan is
tiny compared to the PRC both in population and size. The island's history sets it apart. Taiwan did not suffer a Mao. While running a repressive
regime, the KMT did not have the single-minded ruthlessness of the CCP.
Chiang Ching-kuo and Lee Teng-hui were ready to take the necessary
political steps from which Deng Xiaoping and his successors recoiled. The
American influence played its role. But, with 40 per cent of its exports
now going to China, this often admirable story is overshadowed by the
geo-political orphan-child position in which the island finds itself and
from which the rest of the world will not release it. As a Taiwanese politician remarked to me, 'We have nothing against being an off-shore island;
we would just prefer to be moored off California.'

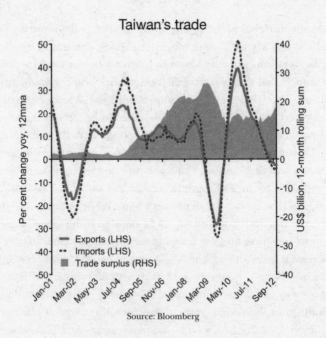

Taiwan's trade

Exports (LHS)
Imports (LHS)
Trade surplus (RHS)

Source: Bloomberg

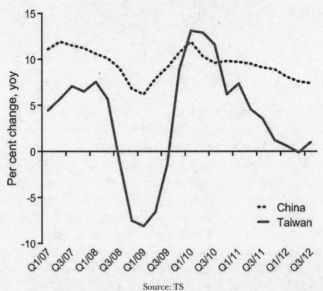

Real GDP growth: Taiwan and China

China
Taiwan

Source: TS

8

POWER CONTROL

Spectacular as it has been, China's growth has spawned a mass of questions and challenges. In retrospect, the first three decades of economic reform may turn out to have been the easy part. It was quite logical that the country should leap ahead given its massive reserves of cheap labour, the abundance of cheap capital from its high savings rate and a friendly global market which welcomed low-cost goods. The pace of expansion has enabled it to absorb its contradictions, but the future is a lot less certain as the regime has to grapple with the problems of maturity, not only economic but also social and political.

The challenges start at the top, with the seven men who make up the Standing Committee of the CCP's Politburo headed by Xi Jinping, Party General Secretary, State President and Chair of the Central Military Commission. Under the Leninist system that operates in the PRC, he and his colleagues in the wider twenty-five-person Politburo stand above the State Council, China's cabinet. This is often ignored or taken for granted in accounts of today's China. Commentators rarely mention Communist Party power, either taking it for granted or appearing to assume it is of marginal importance now that economic policy has shifted so far from Marxism. The government and prime minister are presented abroad as if they have the same powers as in, say, Britain. Hu Jintao and Xi Jinping are referred to as China's President, but not by the more important function of head of the CCP. I have lost count of the number of discussions on the PRC I have attended at which the 'C' word has not been mentioned or has cropped up only in passing. The Party's authority is not as great as it might wish; 'Chinese characteristics' affect politics as well as the economy. But any understanding of how the PRC functions has to start with the movement established in a deserted girls' school in Shanghai in 1921 that fought its way to power twenty-eight years later.[1]

The CCP operates according to its own rules and behind closed doors. In his speech to its Congress in 2007, Hu Jintao spoke of 'democracy' more than sixty times; at the celebrations of the ninetieth anniversary of the foundation of the CCP four years later, he used the word 'reform' forty-four times. There is frequent talk of 'intra-party democracy'. What this means to the leaders is enabling younger more efficient members to replace holdovers from the past and making the CCP a more effective governing organization to avoid the sclerosis that gripped the Soviet Union. Suggestions of real reform are batted away for fear that they might weaken the foundations of the regime.

The Party's Central Committee, consisting of about 300 full and alternate members, is selected by the CCP's National Congress. It holds plenums, usually once a year in the autumn, to discuss major policy matters. It also selects the members of the twenty-five-strong Political Bureau (Politburo) of whom the top figures form the Standing Committee, the top decision-making body in China.

The succession process limits the time the top leadership stays in place to ten years (with an age limit of sixty-nine) to avoid one of the great uncertainties of authoritarian regimes: what happens when the rulers depart? New leaders are singled out a decade before they accede to power. But the process is hidden from public view with the Central Committee voting in secret for members of the Politburo and the Standing Committee.

Since internal disagreements came out into the open during the protests in Beijing and other cities in 1989, Party unity has been a central concern. Open argument is shunned even if many interest groups are at work behind the scenes. The jockeying for power that followed the deaths of Stalin and Mao or which characterised the struggle between Yeltsin and Gorbachev is to be avoided, in public at least, to preserve the façade of the all-wise, all-knowing Party.

However, factions could be identified in the leadership transition at the Party Congress of 2012. Hu Jintao's heirs belong to a group which has its roots in the Party Youth League. It included Senior Vice-Premier Li Keqiang and the Guangdong Party boss, Wang Yang. It leans to the left, for instance backing the building of millions of cheap housing units for the poor and wanting to push through the health programme. The other main group is known as the princelings, consisting of the offspring of First Generation Communist leaders headed by Xi Jinping. These people are the PRC's aristocracy who have gone through its vicissitudes; often brought up in privilege in the early Mao era, they suffered with their fathers during the Cultural Revolution but have now risen to the top to stake their claims to run the nation when Hu and Wen stepped down. A shadowy third group emerged at the Party Congress in November 2012, consisting of officially retired elders around Jiang Zemin, who had stepped down as China's leader ten years earlier. These men in their eighties backed the status quo and blocked the promotion of reformers.

There is considerable fluidity among these groups given the pattern of mentor–pupil relationships which may mean that a princeling owed his initial career to Jiang or may have worked with Hu. Whatever their differences and competing ambitions, unity is the first priority; the price for stepping out of line was shown by the abrupt fall of Bo Xilai in the spring of 2012. Since moving to Chongqing five years earlier, this princeling son of one of the Communist Party's 'eight immortals' had used the mega-metropolis as his springboard to the top, as we have seen. He was as flamboyant as his colleagues were dour, acting like a Western politician on the election trail. When he appeared at the annual meetings of the National People's Congress, the media flocked to him. National leaders including Hu Jintao and Xi Jinping travelled to Chongqing to pay tribute to its expansion. As well as the city's giant development projects, Bo's highly publicised campaign to re-awaken 'red values', combining Maoism with the unsubtle reminder that he came from the Party aristocracy, awakened old anxieties in his fellow Politburo members.

Mass rallies were devoted to singing patriotic and Communist Party songs. An eight-storey-high bronze statue of Mao was put up in the city's university district. The Chongqing *Daily* reported that convicts in Chongqing's jails were set to study Party texts and recite 'red poems'. Cadres were required to spend time working in rural areas in a minor rerun of the Cultural Revolution. Press reports told of a wife awakening her husband from his vegetative state by singing Mao-era songs at him for more than a hundred days and of a cancer patient healing himself by following the same procedure.

Whether Bo actually believed in all of this is uncertain. Rather than marking the emergence of neo-Maoism which some foreign commentators detected, the rallies and 'red songs' were a means of arousing support by a politician on the make. But he had become a tall poppy waiting to be chopped down, a wild card in a system that puts a premium on consensus. Reports that, if he reached the Standing Committee, he wanted the portfolio for internal security heightened the danger his ambition represented for other leadership figures – he had wiretapped Hu when he visited Chongqing. His ruthless anticrime campaign which targeted businessmen as well as the underworld had shown what he was capable of. He had plenty of enemies and Wen Jiabao knew that Bo's father had tried to have him purged after the 1989 protests in Beijing.

In February 2012, those who wanted to check Bo were handed an ideal weapon when the former Chongqing police chief, Wang Lijun, who had been demoted by Bo, drove to the US consulate in Chengdu, capital of Sichuan province, and spilled the beans on his boss. Wang was said to have fallen out with Bo over a corruption investigation of the politician's second wife, Gu Kalai, with some reports saying the two men had come to blows. After 24 hours in the consulate and a US decision not to grant him asylum, Wang was flown to Beijing by officials from the State Security Ministry. One of the revelations he made while in the Consulate concerned a British businessman, Neil Heywood, who had worked with Bo and his second wife, Gu Kailai, and who had died in a hotel in the hills outside Chongqing the previous November. According to Wang, Heywood had been killed by Gu Kailai after a business dispute. The affair quickly spiralled. On March 15, 2012, one day after Wen Jiabao had spoken darkly of the risk of a 'historical tragedy' like the Cultural Revolution unless China adopts reforms, Bo was dismissed from his post in Chongqing.

The story broadened out to cover business Gu had done with Heywood in Britain where newspapers promptly suggested a personal liaison between the two and revealed her purchase of two luxury apartments in London. Her relatives in Hong Kong were said to run a big offshore investment operation. A French architect who had been associated with her was held in Cambodia and flew to China to give evidence. The case attracted unprecedented attention of Chinese websites and in foreign media showing once again the problems the regime has in controlling information, though some leaks were doubtless officially inspired.

After her husband had been suspended from the Party and was being held in a secret location, Gu went on trial in Hefei, capital of Anhui province, chosen as a safe location on the other side of the country from Chongqing. At a seven-hour hearing, which led to her being handed a supsended death sentence, she accepted the prosecution's case that she had killed Heywood by pouring poison into his mouth when he asked for water after getting drunk and vomiting. Official media accounts claimed that Heywood had threatened the Bos' son, Guagua, whom he had previously helped to get into Harrow, saying he would 'destroy' the family if he was not paid $20 million commission on a deal, and then holding the young man as a prisoner.[2]

There were many inconsistencies in the accusation but the line was clearly set. Gu took the blame for Heywood's death, saying that she had a nervous breakdown because of the danger to her son. Then Wang was put on trial. Though found guilty of treason, a capital offence, he got only fifteen years' imprisonment, the leniency due to information he had given the prosecution.

There were rumours of Bo's supporters trying to organize a counter-coup but nothing materialized. Rather than protecting his fellow princeling, Xi Jinping appeared with Hu Jintao to stress top-level unity, and photographs of him with Bo in Chonqing were removed from Chinese websites. In September 2012, the Politburo expelled Bo from the Party, saying he would be put on trial accused of multiple crimes, taking 'huge bribes' and 'improper sexual relationship with a number of women'. This, this statement added, had 'significantly damaged the cause of the Party and the people'. With the wild card from Chongqing removed from play, the factions at the top could manage the leadership transition free from troublesome boat-rocking by an overambitious regional warlord.[3]

As the successor to more than two millennia of imperial top-down rule in which the sovereigns enjoyed quasi-divine status and Confucian rituals and norms regulated society, the Communist Party observes carefully regulated procedures. These have become all the more important since the Mao years given the chaos caused by the Great Helmsman's wilful ways and tendency to ignore any rules that did not suit him. The full Party Congress meets once every five years to elect its Politburo and its top body, the Standing Committee. The Central Committee holds annual plenums in between, and the two state legislatures – the National People's Congress (NPC) and the upper house, the Chinese People's Political Consultative Congress (CPPCC) – meet in full session once a year in March. Only when the Standing Committee members walk out on to the stage at the Great Hall of the People at the end of the Congress do China and the world get the final word on who is up and who is down in the top rankings. They appear in the order of their position as the result of the Central Committee deliberations. The process is opaque in the extreme, but when Xi Jinping, then Party Secretary in Shanghai, came out fifth at the 2007 Congress, it was plain that he was the front runner to become the national leader when Hu stepped down in 2012, at the end of his ten years at the summit. Only because he appeared behind Xi did we know that Hu's protégé, Li Keqiang, was set for the less powerful position of Prime Minister.

Hu had been marked out for the top by Deng Xiaoping as a man fit to head the Communist Party after he quelled protests in 1989 in Tibet while he was CCP Secretary there – he suffered from altitude sickness and is reported to have spent most of his time back in Beijing. So his appointment as General Secretary on 2002 was no surprise though Jiang Zemin showed some reluctance to cede full authority to the younger man and held on to the third of the top three posts, the Chair of the CMC, until 2005.

Hu Jintao was the epitome of the political regime he led, a bureaucrat who was subsumed into the regime he headed. Even his place of birth has been obscured for political reasons: he was born in December 1942 into a modest family of tea traders in Jiangsu province but the official record puts this down as Anhui, where some of his forebears originated, since Jiang came from Jiangsu and somebody decided to avoid speculation about the emergence of a provincial clique.[4]

In his perfectly cut dark business suit and white shirt, Hu sported the thick black hair with not a grey strand that typifies Party chiefs (there is said to be a leadership hair-dye factory but how they repel incipient baldness is not clear). Hu gave nothing away. He met foreign reporters in China on only one occasion – when he said nothing of any significance. He was said to like playing table tennis and ballroom dancing, and to have a photographic memory. There were rumours of a dalliance with a television presenter but no proof one way or the other.

While Mao and Deng represented CCP history reaching back to before the Long March, and Jiang was brought up by a revolutionary hero after his father died, Hu belonged to the new class of political managers. He joined the CCP in 1964, the year of his graduation from Tsinghua University in Beijing where he studied hydraulic engineering and met his wife – they have a son and a daughter. He sidestepped the violence at the university during the Cultural Revolution and, from 1968, held posts in the poor regions of Gansu and Guizhou before being put in charge of Tibet, where he was photographed in a military uniform with a submachine gun held across his chest during the 1989 revolt. Seen by Deng as a coming man, he rose through the party hierarchy to join the Politburo in 1992 and became Vice-President five years later, with a power base as head of the Communist Youth League.

As Party Leader from 2002 to 2012 and State President from the spring of 2003, he has proclaimed the creed of 'Scientific Socialism' and the need to achieve a 'Harmonious Society' in which wealth is shared out equally. The results were sparse and hopes that he might usher in political reform were dashed. A secret body set up in 2003 to consider changes to the constitution produced no results. Hu proved to be a cautious leader who operated like a company chairman, not a risk-taker in the mould of Deng and Mao. He and his fellow top bureaucrats were sometimes referred to as 'shopkeepers' minding the store set up by their more illustrious predecessors in the CCP family, whose children would come to claim their inheritance in 2012.

That said, Hu strengthened Party control while presiding over high economic growth. In his second five-year term, starting in 2007, he presided over a twenty-five-member Politburo that was almost perfectly balanced between representatives of the CCP, the State, the regions and the army and security apparatus and was sensitive to the demands of major interest groups. In terms of personal power, Hu was the weakest leader China has had since 1949 – his failure to get Li Keqiang named as his successor being an example of his lack of ultimate clout. The more managerial style of rule that has been evident in recent years is healthy in moving away from autocracy, but makes hard decision-taking difficult with a tendency to go for the lowest common denominator except when, as in the economic downturn of 2008, strong action is obviously called for. As a result, consensus rules at the top of twenty-first-century China.

The Prime Minister, Wen Jiabao, who ascended with Hu in 2003 and ranked third in the Politburo, was a more interesting figure. Born in 1942, he studied geology and, according to a rare account he gave in 2011 of his early life, came under attack during the Cultural Revolution because his father, who went to the countryside to tend pigs, had been a teacher with a 'bourgeois' class background. In 1960, he added, he carried his father on his back to a hospital where he died. He then came to prominence as head of the Party's General Office between 1986 and

1993. In 1989, he was with Zhao Ziyang, the reformist CCP General Secretary, when he went to Tiananmen Square as the martial-law decree was being signed to tell the protesting students 'We have come too late' and urge them to return to their campuses. Though Zhao was purged, and Bo Xilai's father tried unsuccessfully to get Wen punished as well, he survived, reportedly making himself useful to Jiang when he became the CCP boss. Known for his work rate, he rose through the government ranks under Zhu Rongji, the forceful 1990s Premier, looking after financial and agricultural matters, and enjoyed a natural promotion to head the government in 2003. He was much more forthcoming than Hu, acting as the human face of the regime – earning the nickname of 'Grandpa Wen' – as he rushed to comfort victims of disasters and insisted on the need to control prices and safeguard the interests of ordinary citizens. He reads the texts of the Roman stoics and Adam Smith's *Theory of Moral Sentiments*. Personally upright, he has suffered from the way in which family members, including his wife, appear to have profited from his position, as reported by the *New York Times* in 2012.

Wen's political weight is open to question. When he spoke in 2010 of the need for political and legal reform, he was slapped down by the CCP machine. A critical writer dubs him 'China's Best Actor'. A stand-up comedian in Shanghai does an imitation that has Wen seeking out the dirtiest pair of hands to shake when he gets to a disaster scene and telling the victims, 'I am sorry I am too late,' in an echo of Zhao's words in 1989.

Hu and Wen inherited strong economic growth. China joined the World Trade Organization just before they took over and got through the Asian economic crisis of the late 1990s without major damage. Strong demand from rich countries, high productivity and an undervalued currency pushed up exports. The state sector had been modernized by Wen's predecessor, Zhu Rongji.

They faced their big challenge in the downturn that shaped up during 2008, caused by falling foreign buying of Chinese goods after the financial crisis set off by the collapse of Lehman Brothers compounded the negative effects of anti-inflationary monetary tightening at home and an excessive build-up of inventories around the time of the Beijing Olympics. By launching a 400-billion-yuan infrastructure programme in November

2008, followed by massive credit easing that doubled the volume of new loans in 2009 to 10 trillion yuan, they got China back on the growth path even if their medicine bequeathed major problems in excess liquidity, local-government debt and a growth model tied to big-project spending; in his annual press conference after the NPC meeting in 2010, Wen acknowledged that the country was still facing the most complicated period for its economy and that the most important issues still had to be addressed. Despite the PRC's globalized role, he added that 'our only hope lies in our own efforts'. The downturn of 2008 had made the leaders less confident about relying on the rest of the world to keep the export-led machine moving forward, but the way in which consumption had been dampened down during the decades of growth put them in need of serious rebalancing of the economy.

There were other big problems. Hu's hopes of a harmonious society were undermined by growing wealth disparities. Wen's talk of political and economic reform was quashed by the CCP; anticorruption campaigns had limited effect, even if they claimed some high-profile victims, such as the Party Secretary of Shanghai and the Railways Minister. China's foreign relations were quite primitive: there were widespread protests and the regime showed its repressive side in locking up political critics, notably the 2010 Nobel Peace Prize winner, Liu Xiabao. (These elements in today's China will be explored in later chapters.)

The governing style continued to be as opaque as ever when it came to anything more than displays of CCP solidarity. But it was clear that the top leaders operate atop a complex web of interest groups, some, like the army, part of the official central apparatus but others, like business lobbies, working in parallel with the Party and state. That range of factional pressures made running China more complex than it was when the autocracy was represented by a single man. Like imperial courts in the middle years of a dynasty, the leaders of the Marxist-Market dynasty that has ruled China since 1949 are subject to a range of pressures and complex balancing acts as they pursue their core objective, the preservation of the ruling house. How well they pull this off is central to the future of China.

The new Standing Committee unveiled at the Party Congress of November 2012 was the result of lengthy back-stairs negotiations involving not just the outgoing leadership under Hu Jintao and the incoming team under Xi Jinping, his successor as General Secretary, but also an assorted group of supposedly retired former leaders headed by Jiang Zemin, who had stepped down as Party leader ten years earlier. Xi and Hu's protégé, Li Keqiang, had been safety installed in the Standing Committee at the previous Congress held in 2007 and so moved smoothly into the two senior positions on the Politburo as Hu and Wen Jiabao retired. But there was uncertainty up to the last minute as to whether its membership would now be cut from nine to seven members (it was) and whether two reform-minded officials would be promoted to the top table (they were not). The nature of the Xi–Li leadership, selected to hold power for ten years, will be analysed in the last chapter of this book but they and their five colleagues in the Committee are experienced Party bureaucrats who had made steady, loyal progress through the system. They are not risk-takers and their attachment to the status quo which nurtured them raises serious questions at a time when China faces major challenges and needs economic, social, political and legal reform. Their first policy move was to launch an attack on corruption, a serious problem indeed as we will see, but the campaign faced the basic problem of how high it would go. In common with their predecessors, they face the basic conundrum of whether China can change without shaking the power of the Party.

Like the movement that raised them, these people have 'control' built in to their DNA. In public they usually speak in slogans and their appearances are carefully choreographed. Eight non-Communist 'patriotic parties' are tolerated but they are tiny and under CCP control, known as 'flowerpots' for the regime. The leadership's highest aim, as a former US ambassador, Clark Randt, put it in a cable to the State Department, is to achieve 'the benefits of a market-based economy and limited civil society governed by an efficient, accountable and responsive authoritarian one-party state'. Dominance is not simply a matter of political authoritarianism. Capital markets are controlled, as is the currency. Credit is decided primarily by quotas not the market. State banks lend to politically designated borrowers. The *hukou* registration system regulates the movement of people and labour. All farmland is owned by the state. The law is subservient to the interests of the Party, which has its own feared disciplinary commission. Energy and water prices are fixed by diktat not by the equation of supply and demand. Though Chinese companies and individuals apply competitive mechanisms to their everyday businesses, the superstructure within which they operate is far from the freewheeling vision of a nation hooked on market steroids.[5]

The result is often considerable inefficiencies, for instance in the misallocation of capital and the wasteful use of underpriced water and electricity. If China was truly efficient, the rest of the world would really have to worry.

The extraordinary thing, as in other domains, is that for all its short-comings the PRC continues to do so well, repeatedly heading off disastrous hard landings forecast by economic pundits. That record is subject to significant qualifications which will be analysed later; but, for the moment, the regime can claim success, contrasting itself to fumbling governments abroad. This being the case, the CCP sees no cause to relax their grip, even if some princelings have recently spoken of deep problems and even though Wen Jiabao has acknowledged that too much power is concentrated in the hands of officials.

While its share of output by value fell from 49 per cent to 27 per cent between 1999 and 2009, and the private sector is the biggest employer, the state still accounts for nearly 80 per cent of the country's produc-tive wealth, according to a calculation by the economist Chen Zhiwu. China has around 114,000 state-owned enterprises (SOEs) with com-bined assets of 63 trillion yuan or 30 per cent of the industrial and service sectors. The 123 largest, controlling 90 per cent of assets in key areas such as oil, electricity and telecommunications, are under the state authority, SASAC, that approves stock sales, mergers and legisla-tion. Of the PRC's top global firms in 2010, nearly all are in the public sector. They are run by men and women appointed by the Party who have a 'Red telephone' on their desks connecting them with the CCP hierarchy, the most important of them as powerful as government ministers.[6]

State-owned enterprises are boosted by cheap loans, preferential treatment and monopolistic or oligopolistic positions in their industries as the regime seeks to develop national champions to compete globally. Without such help, their return on equity would be seriously affected; as it is, this stood at 8 per cent in the past decade compared to 13 per cent for the private sector. If the deposit and lending rates of state banks impose a tax on household savings, so be it. The interests of the state, Party and 'Red capitalists' come first.

The public sector is increasingly attractive as a source of jobs at a time when graduate unemployment is almost 30 per cent. More than a million young people sit the annual civil-service entry test, perpetuating the tradition of the imperial examination, which selected the best and brightest to serve the Dragon Throne. Now, as then, competition is intense – in 2010, 16,000 jobs were on offer, one for every sixty-four applicants.[7] Now, as then, the system is not as meritocractic as its admirers claim, given nepotism and corruption.

Party officials in provinces, counties and townships serve the same goals and derive their power and livelihood from continuing supremacy of the CCP. Everything else falls by the wayside, even family history. During the Cultural Revolution, according to reliable accounts, Hu Jintao's father was 'struggled' against by Red Guards until he lost his mind; when his son went to their home area to try to get justice for his father, he was repulsed by local officials and never returned. A sister of Xi Jinping is reported to have been murdered in the ten-year mayhem. The mother of Bo Xilai was also killed or committed suicide at that time and his father, who had been Finance Minister, was beaten repeatedly by Red Guards, his arms twisted from their sockets, his back badly injured when he was thrown in the air to land on a concrete floor. But the sons continue to play the regime game. To get to the top there is only one recipe: to accept that – whatever it has done and whatever its present shortcomings – the Party rules.

Every organization and company of any size has a CCP cell where major decisions are made. The chair of the cell can often be more important than the person nominally in charge of the enterprise. The Party holds itself to be the one organization that can ensure national unity and stability, acting as the modern equivalent of the 'parent officials' who took decisions on behalf of the masses in the imperial era. For all the economic progress of the last thirty years, it still presents the PRC as needing to defend itself against foreign foes plotting to back Tibetan or Taiwanese separatism or to foment disorder. The national anthem warns that 'the Chinese nation faces its greatest danger. From each one the urgent call for action comes forth.' So the only protection against that danger has to be the Communist Party.

Its health and that of the nation are elided in the official discourse. As Hu Jintao said in his speech on the Party's ninetieth birthday, 'We have naturally come to this basic conclusion; success in China hinges on the Party [...] History has fully shown that the CCP truly deserves to be called a great, glorious and correct Marxist political party and the core force leading the Chinese people in breaking new ground in development.'[8]

By its own reasoning the regime is serving the nation by relentlessly suppressing any hint of organized opposition. Democracy, it argues, would risk chaos and threaten material progress. Elections are allowed only at local level and are closely controlled: just a handful of non-CCP candidates are permitted to stand and if, by chance, somebody the authorities do not like wins, he or she is usually disbarred. The fear of popular choice beyond CCP control is such that a hit television talent show, *China Supergirl*, was taken off the air, in part because it might have spread the idea of popular choice.

The state maintains a dossier on every working citizen (except for farmers), which begins when they are at high school and is passed on to employers. This relic from the Maoist era when everybody was organized in a work unit had remained in force during economic reform. The dossiers have a purpose as a social-security register but their true importance is as a control mechanism. Managers and supervisors can open them and add material, but the subjects are not permitted access and so have no way of knowing if their superiors have, for whatever reason, included damaging or downright false information or whether qualifications that could bring promotion have been removed by those anxious to safeguard their own positions.

Media are closely controlled. With no explanation, music websites were ordered in 2011 to remove from their playlists 100 songs, including six by Lady Gaga and others from the Backstreet Boys, Beyoncé and Britney Spears. Despite Bill Clinton's observation that attempts by the Chinese authorities to control the Internet were 'sort of like trying to nail Jell-O to the wall', some 30,000 cyber cops pursue the task. Sites that step out of line are regularly closed down, even if the authorities have more difficulty when the subject matter of online criticism is a social issue, a scandal or an event like the high-speed train crash. Twitter and Facebook are officially banned (though some people still manage to use them) but China's own microblog sites claim 300 million users who are often outspoken in their criticism of officialdom. 'People online seize on anything about officials and corruption, and they don't let up,' a bureaucrat at the State Council Information Office was quoted as saying in August 2011. Fresh restrictions on social media, including the requirement that users must give their real names, were introduced in early 2013 just as the authorities put down a strike by journalists at *Southern Weekly* newspaper objecting to heavy censorship. At the same time, control of virtual private networks was increased to try to enforce the Great Firewall of China. A 2011 Party plenum issued told officials to 'strengthen guidance and administration of social Internet services and instant-communications tools, and regulate the orderly dissemination of information [...] Apply the law to sternly punish the dissemination of harmful information.'[9]

The PRC ranked thirty-fourth out of thirty-seven countries in the Freedom on the Net rankings drawn up by Freedom House in 2011. Wang Chen, deputy head of the Party's Propaganda Department and head of the State Council Information Office, rounded off 2010 by telling reporters that 350 million 'pieces of harmful information' had been deleted from websites in the first eleven months of the year, adding that this had resulted in a 'notable improvement in the online cultural environment'. Google ran into repeated trouble when it declined to conform to censorship regulations.[10]

Anything that concerns the Party has to be made a success, according to the official version at least. When a carefully controlled epic film, *The Beginning of the Great Revival* (a.k.a. *The Founding of the Party*), was released in 2011 to celebrate the ninetieth anniversary of the establishment of the movement, the Propaganda Department issued an instruction that 'no media outlets will report or render negative opinion or news' about it. Ratings sections on websites that review cinema productions were disabled so that bloggers could not express any criticism of it; on one site, 88 per cent of those who commented before the ban gave it only one star. Audiences were bussed in with seats bought by their companies or state bodies and some cinemas were reported to have altered ticket stubs for other films to make it seem that audiences had flocked to see it.[11]

Religion is officially regulated with five faiths allowed: Buddhism, Islam, Catholicism, Protestantism and Daoism – the latter being China's only indigenous creed, with its doctrine of the pursuit of the mystical way, freewheeling belief system and bewildering array of gods and demons (three of its temples are dedicated to Mao Zedong). Buddhism was decried by a late Tang emperor as 'this vile source of errors which flood the empire' whose teachings ran against autocracy and centralization and spawned subversive cults, but it has survived and enjoyed a revival in recent years. More than 1,000 delegates attended a World Buddhist Conference in Beijing in 2006 and an opaque scheme was floated in 2011 for Chinese money moving through Hong Kong to invest $3 billion in developing Buddha's birthplace at Lumbini in Nepal as a 'Mecca for Buddhists' with hotels, a university, an international airport and rail links.

Judaism is not included among the officially approved religions and Jews are not among China's recognized minorities. But several hundred people in the city of Kaifeng in central China claim to be descendants of Persian Jews who settled there when it was the capital of the Song dynasty. One of the streets where they live is called Teaching the Torah Lane and was once home to a synagogue destroyed by floods in 1860. They celebrate Passover and light Sabbath candles but are careful not to get on the wrong side of the authorities; though only ten men are needed for a religious service, they know that gathering in even such small numbers might be seen by the authorities as a potentially subversive act – they were once accused by Mao and Deng of 'causing political trouble'. By Orthodox standards they are not Jewish at all because they trace their heritage through their fathers rather than their mothers.

Since Confucianism is not a religion but a behavioural system, one can be a Confucian and worship any of the approved religions. Each of the five has headquarters in Beijing headed by CCP cadres who report to the State Administration for Religious Affairs. Buddhism, which has a strong appeal to the middle class, has been encouraged so long as it remains loyal to the system and does not veer towards support for the Dalai Lama. Daoism has flowered in the countryside, drawing on age-old roots. The supervision by the state and Party has led the US to express 'particular concern' about religious freedom in the PRC, which brought a counter-blast from the heads of the five main religions accusing Washington of 'attempting to smear the image of China'.

The main problems have been with the fast-growing congregations of Christians, some of whom worship in unauthorized 'house churches'. The clash has been particularly sharp with the Catholic Church which counts an estimated 12 million believers on the mainland. The divergence dates back to the time when the Qing emperors decided that the beliefs of Jesuits working at court were incompatible with their quasi-divine claims. In the 1990s Jiang Zemin set out to normalize relations with the Vatican, which recognized Taiwan rather than the PRC. But there was a clash in 2000 when Rome decided to canonize Catholic martyrs killed during anti-Christian movements in China at a ceremony on 1 October, the PRC's national day. Beijing suspected that it was all the work of Taiwanese Catholics trying to make trouble in order to retain the Holy See's recognition, but the Vatican was reluctant to abandon the island as it moved to democracy in favour of an avowedly atheist regime.

Both the Chinese state and the Vatican insist that they alone have the right to appoint bishops. In 2006 there were three ordinations by the Chinese Catholic Patriotic Association, the state and Party organization, which were not recognized by the Papacy. At the end of 2010, the Association ordained a new bishop in Chengde, north of Beijing; the Vatican did not approve, if only because Chengde is not a diocese it recognizes. The warring parties agreed on the installation of another bishop, Sun Jigen, in a Catholic stronghold in Hebei province, but Beijing insisted on setting the date for the ceremony. Police were reported to have abducted four bishops ordained by Rome to force them to take part. On the day of the event, plainclothes security men lined the road to the church. But the locals had already carried out the ordination on their own. Furious, the authorities detained Sun and two priests for several days.

A new crisis broke out in June 2010 when Beijing ordained a new bishop of the city of Leshan in Sichuan despite warnings from Pope Benedict that he was unacceptable for unspecified 'proven and very grave reasons' (believed to be that he had been having an affair and had fathered a child). The Vatican followed this with what amounted to excommunication. The government then suspended a bishop from Shenyang who refused to take part in the ordination of an officially approved bishop in Guangdong – the Shenyang prelate was guarded by eighty priests who resisted attempts to force him to participate. The confrontation continued in July 2012 with the ordination of a Bishop in Hardin approved by the state but not by Rome. The following week a bishop in Shanghai resigned in protest – to the cheers of his congregation.

The official line seems to be part of the general toughening on opponents apparent since early 2011. 'The regime thinks things should go this way,' a European scholar on the Catholic Church in China told Paul Mooney of the *South China Morning Post*. 'There are no grey areas; no more tolerance about people taking a middle way.' As Cardinal Joseph Zen Ze-kiun of Hong Kong put it, 'At this moment, it's war.'[12]

Since it staged a mass demonstration outside the leadership compound in Beijing in 1999 to demand recognition, the Falun Gong deep-breathing mystical movement, which draws on an assortment of old Chinese beliefs, has been sternly suppressed. The Falun Gong might appear to most outsiders to be harmless even if one cannot accept its claims that its routines can enable practitioners to fly and that modern science is being used by aliens to take over human bodies. As an 'evil cult' it would suffer the fate of 'a rat crossing the street that everyone rushes to squash', official media warned. The movement says that 100,000 of its people have been detained and 3,200 tortured to death. Such figures are unverifiable but there is no doubt of the strength of the repression led by a taskforce, the '601 unit'; an official instruction to police was that there were to be 'no unnatural deaths' among those arrested. In 2001 five practitioners set themselves on fire in Tiananmen Square, their hands held up in meditation; one died. The group's newspaper, *Epoch Times*, which highlights negative reports about the PRC, alleges that the detainees have had organs removed for transplants but there appears to be no independent confirmation of this. The PRC authorities meanwhile link the Falun Gong practitioners and their spiritual 'master', Li Hongzhi, a one-time army grain clerk and trumpeter in an entertainment troupe from north-east China who now lives in the United States, to 'domestic and hostile forces hostile to our socialist government'.

In keeping with its control ethos, the Party proclaims a conservative moral stance. The growing official acceptance of homosexuality, which was until 2001 officially classified as a mental illness, has been a cautious process: organizers of Gay Pride events in Shanghai have run into recurrent problems with the authorities and, while big cities have lesbian clubs and bars, lesbianism is generally a matter of discretion – in the summer of 2012, the main lesbian centre in Beijing was forced to move after complaints from neighbours. In an echo of the New Life campaign of the 1930s, which sought to get Chinese to live cleaner and more seemly lives, periodic campaigns target spitting and loose personal behaviour. When *China Supergirl* was taken off air, despite attracting audiences of 400 million, it was replaced with programmes that 'promote moral ethics and public safety, and provide practical information for housework'. Li Yuanchao, head of the Organization Department, has called on male CCP cadres to 'resist seduction and control the gates of desire', staying away from 'vulgar places' and not engaging paid female escorts to accompany them to banquets. The success rate seems to be about as low as that of Chiang Kai-shek's efforts. A three-day 'sex festival' in Guangdong attracts 300,000 visitors and, as we will see, graft and sex often go hand in hand among Party officials.

Still, the regime keeps trying. The censorship machinery has its head-quarters at the Central Propaganda Department behind an unmarked entrance barrier in a prosperous commercial area of the capital. The courtyard is usually full of smart black limousines, many with military number plates. The interior is bright and modern, with marble slabs alongside high-tech equipment. A slogan on the wall of the main hall urges staff and visitors to be 'diligent as an ox, meticulous as a hair with lips sealed like a bottle, united as one.'

As an example of the nature and detail of the control mechanism take the following set of selected instructions from censorship offices over twelve days in May 2011, as relayed by academics at Berkeley in California who note that such instructions are referred to by Chinese journalists and bloggers as 'Directive from the Ministry of Truth':

31 May

From the Beijing Municipal Government internal document: 'War Time Coordination Mechanism of Intelligence and Information for Maintaining Stability during the June 4th Sensitive Period'
All units are requested to collect and report information regarding potential threats to stability in the capital as well as all work-unit activities conducted during this sensitive period.

28 May

From a provincial Internet-Administration Office
Reporting of news related to the recent ethnic conflicts between Mongol minority and Han majority in Xilinhot is prohibited. No discussion of any form on all micro-blogging sites, blogs, and discussion forums. Violators will be subjected to a RMB 30,000 fine.

From the State Council Information Office
All websites are requested to immediately remove photos and new reports regarding Chengdu bus explosion incident from front pages. Interactive spaces must immediately work on preventing the spread of related information and commentary.

From the Central Propaganda Department to all print and TV media
The serial bombings in Fuzhou, Jiangxi must be referred as '5.26 Criminal Case'. No mentioning of 'administration building' or 'bombing incident' will be allowed.

25 May

From the Central Propaganda Department
In regard to the soon-to-be-released official compensation plan of the deadly Shanghai high-rising building fire, all media are to use copy circulated from Xinhua News Agency. No independent reports will be allowed.

23 May

From the State Council Information Office
Do not hype the so-called 'Principal Fang Binxing shoe-throwing incident' widely reported by foreign press. All websites, including interactive spaces such as discussion forums, weblogs, microblogs, and social media, are requested to immediately remove related articles and comments.

19 May

From the Hubei Provincial Propaganda Department
In regard to today's deadly building collapse in Qiaokou, Wuhan, all media are to wait for an official report. All media are not to conduct follow-up reports.

The litany of censorship is unrelenting and, as above, reaches far beyond politics. In the autumn of 2011 the Hunan Propaganda Department instructed media outlets not 'to hype the serial-murder case in which the killer ate four victims' and its counterpart in Hubei banned reporting of the 'man executed by firing squad found "resurrected" nine years later'. To be deleted were all posts that told of a man who had gone online to brag about having spent 80,000 yuan on a meal while attending a meeting at the Central Party School.[13]

Despite a Chinese tradition of rulers valuing loyal critics who cut through the lies and obfuscations of officials, those who presume to cross the path of the authorities live dangerously. Party members who fall foul of their superiors can be picked up the CCP Disciplinary Commission and held for up to six months in a secret location while they are investigated – they have no right to contact their relatives or a lawyer.

The 2008 Olympics were greeted by some foreign observers as an occasion when the regime might start to relax and liberalize. That was a sad misreading of China's intentions. The Games marked the start of a period of stricter control that has continued ever since. Police activity tightened in the capital and people regarded as undesirable (including Uighur workers) were shipped out of the city. A special area was set aside for protestors, but none of their applications was approved. Riots in Tibet and Xinjiang in the following years led to a further strengthening of security. In an upsurge of police activity in the spring and summer of 2011, human-rights lawyers and dissidents were persecuted. As the scholar, Jerome Cohen, has pointed out, China claims to be building a 'socialist legal system' that protects the rights of citizens, but crushes the lawyers and advocates who could convert the paper promises into 'living law'.

Police turned out in force to prevent any attempt to reproduce the Middle Eastern 'Jasmine Revolutions'. Flower growers were banned from selling jasmine at markets round Beijing while a video of Hu Jintao singing an old song in praise of the flower on a visit to Africa was removed from websites. The international writers' organization PEN reported in 2011 that at least forty-nine authors were in prison, under house arrest or otherwise detained for having displeased the authorities. The number of trials on accusations of endangering state security rose from 306 in 2007 to 466 in 2008 and then to 698 and 670 in 2009–10 involving more than 2,200 people, according to the Dui Hua Human Rights Foundation.

The official mantra to justify repression is quite plain. Not only are those who decline to go along with the CCP guilty of opposing the sole force which can bring China progress, but they also threaten stability and, as the official paper, *Beijing News*, put it: 'Everyone knows that stability is a blessing and chaos is a calamity.' For the regime, there are no halfway houses. As in the imperial regime, dissidence is equivalent to treason. Protests from abroad cut no ice; this is a matter of national security given the elision of the regime and the nation. Liu Xiabao, who would go on to win the Nobel Peace Prize, was sent to jail for eleven years in December 2009 after organizing a pro-democracy petition, Charter 08. His wife was put under house arrest; in a poem to her Liu wrote:

Nothing remains in your name, nothing
But to wait for me, together with the dust of our home.

One of their fellow petitioners, Liu Xianbin, got ten years for writing articles calling for democratic reforms that were judged to amount to incitement of the subversion of state power. Others were put under surveillance or otherwise harassed.

The Nobel ceremony with a symbolic empty chair on which the prize record was placed was denounced by Beijing as a 'farce' and anti-China 'interference by a few clowns'. Western ambassadors in Beijing were given what one described to me as 'a Mao-era harangue' by the Foreign Ministry, which urged governments to boycott the award ceremony (eighteen did so, including Russia, Turkey, Iraq, Iran, Venezuela, Egypt, Tunisia, Morocco, Saudi Arabia and the Philippines).

In 2010 the State Council issued a White Paper entitled 'Progress in China's Human Rights' that filled three broadsheet-newspaper pages and ended with a pledge that the PRC would 'spare no efforts and contribute its due share to ensure the continuous progress of China's human rights'. Visiting the United States in early 2011, Hu Jintao made the first acknowledgement by a PRC leader of the universality of human rights and admitted that 'a lot still needs to be done in China'. But that spring and summer around twenty dissidents were detained without any legal proceedings for months, or put under house arrest. Most were human-rights lawyers, who were often shrouded in black hoods by police so that they would not know where they were being taken. Many were beaten up. Some were forcibly medicated and could not remember what had happened to them. Others were forced to sit or lie immobile for long periods. When released, they were told not to speak about what had happened to them, and most complied.

The phrases 'to be disappeared' and 'to be black-hooded' entered the language. A legislative committee proposed police should be authorized to hold in a secret location for six months anybody who does not cooperate while under house arrest. Such violence against political opponents can be traced back through the Nationalist Republic, which had a much-feared secret-police force, to the First Emperor. China's rulers have never had any truck with the idea of 'loyal opposition' and have used force to repress anybody who tried it. To take some recent examples of what it means in practice:

Chen Guangcheng, a blind lawyer, was imprisoned for four years for 'damaging property and organizing a mob to disturb traffic' after he investigated cases in Shandong in which women had been forced to have abortions; after his release, he was put under house arrest by the local authorities who dispatched thugs to attack him and his wife at home when they sent a video of their surveillance to the United States. His home was floodlit at night and cut off from the mobile telephone networks. But sympathisers made their way to his village, even if thugs and police keep them from seeing Chen and rough them up. A journalist for *Xinhua* tried to visit the village but was beaten up and forced to resign. However, the CCP tabloid, *Global Times*, ran an editorial in October, 2011, which said that reports of abuse of Chen's human rights 'may not be simply invented'. In the repressive atmosphere that prevails, that was a striking admission from an official source. Guards roughed up the actor, Christian Bale, when he tried to visit Chen in December, 2011, in a break from a visit to Beijing to promote a film about the Nanjing massacre of 1937 in which he stars (and which was backed by the Chinese state).

In April 2012, Chen managed to escape from his home and, after a nighttime trek across the countryside during which he fell down 200 times, linked up with associates who took him to the US embassy in Beijing. He arrived there as Sino-US talks were opening attended by Secretary of State Hillary Clinton and Treasury Secretary Tim Geithner but a diplomatic incident was avoided as Chen was taken to hospital for injuries sustained during his escape, and then flown to America where he enrolled as a visiting scholar at New York University. Two months later, the Shandong province police was sacked with *People's Daily* saying local officials should deal with such cases 'more democratically and legally'. But, at the end of 2012, his nephew was sentenced to three years in jail for resisting police who burst into his home; he had been held incommunicado for six months and denied a choice of lawyers.

A month after Chen's flight from China, Li Wangyang, a veteran pro-democracy activist and labour organizer who had been jailed for 23 years for his activities, was found dead in a hospital in Hunan. Torture and ill-treatment meant that Li had become blind and deaf and could hardly walk. He had been under close police guard in the run-up to the anniversary of the 1989 Beijing massacre. The official story was that he had hanged himself but this seemed unlikely given his medical condition. There were street protests in Hong Kong but the story was hushed up on mainland media.

Gao Zhisheng was listed by the Justice Ministry among China's top-ten lawyers in 2001 for his work on behalf of medical-malpractice victims and farmers denied proper compensation for requisitioned land, but his human-rights work then earned him disfavour and he was sent to prison. After his release, his skin had turned black and he could not get out of bed in the morning without help. He, his wife and their two children were put under constant surveillance. Other inhabitants of their block of flats were moved out. Police broke in periodically to assault not only Gao but also his wife, 'tearing her clothing and calling her a beast', according to their daughter, aged twelve, who was also beaten. The lawyer was taken to a police station three times and said he had been hit there with holstered revolvers, tortured with electric batons and burned with cigarettes. In April 2010 he was allowed to return to see his mother at the annual grave-sweeping festival, accompanied by security officers. He told of having been stripped naked and beaten for two days by police. 'The degree of cruelty, there's no way to recount it,' he added to an American reporter. 'For forty-eight hours, my life hung by a thread.' Then he disappeared again. His brother got nowhere when he tried to find out what had happened to Gao. In December 2011, *Xinhua* reported that Gao had been sent back to prison for three years for breaking probation.

Another lawyer, Liu Shihui, was kept under 'residential surveillance' in Guangzhou for 108 days after filming an attempted Jasmine Revolution demonstration in February 2011. His postings on a social network told of police smashing down the door of his house and ransacking the interior, removing books, computer files and equipment, his mobile telephone and a stock-market tracker. His newlywed Vietnamese wife was taken away and held for seventeen days before being sent to her home country. Liu said he was interrogated for five days without sleep until he collapsed. When he was released, he had shed seven or eight pounds. He lost property worth more than 300,000 yuan. When his computer was returned to him he found that the hard disk had been removed, depriving him of professional records dating back ten years. When he sent text messages, they were diverted to a junk-mail site.

Teng Biao, a well-known Beijing lawyer, was picked by police on 23 December 2010 (by coincidence, the day on which the United Nations International Convention for the Protection of All Persons from Forced Disappearance came into force). At the police station, according to his account, he was assaulted. One officer, he wrote, shouted at him, 'You belong to the enemy! You motherfucker won't get out of here again! You traitors, you dogs! Counterrevolutionaries! The Communist Party feeds you and pays you and you still don't acknowledge how good it is! You keep insulting the Party! We will treat you just like an enemy!' Another policeman chimed in with, 'Why waste words on this sort of person? Let's beat him to death and dig a hole to bury him in and be done with it. How lucky we've got a place to put him away here.' Realizing that he was a professor at the China University of Politics and Law (and a visiting Fellow at Yale), the police then released him. But he was detained again for a time in 2011, as part of a round-up of human-rights lawyers during the Jasmine Revolutions begun in North Africa.

Ni Yulan, a lawyer who has handled human-rights cases since 1999, including those of Falun Gong practitioners, was hauled to a police station when she filmed the forced destruction of her home and the eviction of neighbours in 2008. The beating she received was so brutal that she was left permanently disabled and unable to walk. She was then sent to jail where she had to crawl across the floor after her crutches were taken from her. After her release, in 2010, she and her husband, Dong Jiqin, stayed at a hotel without their possessions which were lost when their home was pulled down. But police forced them to leave and they spent fifty days in a tent in a park. After international protests following a film about her, *Emergency Shelter*, made by documentary director He Yang, police put the couple in a dingy, small hotel room from where Ni continued to provide legal advice for petitioners travelling to the capital to seek justice.

Visiting her one evening in early 2011, the journalist Paul Mooney found Ni sitting on her bed tapping at her laptop as her husband lit

candles; they had been without electricity for thirty-seven days and without water for sixteen – her husband and children carried in buckets of
water so that she could wash. The floor was piled with goods donated by
grateful people she had helped. 'I can withstand anything because so
many people support me,' she told Mooney. 'I feel I've chosen the right
path.' In the crackdown that unfurled in the spring of 2011, she and her
husband were detained by police once more and accused of 'causing a
disturbance'.[14] She was sentenced in 2012 to two and a half years while
her husband got two years.

Those who raise awkward questions may find themselves sentenced
without trial to 'reform through labour' as in the case of the teacher in
Sichuan who campaigned on behalf of parents of children buried alive
by the collapse of badly built schools during the 2008 earthquake. As
well as 3,544 instances of arbitrary detention for exercising or defending
human rights in 2010, the Chinese Human Rights Defenders (CHRD)
group reported 118 cases of torture and 36 enforced disappearances.[15]

In 2011 the artist Ai Weiwei, one of the designers of the Bird's Nest
Stadium for the 2008 Olympics, was detained for eighty-one days after
growing increasingly critical of the manner in which China operates. He
recounted that he was held in a windowless cell watched by two guards
and had to ask permission to touch anything, including his own face. His
only exercise was to pace up and down the cell, the guards moving with
him. Ai, fifty-four at the time, was detained as his installations were on
show in London and New York. He was accused of financial irregularities, and was told to pay 15 million yuan in back taxes and fines. In an
unusual public reaction, thousands of people donated money, some
fashioning banknotes into paper planes which they floated over the wall
of his house's courtyard. 'It's like an avalanche,' the artist remarked.

But there could be no doubt that the real reason why he lost the protection he had enjoyed previously from his status as the son of a leading
Revolution-era poet lay in the way he pointed on his blog site and in
interviews to the moral and ethical fault lines running through the
PRC, with a particular focus on the shoddy buildings that collapsed in
the Sichuan earthquake, in which 80,000 people died, and the inade-
quacies of the relief effort. Officials, he wrote, 'close their mouths and
do not discuss corruption'. After his release he was kept under constant

surveillance and refused permission to travel abroad or attend hearing on his appeal against the fine. Nevertheless, he started sending out messages and the Party newspaper, *Global Times*, ran an interview that quoted him as saying, 'I will never avoid politics; none of us can.'[16] Foreign attention to his case made him internationally known, an iconoclastic reproach to the system – at a concert in Beijing at the end of 2012, Elton John dedicated the event to Ai after meeting him.

Another critic, Yu Jie, author of a book entitled *Wen Jiabao: China's Best Actor* (published in Hong Kong but not on the mainland), has come in for softer treatment. He recounts how, during sensitive times, he was escorted to a car by four policemen and taken to supervised accommodation where he is well looked after with what he calls 'minister-level treatment' – all expenses are paid, right down to cinema tickets.

With this mania for control goes a high level of secrecy. China's legislation defines state secrets as 'classified information concerning major policies and decisions of state affairs, national defence and activities of the armed forces, diplomatic activities, national economic and social development, science and technology, activities to safeguard state security and the investigation of crimes, and other items that are classified as state secrets by the state-secret protection departments'. So the 'protection departments' can classify whatever they like as secret.

The budget for internal security now exceeds that for the armed forces – though the latter understates actual spending on military-related projects. In another mega-statistic, the police force numbers 25 million with an estimated 39 million informers. (Though it is illegal, private security employs an estimated 2 million bodyguards with nearly 3,000 companies earning 8 billion yuan a year.) State media reported that no fewer than 739,000 police, security guards and patrols of local residents were mobilized to make sure that there was no trouble when the National People's Congress met for its annual session in Beijing in March 2011. Anxious that this should not be misinterpreted as a sign of worry, the Communist Party's Central Propaganda Bureau issued an instruction that media should not report 'excessive use of public security' and added: 'Do not hype the story "The People's Security Apparatus Fears the People".'[17]

The exercise of CCP power goes with what would be a stultifying degree of bureaucracy if it was not so widely disregarded. China limits to twenty the number of foreign films that can be shown at cinemas each year, but copies of the latest Hollywood hits are on sale in cities across the country within days of their release in the West. The minutiae of the traditional Chinese state live on in its Communist manifestation, but countless businesses operate on the margins of legality and nobody cares, especially if the requisite amount of money has changed hands.

For all the regime preservation measures and the lack of a visible alternative to the Communist Party, large questions hang over its nature and role now that it has ditched ideology in favour of managing economic expansion. It may claim a modern version of the Mandate of Heaven formerly bestowed on imperial dynasties by the gods, and to act as a benign force that rides above the failings of its local agents, but it has had to allow society to move in directions unthinkable under Mao. Nearly 300,000 young people go abroad to study each year. Beijing has underground music clubs and there are more than sixty festivals a year of rock, punk, funk and electronic music. Alternative musicians tour the country and some perform abroad. A gender-bending comic, Xiao Shenyang (Little Shenyang), who may appear in female imperial robes with a Hello Kitty knapsack, reached a television audience of 600 million on the *Lunar New Year Gala*. But Hu Jintao used a Politburo session in 2010 to insist that China must 'resolutely resist' vulgar culture to safeguard the 'great revival' of the Chinese people.

Observers, especially outside the PRC, regularly forecast that China has to become democratic to satisfy the aspirations of its people. But what change has transpired has been very limited, and aimed at strengthening the monopoly political organization rather than opening the system to real competition. At the 2012 Party Congress, an element of choice was announced in voting for members of the Central Committee: in the event, there were just 108 candidates for each 100 seats. The ruling party has eliminated most independent intermediary bodies of civil society. Before village elections in 2011, the *People's Daily* warned that there is no legal basis for 'independent candidates' while the Central Propaganda Department banned media coverage of them. When it outlawed reporting of an independent candidate in Henan, the provincial

Propaganda Department warned that 'foreign forces are participating with ulterior purposes and attempting to overthrow our government'.[18]

The Party has drawn one overriding lesson from the fall of Communism in the Soviet Union and Eastern Europe: the need to maintain its grip and not go in for Gorbachev-style relaxation or renege on its past. Despite the loss of tens of millions of lives as a result of his policies and the economic shambles he bequeathed, Mao is still officially 70 per cent good and only 30 per cent bad. His portrait looks out over Tiananmen Square and appears on all banknotes. Questioning the official version of the past is not permitted. The Party cannot admit error and needs no advice from any external source. As a professor of Tsinghua University in Beijing put it in an article in *Global Times*, 'Firstly, the Party should not give up its leadership of the country during reforms [...] Secondly, reforming should not abandon the principle of public ownership as economic foundation [...] Thirdly, reforming doesn't mean denying previous leaders [...] Fourthly, the reform should not rely on external powers.'[19]

The Party and its state therefore have to remain all-seeing and opaque. Theirs is an ideology of power. They set the rules and are generally above the law. Though ministers may occasionally lose their jobs in the State Council, the Party is not subject to sanctions however it performs. It organizes its succession process internally far from public gaze. It contains competing groups and individuals but they operate behind a screen. It has its own secretive disciplinary process for members, which takes precedence over the law courts. The imperial tradition of distance between the rulers and the ruled is maintained. But the Party's influence is everywhere even if it is not always outwardly evident: as one senior official told the author Richard McGregor it is like God – omnipresent but unseen. It sees no reason why its rule should not continue indefinitely. As a leading Party historian, Li Zhongjie, puts it: 'The Communist Party has built China to what it is today. Many countries in the world are extremely envious. So why can't we carry on?'[20]

Whether all this will be tenable in the years ahead and what the cost of continuing top-down one-party rule will be are the major questions facing China. In contrast with the widespread picture abroad of the PRC as an exemplar of economic freedom, the authorities are frequently at war with markets as they seek to control prices, bank loans, property prices and commerce. Some leaders, such as Wen Jiabao, have acknowledged the need for reform of the political and legal system to modernize the economy and continue to preside over an increasingly disparate society. But the line from the top is plain. Seven months after the Prime Minister spoke out about reform, Wu Bangguo, the President of the National People's Congress, who outranks Wen in the Party hierarchy, declared at the 2011 annual session of the legislature: 'We have made a solemn declaration that we will not employ a system of multiple parties holding office in rotation.' Any change, he warned, would of course mean that 'not only will there be no Socialist modernization to speak of, but the achievements of development will be lost and it is possible that the state could sink into the abyss of internal disorder.' Rather than electoral competition being seen as a positive way of organizing a state and society, it is portrayed by the establishment as a danger that must be avoided at all costs.

'If China imitates the West's multi-party parliamentary democratic system, it could repeat the chaotic and turbulent history of the Cultural Revolution when factions sprung up everywhere,' the state news agency, Xinhua, warned in an article to mark the CCP's ninetieth anniversary in 2011. In other words, by imposing one-party rule the leadership claims to be doing China's people a huge favour. It does not minimize the challenges that lie ahead, in the economy, in the country's demographics, in the environmental crisis or in the difficulty of maintaining social stability. But for those in charge, with their core mindset – inherited from their movement's turbulent past having bred suspicions bordering on paranoia – any significant relaxation of control looks positively dangerous. As it prepared for the 2012 Party Congress, the new leadership's reading list included Alexis de Tocqueville's analysis from 1820 of why Bourbon monarchy fell in France; one reason, he argued, was that it had introduced reforms it could not control. The lesson has been absorbed in Beijing. The heirs of revolution have thus become ardent proponents of the status quo in all matters that might affect their power now – and for as long as they can manage it.[21]

9

HOW CHINA GREW

坚持党的基本路线一百年不动摇

The explosive emergence of the People's Republic on to the world scene stemmed from the realization by the leadership, after Mao's death in 1976, that a fundamental change of course was required. The official story of this, set out in a CCP resolution in 1981, is that it was all Deng's doing. In fact China's annual trade had risen significantly, though from a very low base, after the United Nations voted to transfer the permanent Security Council's seat from the Republic of China on Taiwan in 1971 and the United States dropped its economic embargo. Hua Guofeng, Mao's chosen successor, launched a modernization programme, got rid of the Gang of Four – including Mao's wife, who wanted to continue the Cultural Revolution – and set the stage for Deng's return from the internal exile to which he had been consigned after being stripped of all his posts and branded 'an ugly traitor' in an internal struggle as the Great Helmsman neared his end.

It was Hua who opened the breach in Mao's dam, as is evident from a detailed study by historians Frederick Teiwes and Warren Sun published in 2011. Though he showed great fealty to the late leader, the anointed heir recognized the need for economic development to the extent that he was criticized by some opponents for encouraging the import of foreign machinery and capital. But, crucially, it was Deng who won the political battle between them and so it became even more vital for him to claim sole parentage of the momentous change in keeping with the tradition under which the victors write the history. That said, only a figure with Deng's historical credentials, determination and skills at inner-Party infighting could have pushed through the sustained drive for economic reform.[1]

In his midseventies at the time, Deng had a life story that spanned the history of Communism in China. Purged three times, he had a drive and determination that characterized the political movement to which he devoted his life. He was diminutive and bullet-headed, like a doll that always swings back upright however harshly it is pushed, ready to suffer reverses in pursuit of an ultimate purpose.[2]

As a teenager he was sent by his father from Sichuan to study in Paris; Deng never returned to his birthplace. The school for Chinese youth he was meant to attend folded, and he ended up working in a factory where he was marked down as a troublemaker. He joined the Chinese Communist Party as part of a circle that included Zhou Enlai. He also developed a liking for croissants – after a state visit to France in 1975 he took 200 of the pastries home. He earned the nickname of 'Doctor Mimeograph' for his work printing the Party's journal and tried to organize workers at the Renault factory where he went to work in 1925. Threatened with arrest in 1926, he hightailed it to Moscow where he enrolled at the University of the Toilers of the East run by the International Communist body, the Comintern. At the time, Soviet economic policy permitted private businesses and independent farms of the kind he would encourage in China half a century later.

Having returned to China in 1927, Deng worked under a supposedly progressive warlord, Feng Yuxiang, a hulking figure known variously as the 'Christian General' and the 'Betraying General'. But when Feng lived up to his second soubriquet by abandoning his allies on the left of the Kuomintang and allowing himself to be bought by the party's right under Chiang Kai-shek, the young man was sent to the south-west in an unsuccessful attempt to establish a CCP beachhead there. He then joined Mao in the base in Jiangxi, one of the main centres of resistance to the Chiang regime. He was purged by the leadership for being too close to the future Chairman who was in the doghouse for showing too much independence of the Comintern-approved leadership including Zhou Enlai. Along with Mao, Zhou and other regime icons, Deng participated in the Long March when Chiang's troops forced the Communists at the Jiangxi base to flee across China to a haven in the north.

The 'Little Bottle' (a homonym of his name) acted as a political commissar to huge armies in epic battles of the civil war against the Nationalists and emerged after the victory of 1949 as one of Mao's faithful lieutenants, presiding over brutal land reform in his native south-west for which he was praised by the Chairman. Having proved his loyalty and readiness to use extreme force, he was put in charge of the persecution of alleged rightists who put their heads above the parapet in the mid-1950s after Mao declared that 100 flowers should be allowed to bloom but changed his mind when criticisms of him and the regime rolled in. This pattern of loyalty continued through the ensuing two decades meaning that the idea of Deng as anti-Mao holds little water. Rather, like the older man, he was a supreme power player who would use whatever means were at his disposal to survive and, ultimately, triumph. It took Mao just over two decades; Deng was ready to wait even longer.

So, though he appears to have had doubts about Mao's drive to surpass Britain industrially in the Great Leap Forward of the late 1950s, he was careful not to step out of line. When the Chairman launched his first leadership purge at a conference in 1959 in the resort of Lushan above the Yangtze, Deng found it politic to stay away, pleading an injury he said he had inflicted on himself playing billiards. He once included in a speech an old Sichuan proverb about the colour of a cat being irrelevant so long as it caught mice – a saying that was always to be associated with him subsequently – but on learning that Mao disapproved of its use had the passage removed from the published text. Deng was then a leading spokesman in Mao's attacks on the Soviet Union, which split the two major Communist powers.

Called on to restore order in the later stages of the Cultural Revolution, he once more deployed violence as he had done in the land reforms after 1949: the PLA was sent to deal with ethnic violence in Yunnan and killed more than 1,600 people including 300 women, old people and children as they fled, and trouble on the railways was met with the denunciation of 11,700 workers, the imprisonment of 3,000 and execution of 85.[3]

However, after the Leap finally stuttered to a halt amid the famine that is estimated to have taken more than 40 million lives, Deng, alongside Mao's number two, Liu Shaoqi, took over the reins of recovery to such effect that the Great Helmsman felt the need to reassert himself; this he did with the launch of the Cultural Revolution, aimed at sweeping away the Party bureaucracy and to ensure that the PRC answered to only one man. Liu was harried to death in the persecution inflicted on old-line Communist figures; Deng escaped with ritual humiliation by Red Guards in Beijing, after which he was sent to work in a provincial tractor-repair works. Mao was said to have recognized that the country would one day require the little man's input – 'We need him,' he remarked. Deng was rehabilitated for a time and came out with a plan to modernize industry and boost technology. But he was a constant target for the Gang of Four, and they had cause for exultation when he was ousted once more, in 1976, after being held responsible for an outburst of popular feeling in Tiananmen Square over the death of Zhou Enlai, which was portrayed by the leftists as an anti-regime plot.

When he succeeded Mao as Chairman of the CCP that same year, Hua Guofeng had a difficult line to tread between his desire to boost the economy and his fealty to the late leader. He spoke on several occasions of the need to do 'whatever' Mao had lain down and began to launch a personality cult of his own, even having his hair cut to resemble the Great Helmsman's tonsure. In March 1977 he rejected the idea that Deng should be allowed to rejoin the leadership and said that those who suggested this were 'a small handful of counterrevolutionaries' who, he added bizarrely, wanted to rehabilitate the Gang of Four. Criticism of Deng was, he said, 'a must'.

Hua opted for a 'flying leap' with a grand ten-year plan for 120 heavy-industrial and infrastructure projects using imported technology that was to be paid for by oil exports. He was, however, dogged with problems, including a botched attempt to expand a major steel mill, the collapse of a big oil rig that cost scores of lives, supply bottlenecks, insufficient revenues, inflation as wages rose and the biggest trade gap since the mid-1950s. There were parallels between the new policies and the modernization programme Deng had proposed a couple of years earlier, but it was Hua who was blamed for the failures. Nor did he have the force of personality to withstand the older man, who enlisted the support of veteran cadres, the army and what remained of the Party faithful to form a victorious coalition.

A heavy smoker, bridge player and football fan who talked to foreign leaders with a spittoon placed by his armchair, Deng Xiaoping was an ultimate power player, not much concerned with ideology but focused on getting things done as expressed in his call to 'seek truth from facts'. After becoming China's preeminent leader in 1978 he did not bother with official positions, instead contenting himself with holding just the Chairmanship of the Central Military Commission and of the CCP's Central Advisory Commission. He ruled by political skill, the weight of his long history in the Party and his force of personality – and, when he considered it was needed, ruthlessness. He prized common sense; referring to the 'barefoot doctors' of the Mao era, he observed that doctors should wear shoes. He was direct to the point of bluntness and not only with subordinates: at a state banquet in Washington the actress Shirley MacLaine spoke to him of a Chinese intellectual who had told her how grateful he was for his experience of rural life after being sent down to the countryside during the Cultural Revolution; Deng interrupted to reply, 'He was lying,' and proceeded to lay out the horrors of Mao's last experiment.[4]

At this late stage in life, and with all that he had gone through, he faced a final chance to take control as Hua's flying leap crashed towards earth. Employing a classic Maoist tactic, he used ideology as a tool to set the groundwork for his last assault on his rival. He challenged Hua's devotion to 'whatever' Mao had taught and proposed instead that the late leader's thoughts should be 'an integral whole to guide our Party, our military, our nation and our people' – that is, while they would be respected, they would not act as a brake on change. Hu Yaobang, an open-minded ally who had become head of the CCP School, propagated the idea that 'practice is the sole criterion of truth' – an article with that heading was published in *People's Daily* in May 1978, bringing a stinging telephone call to the editor from a hardline Maoist, Wu Lengxi, who called it 'politically vicious' and 'a merciless call to arms against Marxism and Mao Zedong Thought'.

In 1980 the Politburo decided that Hua 'lacks the political and organization ability to be the Chairman of the Party'. He was replaced by Hu Yaobang. Having won, Deng was not personally vengeful in the fashion of Mao, though he ensured that leading 'whateverists' were moved down several rungs in CCP bodies. Hua lingered on as a powerless Vice-Chairman for a couple of years and stayed on the CCP Central Committee until 2001. He was photographed, obese and asleep, at the 2007 Party Congress and died the following year.

While Deng's skilful political manoeuvres were vital to his rise to the top, the timing was also right – and he knew it. There had been improvements under Mao, notably in the spread of literacy and reduction of infant mortality, which fell from 203 per 1,000 births in 1949 to 84.3 in the 1960s. But, in general, China had been laid low by his experiments, under which it had been more important to be 'Red' than 'expert'. Apart from his huge moral and ethical failings, Mao had brought the country to its knees with the combined effects of the Great Leap Forward and the Cultural Revolution. Poverty was institutionalized. Much of the country was still in a pre-industrial stage. The state was virtually bankrupt. Productivity had slumped. Urban wages were half what they had been under the Nationalist Republic. It took six months' pay to buy a sewing machine. The average calorific intake was only two-thirds of what it had been under the Qing dynasty, with urban residents restricted to four eggs, 100 grams of sugar and 250 grams of pork per month. People grew shorter and thinner; in Guangdong 90 per cent of would-be army recruits were rejected on grounds of size or health. If there was equality in the People's Republic, it was the equality of poverty.

Farmers were hit especially hard: in some places their incomes were only 4 per cent of those in cities and the price the government paid for food was well below cost, removing any incentive to produce. The condition in which Mao left the Party meant that it risked implosion. The strong central-political control that was its lifeblood had been dangerously diluted by the radical shifts of the previous ten years as the Chairman lurched from declaring all-out civil war and encouraging Red Guards to 'storm the fortress' of the state to depending on the army to hold things together and then trying to sideline the PLA. Regions and major cities had peeled off to conduct their own version of the revolution. Productive people were demoralized. Trade was tiny. Though Mao had received Richard Nixon, Zhou Enlai had enraptured Henry Kissinger and Beijing and Washington had agreed on the 'One China' formula to paper over the question of Taiwan, China's foreign relations were still uncertain with the Sino-Soviet split looming over the Communist world.[5]

It was time for a new departure and a new realism by 'seeking truth from facts'. Deng was the right man at the right time. He reached down to the grassroots, starting with the countryside. China's rural masses had backed the Communists as they fought for power in the expectation that would give them land to farm; the victory of 1949 did, indeed, lead to redistribution of farms and punishment of landlords, but this was followed by collectivization on a national and militaristic scale in the Great Leap Forward and Cultural Revolution as the countryside was exploited for the benefit of the urban centres and its inhabitants became the fodder for Mao's social engineering.

Now, farmers were to be largely freed. Though the state retained ownership of land, they were given farming leases rather than having to work in collectives. After they had met quotas for the state, Deng's reforms allowed them to sell their produce, setting in train a boom in the countryside. The 'household-responsibility system' recognized individuals grouped in families. Farm productivity doubled in a decade.

The speed, scale and pragmatism of the revolution launched after Deng gained supremacy at the end of the 1970s masked his basic political inflexibility and his core aim. Though the class struggle was de-emphasized as individuals were empowered to make money and lead better material lives, his fundamental objective as a lifelong Communist stalwart was to strengthen the regime and restore China's greatness with economic growth as the means to that end. The key driver was, and remains, political as the nation's resources are used to buttress the power of the monopoly party which could thereby claim the new Mandate of Heaven to rule the country. As a result, Beijing's policies since the revolution introduced by Deng have to be seen not through the prism of pure economic logic but as a regime preservation exercise in which many other factors come into play and in which guerrilla-style adaptability was a key element

This drove his policy until he faded from the scene after his last hurrah on behalf of economic reform in 1992–93. Political liberalization was never really on the agenda even if there were occasional tantalizing hints and some of Deng's associates saw the need to loosen the Party's grip. But the 'four basic principles' adopted by the CCP after Mao's death remained highly orthodox, consisting of pursuing the Socialist road, the dictatorship of the proletariat, the leadership of the Party and Marxism–Leninism–Mao-Zedong Thought. For the paramount leader the third principle was the key. The 'four modernizations' proclaimed for the PRC by Zhou Enlai at the end of his life and adopted by Deng focused on progress in agriculture, industry, national defence and science and technology; but when the dissident Wei Jingsheng called for a 'fifth modernization' in the form of democracy, and then went on to depict Deng as a 'dictatorial fascist' and compare him to the Gang of Four, he was jailed for eighteen years; news of the sentence was broadcast over factory loudspeaker systems to tell workers the price of political disagreement.

Still, the process took on a momentum of its own in the 1980s and, indeed, had started in some places before becoming government policy. As Deng acknowledged, 'the result was not anything I or any other

172 TIGER HEAD, SNAKE TAILS

comrades had foreseen; it just came out of nowhere'. Once the farmers had been liberated to sell crops and began to grow foodstuffs that made the most money, instead of the staple grains, the next step was to focus on manufacturing and the introduction of market mechanisms and incentives.

The main effect of the manufacturing push was felt initially in the countryside among local economic groupings that had developed as the heirs of the commune and brigade groups established during the Great Leap Forward at the end of the 1950s. A State Council document in 1984 set out 'a new situation' for them in the form of Township and Village Enterprises (TVEs) which were to include 'individual enterprises' as well as entities sponsored by local communities.

The big state firms of the time were ill-fitted to take advantage of the opportunities that opened up. They still existed in the old-style economic world of central planning, Party domination, low productivity, over-employment and lack of responsiveness to demand. The TVEs, on the other hand, were small and nimble, headed by people whose driving aim was to make money and expand their businesses. They swiftly became the main motor of China's growth, their workforce rising from 30 million to 140 million in fifteen years. Privately run and household firms were at the core of the process. From 10.6 million in 1984, TVEs in those two categories rose to 17 million by the end of the decade, whereas the number of collective TVEs remained static at 1.45–1.73 million. The collectives were bigger and dominated the scene in the Beijing and Shanghai regions, but, even then, the household or individual firms employed almost as many people. The private firms did not have the responsibility for ensuring employment and providing welfare borne by SOEs and big collectives. They were able to attract innovative ambitious staff, whereas the large firms were stuck with the worker battalions of the Cultural Revolution. Before long, the rurally based TVEs began to subcontract for urban companies – for instance in producing parts for state vehicle factories. In poorer provinces they reduced poverty and boosted the buying power of grassroots consumers. This suggests that the big state policies behind the China Model and Beijing Consensus have, in fact, put the PRC on a less efficient road to development and improvement and that, as the economist Yasheng Huang

argues strongly, a return to the 1980s model would yield greater benefits and a more harmonious, if less regulated, society.[6]

The successful new entrepreneurs came from outside the framework
of authority and a significant number had suffered under the Cultural
Revolution, giving them a toughness that made them winners in the
commercial world. Inevitably, some overextended themselves or got
into businesses they did not understand; but in general they picked
themselves up and started all over again. The last two decades have
brought the more successful among them far greater riches, but the
early years of growth were the essential phase.

'People of my generation, we were suppressed like crazy in the class
struggle,' as Li Chuanzhi, founder and Chairman of the Lenovo computer company, which has one-third of the domestic market, puts it.
When economic reform dawned, 'finally we could start doing some real
work'. Others were never designated as class enemies but simply wanted
to build businesses and make money.

Liu Yonghao, an archetypical self-made billionaire, was born into a
poor family in Sichuan in the year of the Chinese Communist victory.
He and his three brothers left poorly paid government jobs in 1982 and
sold their bicycles and watches to raise seed capital to put into raising
quails and other poultry. Having done well at that, they moved into
animal feeds with their Hope group, which became one of the country's
biggest non-state enterprises. The brothers split up in 1996 and
Yonghao built his share of the feed business into an even larger outfit
called New Hope, which runs forty factories in the PRC and abroad,
employs 66,000 people and ranks as the world's third-biggest animal-
feed company as well as producing 200 million poultry, 8.5 million pigs
and half a million tons of milk a year. He branched out into banking
through the Minsheng group and invested in logistics, property and
dairy products. The 2011 Rich List put his immediate family's wealth at
41 billion yuan; his eldest brother was also very wealthy, having gone
into industrial materials, aluminium and plastic parts. Liu does not
drink alcohol or smoke and likes to eat pork with bean-curd and chilli
seasoning in the Sichuanese manner.

His modest, 'it's all business' lifestyle is paralleled by that of the even richer Zong Qinghou, head of the Wahaha beverages company, whose net worth was put at $20 billion by Bloomberg in 2012. Born in Zhejiang in 1945, Zong once attributed part of his success to the fact that he does not gamble, drink or play golf – and eats in the company canteen. He puts his average daily spending at 150 yuan, saying, 'I spend less than my employees because I don't have time.' The exception is his taste for Davidoff cigarettes and expensive Dragon Well tea.

Again like Liu, Zong began with menial work but then got into the milk-drinks business and made a fortune. In 2011 he branched out into retailing with a programme to build 100 department stores in smaller cities across the country; his strategy was likened by one of his former managers to Mao's policy of surrounding cities from the countryside as his drinks business took on urban suppliers from the outside. He saw off his French partner, Danone, to which he owed much of his original success, in a protracted dispute about whether he was ripping it off in their joint venture. Eventually he acquired Danone's 51 per cent, after which he issued a barefaced statement that 'China is an open country. Chinese people are broadminded people. Chinese companies are willing to cooperate and grow with the world's leading peers on the basis of equality and reciprocal benefit.'

Deng's other big innovation was the Special Economic Zones (SEZs) drawing on the example of the Asian 'tigers' whose growth far outstripped that of the PRC and set up either close to Hong Kong, as in the case of Shenzhen and Zhuhai, or in outward-looking Fujian. There had been a small experiment in Guangdong in 1978 when a Hong Kong entrepreneur reached an agreement with the authorities in Dongguan to found the Taiping handbag factory for which he put up funds and designs while the mainlanders provided land and labour. According to Hu Yaobang, who served as CCP Secretary in the 1970s, the decision to approve the application from the Guangdong authorities to launch the first SEZ at Shenzhen was taken mainly by Hua Guofeng while 'Deng was preoccupied by non-economic matters'.

Similarly, key reform plans such as the dismantling of farming communes and shifting to export-led growth and their implementation were the work of those around Deng, notably Zhao Ziyang, who was first

Prime Minister and then Hu's successor as General Secretary of the CCP, an open-minded figure by Party standards whose enthusiasm for golf can only have added to the suspicions conservatives felt about him. The old man played the role of conductor of the reform orchestra – or 'mother-in-law', as Zhao put it in his memoirs, relying on CCP control to push through change – Zhao also recalled that 'Deng always stood out among Party elders as the one who emphasized the means of dictatorship.' He often reminded people about its usefulness.' His strength at the centre was essential to keep to the path of change against the opposition of conservatives such as the leading economist Chen Yun, who carried his antagonism to the extent of refusing to set foot in any of the zones.[7]

Plenty of capital was available from China's high savings parked in state banks. Overseas Chinese were keen to invest, especially from Hong Kong and Taiwan, which had already undergone its own economic revolution and was something of an unspoken model for the mainland. For leading Chinese businessmen who preferred to live and keep their companies outside the PRC, putting money into the Dengist experiment was an ideal way of demonstrating patriotism. If much of the money travelled via Caribbean tax havens, well, no worries so long as it ended up in the SEZs in Shenzhen, Xiamen, Shantou and Zhuhai. There was also no shortage of land for development. The use of land to raise cash, which has become a staple of Chinese government funding, was not initially understood by the authorities but, in the mid-1980s, the Hong Kong tycoon Huop Yingdong (Henry Fok) explained to Zhao that if municipalities owned land, they should get permission to lease out some of it to outsiders and thus make money.[8]

Western and Japanese companies provided the technological knowledge necessary for mass production and began to salivate at the prospect of breaking through into the biggest untapped consumer market on earth. Despite the growth in disposable income, however, demand from China's domestic market was too small to support manufacturing on the scale to which the planners aspired. Per capita wealth in 1980 averaged only $200. So the PRC had to look outside for markets in which to sell the goods it was starting to make.

A benign world-trading environment and welcoming markets in

richer countries thus became an essential element in the Deng equation aimed at strengthening China and ensuring continuing Communist Party rule as economics and politics met on a global scale. The PRC also needed to assure foreign companies that by bringing the technologies to the mainland they would reap profits and run no political risk. Hence the patriarch's twenty-four-character instruction to his fellow country-men to keep their heads down, not to make waves and to work quietly as they used imported technology and methods to sell their products at prices Western and Japanese manufacturers could not match.

His desire to get important foreigners on his side was such that, when he visited Washington in 1979 after the establishment of diplomatic relations between the PRC and the USA, Deng felt he had to mention the highly secret preparations for an invasion of Vietnam to Jimmy Carter – and was, no doubt, relieved that the President reacted merely by saying the US would have to advise restraint when the PLA moved. The invasion was not a success and the Chinese were forced to beat a retreat after proclaiming victory, but the American attitude was highly symbolic and there was significantly increased intelligence co-assistance in the ensuing months while photographs of Deng wearing a ten-gallon hat and staring up at basketball stars from the Harlem Globetrotters radiated a folksy image that endeared the paramount leader to the US public

With richer foreign nations welcoming China as a deflationary source of everyday goods, the TVEs boosted their contribution to industrial output from 27.5 per cent in 1982 to 41 per cent six years later, while purely private firms went from practically zero to 6.5 per cent and the state sector's share slumped from 70 per cent to 47.6 per cent. Though Deng closed down the Democracy Wall that had been permitted in Beijing for people to post their views and Wei Jingsheng was jailed, there was a feeling of freedom and a thirst for new ideas among young people in cities. A new dynamism was in the air as they learned about the outside world, apparently with the blessing of the leadership. Students were mesmerized when they saw their first Walt Disney car-toons. The singing group the Carpenters and the crooner Richard Clayderman became symbols of liberation. But old ways persisted in the countryside and in some urban areas. A Chinese author, Lijia

Zhang, recalls that, as a young factory worker in Nanjing, she was not allowed to wear lipstick or high heels or to have dates for her first three years of employment; she earned distrust when she had her hair permed. A woman she knew was sent to a labour camp for three years for having an affair. A concert tour by the pop group Wham was halted when people started dancing in the aisles. Only two Western films were shown, *Gone with the Wind* and *The Sound of Music*.[9]

In 1988 a six-part televised series, *Heshang* (*River Elegy*), lamented China's backwardness, tracing it to isolation and conservatism and pointing to the open cultures of the West and Japan as the way ahead – it ended with symbolic images of the waters of the Yellow River, first home of Chinese civilization, flowing into the open sea. The message was clear: the story of the country's uniqueness as a result of its ancient, glorious civilization was a sham from which the Chinese needed to free themselves. While there was no direct attack on the CCP, the series supported students who had demonstrated against corruption and in favour of democracy and included critical material on inflation, graft and the condition of intellectuals as well as man-made disasters such as huge forest fires and a hepatitis epidemic in Shanghai. The implied question was whether economic growth alone was sufficient or whether more fundamental changes were required. Though the reformist Party leader, Zhao Ziyang, argued that the programme's message was cultural rather than political, it deeply displeased top Party figures who branded it counterrevolutionary, anti-Party and anti-Socialist. When the series was repeated by popular demand, there were significant cuts.

Growth did, indeed, produce mounting problems. Inequalities widened. Inflation spiked to 20 per cent in 1988 after Deng ill-advisedly insisted on lifting price controls. Huge corruption came to light; a major smuggling ring was exposed on Hainan Island. In Beijing and other major cities the younger generation and some of their elders questioned the status quo amid a flowering of independent culture and thought. The net result was the protests in Tiananmen Square in the spring of 1989, which started with commemorations of Hu Yaobang, the reformist former Party leader who died that April. The students who staged a six-week occupation of China's central space broadened out their criticisms to blame the Party for the shortcomings that had developed during the 1980s. Corruption was a main cause for complaint but there was a general alienation from the system which brought the CCP's legitimacy as the true representative of the nation into severe question especially when the students, who enjoyed privileged status in the traditional Chinese order, backed their protests by launching hunger strikes.[10]

The regime's inability to control events was symbolized by the way in which the demonstration derailed one of Deng's main diplomatic strokes, the visit of Mikhail Gorbachev as the result of a rapprochement with the Soviet Union. The Soviet leader had to be smuggled into his meeting with the Chinese by the back door of the Great Hall of the People because the front was blocked by the protestors.

Foreign television crews which had gone to Beijing to cover the visit sent out dramatic reports – 'What a time, what a place, what a story' the US network star, Dan Rather, told CBS viewers. 'It's the people's square all right. More than a million Chinese demanding democracy and freedom, and proclaiming the new revolution.' At one point his network delayed transmission of the last episode of the soap opera *Dallas* to show live coverage from Beijing.[11]

As General Secretary of the CCP, Zhao Ziyang insisted that the young people were acting from patriotic motives; but when he left on a scheduled though ill-timed trip to North Korea, hardliners led by Premier Li Peng pushed through publication of an editorial in *People's Daily* that accused the Tiananmen demonstrators of staging 'premeditated and organized turmoil with anti-Party and anti-socialist motives'. This radicalized both camps. On his return, Zhao sought to reach a compromise but, as he wrote in his memoirs, 'Li Peng and others in his group actively attempted to block, delay and even sabotage the process.'[12]

Deng had tried to regularize the regime's institutions after the wilful aberrations of his predecessor and to promote younger men to senior positions; this included some, such as Zhao Ziyang, who believed that reform should be spread beyond the economy. There had been attempts to increase accountability. Retirement ages were set for senior officials. But the elders still held on to the residual reins of power as the result of a bargain with Deng and they did not know how to react to the swelling demonstrations in big cities. A generation gap divided them from the freewheeling protestors opposite the Forbidden City in the capital. The hunger strikers and their companions were beyond the comprehension of the old men, Zhou Enlai's widow and their younger ally, Li Peng. They had gone through the Long March, the civil war and the Mao era and saw themselves as the guardians of that past. They saw themselves, as the writer Jonathan Mirksy put it at the time, as the 'Founding Members of the Firm'. For his part, Li Peng wrote in his diary: 'From the beginning of the turmoil, I have prepared for the worst. I would rather sacrifice my own life and that of my family to prevent China from going through a tragedy like the Cultural Revolution.'[13]

Given the conspiratorial context in which they had lived for so long, how could they not suspect that the protests were fomented by evil foreign powers working through Chinese 'black hands'? For the semi-geriatric group the maintenance of the regime and of their legacy was paramount. That was their purpose on earth. They were the guarantors of the new Mandate of Heaven; if preserving that cost the lives of some young people who should have known better, what was that to veterans who had lived with violence, sometimes on an extreme scale, all their lives? As Wang 'Big Canon' Zhen, a hardline military figure in the circle of elders whom Deng consulted put it, 'Those goddam bastards. Who do they think they are, trampling on sacred ground like Tiananmen for so long? They are really asking for it.'[14]

The threat to the leadership was all the greater since the protests in the capital were echoed in hundreds of other cities across the country (though not in the countryside) and because in Beijing students had the backing of a million or more of the city's citizens who joined supportive street demonstrations. Blue-collar workers were organizing independent labour unions. CCP members marched, waving banners demanding reform. Fear took over at the top; the hardliners gained the upper hand, castigating Zhao for a speech he had made to a meeting of the Asian Development Bank which they regarded as having shown excessive understanding of the protests and revealed a split in the leadership by saying that the issue should be resolved in a cool, restrained, reasonable and orderly manner.

As Zhao tells it, he went to Deng's home on 17 May for what he thought would be a private meeting during which he would try to persuade the patriarch to adopt a moderate course. When he arrived, however, he found the five members of the Politburo Standing Committee present as well as Deng. President Yang Shangkun suggested imposing martial law. Deng backed him. According to Zhao there was no vote and the decision was illegal – because under Party procedure he should have chaired the session rather than stumbling into it unawares. Another version has it that the Standing Committee *did* vote and split two–two, with one abstention, and that the elders were then called in to make the decision. Whatever the truth, the die was cast.[15]

Though some of the student leaders were ready to go back to their campuses claiming the moral high ground, others insisted on staying put. On the night of 3–4 June the tanks rolled down the boulevard to Tiananmen. Sitting in the courtyard of his home with his family Zhao heard the gunfire: 'a tragedy to shock the world [...] was happening after all,' he wrote. The death toll remains a matter of speculation but certainly went into the hundreds.[16]

The focus, both then and subsequently, has been on the students in China's central square and the killings have gone down as the 'Tiananmen Massacre' (with more guarded writers referring to it as the 'Tiananmen Incident' or the 'June 4 episode'). However, the vast majority of those killed were gunned down not in the square but in surrounding streets or on the boulevard leading to the city centre. The people of the capital had used peaceful tactics to stop two earlier army incursions into the city, erecting barricades, putting sheets of newspaper across the windscreens of military trucks and fraternizing with the bewildered soldiers who had been told they were being sent in to fight foreign-backed fascists but found that they were being offered flowers and ice creams by fellow citizens. For their third attempt the army opened fire to force its way through, shooting at random at residential blocks along the street and killing hundreds.

The PRC authorities insist that the massacre was justified to maintain national stability and economic progress. Deng said it was required to forestall 'the establishment of a bourgeois republic completely dependent on the West'. His family told biographer Ezra Vogel that he never once doubted that he had made the right decision. Zhao Ziyang was put

under house arrest until his death in 2005 – though he recorded his
memoirs and managed to smuggle them out with the help of the son of
Bao Tong, his aide during the 1980s.

Apologists for the repression posit that it saved China from disorder
and, regrettable though it was, ensured that the material growth which
had taken shape in the 1980s continued. As well as ignoring the morality of an unelected power group using force to put down its citizens, this
fails to take account of the extent of the dissatisfaction with the regime.
In 2012, Chen Xitong, mayor of the capital at the time of the massacre,
became the first official to openly regret what was done, with an interview in a book published in Hong Kong in which he called the killings
'regrettable' and 'a tragedy that could have been prevented'. But the
official line was clear, as expressed by Jiang Zemin, the boss of Shanghai
who had been elevated to succeed Zhao. 'The turmoil and rebellion
that occurred in the late spring and early summer of this year was the
result of the combination of the international climate and the domestic
climate,' he told a meeting. 'Hostile forces at home and abroad created
this turmoil to overthrow the leadership of the CCP, subvert the socialist system, and turn China into a bourgeois republic and into an
appendage of big Western capitalist powers once again.'[17]

'If an organization lobbies for the multiparty system, trying to oppose
the leadership of the Communist Party, then it will not be allowed to
exist,' Li Peng told a German magazine. The conservatives, headed by
the elders from the first generation of Communist chieftains along with
the Prime Minister, followed up the army crackdown by launching a
counteroffensive against economic reform – which, they argued, had
proved to be politically dangerous. Old and in poor health, Deng had
trouble countering the challenge. Jiang Zemin, who had been
appointed because of the way he had handled the protests in Shanghai
with minimum violence, swung behind the revisionists.

The collapse of Communism in the Soviet Union strengthened their
case. The growth target was cut in half. Wages were restricted and
poverty reduction went into reverse as the incomes of the least well-off
declined. Measures were prepared to rein in SEZs as the public sector
was boosted. In 1991 the SOE contribution to industrial growth was
back to its level of the early 1980s, that of TVEs was down to 10 per cent

and the input from private enterprises was negative. More than 40,000 cadres were charged with corruption.[18]

Deng, who held no Party or state positions, waited until 1992 to hit back. Then, aged 87, he took his private train to Guangdong and Shanghai to relaunch the drive to the market. His Southern Tour was not reported in the official media but he received an enthusiastic welcome, especially in Shenzhen where a big portrait of him commemorates his visit (photograph at start of this chapter). He insisted on the need to give reform a new start using foreign technology and capital; without economic progress, Deng said, the protests of 1989 would have led to civil war. The economic woes of the recently collapsed Soviet Union added to the case for strong growth. Manufacturers were encouraged to branch out into mechanical and electrical products, and reacted by getting into fresh fields – in one spectacular example, the big Shunde Guizhou eiderdown company switched tracks to become the world's biggest producer of microwave ovens under the name of Galanz. At the end of 1992 growth hit 14.2 per cent and, three years later, mechanical and electrical goods overtook textiles as China's biggest export category.

Under pressure from Deng and seeing the way the wind was blowing, the weathervane Jiang got into line and insisted on the need to 'liberate productive forces'. Foreign money poured in, much from Hong Kong and Taiwan. But the pursuit of the market did not mean political liberalization. If differences of opinion were normal, Jiang said, 'opposition in action is not allowed. Anybody who fails to realize this point is no Communist.' The supreme authority of 'one centre' – Deng – was asserted. The template of economic liberalization and top-down rule lasts to the present day, even if the 'one centre' has become the Party as a whole.

As the patriarch faded from the front of the scene, Jiang's 'Shanghai Faction' took over at the top and pursued all-out growth. Many of the remaining price controls were lifted; in 1994, market pricing applied to 90 per cent of retail goods and 79 per cent of agricultural produce. That led to a fresh bout of inflation, which rose above 25 per cent in 1994 before it was brought under control by the tough-minded Zhu Rongji –

another former Mayor of Shanghai – who then took over from Li to head the government in 1998. The outside world shuffled the killings of 4 June from the forefront of its dealings with mainland China. Britain's Foreign Secretary, John Major, met a senior Chinese official, Qian Qichen, in Paris a few weeks after the massacre. 'Our meeting was civilized and relative straightforward,' Major recalled in his memoirs. 'Although sharp differences were registered between us, we readily identified a way ahead and established a dialogue.' Britain had a particular concern – the handover of Hong Kong scheduled for 1997 – but the desire to find a way to continue working with China was widespread. Though the arms embargo decreed by the European Union after the killings remained in place, it was the economy that counted as Deng had calculated.[19]

Zhu Rongji, who had been purged as a rightist under Mao but, like others, had returned to fight another day, applied harsh medicine. On provincial tours he spoke acerbically of the need for greater efficiency; some state firms used only 35–40 per cent of their capacity at the time but operated as though they were working at full steam. Zhu streamlined government by reducing the number of ministries from forty to twenty-nine and calling cadres to account for the public money they were spending. He threw back reports from provincial officials containing inflated production figures, telling them to 'squeeze the water out' first. An adviser who attended his government meetings over the last two decades recalls that, after asking those present for their opinions, Zhu would brusquely cut off anybody he thought was not contributing useful ideas and then abruptly end the session by telling those who had caught his attention to go with him to continue the discussion and reach a decision. (In contrast, this source adds, Wen Jiabao went round the table patiently noting down what everybody says and then proposes a follow-up weeks later.)[20]

Applying a policy of 'cutting with one stroke', Zhu cracked down on bad lending and uncovered a mountain of bad debt. The main investment trust in Guangdong went bust. Reform of SOEs was pushed through, with staff cuts and improvements to financial management, procurement of raw materials, distribution and sales. But in 2001 Zhu still estimated that 68 per cent of state enterprises cooked their books, reflecting that 'I should be the first official dismissed'. Anywhere from 20 and 40 million people were thrown out of work though, to cushion the impact, some were still paid partial wages or assigned to make-work 're-employment bases'. Urban joblessness was regarded as an inevitable element in a market economy under the slogan 'Reduce the workforce, increase efficiency'. Though the official unemployment rate was kept below 4 per cent, the real level was estimated at 15–20 per cent. The number of poor people in cities rose to 50 million. Demonstrations broke out, especially in the rust belt of the north-east where industrial cuts were particularly harsh. More than 100 people died when protestors set off bombs at a cotton mill in a region of Hebei where significant redundancies had been enforced.

Zhu's focus was on the large industrial groups, especially the public-sector firms that enjoyed complete or virtual monopolies in major areas of the economy and got the bulk of loans from the state banks. The town and village enterprises that had done so much to power growth in the 1980s were reined in, being largely restricted to rural activities at a time when the central-government focus turned to urban development. They were consigned to a low-tech basket while urban firms were encouraged to move up the value chain. The amount of grain rural households were obliged to give to the state was increased, which led people to spend more time in the fields and less on their other activities. In the crack-down on excessive bank loans the informal lending sector, which had done much to pump up places like Wenzhou, was severely restricted.

Some of the biggest state companies, led by the four major banks, prepared to offer shares to global investors by listing on foreign stock markets. This involved a problem in the shape of non-performing loans equivalent to a quarter of GDP, which would have been crippling in Western banking. For the Chinese authorities the solution was simple: the loans were taken off the banks and put into asset-management companies run by the government. These companies issued notes that were acquired by the banks, which were further helped by injections of cash from the state reserves. The idea had been that the companies would be able to dispose of the debt, but they were still saddled with 80 per cent of it a decade later. The cost involved was around $400 billion – another pricey if little-noted element in the Chinese wonder-tale.

Zhu remarked that he would order 100 coffins: 99 for the people he would have shot as he cracked down on economic abuses and one for himself when somebody assassinated him. Corruption was estimated to be costing the economy 4 per cent of GDP annually, and more than 45,000 cases were investigated – leading to convictions for 18,000 people. Jiang called the crusade a matter of life and death and vowed that offenders would be 'punished without pity whatever their rank or fame'. In some cases local officials hit back. In the Guangdong port of Shantou, where tax fraud was estimated to have cost the state 100 billion yuan, a hotel where inspectors from Beijing were staying was burned down. But Zhu never needed his coffin.

In the biggest case, a smuggling ring was uncovered in Xiamen that had brought goods worth 53 billion yuan into the country without paying import duties. It was run by Lai Changxing, an illiterate farmer whose extraordinary rags-to-riches life story, as told in the book *Si Xiao* (*Fierce Smuggler*) published in Hong Kong in 2001, illustrates very well the extremes of shady business in China and of the collusion of officials with people on the make.[21]

Born in 1960 in a poor rural county in Fujian, Lai started out in business with a small enterprise set up by him and his brothers to make screws; he cycled fifty miles to Xiamen to sell them and bring back metal for the factory. In the early 1980s he moved to a larger town and got into printing and making umbrellas. He hit a minor jackpot when land on which he had a lease was re-zoned as part of an industrial area and he was able to sell it for a profit of 2 million yuan. A podgy, unprepossessing figure, Lai moved to Xiamen, where he arranged to import a satellite-telephone system for the city police and was allowed to smuggle in 100 cars as a reward. When the police contact was promoted to head the force in the provincial capital, Lai provided him with half a million yuan in bribes and a BMW.

Having scored his first big success, the Fierce Smuggler went briefly to Hong Kong where he registered a company and bought passports for countries with no extradition treaties with the PRC. He then returned to Fujian with the status of a 'foreign investor'. On meeting the children of an army chief he learned that the PLA wanted computer microprocessors that national security restrictions in the West were making hard to buy abroad. So he arranged to have them brought in through his Hong Kong firm. With military and political protection his career boomed as he imported cars, oil, petrochemicals, plastics, electronic goods, steel, building materials, cigarettes, cooking oil and munitions. The ships carrying them unloaded openly in Xiamen harbour. The operation evaded 30 billion yuan in import duties. Zhu Rongji was furious, calling Lai a 'turtle's egg' or 'bastard', but he was warned off taking action by a senior PLA general, according to the Hong Kong book. It adds that when Zhu and Lai met at a Spring Festival reception in Xiamen the Prime Minister told the crime boss to pay his taxes, stop smuggling 'and that will be the end of the matter'. Lai took no notice. He felt comfortable with his powerful protectors.

Lai said that he had been enrolled in the State Security Ministry. His Mercedes had not only bulletproof glass and a satellite telephone that could call anywhere in the world (this was in the 1990s), but also a red number plate from the General Staff of the PLA. He paid out 10 million yuan a month in bribes and hosted officials at his six-storey Red House where he established his office on the top floor and provided guests with food cooked by a top Hong Kong chef, saunas, karaoke rooms and young women who were paid a basic monthly salary of 10,000 yuan. Among his guests, according to the book, was the local customs chief for whom Lai provided a mistress. Another was China's Deputy Police Minister, who was taken from the airport to a pleasure house where he was introduced to the charming Miss Yang, with whom he spent the next three days. The boss of the smuggling operation bought her out of her job at a foreign public-relations firm and purchased homes for her in Xiamen, Shenzhen and Hong Kong as well as getting her a visa to enter the former British colony on condition that she remained available for the Deputy Police Minister.

Finally, in 1999, a government taskforce was created to close down Lai's operation as part of a broader anti-smuggling exercise authorized by Jiang Zemin. Investigators moved in to Xiamen under a tough female prosecutor, Liu Liying, and raided his premises. They found incriminating lists of corrupt officials but the bank accounts were empty – Lai had moved the cash to Hong Kong.

Two hundred people were questioned. Eighty-one officials were tried

and eleven sentenced to death. Two committed suicide, one by ram-
ming chopsticks down his throat after unsuccessfully trying to kill
himself by cutting his veins with glass from his spectacles. Lai got away
to Canada where he claimed the status of a political refugee, saying he
risked torture and execution if sent back to the PRC. In July 2011, however, a judge in Vancouver ruled that he was a common criminal who
should be sent home. A pledge from the government in Beijing that Lai,
aged fifty-three, would not be executed was enough to convince the
court that he would not be 'at risk if removed to China,' the judge
added. The Fierce Smuggler was flown back to Beijing and sentenced to
life imprisonment in May, 2012.

The Xiamen case was the tip of a considerable iceberg that included
100 officials absconding abroad with funds from Yunnan, a senior official who ran an illegal casino in a trade-union building and road
projects where the State Audit Office found that 15 per cent of the
state funding had gone missing. A former boss of Guangxi province who
had been a deputy chairman of the National People's Congress was
executed for taking 30 million yuan in bribes and the deputy Governor
of Jiangxi was shot after being found in a hotel room with a fake identity card, two envelopes stuffed with cash and a bottle of Viagra. Chen
Xitong, the powerful Mayor of Beijing, was sent to jail for sixteen years
for corruption; but, in an example of how anti-graft crusades are used
for higher political purposes, his fall was primarily the result of a power
struggle with Jiang and his 'Shanghai Faction', who wanted any excuse
to get rid of the competing 'Beijing Clique'. In Shenyang there was the
local Godfather, Liu Yong, operating on a nexus of crime and corruption as described in an earlier chapter.

Despite the crackdowns, major cases of official malfeasance kept sur-
facing and appeared to show that, while Zhu Rongji was serious about
the campaign, corruption was (and is) a historical inheritance given
new life by the way in which the country was growing richer. The weak
legal system and the prevalence of *guanxi* relationships encouraged
dodgy business practices. The state auditor found that the accounts of
two-thirds of state enterprises 'did not truly reflect their financial situation or operational results'. Private business turned up regular cases of
entrepreneurs using connections and sidestepping the law, none more

so than Mou Qizhong, a stocky figure from Sichuan with long salt-and-pepper hair who resembled Mao Zedong.

Mou was celebrated by the government as one of China's top-ten private entrepreneurs and an official 'reform hero'. The son of a finance official, he had questioned Maoism during the Cultural Revolution and was sentenced to be executed but was saved by the change of course after the Great Helmsman's death. His first business venture, which involved making copies of a popular clock, saw him being sent to jail for a year. After his release, he launched into a major barter operation in which he exchanged basic Chinese products, mainly socks, for Russian airliners that he sold to the airline in his home province for a big profit. Becoming a model of the new, thrusting world of Chinese business, he juggled schemes to develop the world's fastest computer chip and to blast a hole through the Himalayas to bring rain to northern China. He got into property and set up US companies to which he planned to transfer assets from state-owned enterprises and then, with American bank loans added, move the money back to the PRC to take advantage of tax breaks for foreign investors. This technique of creating 'fake foreign devils' happened to be illegal. Arrested in 1999, he was given a life sentence for using phony letters of credit from a state company to obtain $75 million in foreign currency.

Under the Jiang–Zhu leadership, China put even more chips down behind Deng's gamble that material progress would cancel out calls for change in the way China was run from the top and for a relaxation of CCP authority. There was no acknowledgement that economic efficiency might be helped by institutional checks and balances, an independent legal system or greater media scrutiny. A global survey by the consultants PWC in 2000 ranked the PRC as the most opaque major country in which to do business. Though the urban housing market was opened to private ownership at the end of the century, suggestions by senior bureaucrats, company managers and scholars that the constitution should be amended to safeguard the sanctity of property were not taken up. One third of the delegates at the annual meeting of the national legislature in 2000 showed their dissatisfaction by voting against or abstaining when presented with reports by the Supreme People's

Court and the Supreme People's Procuratorate – an unusually high number for such a docile body. A poll conducted by the Chinese Academy of Social Sciences (CASS) in 1999 suggested that lagging political reform was the biggest obstacle to China's economic and social progress over the next decade.[22]

But the partial and quite timid political reform policies of the 1980s were halted and CCP rule was reinforced. When survivors of the 1989 crackdown tried to register a Democracy Party of China during a visit by Bill Clinton to the PRC in 1998, they were sent packing and then arrested and jailed (their leader for sixteen years).

Free of Deng's immediate shadow when the patriarch died in 1997, the stout Jiang, with his thick glasses and ready smile, was often underrated, in part because of his obvious pleasure at holding the position to which he had been unexpectedly elevated. He was described as a 'flowerpot' for his way of standing around without apparently doing much and the official slogan used to greet him was hardly inspiring – 'The General Secretary is Working Hard!' He was the first leader of the PRC who had not gone through the Long March and the Civil War with the Nationalists, and did not seem to measure up to the historic personalities who had preceded him as he launched into a karaoke rendition of Elvis Presley's 'Love Me Tender' during the socializing at an international conference. There was embarrassment when he was photographed combing his hair before being taken into an audience with the King of Spain, and stories circulated about his friendships with female associates.

Still, as Party Secretary, State President and Chair of the Central Military Commission, Jiang carried through the second phase of the post-1978 development focusing on growth and boosting exports and presiding over the return of Hong Kong and Macau to Chinese sovereignty. At the annual session of the legislature in 2001, Zhu Rongji put forward an annual growth target of 7 per cent for the following five years – the outcome easily outstripped that, with just over 10 per cent a year in 2003–05. Jiang accepted the importance of good relations with the United States as China became a major supplier to American consumers; at the same time, though, the 'patriotic education' campaign stirred anti-Japanese nationalism in an effort to buttress the regime as ideology fell away and the book *China Can Say No* became a bestseller.

Jiang stepped back from the brink in 1996 when Washington sent in the fleet in a show of support for Taiwan after a mainland war-game against it. Tension rose in 1999 after NATO aircraft bombed China's Embassy in Belgrade and the PRC declined to accept that it had been an accident: 100,000 people demonstrated in Beijing and the residence of the US Consul-General in Chengdu was stormed. But, two years later, Jiang defused a potentially dangerous incident over an American spy plane that became embroiled in a midair confrontation with a Chinese jet and was forced to land on Hainan Island. China won plaudits by resisting devaluation during the Asian economic crisis of the end of the twentieth century. It joined the World Trade Organization in 2001 and benefited from the lifting of tariffs on its exports. The 'opening up' pressed by Deng was no longer subject to any significant ideological challenge – occasional mutterings from the 'new left' about a return to old ways aroused more interest among foreign commentators seeking a new China theme than they did among the Chinese public.

As he prepared to step down in 2002, Jiang promulgated his theory of the 'Three Represents', which, in a regime where slogans count for a great deal, marked an important step by recognizing the role of 'advanced social productive forces' that include the entrepreneurial middle class alongside industrial workers and farmers. The theory laid down that the Party should represent 'the interests of the overwhelming majority', meaning a further move away from the class war proclaimed by Mao with top-level approval for the withering away of ideology.

Jiang's departure was significant for the manner in which he handed over to Hu Jintao, the man designated by Deng a decade earlier as the next leader. Soon afterwards, Zhu Rongji gave way to Wen Jiabao. Jiang's exit may not have been altogether welcome to him and he held on to the third major post, the Chair of the Central Military Commission, for a couple more years. Though Zhu disappeared from public view, making only a brief appearance at a Beijing university in 2011 when he complained about the poor quality of news programmes on state television and then publishing his frank memoirs, the outgoing Secretary remained visible.

Jiang maintained an office in Beijing and staged occasional walkabouts. He put his name to books about information technology, a sector in which his son forged a career; Xi Jinping showed his loyalty to the man whose successor-but-one he was set to become by presenting the volumes to Angela Merkel, the German Chancellor, at the Frankfurt Book Fair. At the 2009 celebrations of the sixtieth anniversary of the foundation of the PRC, television cameras cut to the former leader more than twenty times. In 2011, rumours of his death spread in Beijing and were reported by a Hong Kong television station as fact, but, in October, he appeared at the celebrations of the anniversary of the start of the revolution that overthrew the Qing dynasty appearing weak but certainly not in the grave and there was immediate speculation about the role that he and the remnant Shanghai Faction would play in the leadership changes of 2012–13.

When Jiang quit the Party leadership in 2002 the growth machine was ready to go into overdrive under a leadership that resembled a board of managers rather than a band of revolutionaries. Helped by a low exchange rate, exports had doubled during the 1990s, but to 'only' $200 billion at the turn of the century. The trade surplus rose to $43.3 billion in 1998 but fell to $22.6 billion in 2001. After that, China moved into high gear. GDP growth went into double digits year after year, hitting 11.4 per cent in 2007 when the trade surplus reached $262 billion as the Western (above all American) propensity to spend much and save little boosted exports and dovetailed with the PRC's high-saving, low-spending pattern to produce what looked like global equilibrium masking the fundamental imbalance between the high-spending US and the high-saving PRC.

Fixed-assets investment, mainly in property and infrastructure, jumped by 25 per cent a year. China's appetite for raw materials was insatiable and its overseas direct investment rose nearly tenfold to $26.5 billion between 2003 and 2007. Prices, mainly for food, took off, producing an inflationary spike in 2007.

The year of 2008 was trickier – monetary tightening to combat inflation had an unexpectedly drastic effect on small firms, large inventories of commodities added to excess capacity and, above all, the financial crisis in the West hit the main markets for exports and upset trade. So the leadership reacted with its huge stimulus package announced at the end of 2008, which raised fixed-asset investment by 50 per cent year-on-year as 4 trillion yuan was spent on infrastructure and reconstruction

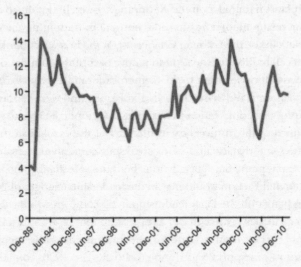

China's real GDP growth rate 1989–2010
Source: CEIC

after the devastating earthquake in Sichuan. This was followed by an opening of the credit tap that produced 10 trillion yuan in new loans in 2009 and 7.5 trillion the following year. The exchange-rate peg to the US dollar, which had been lifted in 2005, was reinstated. After a short dip, the growth rate resumed its onward path and the current account balance showed a twelve-month surplus of $330 billion at the end of 2010, though demand for high-priced commodities and for imported consumer goods went some way towards balancing exports.

China appeared to have found a magic formula, albeit that the magic consisted mainly of throwing an awful lot of money at a problem. Admirers of the Beijing Model were comforted. As the West struggled with low growth, the CCP Leading Group on Foreign Affairs proclaimed that 'the Washington Consensus on economic policy has been discredited' and 'we alone have robust growth'.

By now China seemed to be everywhere, an integral element in the warp and woof of the world – despite, as we will see, its presence not always being welcomed. Its goods were inescapable, whether produced in huge plants like Foxconn in Shenzhen or in small family workshops at the end of the global chain, sold through the trading towers of Yuwi or by traders scouring Africa, the Middle East and Latin America for customers. The PRC manufactured more sombreros than Mexico and provided two-thirds of the world's exports of toys. It turned out more string bikinis than the Brazilians. Ninety per cent of the vuvuzelas blown during the World Cup in South Africa in 2010 came from Guangdong and Zhejiang. Britain's iconic Hornby model trains are made on the mainland as are parts for London taxis. An American writer who tried to do without anything made in the People's Republic found it very hard going (and she may not have been aware of food ingredients such as corn syrup or starch that came from across the Pacific).

The Xinhua state news agency has taken giant displays in Times Square in New York to advertise itself. Chinese 'snakehead' underworld gangs have become a major force on the docks of Naples. Cuban police drive Chinese-made cars. Devout Muslims click prayer beads made in the PRC.

As the regime headed by Hu Jintao got into its stride, the

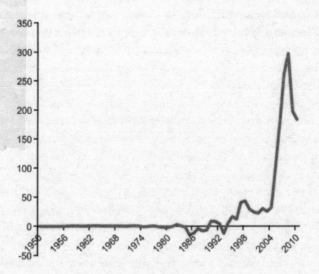

China's trade surplus
Source: CEIC

international balance was changing, tilting from West to East. India was playing its part, and Japan remained the third-biggest economy on earth, but it was the PRC that led the charge. There was suggestion that everything really came down to the Sino-American G2, rather than the world being dominated by groupings such as the G8 or the G20. This was not a characterization embraced by either party, and it ignored many global factors. Still, it was plain that the People's Republic was well on its way to becoming as much an inescapable world power as the United States. Its rise and rise, however, masked a substantial set of fault lines and challenges that begin in the root of its success, the economy. These included rising inflation and a slowdown in export growth. The huge credit expansion that underpinned the stimulus programme threatened to produce a mass of bad debts for banks while government measures to tighten monetary policy severely strained smaller firms that also had to deal with rapidly rising wages. As well as such economic pressures, the social fissures in the PRC were widening and there were shocks such as the high-speed train crash. Later chapters will deal with these elements of today's China; but for the moment, it is time to turn to the past, which, as much as the Dengist evolution of the world's oldest continuous civilization, has made China what it is today, but which has also bequeathed awkward elements that compromise the future.

10

OWNING HISTORY

Given the achievements of the last three decades, the reluctance of the leaders of the People's Republic to engage in experiments that might shake their status quo is understandable. It also fits in with a pattern stretching back for more than two millennia. China had no shortage of power shifts over the centuries but few regime changes. The eight dynasties that occupied the Dragon Throne for more than 2,133 years after Qin Shi Huangdi, the First Emperor, had united what was then China cleaved to the same basic principles. This produced the longest-lasting government system the world has seen – but at a price. Though imperial China was not the immobile monolith it is sometimes depicted as having been, such systems tend, by their nature, to become institutionally fossilized.

The presumption of the right to rule bestowed by the Mandate of Heaven remained in force long after the divine right of kings had faded in Europe. While Britain had its Magna Carta, the growth of parliamentary power, the Civil War and execution of Charles I, the Revolution of 1688 and the electoral reforms of the nineteenth century, China stuck to its imperial system, albeit with different applications by different rulers. The United States and France had their revolutions, and Germany evolved a modern state under the Kaiser, but China stayed as it was under the long-reigning Qing.

There was social and economic movement over the millennia of empire, to be sure. New classes sprouted. Cities rose and fell. People migrated. Agricultural innovations brought new foods and better crop yields. From the First Emperor on, the throne undertook enormous projects, such as the Great Wall and the Grand Canal. Far from being a peace-loving Confucian nation that respected its neighbours, China pushed out into Central Asia, Tibet, Korea and Vietnam. Raiders from the northern steppes meanwhile stormed into the heart of the empire over long periods and the two foreign dynasties, the Mongol Yuan and Manchu Qing, ruled for 356 years between them. The period from the mid-nineteenth century to the mid-1970s was particularly turbulent inflicting a death toll of more than 100 million from revolts, foreign invasions, civil war and Mao's murderous scheme to change the country – not to mention recurrent natural disasters, the last of which, the Tangshan earthquake of 1976 as the Chairman lay dying, killed around a quarter of a million people.

But, for all the disruption over the centuries, the leadership – whether Imperial, Nationalist or Communist – has been loath to embrace reform of the ruling system and successive regimes have borne considerable similarities stretching back to the First Emperor. From that point of view China can claim a unique continuity of its political culture but whether this has been healthy is highly questionable.

Power preservation, often in crude forms, has been the watchword. A line can be drawn from the story of Qin Shi Huangdi burying alive 460 dissenters to Mao and then on to the killings in Beijing on 4 June 1989. On the rare occasions when reform raised its head, reaction soon set in. The attempt by the Guangxu emperor to bring about fundamental change in his Hundred Days of reform in 1898 was quickly undone, both by his own attempt to achieve everything at once and then by the intervention of his aunt, the Dowager Empress Cixi, who told the young man to desist and kept him under palace arrest for the remaining ten years of his life. The overthrow of the Qing in 1912 changed the rulers but brought neither political nor social reform as military strongmen took over. The calls for reform in the May Fourth democracy and modernization movement of 1919 left its legacy among intellectuals and artists but had little effect on the practice of power. Promises of reform by the early Nationalist Republic in the late twenties wilted in the face of harsh realities.

Under the PRC, Mao's Hundred Flowers campaign of 1957, which encouraged people to speak out, led to a mass crackdown when the Great Helmsman found the criticism unacceptable; hundreds of thousands of people were jailed or sent for reform through labour. Having helped to supervise that repression, Deng Xiaoping had the Beijing 'democracy wall' closed down after a year and Wei Jingsheng sent to jail. The wave of protest in the late 1980s was ended when the tanks rolled into the capital on the night of 3–4 June. Today, the repression of political opposition continues unabated.

The repeated triumph of conservativism over reform is one of a number of interlocking strands that link present-day China with a heritage going back more than two millennia. Among them one can identify the stress on national unity and stability which are held to justify the use of force against dissent, mass mobilization of the population, top-down rule and the lack of institutional and legal checks and balances, a mix of Confucianism and Legalism, the recurrent tug-of-war between the central government and the regions, the use of violence to settle disputes, the appeal to China's ancient civilization as a source of uniqueness and exceptionalism – plus the taste for vast infrastructure projects, often with a political subtext. More recently, one can add the desire to use foreign technologies to modernize the nation without ceding autonomy that has its roots in the late nineteenth century. Throughout runs a stress on the centrality of the anointed leader (whether an individual or, today, a political organization) that cannot be gainsaid and can be replaced only by force.

In many ways the First Emperor set the template followed to this day. But Qin Shi Huangdi came only after 2,500 years of mythical history dating back to ruling houses of the twenty-seventh century BC. Even earlier lies the Chinese creation story, which contains no mention of the divine figures prevalent in other cultures. Instead the universe is contained in a black egg broken by its occupant, Pangu, usually shown as a hairy giant with horns on his head. Feeling suffocated, he used an axe to crack the shell, at which point the clear part of the egg floated upwards to constitute heaven while the heavy element stayed below as the earth. Both grew at great speed and were eventually separated by a distance equivalent to 30,000 miles. When Pangu died his voice became thunder, his eyes the sun and moon, his breath the clouds and wind, his hair the stars and his sweat the rain, while his limbs formed the Five Great Mountains of China revered and visited to this day.

Around 2,500 BC, according to tradition, Huangdi, the Yellow Emperor of Shandong, became the father of the Han race. 'To understand us Han Chinese, you must understand that we all see ourselves as the children of the Yellow Emperor,' a leading businessman told me in Hong Kong in the late 1990s. 'That is what binds us together whatever happens, wherever we are and whatever we do.' One may dismiss this as romance tinged with a racial component but the feeling of springing from a common ancestor does serve to underpin the idea of China as special and its inhabitants as imbued with a unique civilizational heritage. Huangdi, naturally, is given many of the traits such a heritage would seek. On top of being a fine and valiant warrior, he was an inventor who taught his subjects how to improve their lives, gave them a written script, good laws, a calculation system and a calendar, as well as evolving a system of internal medicine and playing a musical instrument while his wife offered instructions in silk-weaving.

Moving into recorded history, the Bronze Age Sheng and Zhou kingdoms left plentiful archaeological remains of their achievements and developed writing systems on oracle bones that led to present-day Chinese characters. From around 700 BC the decline of the Zhou, the first rulers to claim the Mandate of Heaven and the first to use eunuchs as court servants, led to two lengthy periods of instability and dislocation: the Spring and Autumn Period followed by the Warring State Period, which lasted from 403 to 221 BC. Though this was a time of considerable intellectual debate and thinking – by Confucius among others – about how states should be run, the weakening of Zhou rulers produced fragmentation as local strongmen operated autonomously, another trend that would recur periodically through the nation's history.

Thirty-five years after the death of the last Zhou king, Shi Huangdi took the name of the First August Emperor, having expanded the reach of his militaristic state of Qin with a series of victories over rivals. He claimed to rule all China as it existed at that point as a unified domain rather than being simply the king of one part of it who had managed to conquer the rest. There was no limit to his ambition as he melded together the previously warring states. In the words of an inscription on big stone tablets in eastern China:

> Wherever the sun and moon shine,
> Wherever one can go by boat or by carriage,
> Men obey the orders
> And satisfy his desires.

Qin Shi Huangdi's power base was in the basin of the Yellow River in Central China and his capital at Chang'an near what is now Xi'an. His empire's frontiers reached north to what is now Inner Mongolia and to Liaoning in the north-east, south to Hunan, Jiangxi and Zhejiang, and west to Sichuan and Gansu. Though this is only a fraction of modern China, the First Emperor embodies many of the elements that ran through the following twenty-two centuries. It does not matter if everything written about him was strictly true. He has stood as an icon for China, with the tenets of his rule becoming the hallmark of successors.

To command such a large domain as a united entity he imposed standardization – of written script, money, weights and measures, the width of roads and carriage axles. The use of extreme violence against opponents was carried over from the bloody campaigns that swept him to power as his armies demolished enemies 'like a silkworm devours a mulberry leaf'. He initiated huge building projects, including his palace with the nearby burial mound, still unopened but reputed to contain a great copper ceiling set with jewels to represent the stars and streams of mercury to stand for the rivers and seas of China, plus an elaborate defensive system whose secrets were protected by the expedient of having all the workers from the project buried alive with the emperor together with his wives and concubines. Nearby lies the home for the Terracotta Warriors, who would guard him in the here-after.

Qin Shi Huangdi had 4,700 miles of roads built – more than the Romans – and started work on the Great Wall to keep out raiders from the north. Land reform was implemented to ensure reliable food supplies for the army. To provide labour he ordered forced mass mobilization of the population; nearly 750,000 men were conscripted to build his palace and tomb, and it was said that one man died for each metre of the Great Wall.

He adopted Legalism, the creed that holds that man is fundamentally bad and needs to be kept in check by fear of draconian laws. 'In an orderly country, punishments are numerous and rewards rare,' a Legalist posited. It was all for the people's good. As another exponent of the creed explained with questionable factual evidence: people like water but fear fire; so many are drowned but few are burned and the law should be fire rather than water. To reinforce his rule the emperor ordered the burning of ancient texts expressing ideas that did not con-form to his precepts and, according to tradition, buried alive the scholars who dissented from his views. As he grew increasingly paranoid, he made it a crime to reveal his whereabouts – setting a standard for secrecy that pervades the country's leadership to the present day. Not surprisingly Mao was a great admirer, remarking that he had done away with far more of the intellectuals he despised than the First Emperor, whom he echoed in efforts to beat the Chinese into a single mould as they were press-ganged to carry out grandiose construction and economic projects.

The highly practical First Qin also embodied the superstitious side of China that thrives to this day. He listened to soothsayers and shamans. He sought elixirs to grant him everlasting life. He was on a trip to seek a way to achieve eternity when he died in 210 BC after eleven years on the imperial throne.

The death of the First Emperor set another pattern that is by no means unique to China but recurs regularly: internal faction fighting after the passing of the strong man. Qin Shi Huangdi's adviser, Li Si, kept the news of his death secret; it was high summer and, when the body was transported back to Chang'an, a cartload of fish trundled alongside to account for the smell. Using the time at his disposal, Li Si forged a document said to be from the emperor ordering a liberal-minded prince to commit suicide and installing a more pliant younger son on the throne. But the new ruler, a sybarite under the influence of a court eunuch, had Li Si executed in a wholesale purge of Qin Shi Huangdi's leading followers. Taxes were increased; peasants rebelled; prices rose; banditry became common. The empire fragmented. When the ruler tried to stand up to him, the eunuch took over the palace and made the young man kill himself, putting in his place a nephew who reigned for forty-six days, after which the main force of rural rebels took power and founded the Han dynasty, the longest imperial ruling house.

The new emperor, Gaodi, was one of the great figures of Chinese history, an excellent military strategist who restored national unity, reformed the economy and relaxed the extremes of Legalism, introducing Confucianism and seeking popular support in place of the First Emperor's despotism. His strength made him an iconic dynastic founding father. A peasant by origin, he showed his earthiness in his language and by urinating into a scholar's formal hat. He punished merchants who were blamed for profiteering and speculation, forbidding them to hold official positions, ride in carts or wear silk – the Confucianism he adopted relegated business people to the lowest social rank, below scholars and farmers. But he also initiated the appeal to the supposedly glorious past, in his case the early Zhou, by initiating court rituals that harked back half a millennium to form a connection with the original Sons of Heaven.

The dynastic cycle was played out again and again over the following centuries, though usually in a more protracted form than the fall of the Qin. Strong men, often leaders of rebel forces, would use revolts and military campaigns to take over as the preceding ruling house was brought down by disasters and internal weaknesses; again the pattern can be seen in the victory of the PLA in 1949 propelling Mao to supreme power. In most cases the founders of dynasties and their immediate heirs would fare well, but then the difficulties of ruling China, court intrigues, natural calamities and foreign intervention would set the scene for another change of ruling house as the occupants of the throne grew increasingly less authoritative and charismatic. The parallels are imperfect but one might speculate as to whether the consensus leadership that rules today from its compound by the Forbidden City in Beijing reflects characteristics of later generations of emperors and faces some of the same challenges. But then the current dynasty has only been in power for six decades, whereas the Han lasted for four centuries, the Tang, Song and Ming for around three each and the Qing for more than two and a half.

The result of the dynastic cycle was an underlying fragility and nervousness despite the seemingly perennial imperial system – rather akin to the shorter-term truism today that successful businesses last for only three generations (those being that of the strong founder, the son who manages the business and the grandson who wastes the accumulated capital and ends up ruined). That easily bred paranoia and the attempt by each dynasty to insist that every child of the Yellow Emperor owed it loyalty. This, in turn, meant that dissent was outlawed while the adoption of Confucianism never replaced the harsher uses of Legalism to regiment the population. The teaching of Confucius's leading follower, Mencius, that heaven granted the right to rebel had little appeal for those in power and was invoked retrospectively after the fall of a ruling house that was held to have lost the Mandate of Heaven, its bad behaviour meaning that it had failed to pursue the correct relationships with its people. By and large, China has been ruled by the Legalist fist concealed in the Confucian glove. Today, the regime encourages people to follow the teachings of the sage but its treatment of dissent shows the legacy of Qin Shi Huangdi.

History is always political but nowhere more so than in China. The writing and rewriting of the accounts of the past to suit the political requirements of the present forms another clear line over more than 2,000 years. Today it is not simply that there is no tolerance for any variation from the official version of such major events as the Beijing massacre of 1989 or the catastrophic man-made famine around 1960. The control dynamic applies across the board of the past. A professor who suggested a re-evaluation of the official version of the Boxer Rising was sanctioned. In 2011 the President of the well-regarded magazine *Nanfengchuang* (*South Wind Window*) was demoted after it published an interview with a Taiwanese historian who recounted well-known episodes (at least outside China) in which Sun Yat-sen, the Father of the Republic, sought deals with the Japanese to cede Chinese territory in return for their backing when he was trying to launch a military expedition against the warlords controlling Beijing. Officials told the magazine's editorial committee that the story was 'anti-government and anti-Communist Party'. No matter that it was right.

The revolt against the Qing of 1911–12 remains a tricky issue for the Communist regime, which likes to see itself as the only true revolutionary force. Though the centenary of the rising in Wuhan was marked by the leadership (joined by Jiang Zemin) in October 2011, the first performance in Beijing of an opera on Sun Yat-sen was, at the same time, abruptly cancelled 'for logistical reasons'. Such control of the past has a very long history. On taking the throne dynasties had accounts written of their predecessors that inevitably painted them in a bad light in contrast to the heroes blessed by divine favour who had taken power. (Shakespeare did the same for the rulers of his day, of course.) This was not simply the usual practice of monarchs and governments blaming those who had gone before for the woes they inherited. In China it had a more powerful purpose. It was essential in order to explain why the previous ruling house had lost the Mandate of Heaven but that this did not compromise the continuation of the imperial system. The highly coloured biographies of rulers written for the early Han by the first known Chinese historian, Sima Qian, set the model. Did the First Emperor actually bury alive those hundreds of scholars after burning the ancient texts of which he disapproved? Some recent Western scholarship doubts the interments. We will probably never know the truth. But Sima Qian set down an account that lives on.

After China's only female emperor, Wu Zetian – an extraordinary feminist ahead of her time – was forced to abdicate and died in 705, her Tang successor had lurid tales penned depicting her poisoning her rivals right, left and centre, having their arms and legs amputated before the remaining bodies were thrown into wine vats or pig pens and, as she aged, taking so many aphrodisiacs that she grew an extra set of teeth. The image of Wu leading her female followers up a holy mountain previously reserved for men and then descending into slaughter and lust animates television dramas and biographies that rely heavily on the words 'may have' and 'was said to'.

Such lurid tales dramatize the dangers of ruling. The story of the end of the last ethnic Han dynasty has the Ming emperor, who was facing widespread revolts against famine, corruption, high taxation and harsh officials, being abandoned by his generals as a rebel army entered Beijing. He called a council at which 'all were silent and many wept'. The ruler got drunk and ran through the Forbidden City telling the women to commit suicide as his wife did. He cut the arms off one of his daughters, and killed his concubines. At dawn he ascended the hill behind the palace to hang himself as Manchu forces rode in to defeat the rebels and establish the Qing dynasty. Did it really happen like that? Nobody can tell. But Chinese history is replete with dynasties crashing to disaster. No wonder that paranoia and power go hand in hand.

Mao's rise is painted as an inevitable historical event, with the future Chairman donning the Marxist Mandate of Heaven while the Nationalists showed themselves unworthy to rule. The distortions start with the founding of the CCP in 1921. The exhibition at the Shanghai house where this began shows Mao looming over his colleagues – in fact he was only a provincial representative. The men who really ran the

Party in its early days have been airbrushed from the official record. The Long March of 1934–35 is depicted not as a desperate escape from Kuomintang forces marked by defeats, desertions and discord, but as a heroic founding narrative during which Mao emerged as the fount of all wisdom to which Zhou Enlai and others rallied. The war with Japan is the regime's second great saga, despite the fact that, contrary to its version, the Nationalists did much more fighting than the People's Liberation Army and won more victories even if they lost most of China. The dozen years spent by Mao and his colleagues in their base at Yan'an provide a third historical plank for the regime as a period in which Communism Chinese-style was forged far from the corruption of the cities, with high productivity and selfless devotion to the cause; the brutal purges and growing of opium to raise funds are among issues left unmentioned. Finally, victory in 1949 is presented as a rising of the Chinese people to sweep the CCP to power when it was actually more of a military triumph by an army better organized and led than its opponent, and with plentiful modern weapons.[1]

Mao is officially classified as 70 per cent good, 30 per cent bad, and the Cultural Revolution is admitted to have been a catastrophe. But the founder of the latest dynasty presents an obvious and continuing problem. How does a regime in which people are shaking off the enforced conformity of the early decades of Communist rule account for the anti-rightist campaign of 1957? How does it explain the Great Leap Forward, which aimed to boost industrial and agricultural production in unheard-of proportions and had what seems today the quaint target of surpassing Britain economically in fifteen years? China was transformed into a mass of communes as farmers lost the plots handed to them in post-1949 land redistribution. Backyard furnaces were established to turn out iron and steel. Targets were ramped up remorselessly. Mao declared that 'one day equals twenty years' in the race for growth. The resulting chaos and misguided policies led to the great famine around 1960 in which the deaths of 40 million people were abetted by official indifference and thuggery by card-carrying cadres.[2]

What followed bears no easier explanation: after being forced into temporary retreat for a few years Mao hit back with the launch of the Cultural Revolution in 1966, aiming to topple what he saw as an excessive bureaucratic Party leadership under his number two, Liu Shaoqi, and the loyal but realistic Deng Xiaoping. The next ten years brought the country to its knees as Mao switched course in alarming, irrational fashion creating the social, economic and political chaos of the Cultural Revolution.

Yet the Chairman remains the key figure of the People's Republic. His portrait looks out over Tiananmen Square. His face is on all banknotes. Buffeted by progress, some older people look back fondly to a previous era, forgetting the woes it brought. In Chongqing, Bo Xilai was able to build on patriotic sentiment by organizing the singing of 'Red Songs'. Acknowledging the truth about the Maoist era would face the Party with an extremely tricky problem since it loyally followed the Great Helmsman through all the disasters he visited on the country. There were occasional dissenting voices but they were slapped down. We have seen the fate of those who spoke out during the Hundred Flowers episode. In 1959, Mao's old comrade-in-arms Defence Minister Peng Dehuai was purged after raising criticism of the Great Leap. During the Cultural Revolution many old CCP figures were relentlessly 'struggled against' by Red Guards in mass-persecution sessions. A Party plenum condemned Liu Shaoqi as a 'highly venomous renegade' and 'exceptionally big bastard' with Zhou Enlai reported to have remarked: 'This one can be executed.' Liu was kept in solitary confinement on short rations in an unheated building and then deprived of medicines and refused hospital treatment before dying in November 1972 – his uncut hair was said to have grown to a foot in length.

At Mao's urging, the Party accepted as his heir the civil war Marshal, Lin Biao, promoter of the Chairman's Little Red Book and a man subject to manifold phobias including moving air and running water, which was said to induce diarrhoea in him – Mao's doctor said he never bathed but was rubbed down with hot towels and squatted on a bedpan rather than using a lavatory. After Lin died in a plane crash fleeing from what may or may not have been a coup attempt engineered by his highly ambitious wife and son, the CCP accepted as the new putative successor a young radical from Shanghai, Wang Hongwen, to whom Mao had taken a shine but who had none of the skill or experience needed to run the country.[3]

Even if it wished to, the Party cannot blame the Cultural Revolution simply on Mao's madness. It went along; and, if it is always correct, then simply describing those ten years as a time of disaster is not enough. Historical truth and infallibility are uneasy bedfellows, so truth has to go out of the window.

Not that Mao is the only problem the Party has with history. The anniversaries of the massacre in Beijing on 4 June 1989 remain a highly sensitive time. The memoirs of the reformist Party leader Zhao Ziyang showed him still as a true believer who could not understand how his opponents had bent the rules to ditch him. Though he may appear naive, he has a point which those in power subsequently would be hard put to explain away. When Zhao died in 2005 the news was relayed to the public in a two-line report from Xinhua. The leadership declared 'a period of extreme sensitivity', put the PLA on alert, formed an Emergency Response Leadership Small Group and ordered travellers heading for Beijing to be screened. His close associate, Bao Tong, who was criticized by conservatives in 1989 for wearing jeans, remains under virtual detention in his sixth-floor apartment in western Beijing.[4]

Though Hong Kong is the only place where the dead are publicly remembered, there was a strange occurrence on June 4, 2012 when the Shanghai stock exchange index closed down by 64.89 points, echoing the 6-4-89 date of the massacre. There have been reports that Wen Jiabao has raised the matter of reopening the official verdict, but the regime remains intent on owning this part of its history, like all others. An elderly campaigner whose son was killed in the massacre is dogged by police when she goes to the spot to honour him. A newspaper in Chengdu that ran a classified advertisement paying tribute to 'the mothers of June 4' without its staff grasping the reference suffered official sanctions. Blank looks are the response from young Chinese to whom Westerners show pictures of the events and of the white-shirted man who stood up to the tanks. The intersection on a ring road where much of the killing took place is now awash with modern tower blocks, a McDonald's, the Orient Beautiful Women's Gym and the Dongying Beauty Shaping Club; when I went there around the twentieth anniversary of the killings, the main feature was a huge advertising panel featuring David Beckham.

The events of 1989 have their resonance more directly with today's leadership. Wen Jiabao was photographed standing behind Zhao Ziyang when he went to the square in an unavailing effort to get the students to return to their campuses and avoid bloodshed, while Deng marked Hu Jintao out for promotion on the basis of the repression of protests in Tibet that year when he was in charge of the Himalayan region. The son and daughter of the now aged Li Peng hold significant positions. The PLA has a reputational issue having fulfilled its role as the Party army ready to act against the people.

The regime's hope is that people forget what happened in 1989, and that the young do not learn about it, as Chan Koonchung sets out in his fine novel, *The Fat Years*, which has not been published in China. In the book, the rulers have induced national amnesia about events similar to those of 1989 as their country has raced ahead of the West; an official explains that this is what the people desired – 'If [they] had not already wanted to forget, we could not have forced them to do so.' It is an apt metaphor for the way in which the regime calculates that growing prosperity will wipe out its failings, past and present. That has not yet been achieved but such a prospect makes control of history essential.[5]

So, like dynasties before it, the CCP denies what it wishes to hide and extols what it sees as positive for its cause. As we will see, this creates a climate of falsehood that runs far more widely through the People's Republic and creates the constant risk that history and the truth will bite back.

11

SHADOWS OF THE PAST

For all the evasion of the realities of the recent past, there is another sense in which China's modern history comes to the aid of the regime. To see why that is the case one has to go back over the centuries, starting with the 125 years before economic reform gave the PRC a fresh economic start that led to the social changes of the past three decades.

No country has suffered such protracted bad times on such a scale as China from the mid-nineteenth century to the end of the Cultural Revolution. The official version blames this primarily on the 'century of humiliation' at the hands of foreigners, beginning with the British incursion in the First Opium War of 1839–42. The imposition of treaty ports in which Europeans, Americans and then Japanese could do business freely under their own laws was undoubtedly an exercise of colonialism often conducted brutally and combined with the 'muscular Christianity' of some missionaries.[1]

The opium trade that lay behind Britain's predatory policies was an abomination. But the foreign enclaves, notably Shanghai, became the most materially advanced places in the country, with electricity, sewage, freedom of movement, global trade links and a fairly independent legal system. Their appeal was such that the bulk of the population of the International Settlement and French Concession in Shanghai (to take two examples) were Chinese who found them better places to inhabit than the native section of the city. 'In the international settlement,' one Chinese wrote, 'the roads reach everywhere. In the [native] city, the roads are narrow. The international settlement is exceptionally clean. Its cars do not leave a cloud of dust. People who live there think of it as a paradise. In the [native] city, although there is a street-cleaning bureau, the stench from the river attacks the nose, and latrines lie adjacent to one another [...] the difference between the city and the international settlement is that between heaven and earth.'[2]

The mutual incomprehension between the Chinese and British was complete. The Qing were focused on land, not the sea, and did not grasp the way in which global trading systems backed by naval power had changed the world balance or see how backward their military forces were. The foreigners were no threat to the dynasty; the emperor at the time of the First Opium War remarked that they were 'not worth attending to' and senior mandarins dismissed the British as 'an insignificant and detestable race [...] in the class of dogs and horses.'[3]

However, the 'century of humiliation' narrative is only a partial explanation of China's transition from the zenith of the Qing dynasty around 1800 to the status of the Sick Man of Asia by 1900. The greater threat to the dynasty and to its claim to offer stability and unity in return for obeisance sprang from internal weaknesses that bubbled to the surface from 1850 onwards. Territorial expansion and population growth stretched the imperial treasury and the civil service. A succession of huge midcentury rebellions spread across the empire, sparked by peasant discontent, the decline in central authority and separatist aspirations.

The largest, by the Taiping, who originated on the border of Guizhou and Guangdong, espoused a creed that mixed Christianity and a form of primitive Communism with the sharing of land and wealth, gender separation and a ban on opium. As a Taiping song put it:

> Those with millions owe us money.
> Those who are half-poor half-rich can till their fields.
> Those with ambitions but no cash should go with us.
> Broke or hungry, Heaven will keep you well.

Hong Xiuquan, the leader of this search for a Heavenly Kingdom on earth, was a village teacher in his late thirties who, during what appeared to be a depressive fit after failing the imperial civil-service examination, convinced himself that he was the son of the Christian God who had ascended to heaven. God had charged him with eradicating demons on earth, which he identified as the Qing. The rulers, a Taiping tract declared, had 'unleashed grasping officials and corrupt subordinates to strip the people of their flesh until men and women weep by the road-side [...] the rich hold the power and the heroes despair.'

The Taiping surged north in 1851 and, despite some defeats along the way, took the imperial southern capital of Nanjing to establish their capital there, massacring the Manchu inhabitants and crowning Hong as their supreme leader. Under the command of some impressive generals, their armies roamed through a dozen provinces, getting as far as Sichuan and Tianjin before the Han gentry came to the dynasty's aid, raising local forces and gradually gaining the upper hand, in places with the aid of foreign mercenaries. There was no quarter on either side. 'All who resist us are [...] idolatrous demons and we will kill them without sparing,' Hong declared while the main gentry leader, Zeng Guofan, a devoted Confucian from Hunan, warned his opponents that 'every person will be crushed'.[4]

The Heavenly Kingdom sank into bloody internal feuds. Its rulers gave up their original egalitarian pledges in favour of high living, rather than ruling; Hong preferred to spend time with his sixty-eight wives and listening to music played on an organ taken from a Christian church to his palace. The best Taiping general, Shi Dakai, left Nanjing after rivals killed his wife and daughter and wandered with an army through western China before being cornered by imperial forces; he surrendered on condition that his men were spared and 4,000 were allowed to escape but 2,000 were slaughtered as they slept and their commander was sliced to death. In 1864, forces under Zeng Guofan encircled Nanjing. The city had no food; Hong died – probably after eating poisonous weeds that he proclaimed to be manna from Heaven. Nanjing fell and a bloodbath ensued, as it did in other cities taken by the pro-imperial forces. More than 20 million died in the fourteen years of the Taiping revolt.

At the same time, the Qing were also rocked by a British–French punitive expedition against Beijing in 1860 – launched after fresh incidents involving traders and because China was alleged to have breached the Treaty of Nanjing, which had ended the First Opium War. The emperor was forced to flee to his hunting estate to the north, where he died amid a succession crisis. The Summer Palace was ransacked by the foreign troops; one of them, Charles Gordon (later to become famous as 'Chinese Gordon' before dying in the Sudan fighting the revolt led by the Mahdi), lamented in a letter to his mother that 'these palaces were so large, and we were so pressed for time, that we could not plunder them carefully'. He went on to help Zeng's forces defeat the Taiping at the head of a mercenary force known as the Ever Victorious Army.

As if this was not enough, Xinjiang seceded under a Muslim leader, Yakub Beg, while another Islamic group declared an independent kingdom in Dali in the south-west. A vast army of bandit horsemen known as the Nien fought lightning campaigns from the east coast to the vicinity of Beijing. Imperial order was eventually restored but only at the price of the throne ceding authority to the provincial gentry and the armies it raised to make up for the deficiencies of the Manchu forces. The Dowager Empress Cixi emerged as the main power at court until her death in 1908, but she had little idea of how to cope with the challenges facing China as the modern world intruded and the Han gentry became increasingly disillusioned with their rulers. As convinced Confucians, men like Zeng venerated the established order: everybody should know their social rank and keep to it, he said, just as hats and shoes were not mixed up. But the gentry leader worried that the court was promoting functionaries for their 'smart demeanour and smooth speech' rather than their ability and that officials were shirking their duties and 'shilly-shallying'.

The Nien rebellion subsided after one of Zeng's protégés, Li Hongzhang, who had fought the Taiping and who would go on to become the leading figure among the late-century economic modernizers, applied a strategy known as 'strengthening the walls and cleaning up the countryside' – in other words encircling the rebels, depriving them of food to the point at which they resorted to cannibalism, and then killing them. A final Nien thrust took its army to within eighty miles of Beijing but it was turned back by forces under Li and Zuo Zongtang, another gentry general from Hunan. In August 1868 the last Nien leader dashed into a river on his horse and was drowned. However, the Shandong–Henan–Anhui triangle that had bred the revolt remained unsettled and would later provide many members of the Boxer Rising; but, for the moment, imperial rule was restored.

Another imperial army surrounded the Hui Muslims' capital in Dali at the end of 1871. The leader of the revolt donned his robes and swallowed a lethal dose of opium as he was carried in a yellow sedan chair to the enemy camp. He was dead on arrival but his head was cut off nevertheless and a ferocious attack took the city; all Muslims were killed and more than 20,000 ears were sent back to Beijing as a sign of the victory.

The gentry general Zuo Zongtang led the re-conquest of Xinjiang (after its leader sent an unanswered appeal to Britain to act as peacemaker). His 'Go West' policy got imperial backing when he pointed out the danger that Russia, which had already moved into the frontier zone on the Ili River, would expand further if China did not reassert itself. After raising loans from the Hong Kong and Shanghai Bank, Zuo led a 60,000-strong army on a methodical campaign in 1876 into Uighur territory that reached the rebel capital of Kashgar, where Yakub Beg committed suicide. The sinicization of the region began as Han moved in and Chinese ways were imposed on the local people.

After the shocks of the four major rebellions, which had been accompanied by a string of smaller risings, the economy revived for a time. Li Hongzhang, an imposing figure of a man and an accomplished scholar who became, in effect, China's foreign minister, led fellow Self Strengtheners to develop industry, arsenals, mines and railways by importing foreign technology and experts as the PRC would do nearly a century later. But their efforts were tiny compared with China's industrial backwardness and they were always dependent on imperial favour and finance. The country which had once invented so much now lacked entrepreneurial spirit. Finance was weak. The institutions that promoted change in the West, such as an independent legal system and at least partially representative government were lacking. There was no significant middle class. Confucianism placed merchants and their ilk at the bottom of the social order. Corruption wormed away at new enterprises. Resources were far from the manufacturing centres. Cixi and her court were not convinced of the benefits of industry and many Chinese regarded such innovations as the railways as devilish devices designed to disturb the spirits of their ancestors. A listing by the historian Immanuel Hsü of the new undertakings set up in 1885–95 shows a total of seven textile plants, three iron works, two match factories, two mints, one paper mill and three mines, one each for gold, coal and iron.[5]

The authority of the throne was severely undercut and Han Chinese began to condemn their rulers as failing to uphold the values that made China unique. Catastrophic defeat at the hands of the rising Asian power, Japan, in 1894–45 was a fresh shock to the system, and led to the empire being compared to a 'vast jellyfish' unable to come to terms with modern conditions. The young Guangxu emperor, chosen for the throne by Cixi before she went into semi-retreat at the Summer Palace, reacted to the humiliation by launching a headlong quest for change in the Hundred Days of Reform in 1898, issuing decrees to change everything from education to the military, from agriculture to freedom of the press. The bureaucracy was horrified and the sheer speed and scale of the reform effort meant it quickly became completely unrealistic. The Manchu nobles and senior Han army generals closed ranks against change. Cixi returned to the Forbidden City, stopped the reform pro-gramme and consigned the emperor to spend the rest of his life cooped up in the Summer Palace.

The dynasty then made things even worse for itself by siding with the anti-foreign Boxer movement, which surged out of the Nien heartland in Shandong. There was fresh humiliation at the hands of the interna-tional force that marched on Beijing in 1900 to lift the siege of the Legation Quarter by the Chinese forces and Boxers, forcing Cixi and the emperor to flee on a long and painful exodus through western China while a huge indemnity was imposed that helped to ruin the national treasury for decades to come.

The ruthless incursions by British, Japanese, Russians, French and Germans as they 'carved up the melon' were certainly a cause of national weakness but the prime causes were the inability of the Qing to evolve a modern state, popular discontent that erupted in the mid-century revolts but simmered on during the ensuing decades among the Han, and the resulting racial divide between rulers and ruled.

When the Qing were finally overthrown by the revolution of 1911–12, there was no new political system to guide the nation forward. Sun Yat-sen, the revolutionary from Guangdong who had campaigned so tirelessly against the Qing, spent ten weeks as President of the Republic. He presided over a chaotic government whose remit did not reach much beyond its headquarters in Nanjing, but then handed over to a military strongman, Yuan Shikai. Sun chose not to participate in China's first parliamentary elections, held in early 1913. The Kuomintang scored a big victory in his absence under a young politician, Song Jiaoren, who had locked horns with the Father of the Republic – Sun was a believer in authoritarian leadership, even if he was not able to practise it, but Song wanted a parliamentary democracy. The argument became moot when Yuan's agents assassinated the younger man as he boarded a train in Shanghai to go to Beijing to claim the premiership.

After that Yuan declared himself emperor, though the opposition he encountered soon forced him to step down from the throne. Following his death in 1916, China lapsed into anarchy on a national scale under the rule of regional warlords. The May Fourth reform movement, which broke out in 1919 after China was humiliated by the Allies at the

Versailles Peace Conference by the transfer of former German concessions in Shandong to Japan, left its intellectual legacy but made little practical progress in its efforts to wean the country on to an iconoclastic path of democracy and science. Sun retreated to Guangzhou (Canton) to head a wobbly republic he set up with the backing of petty warlords but which then enlisted Soviet aid and formed a Kuomintang–Communist Party alliance. He died in 1925, after offering territorial concessions to the Japanese on the basis that they would agree to help him reunite the nation and floating a scheme by which the United States, Britain, Germany, France and Italy would send in forces to wrest control of provincial capitals, railways, ports, rivers and the telegraph from the warlords and run them for five years. Neither proposal got anywhere but they shed an interesting light on the proponent of Chinese nationalism who still knew how much ground his country had to make up.[6]

His successor, Chiang Kai-shek, realized Sun's dream by leading the victorious Northern Expedition from the South which, to general surprise, defeated some major warlords, took Wuhan, Nanjing and Shanghai and enabled him to form the Nationalist Government in Nanjing in 1927, co-opting some militarists and turning the Kuomintang on a right-wing course. Ambitious plans were laid for sweeping reforms and national development. Shanghai blossomed. But implementation of the government's programme was poor and most of the country was left behind as the Nationalist regime was bogged down by recurrent regional revolts, lack of cash, ineffectiveness and corruption. There were huge national disasters. China was led by a general – later Generalissimo – who was a poor military tactician but an expert at political manoeuvre, and aimed to establish a regime best described by the historian Frederic Wakeman as 'Confucian Fascism'.

In 1931 the Japanese army seized Manchuria and expanded steadily into northern China. Chiang concentrated on trying to wipe out the Communists, who had been allied with the Kuomintang after the foundation of the CCP but on whom Chiang turned in a bloody White Terror in 1927. The Nationalists managed to force Mao and other leaders to flee from their bases in southern and central China and to undertake a series of long marches to their haven at Yan'an in the north. Unrelenting, Chiang – a martinet who hated to change his mind – prepared a final assault from the city of Xi'an.

But the commander of the offensive, Zhang Xueliang, the 'Young Marshal' and former warlord of Manchuria who had been driven out by the Japanese when they occupied his homeland in 1931, came to believe that China should unite to combat the Japanese (and regain his territory). So he engaged in secret negotiations with the supposed 'enemy of the heart' and kidnapped Chiang when he visited Xi'an at Christmas 1936. After this, Zhang did not know what to do next. Having initially relished the thought of putting Chiang on trial before a people's court, the Communists in Yan'an received instructions from Moscow that they should get him freed, since Stalin saw the Generalissimo as the best national leader for China. Mao's lieutenant, Zhou Enlai, travelled to Xi'an and joined in negotiations that ended with the liberation of Chiang and an uneasy common front against the invader; this alliance frayed with the years and broke apart after Nationalist troops attacked Communist forces in the Lower Yangtze at the beginning of 1941.

Chiang had not been as passive towards the Japanese as was often supposed. He had laid defence plans and modernized some army units. But it proved to be too little when Tokyo's forces launched all-out war after a clash outside Beijing in July 1937. Nationalist forces in northern China were routed though they put up an epic three-month struggle in Shanghai. After being defeated there in November 1937, the Nationalist forces retreated up the Yangtze to the capital of Nanjing, which was then abandoned. This opened the way to a huge massacre by Japanese troops in the Rape of Nanjing; estimates of the death toll range from 80,000 to the official Chinese total of 300,000 with horrific acts of savagery by the invaders.

The Generalissimo moved his capital to Wuhan, where something approaching a government of national unity was formed with the Communists and other political groups. Chiang sought to halt the enemy advance by having the dykes on the Yellow River breached to flood farmland where some 6 million people lived. The Nationalists won a notable victory in the town of Taierzhuang by the Grand Canal but the Japanese rolled on before long and the government fled Wuhan for Chongqing, safe behind the Yangtze Gorges, a city described by one visitor as resembling 'a junk heap of boxes piled together', where for seven years it waited for Japan's defeat. American aid was forthcoming after Pearl Harbor at the end of 1941 but Franklin Roosevelt avoided sending troops to China.

Great throngs of refugees crisscrossed the country, often in terrible conditions, strafed by Japanese planes, subject to gouging by Nationalist forces. A devastating famine ravaged central China in 1943. The Japanese took over all the major cities east of Sichuan, acting with extreme brutality as they launched campaigns such as the 'Three Alls': kill all, burn all, destroy all. The Nationalists won some further victories, notably at Changsha. The Communists launched one major attack, the Hundred Regiments offensive of 1940, which was a flop. Many stretches of rural China remained outside the permanent control of the invaders, but the country as a whole was devastated and that devastation was ratcheted up when civil war broke out between Nationalists and Communists after Japan's defeat in 1945.

Aided by the Americans, Chiang's forces did well initially and forced the PLA back to the north of Manchuria. But the Nationalists' own incompetence, and the superior skills of their opponents helped by the Soviets, plus a temporary ceasefire imposed by the Americans when the PLA was on the ropes, caused them to lose ground. Successive major victories in Manchuria, including the starvation siege of one large city, opened the way for the Communists to advance on Beijing and Tianjin, which surrendered. A huge battle in eastern China at the end of 1948 brought another major victory. Chiang had already prepared his bolt-hole in Taiwan and, after Nanjing fell, formally resigned from his state posts, though he continued to pull the strings from not so far behind the scenes. By the end of 1949, however, the situation had become impossible and he flew out of Chengdu to his new island home, taking with him the Republic of China.

The long era of twentieth-century wars had exhausted China, and the new regime was seen by many – including non-Communists – as the much-needed fresh start after decline stretching back for 100 years or more. China was soon plunged into another war but this time beyond its own borders in Korea as it sought to assert its rebirth and to resist the possibility of US forces establishing themselves on its frontier. Domestically, the country underwent its first true revolution as land was redistributed to peasants and the state took over business. The mass-mobilization techniques used by the Communists in Yan'an and during the civil war became a hallmark of the regime. Mao's personality cult, which had been nurtured since the Long March, engulfed the nation. The New China born in 1949 was never a liberal place but the rush to enable the People's Republic to 'stand up' bred a degree of popular enthusiasm for the new project. However, the criticism enunciated during the Hundred Flowers liberalization tilted the regime towards repressive control that was soon combined with the wild adventurism of a leader trying to pursue utopian goals but plunging his country into disasters which grew ever more enormous as he refused to admit to error.

The Maoist catastrophes formed a climax to the century of turbulence and tribulation endured by China's people. Nobody can say for sure how many people perished as a direct or indirect result of the Chairman's policies but it is certainly more than 60 million. It was a terrible conclusion to a terrible century and a quarter of extreme woe.

The post-Mao story has many fault lines, and includes the decision by the leadership to unleash tanks against its own people in 1989. But there can be no doubt that, for all the problems they face, most Chinese today know that on the whole this is the best era in which to live in their country for a very long time. Hu Jintao, Wen Jiabao, Xi Jinping and their colleagues have problems with modern historical comparisons because of the legacy of the first three decades of the PRC. But one of their greatest strengths lies in what went before. To that extent, history does serve the regime, though not in ways that it can fully exploit.

They can use the past as evidence that they offer a greater degree of stability than was enjoyed in the period from 1850 to 1976. Equally, the need for national unity can be invoked in an effort to justify the occupation of Tibet and Xinjiang. History serves China's rulers in other ways, too. They can revel in its length and achievements. The country houses the world's oldest continuous civilization, stretching back to beyond the oracle bones of the Shang dynasty 3,500 years ago; its current length is officially put at 5,000 years, give or take a few centuries. Its imperial system lasted for more than two millennia and produced a unique meritocratic civil service selected by competitive examination – even if, as always, those whose parents and grandparents had already risen in the social scale were most likely to succeed.

China has perhaps the richest set of cultural traditions on earth, with a plethora of inventions from gunpowder, movable type and the use of paper to wheelbarrows, umbrellas and the compass. The Great Wall, started in primitive form by the First Emperor but built mainly much later, is one of the world's best-known landmarks (albeit that a Chinese astronaut disproved the long-held belief that it was the only man-made structure that could be seen from outer space). The Terracotta Warriors are a great global treasure, making periodic trips to be shown at faraway museums. Martial-arts films have brought the sagas of legendary warriors, princesses and great rulers to audiences round the planet. Confucius is a familiar name to people abroad who have little idea of the teachings attributed to him or how they were adopted as a national behaviour system. While the Forbidden City, having been built in the early fifteenth century when the Ming moved the capital from Nanjing, is really not so very ancient, it is nonetheless a site of majesty and power.

This history has led to the depiction of China as a 'civilization state' rooted in Confucian traditions. These urge one to deal with others as one would wish them to behave to oneself, advise rulers to pursue benevolence and require subjects to show filial piety not only to their fathers but also to all those in authority. This is said to give China a unique advantage when compared to Western nations with less historic ballast. Such a view is encouraged by the authorities who find filial piety towards the regime an estimable commodity, and who reserve for themselves the power to define the benevolence given in return for obedience – in line with the sage's observation that 'When a ruler loves anything, those below him are sure to love it more.'

In reality, China's history is far from the perpetual unrolling of a civilization over the centuries and most of its cities are singularly bereft of the legacy of the past to be found in, say, the architecture of London, Paris, Rome or Boston. It has been interspersed with lengthy periods of disunion and anything but civilized rule long before the disruptions of the century and a quarter before Mao's death. The idea that China has always been the same geographical shape is another fiction: if that were the case, why is the Great Wall outside Beijing rather than on China's far frontiers? Under the pressure of foreign incursions, the borders of the empire fluctuated – the Song dynasty spent 150 years ruling half the country from Hangzhou. Tibet and Xinjiang have been independent or beyond the control of the central Chinese government for long periods. The northern regions now contained in the PRC went their own way under tribal leaders who threatened imperial dynasties rather than being their servants. Hong Kong was ruled by the British for a century and a half and Macau by the Portuguese for longer. Taiwan, once a Dutch colony, was occupied by the Japanese from 1895 to 1945 and has been beyond Beijing's control since 1949. Manchuria was dominated by either Russia or Japan for half a century.

Within its borders, Chinese unity was an empty concept for three and a half centuries of virtually incessant warfare and instability after the fall of the Han in 200. The country was only 'one' during 570 of the 1,350 years covered by the eleventh-century historian Sima Guang. As well as the protracted wars between regional barons, the end of the Han marked the growth of millennial sects headed by the Yellow Turban agrarian rebels who were linked to a Daoist group that believed in equal rights for all and equal distribution of land. In the following centuries, similar sects and cults repeatedly disturbed the veneer of national unity. At court the supposedly national power structure was dented by regional barons, warlords and, from time to time, the influence of eunuchs.

The country's volatility was well demonstrated by the history of the city of Luoyang on the central China plain, which had been chosen as its seat by the Eastern Zhou ruling house as far back as 771 BC. The Han made it their capital in 25 AD. During a revolt in 189 it was burned down. Rebuilt a decade later, it flowered until it was caught up in civil wars and sacked in 311. Han rule was restored in 416 but tribes from the north took Luoyang seven years later, only for the Song to drive them out seven years after that. At the end of the sixth century the city was re-established as the imperial capital and enjoyed three decades of prosperity, during which it expanded with fine roads, water channels, an imposing palace and a thriving Buddhist culture. Then another group of raiders from the north stormed in and massacred inhabitants. Finally, in 534, Luoyang was abandoned. At the start of the seventh century the Sui emperor Yang Di put two million labourers to work on a new city nearby, on the site where today's Luoyang stands. As a general-poet lamented during one of its periods of destruction:

> How desolate in Luoyang,
> Its palace burned down,
> The walls fallen in ruins,
> As brambles climb to the sky . . .
> There are no paths to walk,
> Unworked fields have run to waste . . .
> Lonely in the countryside,
> A thousand *li* without one smoking hearth.[7]

Celebrated as one of the high points of Chinese civilization, the Tang dynasty, which ruled from 618 to 907 AD, was marked by repeated upheavals that show just how unstable and divided China could be even when not formally in a period of disunion. The first Tang ruler, a northern general who took the name of Gaozu, came to power by overthrowing the short-lived Sui dynasty. He spent much of his eight years on the throne bringing rival factions under control, and then abdicated in favour of second son, Taizong, who is generally painted as the paragon of an emperor – a scholar who encouraged the arts (including the famed Tang horse sculptures – the dynasty built up a stock of 700,000 steeds for the army). A great warrior, he entered the capital of Chang'an in golden armour followed by two rebel leaders he had captured and 10,000 heavily armed cavalry. A workaholic devoted to his country, he had documents pasted to the walls of his bedroom so that he could work if he awoke at night. He staged successful campaigns against the northern tribes, swept through Xinjiang into Central Asia, and sent a Tang princess to marry the King of Tibet with whom he signed a twenty-year peace treaty. As he aged, however, Taizong displayed the habitual signs of excessive power, spending more time hunting than working and indulging in lavish buildings – he was said to have had one which had required two million man-days to construct demolished because he found it too ostentatious and its location too hot.

His son, Gaozong, fell for the charms of one of his father's concubines, Wu Zhao (later Wu Zetian), who rose relentlessly to the top and declared her own dynasty, the Zhou, at the end of the seventh century, becoming China's only woman emperor and, as mentioned earlier, providing a rich vein of folklore about her bloody disposal of rivals and her lascivious sexual appetites.

In the following century, An Lushan, a forceful general born into a northern tribe, manipulated Tang court politics to enable him to rule over much of north-east China as a virtually autonomous fiefdom before launching an eight-year rebellion after the promotion of a rival as Chancellor in the imperial capital of Chang'an. His forces surged south to take Luoyang where he declared himself emperor. They then took Chang'an after the emperor had fled south. An became increasingly despotic and foul-tempered and was assassinated in 757 by his eldest surviving son, who feared that his father was planning to pass his heritage to a younger offspring.

The new emperor lasted for two years before he was executed by his father's leading general, Shi Siming, after a series of defeats by Tang forces. Shi proclaimed himself emperor but was taken prisoner in 761 by his eldest son, Shi Chaoyi, whom his father had threatened to kill for not having completed work on a fort. An associate of the younger Shi strangled the father and the son proclaimed himself emperor. But he, too, lasted for only two years, suffering repeated defeats by Tang armies and losing Luoyang. Rejected by his generals, Chaoyi fled towards his family's northern tribal heartland but was intercepted by Tang soldiers and hanged himself. One of his commanders had his head cut off and delivered to the Tang. The toll in the extended conflict is estimated by Professor Steven Pinker of Harvard to have resulted in more deaths in relation to the global population of the time than any other war or disaster, equivalent to 429 million in twentieth-century terms.[8]

The fall of the Tang in 907 led to another half-century of division, known as the era of 'Five Dynasties and Ten Kingdoms', when China was divided among warlords and millions of bandits ran amok. The Song dynasty restored unity and order but came under growing pressure from northern tribes, which took over a wide belt of territory running from Inner Mongolia to the Eastern Sea. In 1126 the Jin people from Manchuria took the Song capital of Kaifeng, laid waste other major cities and captured the emperor, forcing the dynasty to flee to Hangzhou in the south as China was once more divided. Then came the Mongol invasion, which defeated the Southern Song in a three-week naval battle in which the Chinese lost 800 ships and 100,000 men died. For the first time, the whole country came under alien rule and it was very foreign – the rampaging, fast-riding Mongols were from a completely different background to their subjects and resisted sinicization. Their Yuan dynasty lasted for only eighty-nine years and left few traces, even if its summer capital of Shangdu bequeathed a literary landmark in Samuel Taylor Coleridge's imagined Xanadu (and the home of Charles Foster Kane).

The Ming, who took the throne in 1368 at the head of rebel armies and secret societies, restored Han rule but the death of the dynasty's first ruler, Hongwu, was followed by civil war between the heir and his uncle, who emerged victorious as the forceful emperor Yongle – ruling for two decades and moving the capital from Nanjing to Beijing, where he built the Forbidden City. Facing renewed pressure from the Mongols, the mid-fifteenth-century Ming ruler Zhengtong launched a campaign against his northern foe which was a huge disaster, with many of his half-a-million-strong army killed. Satisfied with capturing the emperor, the Mongols went back to their homeland and did not repeat their invasion of China. When Zhengtong was released, his successor sent only two horses and a sedan chair to bring him home, and he was kept in detention for six years before being restored to the throne.

China subsequently developed under one of its longest serving rulers, Wanli (1573–1620), with the import of new crops, tax reform, the growth of manufacturing and trade. But the court became increasingly dissolute as Wanli spent enormous sums on palaces and tombs and corruption soared. There were renewed threats from the Mongols, the Jurchen (precursors of the Manchu), minority tribes in the south-west – and the Japanese, who invaded the Chinese protectorate of Korea. Under Wanli's successors, eunuchs became increasingly powerful at court, much resented by officials and the Han gentry. When a eunuch called Wei Zhongxian assumed power, with the apparent blessing of an illiterate emperor, and had six Confucians who had tried to instil old values beaten to death, it was assumed that the Ming had lost the Mandate of Heaven – a conclusion helped by high taxation and Wei's reign of terror. As large bandit gangs rampaged round the countryside, a rebel army marched into Beijing but the Manchus rode down from the north to oust it and claim the throne.

The way in which the later Qing lost control of large parts of China for protracted periods in the middle of the nineteenth century has been recounted, as has the depressing story of the subsequent warlord period of the Nationalist Republic. Against such a historical story, it is difficult to view China as resting on a sustained record of national unity. The aspiration may have been there and may feed contemporary accounts, but the reality was, all too often, otherwise.

If the image of China as an eternal united nation existing within set frontiers needs serious modification then so does the notion that for most of its history under the empire it was isolated from the world, a giant living on its own in a deep sense of self-satisfaction unwilling to engage with other nations and free from foreign influences, somehow uniquely 'Chinese' in its Confucian culture.

External links date back to the Neolithic era, when the jade used in religious rituals in China was imported from present-day Burma to the south and the Tarim Basin to the west. Around 2,000 BC the techniques of metallurgy entered China across the steppes from the Black Sea. The discovery in the Tarim Basin of Caucasian mummies wearing clothing originating from central Asia bear witness to the flow of people from the west, while China's cultivation of the silkworm gave it a valued export. The Silk Road ran from Xi'an to Central Asia and Europe well before the birth of Christ and was used by travellers of many nationalities; the marvellously preserved sculptures and wall paintings in hundreds of caves near Dunhuang, which first flourished more than 2,000 years ago as a key garrison town on the trading route, bear witness to the presence of non-Han merchants and travellers. They lie on the route along which Buddhism entered the country around 150 AD. The foreign religion was subsequently promoted by non-Han rulers who

wanted to limit the influence of Confucianism – 'Buddha being a bar-
barian god is the very one we should worship,' as one of the tribal
chieftains from the northern steppes put it. Islam was brought to China
in the early seventh century by companions of Muhammad who had
advised, 'Seek for knowledge even unto China.'

Merchants from Shanxi on the northern edge of the Han lands
traded food, furs and other commodities with peoples living far away to
the north and west. Arab and Persian traders set up communities in
major inland cities and along the coast; Guangzhou had four mosques.
The Jews from Persia whose descendants still live in Kaifeng settled
there around the end of the first millennium, marrying Chinese women
and establishing the community that provided the empire with mandarins and military officers.

Under the Southern Song (1127–1279), a Muslim was Director
General of Shipping, and more than 5,000 of his co-religionists were
invited in from present-day Uzbekistan as a protection force against foreign raiders. The Mongol Yuan dynasty that followed made even more
use of foreigners to balance the influence of the Han while importing
its native habits with it. Persians and Arabs held official posts, particularly in dealing with finance and taxation. Muslim scholars were
employed at court. Even if some believe that Marco Polo never made
his celebrated journey and merely retailed the stories of others, envoys
and traders from Venice, France, the Vatican, the Middle East and
Flanders certainly travelled to do business in China at that time. The
great Muslim traveller Ibn Battuta visited Fujian and Hangzhou in the
mid-fourteenth century. The emperor who founded the Ming dynasty
in 1368 employed six Muslim generals, including one who clinched a
decisive victory against the Mongols in their northern homeland.
Under his son, the Yongle emperor, the Muslim eunuch admiral Zheng
took huge Chinese ships to the shores of Africa in the early sixteenth
century and, enthusiasts would say, also reached to America and
Australia before Yongle's successors decided that China should not be
a maritime power and banned even trade with Japan.[9]

In 1571 Spanish traders exchanged silver from their country's possessions in South America with Chinese merchants for silks and
porcelain in probably the first three-way global commercial

transaction. The import of new crops from the Americas gave an important boost to food supply.

After the Manchus had established a new foreign ruling house in 1644, China was linked to other parts of their far-flung multiethnic, multicultural empire. Jesuits thrived at the early Qing court after Matteo Ricci was allowed to travel to the capital, where among many others he met a Jew from Kaifeng and spread news of the existence of the community there. Ricci, a consummate diplomat as well as a painter who also introduced the art of perspective to Chinese painters, was succeeded by fellow missionary diplomats Adam Schell von Bell and John Schneck before the emperor decided that the claims of the Pope were incompatible with his own pretensions.[10]

The eighteenth-century European vogue for *Chinoiserie* brought porcelain, tea and Chinese art to Europe; the parks of stately homes were adorned with pagodas and pavilions and Chinese wallpaper became a fashionable adjunct for grand homes. Canton may have been the only port authorized to conduct foreign trade with the strangers; there were measures to deter Chinese from unauthorized fraternization including death. Still, plenty of unlicensed ships sailed from Fujian and other coastal areas. Migrants from the mainland established Chinatowns round the globe, laboured on the Gold Rush in the United States and ran the iconic Chinese laundries in Western cities.

In the mid-nineteenth century as many as 5,000 cases of Chinese tea passed daily through the Russian frontier post of Kyakhta, south of Lake Baikal. Long caravans guarded by Cossacks trekked to western Russia and returned with furs, precious metals and European goods – the Shanxi merchants controlled their distribution in the Middle Kingdom and established branches in major Russian cities, almost certainly learning banking practices there, which they brought back to China where they became the predominant financial operators in the late imperial era. An early nineteenth-century Chinese writer recorded that 'every year Shanxi merchants transport countless silk, cloth, tea, sugar, cigarettes and china to Lanzhou and Xinxiang or, through Kyakhta to Russia, to their branches as far as Moscow and St Petersburg.' One 'Tea Road' stretched from Beijing to the Russian border and then on to the west of the country; another snaked up the Himalayas from Yunnan.[11]

Under the concessions forced on the Qing by defeat in the First Opium War and extended after the 1860 punitive expedition to Beijing, the British, French, Russians, Germans, Japanese and Italians established themselves across China; most gathered on the coast but some journeyed to 'up-country stations' and mining towns. They were joined by missionaries who, though notoriously unsuccessful at conversion, affected the ordinary lives of the Chinese around them as they ran schools, hospitals and orphanages.

After the fall of the Qing, the military strongman Yuan Shikai engaged an American adviser, F. J. Goodnow, who egged him on in his short-lived spell as emperor. Some of the warlords who ruled China after Yuan's death in 1916 also took on foreign advisers. The 'Old Marshal' of Manchuria kept a cellar of fine French wines and his son, the 'Young Marshal', engaged the Australian journalist W. H. Donald as an adviser. The murderous 'Dogmeat General' of Shandong ate off a forty-piece Belgian dinner service, offering honoured guests French champagne and what the *New York Times* correspondent described as 'sound brandy'. Sun Yat-sen saw models for China in the British educational, legal and urban facilities of Hong Kong and its lack of corruption. The 'Father of the Republic' lived for a time in a European-style house on the rue Molière in the French Concession of Shanghai with a croquet lawn and a fine collection of English-language books; he also had a bodyguard from London's East End, Morris 'Two-Gun' Cohen, and signed his will with a Waterman pen. Elsewhere in the French Concession, the fledgling Chinese Communist Party opened its inaugural meeting in a deserted girl's school but moved on when snoopers who may have been police agents looked in.

Russian and Dutch emissaries sent by Moscow acted as midwives in the birth of the Communist Party in Shanghai in 1921. Two Soviet emissaries, Mikhail Markovich Grunzeberg and General Vasilii Konstantinovich Blyukher, who went under the pseudonyms of Borodin and Galen respectively, advised the Kuomintang in Canton – the first reshaping Sun Yat-sen's party on Leninist lines and the second providing the strategic genius for Chiang Kai-shek's Northern Expedition.

Sun Yat-sen was treated for his terminal liver cancer at an American hospital in Beijing and, on the Northern Expedition in 1926, the dental clinic where Chiang Kai-shek had an impacted wisdom tooth treated was run by Yale University in the Hunan capital of Changsha. Later, the 'Young Marshal' of Manchuria was cured of his morphine addiction by an American physician. Shanghai's powerful Song family were converts to Methodism; the Generalissimo joined them in their Western faith after pledging to do so if he was saved from an impending battlefield disaster – which he was, by a snowstorm.

After he sent the Soviets packing in 1927 Chiang took on a succession of German military advisers while foreign experts flooded in to the capital of Nanjing to give advice on the economy, the constitution and city planning; Henry Ford was listed among the advisers, though he accepted only on condition that he did not have to visit China. Foreign influences in the concessions affected young Chinese, who read Western books, worked for European, American and Japanese companies, built a thriving film industry, travelled abroad, attended tea dances and dressed in flapper frocks and blazers. American-educated Madame Chiang Kai-shek spread the China message in the US media. The Nationalist regime saw the rapid development of China's institutional links with the rest of the world as its diplomats played a significant role in international bodies. China exports expanded. Though the tea and silk industries were hit by foreign competition, the historian Robert Bickers has pointed out that 90 per cent of egg products imported into Britain before 1941 came from China – so 'the chances were very high that British consumers of biscuits, cakes, sweets or ice-creams ingested something made in China'. Shanghai was a global trading centre, absorbing foreign influences to form a bridge between China and the rest of the world, visited by Bertrand Russell, Charlie Chaplin, Bernard Shaw, Aldous Huxley, Charles Lindberg, Douglas Fairbanks Jnr and Noël Coward.[12]

The Communists adopted a political philosophy of a German thinker and were advised from Moscow. At one point, after Chiang launched his 'White Terror' against them in 1927, the Party's official leadership moved to the Soviet capital (Mao was in semi-disgrace in the Jiangxi base in south-east China at the time). A German adviser, Otto Braun, was a dominant voice in urging a frontal military strategy against Nationalist attacks before this proved disastrous and Mao's guerrilla tactics won the day during the Long March. It was the Comintern in Moscow that issued the instruction to get Chiang Kai-shek freed after the Xi'an kidnapping in 1936. An American journalist, Edgar Snow, was chosen to write the first biography of Mao for the world. His compatriot Agnes Smedley danced with the PLA commander, Zhu De, in Yan'an and the Canadian Norman Bethune and Lebanese-American George Hatem provided medical expertise.

During the Second World War the Nationalists drew heavily on American supplies and financial aid. Though Roosevelt was careful not to commit US troops to the China theatre, he sent a leading general, Joseph 'Vinegar Joe' Stilwell, on an impossible mission to be Chiang's Chief of Staff. Stilwell began his tenure by telling the American journalist Theodore 'Teddy' White: 'The trouble in China is simple; we are allied to an ignorant, illiterate, superstitious peasant son of a bitch.' In his diary he called the Generalissimo 'the peanut', and later 'the rattlesnake'. Stilwell aggravated his case by forming a good opinion of the Communists to balance his disdain for the Nationalists and was eventually replaced by a more emollient military man, Albert Wedemeyer.

High-level American figures shuttled through the Nationalist capital of Chongqing, including Vice President Henry Wallace and Roosevelt's presidential opponent in 1940, Wendell Willkie, who had a dalliance with Madame Chiang. American pilots joined the Nationalists on a free-lance basis in the Flying Tigers force headed by the 'good ole boy' Texan Claire Lee Chennault, who fought ceaselessly with Stilwell and tolerated a brothel for his fliers in their base in southern China. A team sent to Yan'an by the US, known as the 'Dixie Mission' since it was operating in what Washington's Nationalist ally regarded as enemy territory, relayed favourable reports in ignorance of a terror-laden Rectification Campaign launched by Mao at the base to consolidate his power. (The diaries of the Comintern agent were less admiring as he recorded the PLA's reluctance to fight the Japanese and the growing of opium to raise revenue.) Roosevelt described the Communists as 'what we'd call agrarian socialists' and the OSS, the forerunner of the CIA, at one point proposed arming and training PLA troops, a project that Chiang quickly squelched. Mao wondered about visiting Washington.

Madame Chiang did so on a highly successful trip in 1943, during which she stayed at the White House (where Roosevelt put a card table between them so that she would not 'vamp' him), addressed rallies in Madison Square Garden and made an appearance at a gala evening at the Hollywood Bowl attended by an army of film stars. Henry Luce, head of the Time–Life magazine empire, who was born in China to missionary parents, was a diehard supporter. Congress rose to its feet to applaud the visitor when she addressed a joint session.

After the defeat of Japan, Harry Truman sent George Marshall, the US Chief of Staff during the Second World War, on a year-long mission to try to bring the Nationalists and Communists together; each side played the visitor for its own benefit and the future Secretary of State finally recognized the impossibility of his task. The truth was that Chiang and Mao, who met fruitlessly in Chongqing in 1945 under US auspices, were both intent on resuming the struggle for the mastery of China that dated back to 1927.

They both looked to support from outside the country. The Kuomintang armies depended on US transport, arms, logistics and money as well as the backing of friends in Congress. The Communists received Soviet training and weapons when they were pushed back in Manchuria in the early stages of the conflict; their final victory was aided by the American weapons they captured – Mao was driven in to Beijing to proclaim the People's Republic in a Dodge limousine and PLA troops entered the city in captured US trucks.

The Communist triumph ended China's engagement with the West as Mao decided to lean to the USSR. Anyway, Truman was fed up with the Nationalists, refusing to intervene to stop the PLA's advance and cold-shouldering Madame Chiang when she visited Washington. But a PRC–US rapprochement seemed highly unlikely and was soon ruled out by the Korean War, in which the two nations fought one another.

Mao's destination on the first trip he ever made outside China was Moscow, in December 1949, to negotiate a treaty. He was given a splendid welcome – though he showed anxiety during the journey, staggering white-faced and pouring with sweat as he walked along the platform in Sverdlovsk (he had suffered a similar attack after meeting Chiang in 1945).

Following the initial festivities Stalin left the visitor alone in his dacha, where he exclaimed: 'I have only three tasks here. The first is to eat; the second is to sleep; the third is to shit.' Still a Treaty of Friendship, Alliance and Mutual Assistance was concluded. China received a loan and industrial aid, albeit less than Mao had hoped for, and a secret clause recognized Manchuria and Xinjiang as falling on to the Soviet sphere of influence, though this meant little in practice. China followed the USSR in carrying out Five-Year Plans and adopted Stalinist heavy industrial policies while it nurtured links with foreign Communist nations. Meanwhile, across the Strait, the Korean War made Taiwan into a front-line bastion of anti-Communism as the US poured in not only money but also advice on developing the economy that saw the island move ahead of the mainland.

Not that Moscow was not helping Mao. More than 1,000 Soviet advisers went to help modernize China, including assistance for the PRC's atomic-weapons programme. Mao made another trip to Moscow. The true period of isolation came only after 1960, when the Chairman found Khrushchev's revisionism unpalatable. Amid Siberian border clashes, and after a war with Moscow's friend India, Beijing broke with the Kremlin. Mao then led his country on its own path, ending up with Albania as its only stalwart support along with assorted liberation movements in Africa and Latin America that looked to Beijing for aid and inspiration.

By the early 1970s isolation was less and less attractive. Richard Nixon's visit to China in 1972 produced little in practical terms but was the start of a watershed prompted in the short term by a mutual desire of both the President and Mao to get the better of the Soviet Union and, in the longer run, by the realization that the PRC could not stand aside from the world community. Yet it took another seven years before formal diplomatic relations were established with the USA after the Carter administration decided to switch recognition from the Republic of China on Taiwan to the People's Republic in Beijing. That was followed by Deng's triumphal visit to the US and the development of Sino-US relations which, however testy they may become at times, are probably the most important links in today's world.

The pattern was set when, soon after returning home and while welcoming American assistance in building up China, Deng clamped down on the Democracy Wall in Beijing and dissenters were sentenced to long jail terms. China was an integral part of the world it had never really left for any protracted period. At the same time, the Communist Party would put its own preservation first. For China's leaders, engagement with the world does not mean accepting foreigners' views of what is good for China. That leaves the rest of the globe to puzzle over what to make of today's PRC and how to deal with it.

12

THE WORLD AND CHINA

The simple answer to the first part of that last conundrum is that, in general, governments are at a loss as to how to respond to the rise of China, especially now that Beijing has abandoned Deng Xiaoping's twenty-four-character prescription to adopt a policy of 'biding time and hiding one's talents' while the PRC concentrated on its economic rise. Deng was content to work within a US-led global world as China grew, but the leadership in Beijing and its citizens – and army – now feel that their success entitles them to adopt a higher profile in pursuit of their 'core interests'. These are defined narrowly as consisting of the preservation of the domestic system, continuing rule over Tibet and the recovery of Taiwan – a Xinhua news agency commentary in September 2011 also included sovereignty over the islands and waters of the South China Sea, and subsequently Beijing added a crop of uninhabited islands off Japan. In addition, the PRC insists on free access to raw materials and denies the right of other countries to comment on its internal record on such matters as human rights, Tibet or Taiwan.[1]

Foreign powers can surely have qualms about the ascent of a state that operates so much to its own agenda and follows its own norms, but geopolitical and economic realities impel them to pursue a working relationship. The United States, the nation with most at stake, seeks to engage the People's Republic while hedging its bets by retaining an ability to confront the rising power in the case of a major crisis. Most presidents have stressed the first: George W. Bush started by portraying China as a competitor but then switched to a more conciliatory tone; Barack Obama emphasized that the two had a mutual interest in cooperation. But there is a constant tone of uncertainty about the PRC's long-term aims in US policy, especially when, as on Obama's visit to the mainland in 2009, his hosts were clearly in the driving seat, reflecting their growing confidence vis-à-vis a power that they see as facing long-term decline. The situation remains as set out that year by Clark Randt, the ambassador in Beijing; 'Just as no one in 1979 would have predicted that China would become the United States' most important relationship in thirty years, no one today can predict with certainty where our relations with Beijing will be thirty years hence.'[2]

The relationship stretches from economic and monetary affairs to regional security, from environmental pollution to trying to paper over a fundamental difference in values notably over human rights and freedom. When they meet, President Obama makes the point that liberalization would help the PRC but Hu Jintao is not impressed. Still, each of these great states depends on the other to the point at which it has been suggested that they constitute a G2 at the centre of global affairs. When he accompanied Richard Nixon on the ground-breaking trip to see Mao in 1972, Henry Kissinger was reported to have told the President that trade would never amount to much and so could be handed as a placatory bone to the State Department, which he had sidelined from the China opening. In 2010 the mainland's trade surplus with the US totalled $273 billion, which was $90 billion more than its overall surplus; in other words, if the US stopped buying its goods the PRC would run a trade deficit.

The uncertainty of which Randt wrote produces mixed signals from the American side. On her first visit to the PRC after taking office in 2009, Secretary of State Hillary Clinton pledged to continue to press on human rights and Tibet, but said this could not interfere with coopera-tion on the economy, climate change and security. In a magazine interview two years later she depicted China as pursuing a 'fool's errand' in trying to stem the tide of history with its 'deplorable' crackdown on dissent. But 'we live in the real world', she added.[3]

US government cables made known through Wikileaks show a rising pattern of concern at the competition China constitutes, especially since the financial crisis led Beijing to conclude that American power was waning. The smiles that accompanied a visit to China by Vice President Joe Biden in August 2011 were accompanied by a much tougher Chinese attitude behind the scenes. In congressional testimony that same year, Clinton warned of declining American influence – particu-larly in the Pacific. To some, it seems as though the PRC is already number one. Though their economy is four times bigger than China's, a survey in 2011 reported that 47 per cent of Americans regarded the PRC as the world's top economic power; 31 per cent named their own country.

China's military build-up – and particularly the development of its fleet – poses an obvious challenge to the strategic supremacy exercised by the US in East Asia since the defeat of Japan in 1945. Beijing reacted badly when Washington declared that freedom of navigation on the 1.3-million-square-mile sea was a national interest, and Clinton referred to her country as a 'resident power' in East Asia. It has been alarmed by Obama's adoption of a 'Pacific pivot' as a major plank of US foreign and strategic policy, lining up with regional powers such as Japan, South Korea, Vietnam and the Philippines. As Professor Wu Xinbo of Fudan University in Shanghai put it to Robert Gates, then the Defense Secretary, at a regional security dialogue in the summer of 2011: 'While the United States may take access to every part of the world for granted [...] China may find the United States' activities intimidating and intrusive.' For his part, Gates expressed 'growing concern' about China's behaviour, but said it had not yet undermined the mainland's claim to be pursuing a peaceful rise – 'yet' being perhaps the operative word.[4]

Other states – notably Vietnam, which the PRC invaded in the thirty-eight-day war in 1979 – have become increasingly concerned about the PRC's regional role. Tension rose in the summer of 2011 when a Chinese patrol vessel cut the underwater cables of a Vietnamese survey ship. There was a rolling series of weekly street protests in Hanoi (police did not intervene until the eleventh) and the Foreign Ministry complained about a 'serious violation' and PRC attempts to turn the sea into its 'home pond'. Playing a hard–soft game, the PRC adopted more emollient language, sending a high-level military mission to Vietnam and holding a regular session of cooperation talks. But it also then dispatched a 400-tonne 'fishing-enforcement ship' to the disputed Paracel Islands, to 'safeguard China's maritime sovereignty and fisheries interests'.

Maritime disputes between China and Japan have escalated since 2010, especially over sovereignity on small uninhabited islands off the Japanese coast, as set out later in this chapter. After a Japanese Defence White Paper described the PRC's attitude to its neighbours as 'assertive', Yukio Edano, the Chief Cabinet Secretary, said that China's military build-up and increased PLA activity were matters of concern. At the end of 2011, a trawler captain from the mainland fatally stabbed a Korean coastguard who led a boarding party when the ship operated in territorial waters. Nor is Seoul happy with Beijing's failure to rein in North Korea. Though the President of the Philippines, Benigno Aquino III, paid a visit to Beijing in September 2011, his administration ordered tighter maritime security after China unloaded construction material and set up military outposts on several reefs both countries claim as its territory. Manila strengthened its small navy with a cutter warship, and six training aircraft from the US. Fresh clashes broke out in mid-2012 between Chinese trawlers and Filipino vessels in the disputed Scarborough Shoal area of the South China Sea as Aquino's administration sought closer defence ties with Japan and the US.

Australia negotiated an agreement to allow the US to expand its military presence in the country with an expansion of joint exercises, training and access to bases followed by the posting of 250 American troops to the north of the country, a figure due to rise in time to 2,500. Taiwan announced that it was strengthening the defence of one of the Spratley Islands, which it holds and which may sit on top of valuable energy reserves. India also became involved, in July 2011, when one of its amphibious assault craft was intercepted by a Chinese vessel by radio in international waters after a port visit to Vietnam and asked to explain its presence. Two months later New Delhi said it was stepping up energy cooperation with Vietnam just as Beijing repeated its claim to 'indisputable sovereignty' over the South China Sea. When an Indian oil company, ONGC, then moved to drill in a big oil block off Vietnam, the CCP tabloid *Global Times* thundered that Beijing should use 'every means possible' to prevent this.[5]

Given China's dependence on energy imported through the South China Sea, and the desire of its big oil firms to get access to deposits there, the PRC will continue to press its case with a mixture of force and diplomacy. In 2012, its muscle was evident when Cambodia, which receives aid from Beijing, prevented a South East Asian Summit it was hosting from expressing concern about China's assertive regional policies and blocked an attempt to produce a joint policy on the South China Sea. The PRC's long-term aim is to become the dominant power in the region without needing actually to use its military power – to 'win without fighting', as the traditional military theorist Sun Tzu put it – or to encircle its neighbours in Maoist guerrilla fashion, leaving them with no alternative but to go along with its wishes. It insists on dealing with East Asian nations one by one, aiming to maximise its clout case by case.

Yet the immediate effect of the tension of 2010–13 was to bolster America's position as smaller East Asian states looked to it for protection, coinciding with tougher rhetoric from President Obama who told China 'enough's enough' and launched a proposal for a Pacific free trade area which would not include the PRC. Given the mainland's economic weight, the prospects for that initiative looked quite doubtful but, strategically, East Asia is not ready to ditch the US for a revival of the imperial-era 'tributary system' centred on Beijing. Though Japan and South Korea agreed in 2012 to negotiate a free trade agreement with the PRC, both remain firmly in the US security orbit. Vietnam ignored a call by China to refuse to allow an American aircraft carrier to put in at one of its ports and received Defense Secretary Leon Panetta in June, 2012. The Philippines and Taiwan look to Washington for protection. So, though they need China economically, East Asian states are far from ready to move outside the post-1945 US strategic umbrella. Given the strong American naval presence in the region, that leaves Beijing facing the not-fanciful possibility that it may be Washington and its allies that carry out the Maoist encirclement strategy.

Important as the regional strategic situation is, the core of the US–China relationship is economic and – notwithstanding the way in which it has mushroomed in the last three decades – this contains a fair number of friction points such as the disclosure the US uniforms for the 2012 Olympics were made in China, prompting incendiary comments from American legislators. Chinese money has been largely welcome at US financial institutions; China's sovereign-wealth fund paid $3 billion for a 10 per cent stake in the American private-equity firm Blackstone. But other Chinese entities have been blocked or have walked away from proposed deals when they sensed the opposition they faced – particularly in the priority area of information technology, where the Committee on Foreign Investment in the US (CFIUS), chaired by the Treasury Department and including defence and intelligence officials, has taken a tough line. (It gives no explanation for its decisions.)

    Huawei's efforts to expand in the US have run into accusations that it may have connections to the PLA (dating back to its founder's army service) and to the Chinese state, and thus represents a security risk. Distrust was heightened by a suit it settled in 2011 alleging that it had worked with a company set up by a Chinese-born former employee of Motorola who stole trade secrets. The FBI said a Chinese woman who had just left Motorola was caught at Chicago airport in 2007 carrying 1,000 stolen documents from the US company. A separate suit against her and Huawei charged that she and others were secretly engaged in product development for the Shenzhen firm while employed by Motorola. The company strongly denies being under military influence and that its equipment could be used to monitor communications on networks it supplies as has been alleged. In October 2012, a congressional panel warned that Huawei and the big Chinese ZTE electronics firm posed a security threat and should be barred from US mergers or acquisitions. Whatever the truth, Huawei has the classic problem of proving a negative, as one of its executives noted in a conversation at the corporate headquarters.[6]

Though Chinese firms have invested in thirty-five of the fifty states, this has mostly been small beer. In 2011 the US ranked tenth among destinations for outward investment from the mainland. The oil group CNOOC abandoned one of China's highest-profile overseas bids – for Unocal of California – after being painted as a tool of the state and the Communist Party. The political charges were sufficient to derail the deal. As the man who organized Unocal's defence put it, 'We are not competing with this company; we are competing with the Chinese government. I think it's wrong.'[7]

Yet business goes on in sometimes unexpected ways. In 2010 the US International Trade Commission upheld tariffs of 63 per cent on imports of steel pipes from the PRC on the grounds of unfair pricing and government subsidies that made it impossible for American firms to compete. One Chinese firm involved was Tianjin Pipe, which had been able to borrow from Chinese state banks at a preferential rate. Its sales for the US slumped after the tariffs were raised. But it then emerged that the company was going to build a plant in Texas to produce half a million tons of pipes from recycled scrap metal each year. The project is set to employ 600 people and would enjoy tax breaks from the Texas government of former presidential candidate Rick Perry.[8]

At government level the economic link is embodied in China's holdings of almost $2 trillion in US securities. Most of these – some $1.13 trillion as of the autumn of 2011 – are in Treasury bonds, especially since Beijing cut back on its holdings of paper issued by the mortgage agencies Fannie Mae and Freddie Mac. The proportion of PRC reserves held in dollars has dropped to 60 per cent from 71 per cent in 2005, according to data compiled in New York. (In China, the figure is a state secret). Still, the hoard of T-bonds is equal to that in the hands of US households and hedge funds, and compares with $884 billion held by Japan.[9]

The mountain is the result of currency controls that mean that the central bank, the People's Bank of China (PBoC) 'sterilizes' dollars earned by importers by exchanging them for securities in yuan. This enables it to control the value of the Chinese currency through the exchange rate it applies, but leaves it sitting on a great pile of greenbacks that cannot be used domestically as a national savings reserve. It invests this treasure in the only market big enough to absorb them: the United States. This creates unhappiness all round. America is seen to depend on a poorer country that is regarded by some of its citizens as a foe. The Chinese see their national savings tied to a declining dollar and wonder why their money is funding a foreign power rather than being used for domestic development. But if the PRC began to sell its T-bonds, or cut down its purchases significantly, the dollar would plummet, reducing the value of its remaining holdings. Like the United States and the Soviet Union during the Cold War, the two countries face mutual assured destruction – in this instance monetary rather than nuclear – if they change their policies. Until the leadership decides to make the yuan convertible, the PRC is caught in a dollar trap and Hillary Clinton is reduced to appealing publicly to the Chinese not to stop buying her country's bonds.

The PRC's purchase of US securities has enabled the much richer nation to keep interest rates low as well as funding the federal deficit. That made it easier for Americans to go on their buying spree in the early years of this century, which was also helped by all those cheap goods flooding in from the mainland. This confirmed the pattern by which the world's wealthiest major country consumes more than it produces while the world's fastest-growing major economy works the other way round. Both sides needed the equation: the US to keep prices down and provide cheap cash; China to ensure that it has a strong market for its exports across the Pacific.

But the PRC now finds itself in the dock, accused of playing irresponsibly on the global imbalance between high consumption in the US and high savings in China. If China spent more at home the flow of monetary narcotics would dry up and Americans would be less tempted to spend too much, the argument goes. One might object that the first duty lay with the users to cut down on their addiction, but the buck-passing thesis has taken root – a headline in the *Financial Times* in August 2011 spoke of China as 'a sanctimonious drug dealer' when it came to US debt.

The problem is not so much that China lends and America borrows, but that the PRC's holdings of T-bonds has risen from around $100 billion at the start of this century to more than $1,100 billion today. So long as the mainland trade surplus continues, the amount will increase further. Even moves to expand the use of the yuan in international trade result only in a further addition to the reserves.[10]

China, naturally, rejects accusations of bad behaviour, insisting that the US must put its own house in order with none-too-subtle references to the way in which its own credit and infrastructure-stimulus programme launched at the end of 2008 bucked up its economy far more than the quantitative-easing programmes carried out by the Federal Reserve – which Beijing thoroughly disliked for injecting what it sees as destabilizing global liquidity. Li Yong, the Deputy Finance Minister, accuses the US and other rich nations of seeking to make China pay for their economic recovery by printing money that feeds inflation and increases prices for the commodities the PRC needs.

In 2010 China's ratings agency, Dagong, drew attention to 'long-standing accumulation of the contradictions in [the US] economic system [that] will lead to the long-term recession of its national economy, fundamentally lowering the national solvency' and anticipated the Standards & Poor's agency by a couple of days in downgrading the US credit rating – Dagong cut it to a single A while S&P took it from AAA to AA+ in August 2011. After that, Xinhua warned, 'the days when the debt-ridden Uncle Sam could leisurely squander unlimited overseas borrowing appear to be numbered. To cure its addiction to debts, the United States has to re-establish the common-sense principle that one should live within one's means.' Taking a sniffy view of the US process, *People's Daily* wrote that: 'What's near the cliff edge isn't the world economy, it's the politics in Washington.'[11]

For all the sermonizing, however, China is caught. If the US did significantly tighten its belt, Chinese exports would be hit. One great fear expressed by government advisers in Beijing during 2010–11 was of a double-dip recession in the West; the prospect of slow recovery in the US and a severe decline in the crisis-wracked euro-zone sent markets and commentators into a swoon in the autumn of 2011 even though the PRC had registered rising trade surpluses in the second and third quarters of the year. The coming collapse of China was taken to be on the cards once again even if had not materialized in the past. Though Beijing's long-term policy is to lessen dependence on exports as domestic consumption rises, that point has not been reached. Until it is, China will disapprove of American behaviour but depends on the sinner not recanting, and markets will run scared when the mainland's external environment turns chilly.

Meanwhile the miscreant across the Pacific has its own complaint that currency controls are used to undervalue the yuan, giving Chinese exports an unfair edge, destroying American jobs and adding to global imbalances. The yuan was formally de-pegged from the dollar in 2005–08 and again in 2010. In the first period, its value rose by 20 per cent. In the two-and-a-half years after it was linked to a 'flexible' basket of currencies in June 2010, the increase was 9.7 per cent in nominal terms and 12.6 per cent adjusted for inflation. A determined group of Senators has repeatedly put forward legislation to slap punitive tariffs on the PRC as punishment for its mercantilism: the Senate passed anti-China legislation in October 2011, leading China to warn that it could lead to a trade war. Though the bill faced free-trade sentiment in the House of Representatives and the White House, it was still a sign of the strength of feeling. The two countries have already taken action against each other on products ranging from cars and tyres to poultry and steel.

In a speech in the autumn of 2011, Hillary Clinton said that as China was pursuing an economic policy that sought 'to game the system to their advantage and our disadvantage, it is fitting and timely for us to be standing up and saying "this is not acceptable".' Ben Bernanke, Chairman of the US Federal Reserve, expressed concern that an undervalued yuan was blocking global recovery in the second half of 2011. 'Having embraced free enterprise to some degree, the Chinese government and Chinese companies have quickly derived the benefits of ignoring the rules followed by others. China seeks advantage through systematic exploitation of other economies,' Republican presidential candidate Mitt Romney wrote at the same time, pledging, if elected, to brand the PRC as 'the currency manipulator it is' on his first day in office. From a different political position, Paul Krugman, winner of the Nobel Prize in Economics and a liberal *New York Times* commentator, argues that 'Chinese currency policy is a lose-lose proposition, simultaneously depressing employment here and producing an overheated inflation-prone economy in China itself.'[12] However, the IMF said in 2012 that the yuan was only moderately undervalued and at the end of that year the US Treasury Department, while saying that it was 'significantly undervalued', declined to brand the PRC as a currency manipulator.

The argument overstates the importance of the currency. During the appreciation of 2005–08, Chinese exports to the US boomed. As for domestic inflation, that is driven mainly by food of which China imports little. The government worried more about a rising yuan increasing the flow of 'hot money', betting on appreciation and adding to domestic liquidity at a time when it was trying to get the money supply under control.

Chinese officials point out that their country experienced inflation above 6 per cent in 2011 while prices in the US were quite flat; so if one adds 4–6 per cent annual inflation to a nominal yuan appreciation of 4–5 per cent a year, the real result was 8–11 per cent – which is, they say, as much as Washington can expect. While periodically wagging its finger at Beijing on the issue as in Clinton's 'gaming' speech, the Obama administration remained quite cool, declining to brand the mainland as a currency manipulator, which would have opened the way for sanctions, and moving the quarrel to the back burner.[13]

At least some of the US companies operating in China are on the PRC's side, even if they do not like to say so too openly. A survey by the American Chamber of Commerce in China in 2011 found that 17 per cent of its members said yuan appreciation was the greatest risk facing them. The 'Smiley Curve' for goods put together in the People's Republic for big American corporations such as Apple means that the vast bulk of profits come in origination and the final sales and marketing – not in the middle, where China does the manufacturing. A study by the Asian Development Bank calculated that only 3.6 per cent of the overall cost of an iPhone occurs in the PRC, compared to a profit margin for Apple of 64 per cent when the devices are sold in the USA with a small notice on the back reading 'Designed by Apple in California – Assembled in China'. iPhones imported to the US from China contributed $1.9 billion to the trade gap if counted by country of origin but, as Pascal Lamy, Director-General of the World Trade Organization, notes, assessing the US deficit on the grounds of national content can cut the headline total by half, if not more. On top of that there is the question of whether the most advanced major economy on earth could, or should, go back to making the things it imports from China rather than boosting advanced productivity and high-tech sectors.[14]

Hu Jintao may say, as he did when he visited Washington in 2011, that the current international currency system is the product of the past, but China has no alternative to offer. As in other fields of its international relations, it knows what it does not like but lacks the means and imagination to shift the goalposts. It has set up currency-swap arrangements with half-a-dozen countries, including Argentina, South Korea, Malaysia and Indonesia, encourages use of the yuan in trade and is experimenting with the 'internationalization' of its currency through Hong Kong. Yuan deposits at banks in the former British colony rose fivefold in 2010 to 314.9 billion and increased further to 554 billion in the first half of 2011, after permanent residents were permitted to buy up to HK$20,000 of renminbi a day – though the growth then tapered off. (The Bank of China in the United States also offers yuan accounts, telling potential customers that they may profit from a currency appreciation bigger than the interest they could obtain from a savings account in dollars with an American bank.) McDonald's and Caterpillar led the way, issuing 'dim sum' bonds denominated in the mainland currency. In August 2011 China floated a sale of bonds worth 20 billion yuan in the former colony and, in late 2011 the state-owned Baosteel group became the first PRC firm to sell yuan bonds directly to foreign investors. On a brief visit, Vice-Premier Li Keqiang announced half-a-dozen measures to increase the flow of the currency in and out of the mainland; meanwhile in September 2011 China agreed that London should become an offshore trading centre for the yuan.

But serious questions hang over the policy. As long as the PRC has a trade surplus internationalization will end up further boosting the People's Bank of China dollar holdings and open the door to speculative arbitrage between currency values and interest rates. More generally, is the leadership really ready to give up control of its currency? The President of the EU Chamber of Commerce in China, Davide Cucino, told reporters in 2011 that PRC officials had spoken of full convertibility by 2015, but the Central Bank Governor responded that there was no timetable. Slow movement appears in keeping with the mindset of mainland leaders and, while the yuan will loom larger globally, an increasingly unhappy China looks doomed to continue to live in a dollar world.

If the US and China have the world's most important relationship, the European Union is the mainland's biggest trading partner. The EU pursues a 'strategic partnership' with the PRC. London is bathed in red light for a visit by Hu Jintao and Chinese lanterns are hung out for Wen Jiabao in Rome. Europe welcomes hints from Chinese leaders that the PBoC may prop up troubled euro-zone members on top of the estimated $500 billion it holds in bonds of EU countries, even as Wen wags his finger and tells them that they 'should put their own houses in order'. Europe's less prosperous industries seek investment from the mainland. Chinese car firms have acquired Volvo and the iconic MG brand, and signed a rescue package for Saab.

The state company Cosco has a $4.2 billion, thirty-five-year lease to run a terminal at the Piraeus port in Greece, while Chinese firms operate wind-power farms in Romania and a special economic zone in Sofia. The Ping An insurance company has taken a share in Belgium's Fortis bank. In Britain, where Chinese takeaways overtook fish-and-chip shops in numbers in 1976, the CIC sovereign-wealth fund has a 1 per cent stake in Barclays Bank and has bought into water and airport companies while Chinese purchasers have boosted the London real-estate market with an average spend of £6.5 million per property. The *Economist* puts mainland holdings in the top 100 companies on the London Stock Exchange at $18.6 billion. When Wen Jiabao visited in 2011 (finding time to go to Stratford-upon-Avon for a special staging of Shakespeare),

China's ambassador, Liu Xiaoming, made a remark that reflected the changed balance between the PRC and the country whose economic strength Mao took as the benchmark for the Great Leap Forward. 'We really need to identify flagship projects,' he said, singling out high-speed rail given his country's 'knowledge and experience'.[15]

The Haier household-equipment firm is developing a plant in northern Italy that is designed to be the springboard to make it one of the five biggest makers of white goods in the continent by 2014. A Chinese tycoon with a pet cat called Little Sister Big Eyes announced plans in 2011 to buy a large tract of Iceland to develop a $100 million tourist and golf resort. In Norway a Chinese firm paid $2.2 billion to purchase a maker of polysilicon for solar panels while the state group Sinochem invested $3.1 billion to buy a 40 per cent stake in an oil field held by the Norwegian Statoil group off Brazil. PetroChina paid $7.3 billion for Swiss-based Addax Petroleum.[16] Chinese companies have bought a big German machinery maker and invested in a bank in Georgia.

The Chinese presence in Europe is accompanied by illegal immigration organized by 'snakeheads' on the mainland who smuggle people to the West by hiding them in boats, trains, trucks and containers. There have been tragic cases. Fifty-eight people suffocated to death in the back of a truck trying to enter Britain from the Netherlands in 2000; some had paid £30,000 for the trip. In 2004 twenty-three Chinese drowned after being caught by the tide in Morecombe in England while they collected cockles. The Belleville district of Paris has taken on a strongly Chinese aspect, with sweatshops staffed by migrant workers, 'black money' changing hands and occasional attacks by racist French gangs. In Italy police raids in the summer of 2011 seized 25 million euros in assets from Chinese firms in the Prato region, where 4,000 Chinese businesses compete on price, employing illegal mainland immigrants at low wages and sending undeclared money to the PRC.

For all the deals mentioned above, and despite the media excitement about prospective agreements when Chinese leaders visit Europe, some projects have not turned out well. Chinese builders had to stop work on a $447-million motorway project in Poland when it was discovered that the costs had been miscalculated. The Iceland project was blocked amid concerns that it was a part of a bid by the PRC to expand its shipping links or a cover for a listening post in a strategic NATO area. A Tianjin company lodged the highest bid for a Dutch maker of fibre-optic cable that supplies NATO forces; after an Italian rival hired a lobbying firm to spread the word that the Chinese firm was secretly backed by the state, it abandoned the bid. Though the use of Hong Kong and tax havens makes it impossible to accurately track the flow of outward funds from the PRC, the evidence suggests that Europe has not been as much of a magnet for mainland investments as was hoped. German investment in the PRC is thirty times China's registered investment in Europe's biggest economy.[17]

China would like the EU to lift the arms embargo imposed on it after the 1989 killings in Beijing and to grant it the status of a full market economy, which would shield it from anti-dumping cases. The first is a highly politicized issue on which Europeans do not agree, while the second would deprive the EU of a weapon cherished by its producers of lower-cost goods; it holds the record at the World Trade Organization for anti-dumping cases against China and slaps prohibitive duties on Chinese goods such as bicycles.

Unable to make much headway on those broad demands, the PRC cherry-picks between European nations in line with the idea evolved by late imperial statesmen of playing the barbarians off against one another. It is helped in this by the EU's internal divisions between free traders and protectionists, and between those states that favour a tough line on human rights and those that wish to be more accommodating. Visiting officials tantalize the Europeans with talk of investment, but most Chinese money goes to familiar recipients – Airbus planes, German machinery firms and French and Italian luxury goods. Europe does not know where it stands and is aware of the problem. 'In a remarkably short space of time, complacency has been replaced to a large extent by anxiety,' as French political scientist François Godemont puts it.[18]

Japan's relations with the PRC are enormously complicated by the history of invasions since the war of 1894–5, when the power that had traditionally lived in the shadow of the Middle Kingdom humiliated

China militarily and became the prime modernizing nation in Asia. The number of people, most of them civilians, killed in Japan's full-scale invasion of China from 1937 to 1945 will never be known but may have reached 20 million. Sagas of resistance to the invaders are a staple of Chinese television. Tokyo's failure to offer a wholehearted apology for its barbarous conduct, the presence of strident right-wing nationalists and the way in which some of its politicians continued to pay homage at a shrine containing war criminals mean that anti-Japanese sentiment regularly bubbles up on the mainland – despite Mao once telling a delegation from Japan that the Communists would not have won the civil war had it not been for the social and economic dislocation caused by the eight years of conflict.

Japan's post-war recovery was an obvious reflection on the backwardness and failures of the first three decades of the People's Republic. Today, resurgent China looms larger in the East Asia strategic balance than the politically quiescent power across the sea. Japanese companies profit greatly from low-cost manufacturing on the mainland and China has become their biggest export destination. But efforts launched in 2006 by Hu Jintao and the then Premier, Shinzo Abe, to complement the economic links with a deep political relationship have not borne fruit. An attempt to write a joint history of modern times fell apart.

The mutual distrust was well reflected in a 2010 survey by the *Yomiuri Shimbun* newspaper and a magazine published by the Xinhua news agency. This found that 87 per cent of Japanese and 79 per cent of Chinese considered the other country untrustworthy. The number who thought that relations between the two nations were bad represented a big jump since earlier polls. Nearly 80 per cent of Japanese respondents said they believed China could pose a military threat to Japan.[19]

Anti-Japanese sentiment is not simply held by those old enough to remember the 1937–45 period. Many young people join demonstrations against perceived Japanese misdeeds.

When a Chinese trawler brushed with Japanese coastguard boats in the autumn of 2010, Beijing unleashed a high-level diplomatic offensive against Tokyo. Wen Jiabao refused to meet his counterpart on the fringes of a United Nations session in New York. The PRC cut off exports of rare earths vital for high technology manufacturing. However, Beijing evidently decided enough was enough. Despite a call by anti-Japanese organizers, protestors failed to turn out in force to shout abuse at the Japanese Embassy: after a small demonstration on a Saturday, the street by the legation beside Ritan Park in central Beijing was choc-a-bloc with police wagons the following day but the police had nothing to do except to sit in their trucks or huddle on the pavement, smoking, eating and chatting in the sunshine – nobody turned up. Tokyo reacted by freeing the trawler captain and saying as little as possible.

While using the mainland as an assembly centre for products that are then re-exported, as well as increasing their sale to PRC consumers, Japanese companies have been leery about accepting Chinese invest-ment. The experience of Kawasaki in seeing its high-speed train technology 'indigenously re-innovated' stands as a warning to others. Remaining under the US strategic umbrella as they have since 1945, suc-cessive governments in Tokyo have been neither able nor ready to forge a China policy that goes beyond the economy and the hope that friction will not boil over. There was, however, a sign of some toughening in 2011 when a White Paper drawn up by the Defence Department in Tokyo and approved by the Cabinet described China as 'overbearing', expressed anxiety about the mainland's arms build-up and praised joint operations with the US forces that would 'further deepen the Japan-US alliance in the future'.

When Japan got a new Prime Minister, Yoshihiko Noda, in August 2011, Xinhua immediately came up with a scolding list of what he must do with regard to the PRC. Japan, it said, had to be blamed for the fact that there were disputes between the two nations. Apart from the way in which some of its right-wing politicians sought to cover up their country's record on the mainland, 'Tokyo has managed its relationship with Beijing without due respect for China's core interests and legitimate demands for development.' It went on. 'To improve the relationship between the world's second- and third-biggest economies, Noda's cabinet has to care-fully craft and implement a proper policy in treating Japan's war past to soothe the resentment among the Chinese public toward Japan.' Tokyo, it added, had to accept PRC sovereignty over disputed islands, and 'acknowledge China's legitimate requirement for military moderniza-tion'. The keys to better relations were in the hands of Japan and 'substantial measures' were expected. Beijing, it was clear, felt it had only to sit back and wait for its demands to be met. The era when the Qing court looked down on the Japanese 'dwarf bandits' suddenly seemed not so far away. Deng's low-profile policy was truly dead and buried. But the only reaction from Tokyo could be to tighten the American embrace.[20]

The escalating row over the uninhabited islands known to the Chinese as the Diaoyu and to the Japanese as the Senkaku heightened tension as demonstrators trashed Japanese shops on the mainland and the new Liberal Democratic government in Tokyo took a more assertive line in late 2012 and early 2013, especially after Chinese military planes began to fly over the islands. Previous spats involving Chinese trawlers intruding into waters claimed by Japan had been easy to clear up but now high-profile issues of state sovereignty and national pride were concerned and neither the new leadership in Beijing nor the incoming administration in Tokyo was in a mood to back down.

China remains at arm's length from its fellow BRIC state India, with which it fought a war in the Himalayas in 1962 ending in victory for the PLA. Though Buddhism travelled to China from India, the history of the Asian giants is one of distance through the centuries as they looked in different directions on either side of their 2,000-mile Himalayan frontier. Today the two nations, which between them contain nearly 40 per cent of the world's population, and which both have nuclear weapons, seem uncomfortable with one another.

India's Prime Minister, Manmohan Singh, spoke in 2011 about China's 'new assertiveness'. India worries about the PRC's efforts to seek a foothold in South Asia. Indian military commanders warn of a 'collusive threat' from China. Before Wen Jiabao embarked on a visit to India at the end of 2010, Zhang Yan, the PRC ambassador in New Delhi, called relations 'very fragile'. Bilateral trade has risen sharply, to $60 billion, but that has produced a large surplus for China. Little has come of the cooperation spoken about by leaders of the two countries in the 1990s, in which Indian software was meant to meld with Chinese hardware to form 'Chindia'. India slaps occasional bans on Chinese imports and complains about restricted access for its goods to mainland markets. The two countries compete for raw materials, and India restricts its sales of iron ore to the mainland.[21]

Territorial disputes persist. New Delhi does not like China strengthening its military presence and communications in Tibet. Beijing is unhappy at India providing a home for the Dalai Lama. New Delhi's rapprochement with Washington – and with Vietnam – is viewed with suspicion in Beijing while India is riled by the PRC's reluctance to back its bid for a permanent Security Council seat and its links with Pakistan. After visiting India Wen flew on to Pakistan, where he signed economic agreements that far outstripped those he had finalized in New Delhi.

Chinese damming of rivers that flow down from its Himalayan territory into India is a further cause of concern. There is the political divide which would be heightened if Beijing sought to divert the water towards itself. There is the political divide between a democracy and an authoritarian state. Chinese tend to regard Indians as messy, disorganized and probably dirty people incapable of getting their act together, while Indians see the Chinese as regimented mice doing what they are told without any of the individuality that marks their own country. None of this means direct conflict is likely. Relations blow between lukewarm and blustery. In 2010 there was a freeze in military exchanges but, after a year, a high-level Indian delegation visited China from New Delhi and then, in 2012, the two countries agreed to step up their defence and security dialogue and set a trade target of $100 billion by 2015.

Still, competition is inherent in their separate paths of development and different systems. The two countries are constantly compared as analysts swing between them in their forecasts of which will grow fastest. Advocates for India point to its democracy, legal system and favourable demographics with more young people than China in a population that is forecast to overtake that of the PRC by 2030. The relative strength of Indian domestic demand also makes it less reliant than the PRC on exports and so provides protection from a global downturn. The metaphor of India's tortoise overtaking China's hare when it runs out of breath is sometimes invoked. However, as things stand, the PRC has the edge with significantly greater per capita income and stronger economic indicators. It enjoys higher levels of literacy, with a ratio of teachers to students three times that of India and average schooling of 7.5 years compared with 4.4 in its neighbour across the Himalayas. China also shows much lower rates of poverty, child mortality and malnutrition. As has become increasingly apparent, India cannot claim the moral high ground when it comes to corruption. The ball appears firmly on China's side of the net.[22]

From Australia to Africa via Brazil and Venezuela, nations rich in resources love the orders they receive from the PRC. Oil comes from Saudi Arabia, Angola, Iran, Russia, Sudan, Kazakhstan, Venezuela and the Caspian Basin, iron ore from Australia and Brazil, coal from Australia, Indonesia, South Africa and Mongolia. Mainland firms are investing in shale gas in Oklahoma and have sunk more than $30 billion into energy firms in Canada including the $15 billion acquisition of the big Nexen group at the end of 2012. Boosted by its buying of metals, energy and animal feed, China's annual trade with Latin America has reached $118 billion, twelve times the amount for 2000, and the PRC invested $25 billion there in 2010, 40 per cent of its total for the year.

Russia, which has been a big supplier of timber from its eastern forests, hopes to be a major source of the natural gas needed by the mainland to lessen its dependency on coal. But relations between the two giant neighbours remain at arm's length with the PRC unwilling to become reliant on energy from its northern neighbour and Russia concerned about the spread of Chinese influence across its Siberian frontier. Politically, the Putin–Medvedev administration has the galling experience of watching China's political rise, about which it can do nothing, and seeing the Washington–Beijing relationship outweighing that between Washington and Moscow in the global scales.

But there is another side to the embrace of China by countries that have got the thing under their soil that it wants to buy. Round the world, makers of everything from shoes to steel fear its competition. Brazil, which occupies first place to China's last in the BRIC formulation of major emerging economies, with Russia and India in between, is a good example of the China dilemma. It enjoys the strong revenues it earns from selling iron ore and soya to the mainland. China was the destination for the first trip abroad by Brazilian President Dilma Rousseff after she took office in 2011. At $65 billion, bilateral Sino-Brazilian trade in 2010 was $11 billion above the figure for commerce with the US, traditionally Brazil's main partner. The revenue from trade with China helped to fund social spending under Dilma's predecessor, Lula da Silva. The country's richest man is building Latin America's biggest port, dubbed Highway to China. The mining company Vale, which draws almost one-third of its revenue from sales to China, has inaugurated a new class of 400,000-ton bulk carriers called Chinamax, though the PRC shipowners told mainland companies not to use the ships to safeguard their freight rates.

But Brazil feels threatened by cheap Chinese goods undercutting its domestic manufacturers. It registered a shortfall in trade with China in manufactured goods amounting to $23.5 billion in 2010, forty times as much as seven years earlier; the volume of shoe imports doubled to 34 million pairs between 2006 and 2008. Mainland firms, primarily state-owned, account for one-third of foreign investment in the country – the Chinese started with plants to turn out cheap goods and then moved up to making cars and more advanced products, leading the government to impose restrictions to limit PRC inroads.

This did not halt China's onward march. The Sinopec oil group paid $7.1 billion for a 40 per cent stake in a major Brazilian energy company. The PRC loaned the oil company Petrobras $10 billion for deep-sea exploration. Chinese state firms paid $1.95 billion for a stake in a big supplier of the rare earth niobium. Foxconn plans to make iPods in Brazil. The ZTE information-technology group is to build an industrial park outside São Paulo. A state-owned grain group from Chongqing is investing $500 million in a soybean base in Bahia.

Brazil has become heavily and perhaps dangerously dependent on sales of raw materials and food to the PRC – as have Chile and Peru, which respectively send 23 and 15 per cent of their exports to China. Primary commodities have doubled their slice of Brazilian exports in the last decade to 43 per cent, while the share of manufactured goods has dropped from 58 to 38 per cent. Is Brazil's future to be China's provider? And what happens if demand from the mainland slows down? On the other side of the coin, is Brazil ready to allow Chinese companies to move into its manufacturing sector or will pressure from local firms to limit the penetration lead to stepped-up government measures? If so, how will Beijing react?

One pointer was provided by a spat between the PRC and Argentina. To protect domestic industries the government in Buenos Aires imposed a ban on imports of Chinese footwear and dyes. In retaliation the PRC upped the standards required for soya-bean oil it buys from the Latin American nation. As a result, Chinese purchases from Argentina fell by 42 per cent year-on-year while PRC exports as a whole went on growing. Buenos Aires lifted its ban and business resumed. It is hard to stand up to China when it is so big a player.

Australia has been another enormous beneficiary of China's rise. Exports to the mainland account for some 21 per cent of the country's overseas sales; for iron ore it is closer to China than Brazil, which reduces shipping costs. At one point in 2007, a quarter of the world's biggest bulk freighters were moored off New South Wales waiting to take coal and ore to the PRC. As an Australian political scientist put it, PRC demand means that 'we are looking at a boom like we have never seen before in our history'. China has put $5 billion into an Australian mining company that is due to deliver 1 billion tons of coal to the mainland over the next thirty years. The mainland's Citic Resources has a 24 per cent stake in one of Australia's big coal companies, Macarthur. Another state enterprise, Chinalco, holds a 9 per cent interest in the major British–Australia mining firm, Rio Tinto, and has tried unsuccessfully to double its stake. The Australian dollar rises on news of China's growth but there is also regular questioning: in 2011 Barnaby Joyce, the opposition leader in the Senate, railed against 'Australia's prime sources of wealth being hijacked by a foreign government'. A poll by the Lowy Institute of Sydney in the spring of 2011 showed that 57 per cent of those questioned thought too much Chinese investment had been allowed in the country.[23]

For many developing economies China has become an essential partner, made all the more attractive for repressive regimes and rogue states by its lack of scruples about the nature of the governments with which it deals. Mainland firms are building roads and developing refineries in Iran, which in return supplies oil with barter used to get round sanctions. Long-term contracts guarantee the PRC natural gas from Turkmenistan and Burma. It has invested heavily in Venezuela's oil industry and has agreed to help develop Cuba's offshore energy industry. In Afghanistan,

China has signed a twenty-year lease on a copper mine in the Logar Plain twenty-five miles south of Kabul, the biggest open-cast mine outside Africa; the plan is to blow up a mountain and Buddhist temples there to get at deposit estimated to be worth £45 billion. Given a shortage of land and water at home, China has bought land in Africa and Latin America – including 2.8 million hectares in the Democratic Republic of Congo to grow palm oil for biofuels.[24]

China's trade in Africa rose to $127 billion in 2010 from $10 billion ten years earlier and its total investment to $40 billion. It has taken a 20 per cent stake in Chartered Bank of South Africa for $5.5 billion, but its main interest in the continent is for raw materials. Chinese companies have stakes in an iron-ore mine in Sierra Leone that contains resources estimated at 12.8 billion tons. Chinalco and Rio Tinto are working together on another major deposit in Guinea. Angola is China's second-biggest supplier of oil after Saudi Arabia.

Helped by largesse that includes a $98-million loan to set up the Robert Mugabe School of (Military) Intelligence, the PRC has clinched minerals deals in Zimbabwe, where a company from Anhui mines diamonds. Beijing nurtured relations with Sudan as an oil provider, feting its ruler on a state visit at a time when he was under indictment for crimes against humanity; but the state oil group CNPC has a 40 per cent stake in three major oil blocks in the world's newest state, South Sudan, buying 60 per cent of its output and building the pipeline, refinery and export terminals through which the oil passes.

In return for access to natural resources, China lends money and builds roads, railways, airports, bridges, military installations, hospitals, sports stadiums and official buildings. It is paying for a $200 million headquarters for the African Union in Addis Ababa, has put up a new home for the parliament in Lesotho, and agreed to provide the Democratic Republic of Congo with 32 hospitals, 145 health centres and 2 universities in return for copper and cobalt. It plans to sink $23 billion into the development of oil refineries in Nigeria and $20 billion into construction in Algeria. It has signed a package for $13 billion in loans for infrastructure and energy projects to Ghana in return for oil and gas, and pledged $234 million for Ethiopia's shipping line to buy nine ships from Chinese yards. Mainland investments in Zambia exceed

$2 billion; Labour Minister Austin Liatao described the Chinese to the *New York Times* as 'the cow that gives us milk'. The Chinese Embassy says the PRC has been responsible for two-thirds of new construction in the country and had created 25,000 jobs in a country racked by high unemployment.[25]

China's readiness to make such assistance available through low-cost loans without strings other than the provision of raw materials in return has been a blow to efforts by the World Bank to get poor nations to reduce their debt and accept conditions of transparency and improved governance. The Global Witness international watchdog and the *Economist* report that much of the trade in oil and minerals with Angola, Guinea, Zimbabwe and other countries is controlled by a mysterious syndicate based in Hong Kong. On a visit to Burma in late 2011, Hillary Clinton urged poor states to be 'smart shoppers' when it came to accepting Chinese aid and to 'be wary of donors who are more interested in extracting your resources than in building your capacity'. But the lure of cheap cash from the PRC remained a potent arm in China's global development.[26]

'China is a very aggressive and pernicious economic competitor with no morals,' according to a cable sent from the US consulate in Lagos relaying the views of Johnnie Carson, Assistant Secretary of State for African Affairs, during a visit to Nigeria. Thabo Mbeki, the former president of South Africa, warned of a 'new colonial relationship' with the PRC. His successor, Jacob Zuma, spoke reassuringly of 'a mutually beneficial kind of relationship [...] different from former Western colonialists [who took] things by force,'[27] but, at a China-African summit in Beijing in July 2012 warned that the relationship was unsustainable in the long run.

More than a million Chinese are doing business across the continent, most of them in small enterprises. Individuals run shops, restaurants, trading companies, workshops and farms. It is estimated that a quarter of the eggs sold in the Zambian capital of Lusaka come from Chinese suppliers and Chinese chicken farmers sell thousands of birds each week in the city, crowding out local produce. PRC companies operate mines, logging outfits and mobile-telephone networks. China's presence arouses resentment in countries like Tanzania and South Africa as its traders offer cut-price goods and branches of PRC banks provide its nationals

with cheap no-collateral loans. The habit of bringing in mainland workers, reportedly including prison convicts, heightens unpopularity. In
some places clothing factories run by mainlanders and Taiwanese have
driven locals out of business. Mainland shippers run contraband wood
from Tanzania and Mozambique. Most ivory smugglers detained at
Nairobi airport are Chinese. Trawlers from the People's Republic roam
through fishing grounds off southern Africa. There have been clashes in
Algeria between Chinese and local people.

Standards at Chinese-run enterprises come in for recurrent criticism.
In Zambia forty-nine workers died in an explosion in a factory run by a
PRC firm. Workers at uranium mines operated by Chinese in Zambia
and Niger have no protective clothing and live in camps where radiation
levels are high. Nor are the buildings put up with PRC aid always well
made; in Angola rains washed away a Chinese-built road, and a hospital
built by a mainland contractor had to be closed when cracks appeared
in the walls a few months after its grand opening.[28]

In Zambia hundreds of miners working at the Chinese-owned Collum
mine demonstrated in 2010 about conditions and pay. They said they
had to walk 1,000 steps to get to the coal face, laboured in the dark with
no safety protection or protective masks. They were expected to work
seven days a week. Roofs collapsed underground and there was little or
no ventilation 200 metres down. Accidents were common and promises
of increased wages had not been fulfilled. The managers replied that
the workers had four to five days off a month and were 'kind of lazy'.

As the protestors advanced on the mine head, two Chinese managers opened fire with shotguns; a dozen workers were wounded. The
Zambian President condemned the shooting. A minister said the miners
were being 'treated like animals' and paid 'slave salaries'. The two
Chinese were charged with attempted murder – but in April 2011 prosecutors decided to drop the case after the government in Lusaka
brokered an agreement. 'My clients are very happy,' the Zambian
lawyers representing the two managers told reporters. 'The whole case
is really about a clash of cultures, people from conflicting backgrounds
who don't understand how to deal with each other.' An official of the
mineworkers' remarked: 'Unfortunately we don't have better investors
than the Chinese.'[29]

In the autumn of 2011 Michael Sata won the Zambian presidential election. As opposition leader, he had been sharply critical of the Chinese presence, attacking PRC companies for importing mainland workers and for reducing local employees to the status of 'slave labour'. But his first official engagement after his election was to receive China's ambassador and confirm that PRC firms were welcome to invest in the country – so long as they respected national laws. In the following weeks a series of strikes broke out at Chinese-run mines. In a sign that government pressure was having an effect, a Chinese company agreed to reinstate more than 1,000 workers it had sacked for stopping work to back a demand for wages to be doubled. However workers at the Collum mine rioted in the summer of 2012 for the implementation of an agreement to raise wages and killed a Chinese worker. Some commentators wondered if the Chinese would lose patience and shift to other mineral-rich nations that would provide them with better-quality mines and less hassle.[30]

13

CHINA AND THE WORLD

China's global involvement means that it is increasingly caught up in events beyond its control. In the spring of 2011 it evacuated an estimated 38,000 Chinese from Libya, where it had three times as many workers as Europe employed on $19 billion worth of contracts in infrastructure and the oil industry. Beijing has sent an advanced missile frigate to help combat pirates off East Africa. It found some of its citizens taken hostage by Taliban fighters who attacked a base in Pakistan where they were employed. The PRC has been the biggest contributor of peacekeeping forces to the United Nations among the permanent members of the Security Council, having sent more than 17,000 troops to join nineteen operations since 1990.

It uses its influence at the international body to protect nations with which it has nurtured economic relations or to limit international action in line with its insistence on the paramount principle of non-interference in the internal affairs of states. It sees the UN as a means of checking the influence of the United States and associating itself with non-Western nations. Though it did not block action against the Gaddafi regime in Libya after the Arab League and African Union backed such a step, Beijing (together with Moscow) applied the doctrine of non-interference by vetoing UN sanctions against the Syrian regime in 2011-2012 as the Assad adminstration used maximum violence to quell the popular uprising.

China is developing a 'string of pearls' on the sea route from the oil-providing states of the Gulf with ports in Pakistan, Sri Lanka – where it backed the government against the Tamil Tigers – and Burma. It plans to drive a high-speed rail track through Laos to Thailand to strengthen links with those two countries and open the route to South East Asia. The PRC accounts for half the foreign investment in Cambodia, where its engineers have built a container port, bridge and highway, though a PRC grid firm pulled out of dam projects after protests by local fishermen. It turned Burma into a client state, both for its natural resources and strategic position and as a transit point for oil. Three members of the Politburo visited the neighbouring dictatorship in 2009–10 and leaders of the military junta are honoured guests in Beijing. The Wa region of Burma, by the border with Yunnan, is on the PRC's electricity grid. Trade flourishes in frontier towns that are more prosperous than Rangoon. Chinese involvement is increasingly resented, however. There have been clashes between the Burmese army and tribal militia over Chinese hydropower projects along the Irrawaddy River, one of which was suspended in the autumn of 2011.

But Burma's reform programme now faces China with the challenge of competition from other powers that have opened relations with the evolving state, notably the US and Japan. President Obama's visit at the end of 2012 represented a direct attempt to 'pull Myanmar off the China track', as the PRC's *Global Times* put it.[1]

In Pakistan, with which it has a free-trade agreement, China is building a major port at Gwadar close to sea lanes to the Middle East, which will be linked by rail and a possible oil pipeline to Xinjiang and will provide a listening post on a sensitive maritime region. It provides Islamabad with nuclear-power stations, military jets, and modernization of the Karakoram highway across the mountains from Xinjiang as well as dams, including a $15 billion project on the Indus River. However, in the autumn of 2011, a Chinese company pulled out of a $19 billion investment (Pakistan's biggest) to develop a big coalmine as well as power and chemical plants over a twenty-year period because of security concerns. Still, in an unsubtle attempt to play off the PRC against the US, Prime Minister Raza Gilani praised the mainland as an 'all-weather friend' and President Ali Zardari said the relationship was 'not matched by any other between two sovereign countries'. Raising the hyperbole, Pakistan's ambassador in Beijing proclaimed their friendship to be 'taller than the Himalayas and deeper than the oceans, stronger than steel, dearer than eye-sight, sweeter than honey'.[2]

In 2012, Beijing moved to develop relations with Afghanistan while buttressing its links with the "stans" of the former Soviet Union. The Shanghai Cooperation Organization (SCO), linking it with Kazakhstan, Kyrgyzstan, Russia, Tajikistan and Uzbekistan, acts as a strategic hedge in a region that supplies 10 per cent of the mainland's energy imports through pipelines rather than long sea voyages. At the SCO summit in Beijing in June, 2012, where Afghanistan was granted observer status, Hu Jintao hailed the grouping as ' a fortress of regional security and stability and a driving force for regional economic development'. In return for oil, gas and uranium, the PRC has underwritten road, railway and telecommunication development in Kazakhstan to the tune of $10 billion; it now controls a quarter of the nation's oil output while Chinese firms are working on a $1-billion expansion of an oil refinery in the west of the country and a pipeline to Xinjiang set to carry 20 million tons of oil a year by 2013.

To the north, China is the major customer for Mongolia's mineral wealth, though the home of the Yuan dynasty seeks to play Russia off against its southern neighbour and to prevent itself becoming an economic satellite of the PRC. South Korea is a major economic partner. China has a free-trade agreement with the ASEAN nations of South East Asia. In its role as the biggest of the BRIC economies, it hosted a summit of the four acronymic nations, plus South Africa, on Hainan Island in 2011, which produced nothing concrete but symbolized its world role. Despite this spread of activity and interests, Beijing has not evolved a coherent global policy beyond defending its 'core interests' and assuaging its thirst for natural resources.

A senior official, Dai Bingguo, has defined the target as being to 'preserve its fundamental system and state security'. That is hardly a target befitting of a true superpower; nor does it suggests how the PRC will modify a world shaped by US leadership. The Central Committee has laid down that foreign affairs should 'hold economic construction at its core' but, as the scholar Yan Xuetong has pointed out, 'a political superpower that puts wealth as its highest national interest may bring disaster rather than blessings to other countries'.[3]

China wants to make its voice heard internationally. It seeks *huayuquan*, or the 'right to discourse', but on its own terms and without meaningful debate. Nationalism is on the rise, evident in the strident comments on Japan in the islands dispute, the often radical positions taken by the Party's tabloid, *Global Times*, and in such campaigns as the (unsuccessful) attempt to have the Hollywood animated film *Kung Fu Panda*, which is set in ancient China, banned on the grounds that it 'twists Chinese culture and works as a tool to "kidnap" the minds of Chinese people'. As the bestselling book's title suggests, China can say no – and nationalists think it should do so more often. In that context, amid jockeying for leadership positions in the renewal of the Politburo and government in 2012–13, there are no dividends for politicians who seek compromise on foreign affairs and every encouragement to strike a hard line, evoking nationalism as a useful regime prop amid economic uncertainties and the US Pacific challenge.[4]

China's approach to the world does not embody the evangelical element in American foreign policy; some foreigner observers may admire the China Model but Beijing does not try to sell it in the way the US has aimed to spread democracy and market economics. Having set its claims to Tibet and Xinjiang in stone, the PRC does not have expansionist territorial ambitions either. It may well wish to re-create the tributary system under which neighbouring countries recognized its supremacy as a basis for trade but it does not aim to follow the European model of colonization. What it wants, above all, is to be able to use the rest of the world to achieve its domestic development and to be able to go its own way without being obstructed by the moralizing of others.

Its foreign policy is essentially opportunistic. The leadership seems ill-prepared to grasp the strategic opportunities created by the current international situation and to mould them into an encompassing code of practice, notably with the United States. Despite the jousting over the South China Sea, the PRC has no interest in engaging in the kind of direct global competition with the superpower that was pursued by the Soviet Union in the Cold War. Beijing benefits from the 'operating system' overseen by the US that maintains the security of world trade, and shares with America common interests in global prosperity, open commerce and as stable a position as possible in the oil-producing Middle East. Yet the two sides do not share a sufficient communality of interests, values and objectives to form the basis for a wider under-standing to underpin the future. It is hard for rising China to admit that, as Barack Obama put it when meeting Hu Jintao in 2011, its success has depended, in part, on 'decades of stability in Asia made possible by America's forward presence in the region and global trading championed by the US'.[5]

For American 'realist' analysts, a financially troubled US risks finding itself on a path of declining influence in the face of a rising power that is larger than its opponents in the Second World War and more efficient than the USSR. That leads, of course, to the argument for Washington to maintain high military spending to enable it to push back against any expansionism by Beijing. But the PRC's weaknesses also have to be taken into account in any balance sheet between the two great powers. The PRC's shortage of natural resources is not going to be significantly reduced by efficiency measures; even if these are effective, which is far from proven, China will require even greater quantity of imported oil, iron ore, coal, gas and other minerals. The transport channels through which these pass are vulnerable to attack, most obviously in the Straits of Malacca but also out on the ocean or on long rail links. Pipelines can be burst. Naval blockades are not necessarily a thing of the past, and America has by far the most powerful navy on earth.[6]

Closer to home China is 'a regional power without a regional policy', in the words of the scholar Steven Levine. It would like to be the central state in Asia but its policies are little more than a series of bilateral relationships, driven either by immediate material considerations or by a self-defensiveness that echoes Cold War attitudes. On the wider global stage Beijing may proclaim its goal of creating a 'harmonious world' and promoting multi-polarity but its practices do little to achieve that. It denounces 'hegemony' (i.e., US power) but does not use its position at the United Nations to champion the granting of permanent Security Council seats to Japan, India or Brazil. At G20 summits it does not put forward proposals to recalibrate the global economic and monetary systems beyond vague talk of the need for a new reserve system to replace the dollar. Historically the world financial system has hinged on the main creditor nation – Britain or the US in the past. But a 'yuan standard' is nowhere in sight as China shelters behind currency and capital market controls. If it turns out that the West, particularly the United States, is indeed losing its position of leadership, the People's Republic seems singularly ill-equipped and unready to step up to take over.[7]

Chinese foreign-policy experts reflect the uncertainty that envelops their country's approach to the world. 'China's grand strategy is still a field to be ploughed [as its] power and influence relative to those of other great states have outgrown the expectations of even its own leaders,' as Wang Jisi, Dean of the School of International Studies at Peking University, puts it. Pan Zongqi, Professor at the School of International Relations at Fudan University in Shanghai, defines the PRC's role as that of 'a responsible and constructive reformist', which is 'an active promoter and indeed shaper of the international system'. Gong Li, the global strategy director at the Party School, sees the United States struggling with the challenges of its economy, Afghanistan, Iraq, North Korea and terrorism, all of which will take their toll, but argues that China should remain cautious because it is still no match for the superpower.

One school of thought holds that China's success is enough to be getting on with, and that it should simply 'earn credits' for its progress from the rest of the world. Others see the United States as owing a debt to the mainland for having bought so many of its government bonds, and regard its failure to act accordingly as a form of betrayal. Some Chinese analysts advocate a triangular relationship with Europe and Russia to balance US power or, alternatively, believe it should concentrate on developing relations with Central Asia and Indochina. Those who look back to the decline of imperial China consider that foreign policy must be conducted from a position of strength, both military and economic, and invoke a 'century of humiliation' to assert that foreign powers owe China a debt from the past.

The scholar David Shambaugh has identified foreign-policy camps, starting with populist, xenophobic, Marxist 'nativism' and moving on to the dominant 'realist' group and those who think Beijing should concentrate on relations with the major powers and pay less attention to the rest. Then there are thinkers who put Asia and the developing world first; and so to 'selective multilateralism', which would expand China's global involvement gradually and only where national-security interests are involved, and 'globalism', which holds that the country must shoulder responsibility for addressing a range of world-governance issues in keeping with its size, power and influence. The weight of each of these groups varies and none is dominant; but, Shambaugh notes, 'globalism has lost the debate', which faces the rest of the world with obvious problems.[8]

On his visit to the United States in 2011, Hu Jintao was firm: 'We should abandon zero-sum Cold War mentality, view each other's development in an objective and sensible way, respect each other's choice of development path and pursue common development through win-win cooperation. We should respect each other's sovereignty, territorial integrity and development interests and properly address each other's major concerns.' He and his colleagues have no interest in assuming the global responsibilities implied in the concept of a G2 with the United States; indeed, such an idea is seen as a potential trap designed to ensnare the People's Republic and to divert it from its core concerns. Nor do they show much interest in joining a rules-based system for Asia, as promoted by Washington. The current 'hodgepodge' (to use Hillary Clinton's phrase) of regional arrangements suits Beijing quite well, allowing it to pick and choose, to avoid commitments which it might come to regret and to ensure that its own interests always have primacy while its growing strength intimidates smaller neighbours. The appeal of such an approach is evident, but it is not the agenda for a great power, even if it reaches back into history for a foundation that has become part of the national mantra and is often accepted with little questioning abroad.[9]

China shows extreme sensitiveness when it perceives that it has not been accorded full respect. The problem is that Beijing's definition of respect extends to requiring foreigners to gag themselves when their values are in conflict with those espoused by China on matters such as Tibet, Taiwan and human rights. Foreign leaders who dare to receive the Dalai Lama are told that they have 'hurt the feelings of 1.3 billion Chinese'. After Nicolas Sarkozy met the spiritual leader when France held the rotating presidency of the EU, Beijing cancelled a summit with the EU. A White House meeting between Barack Obama and the Dalai Lama brought reprimands from China for having 'grossly interfered in China's internal affairs' and breaching mutual trust between the two nations. The French retail group Carrefour suffered a boycott when it was accused of backing the Tibetan cause. Norwegian exports of salmon and trout to the PRC dropped sharply after the award of the Nobel Peace Prize to the imprisoned Liu Xiabao.

However, the PRC's bark is not always followed up by a bite. Beijing thunders against US arms sales to Taiwan but has taken only limited countermeasures and has not imposed threatened reprisals against the companies concerned, whose non-military cooperation it needs in its development plans. In the summer of 2011 its reaction to a repeat White House visit by the Dalai Lama was remarkably restrained, as if it had decided that calmer relations with Washington were in order at the time. While the Chinese ate less Norwegian fish after the Nobel award, a state company went ahead with the acquisition of a stake in an energy field held by Norway's Statoil group. Carrefour soon resumed normal operations.

China knows what it does not want others to do, but finds it hard to frame its policy in a more positive manner beyond the provision of markets and raw materials. If a definition of a great power is the ability

to set out norms that others find attractive, China is singularly defi-
cient. This state of affairs is further complicated by the way in which
foreign policy is shaped by the interests of a variety of parties ranging
from the Communist Party Leading Group on Foreign Affairs through
the State Security Ministry and the PLA to the National Development
and Reform Commission (NDRC), the main economic planning body,
and the Commerce Ministry representing exporters. Then there are the
heavy-industry and energy lobbies as the state oil companies expand
globally and China ramps up its imports of coal and natural gas. The
CCP's Propaganda Department is concerned with the country's image.
The Finance Ministry and the People's Bank of China have views on
international monetary and currency policy that, given the nature of the
country's foreign involvement, spill over into broader policy areas.
Nobody is quite sure how much clout the Foreign Ministry carries in
decision-making but it is not thought to be great.

This complex of different interest groups easily leads to confusion or
a failure to adopt a clear position. The PRC remains apparently unwilling, or unable, to bring its 'Little Brother' in North Korea to heel,
leading officials to describe their neighbour as a 'spoiled child'. It says
it wants to make the post-1945 global system more equitable but
opposes the granting of permanent Security Council seats to Japan or
India. Though China allowed the UN no-fly-zone resolution on Libya
to go through, it made clear that it could still criticize action by NATO
powers if things did not go according to its wishes. It then pursued a del-
icate balancing act between maintaining relations with the Gaddafi
regime and talking to the rebels. Hu Jintao upbraided President Sarkozy
over the air strikes and PLA generals sounded off in private to visitors in
the presence of an apparently approving Xi Jinping. A PRC firm, meanwhile, offered to sell weapons to the dictator, though the deal was not
concluded.[10]

Hu Jintao has told Chinese diplomats that they need to 'build a more
congenial image'. Improving China's image abroad was a main theme
of a Party plenum held in the autumn of 2011. Beijing pursues 'soft
power' through cultural missions and a network of Confucius Institutes
abroad, bestowing funds on festivals that celebrate its civilization and

brush awkward issues under the carpet. It lends out pandas and stages shows that highlight its history. It has committed to spending 50 billion yuan on its international broadcasting, including a second English-language television channel and a doubling of the shortwave-radio output from a transmitter in Texas. (This at a time when the BBC has stopped its Chinese-language service.) The state newspaper *China Daily* has launched international editions. When Hu Jintao made a state visit to the US in 2011, China bought space on giant screens in Times Square in New York to show a glossy film of its star entrepreneurs, actors, athletes and astronauts. The prominent academic Yuan Xuetong argues that China should develop its moral authority to buttress its place at the top of the hierarchy of nations he sees dominating the world.

But the authorities prefer scale and spectacle as at the Beijing Olympics and the Shanghai Expo (even if the latter ended up with debts of 19 billion yuan). When they decide to put on a spectacle to impress the world, they push the boat way out to display their nation's renaissance of the *shengshi* age of wealth and greatness before decline set in during the nineteenth century. Impressive as such displays are in scale, they reflect, above all, careful regimentation just as the push to charm foreign public opinion is the result of state planning offered strictly on China's terms. The contribution of the private sector, of individual writers and artists, which has done so much to spread Western culture round the globe, is missing. A benevolent image is somewhat tricky when the country's best-known international artist, Ai Weiwei, has been detained after criticizing the regime and when one of China's only two Nobel laureates for literature, Gao Xingjian, has chosen to take French citizenship (the other, Mo Yan, who won the prize in 2012, remains within the system and is careful not to stray far from the official line). The President of the Norwegian Nobel committee said the long prison sentence passed on Liu Xiabao had 'solved the problem' of how to recognize Chinese dissidents since 'automatically he became [...] a universal symbol of human rights'. Once again the imposition of Party power took precedence over everything else, and 'soft diplomacy' suffered a large shot in its foot, made all the more evident when an attempt to set up a Confucius Prize to rival the Nobel ended in fiasco. A veteran Kuomintang politician from Taiwan, Lien Chan, who had held talks to smooth cross-Strait relations, was chosen as the first laureate in 2010. But he was not informed and did not turn up for the ceremony in Beijing at which the 100,000-yuan prize was handed to a small girl for unexplained reasons. In September 2011 the Chinese prize was scrapped with an explanation that it had 'violated relevant regulations' but its organizers still went ahead and gave the second year's award to Vladimir Putin.

Nor is the talk of harmoniousness and congeniality helped by China's military build-up. The PLA's capacity remains far behind that of the United States. Data from 2009 show it accounting for 6.2 per cent of global military spending, ahead of France and Britain but far behind the 43 per cent for the US. A leading Chinese general says the PRC needs to double spending on its armed forces from 1.4 to 2.8 per cent of GDP to close the gap. The official PLA budget rose by 11.2 per cent in 2011 to the equivalent of $106 billion (though that figure is an under-statement, since it does not cover all military-linked projects) and it is forecast to increase by almost 150 per cent by 2015. Even so, China is anxious to play down its military expansion.

When the Pentagon issued an assessment in 2011 the PRC was on track to forge a modern military force by 2020, Xinhua responded by describing this as 'an utterly cock-and-bull story'. But Beijing does protest too much, for it is hard to ignore the expansion of spending on armed forces numbering 1.5 million troops and the drive to master advances in technology for military applications. The PRC shoots down satellites of the type used for military-command systems, sends submarines to pop up amid American fleet exercises, puts new fighter planes into service and develops its navy. While the US Defense Secretary was having talks with Hu Jintao in 2011, the air force showed off its stealth fighter. The PLA's ability to watch targets from space is almost equal to that of the US forces, according to a report by a Washington think tank, though this seems to be a considerable exaggeration.[11]

The Pentagon says the mainland is increasing spending on nuclear weapons and long-range missiles able to reach targets beyond Guam. In 2008 General Ma Xiaotian, Deputy Chief of the PLA General Staff, was quoted as telling US officials that the growth of the PRC's nuclear force was 'an imperative necessity' and that there could be 'no limit on technical progress'. A new base to house nuclear-powered ballistic-missile submarines has been built at Sanya on Hainan Island. An anti-ship missile dubbed the 'Sizzler' by NATO can be launched from submerged submarines and is reported to fly at three times the speed of sound over a 200-mile range. Another missile, the Dongfeng, is being developed to hit a carrier 2,000 miles away. The fleet air arm is being expanded to 200 planes.

The expansion of the navy and air force was originally spurred by the PLA's desire to be able to invade Taiwan if Beijing decided to use force to try to achieve reunification, especially after the US navy blocked the Strait during the crisis that erupted in 1996 when the PLA fired missiles into the sea off the island. But it now has wider implications as China implements its version of the thesis advanced by the American strategist Alfred Mahan on the link between a powerful navy and the development of international trade. In 2011 the PRC conducted sea trials of a modernized 67,000-ton aircraft carrier bought for $20 million from Ukraine – supposedly to use as a floating casino off Macau but now converted to military purposes. There is uncertainty about whether the PRC should build its own carrier, a highly complex job that would test its technologies to the full, but some reports say that work is already under way as part of a ten-year navy-modernization programme. However, the PRC is still a long way from being able to rival the US navy – it managed to get jets to land and take off the ship only at the end of 2012. The single carrier is an assertion of China's ambitions rather than a significant factor in the East Asia strategic balance.

Still, the PLA sees naval expansion as a means for the nation to project itself. Beijing wants to be able to counter any attempt by India or the United States to control the sea lanes that bring it oil from the Middle East. Eighty per cent of such imports come through the Malacca Straits, which will remain a potential choke point even after a pipeline is built from the Burma coast to Yunnan. So the ability to intervene to ensure freedom of navigation if this is threatened is highly important. Strategically, China views greater naval force as a means to free itself from the confines of the chain of islands, including Taiwan, that runs

south from Japan to the Philippines and on to the US base at Diego
Garcia, and a second chain further away that stretches from Japan to the
Marshall and Bonin Islands, including the American strongpoint of
Guam.

This desire of the People's Republic to become a blue-water ocean
power in the region is entirely normal and natural, but it poses an obvious test to the regional-security system in place in East Asia since the
end of the Second World War. Admiral Mike Mullen, the Chairman of
the American Joint Chiefs of Staff, spoke in 2011 of Beijing seeking
'access denial' to push the US out of the area. Traditional US allies
from Japan to Australia cannot avert their eyes to the possibility that
their economic ties with the PRC will come into conflict with their
strategic and political positions. 'Differences between us are still stark,'
Mullen said after visiting China in mid-2011.[12]

With 2.3 million troops, 2,000 aircraft, 80 surface vessels and 70 submarines, the PLA is officially described as 'defensive in nature' as 'China
unswervingly takes the road of peaceful development'. But, like every
other element of the power structure, it has a political role to play at the
behest of the CCP – which, in Leninist fashion, insists that it remains
under civilian control, with Xi Jinping now heading the Central Military
Commission to ensure Party command of the gun. Eighteen per cent of
Central Committee and two of the twenty-five Politburo seats are
occupied by PLA members, giving the military a limited say in policy
formulation.

The forces nurture a powerful narrative that gives them a central place
in the regime and the creation of the People's Republic, followed by the
way the PLA was called in by Mao to cope with the excesses of the Cultural
Revolution and then, in the official version, saved the PRC by cracking
down on the protestors of 1989. Naturally the PLA presents itself as serving the people and nation as it undertakes tasks set out in official
statements that stress its role in disaster relief at home and abroad, in
helping maintain law and order, solving 37,000 criminal cases in 2010 and
seizing 3,845 illegal guns, digging wells, dredging waterways and planting
11 million trees a year. A White Paper issued in the spring of 2011 gives
'maintaining social harmony and stability' as one of its main aims in

addition to 'upholding national security and unity' and subduing 'all subversive and sabotage activities by hostile forces'.

But, as a senior PLA political officer, Zhang Weibing, restated in its theoretical journal, it is primarily a Party army with 90,000 Communist cells. In June 1989 it acted against the people in Beijing to save the CCP leadership, and its troops swore loyalty oaths to the ruling movement. A recent article in the *People's Daily* by the Commander and Political Commissar of the strategic missile force stressed that the PLA 'should promote obedience in the ranks towards the Communist Party of China'.[13] In the wake of the Bo Xilai case, the party stressed the need for the PLA to be loyal to it amid fears that some generals had been ready to side with the fallen politician.

The corollary of this is that, though civilian control of the military is enshrined, the PLA enjoys weight in the regime that sets it apart from professional, apolitical armies in the West. The evocation of heroic battles of the past and the PLA's goose-stepping parades reinforce nationalism and sabre-rattling. Military-style campaigns remain part of the regime's culture, even if they are no longer as vast and brutal as they were under the Great Helmsman. As the history of China shows, the past is filled with martial acts that undermine the veneer of Confucian reasonableness. In a recent book entitled *The China Dream* Senior Colonel Liu Mingfu called for the PRC to focus on building up its military strength while the United States suffers from economic problems. In the preface to another book published in 2011, General Liu Yuan, Political Commissar of the PLA's General Logistics Department, declared that 'history is written by blood and slaughter' and described the nation-state as 'a power machine made of violence'. He added: 'Military culture is the oldest and most important wisdom of humanity'. Not content with that, the general, the son of Mao's onetime number two who was purged and left to die in the Cultural Revolution, slammed General Secretaries of the CCP 'recently and in the past' for having betrayed it. Another general, Luo Yuan, has advocated the dispatch of hundreds of fishing boats to fight a guerilla war at sea for territories claimed by the PRC.

No wonder foreign analysts worry about the thinking and ambitions of the coming generation of army leaders. Civilian politicians remain in

charge but the PLA's political position and the readiness of senior officers to speak out sets a 'boundary of the permissible' about how far they
can go in distancing themselves from the demands of the military,
should they wish to do so.

Concern about China's offensive potential is heightened by allegations of widespread 'vacuum-cleaner' espionage abroad, both on behalf
of the military and by companies, and by the PRC's cyber-war and hacking abilities. Officials deny any involvement of the state or army, and say
it is the work of individuals whom the authorities would like to catch.
However, it is hard to believe that in a system such as that on the mainland the widespread and long-lasting hacking reported by Western
investigators could continue without approval or encouragement from
the security agencies. The *Financial Times* reported in October 2011
that the PLA had set up thousands of units in the previous decade in
technology companies and universities to form 'the backbone of its
Internet warfare forces'. Some attacks have been traced back to the city
of Jinan in Shandong, which houses a base for the national-security
arm of the People's Liberation Army. Mike Rogers, Chairman of the
House of Representatives Permanent Select Committee on Intelligence
in Washington, charged China with staging 'a massive and sustained
intelligence effort by a government to blatantly steal commercial data
and intellectual property.'[14]

In 2006–07 West European governments spoke openly of Internet
attacks from China and the head of Britain's security service wrote to
300 corporate chief executives and security advisers alerting them to the
threat from China. A US government report in 2009 quoted the defence
contractor Northrop Grumman as listing thirty-five significant cyber-
attacks from the mainland against Western or Taiwanese targets. The
following year, Canadian researchers uncovered a spy network using
1,300 computers, many of them in China, and said they had penetrated
government systems. There were also reports of hacking into major oil
and gas companies, the Lockheed defence-equipment company, the
US electricity grid and the personal computer of German Chancellor
Angela Merkel.

Then Google, which had pulled back from the PRC because of hacking into Gmail accounts of dissidents and Chinese censorship, reported

that hundreds of users of its Gmail service had been 'phished' by cyber attackers who sent out fake emails to get access to passwords. The targets, the company said, were senior government officials in the US and several Asian countries, military personnel, journalists and Chinese political activists. Denying the charges through the *People's Daily*, Beijing accused Google of having become a 'tool for political contention' by 'deliberately pandering to negative Western perceptions of China'.

But the accusations continued to pile up. In the summer of 2011 the Internet-security company McAfee released a report listing infiltration over five years of seventy-two organizations, including governments, companies, the United Nations, the Association of Southeast Asian Nations (ASEAN), the International Olympic Committee and the World Anti-Doping Agency. The attacks, dubbed 'Operation Shady RAT', were believed to originate with 'one state actor', McAfee said. It did not name any country but an expert who was briefed on the hacking said the evidence pointed to the PRC, which again denied the accusation in a comment in *People's Daily*. This stated that 'linking China to Internet hacking attacks is irresponsible' and charged that it was, itself, hit by nearly 500,000 cyber-attacks in 2010, nearly half originating overseas, with 14.7 per cent from the US and 8 per cent from India.

Though there is a danger in automatically fingering China as the villain in Western security breaches, the threat seems plain and the source is likely not to be run-of-the mill hackers who prefer to go for bank accounts and credit cards. The potential for attacks on such vital elements to the functioning of a nation as the electric-grid control system is an obvious danger that reaches beyond military hardware. In November 2011, the US administration formally accused the PRC (along with Russia) of seeking to steal American technology.

Such factors, on top of the worries about China eating everybody else's economic lunch, induce a decidedly mixed attitude towards the People's Republic round the world. A global survey by the Pew Institute in 2011 reported that more than 60 per cent of those questioned had a favourable view of the PRC in Pakistan, Kenya, Indonesia, Russia, Ukraine and the Palestinian territories. The figure for Britain was 59 per cent and the US 51 per cent. Scores of below 40 per cent were recorded in Mexico, Germany, Japan, India and Turkey. Another poll for the

BBC published in 2011 and covering twenty-seven countries, showed that, while China was popular in Russia, Latin America and Africa, negative opinions prevailed in the US (51 to 36 per cent positive), Canada (49–35) and Britain (46–38) and even more strongly in Germany (62–24), France (64–26) and other major Asian powers – India (52–25), South Korea (53–38) and Japan (52–12).[15]

Even if respondents in such polls do not follow the ins and outs of the PRC's policies, what they know is clearly sufficient to breed concern about the rising power. The spread of opinion echoes the divisions among commentators mentioned in the opening chapter and the ambivalent sentiment in countries that benefit from the mainland's investment and purchases but would rather that the Chinese were not so expansive. The lack of a clear global vision from its leadership, the great focus on domestic development and the multiplicity of interest groups at work make it a volatile player that may lurch alarmingly when it considers its narrowly defined national interests at stake. For a nation that can look back to such a long history, the People's Republic is, in many ways, still in an adolescent phase as an actor on the world scene. That worries the governments with which it deals but how China operates internally is also a cause of concern for the people with whom it does business and whose experiences throw valuable light on the PRC's integration with the world.

14

THE LAST FRONTIER

Roberto C. Goizueta, Chairman and Chief Executive of Coca-Cola, may have been guilty of hyperbole when he hailed the opening of a bottling plant in China in the 1990s as possibly 'one of the most important days in [...] the history of the world'. As he passed through Hong Kong a few days later he told me that he could not stop himself thinking of the day when every Chinese household would have 'at least one can of Coke in the ice box' – even if most did not have a refrigerator at that time.

The other side of China's outward economic expansion has been the attempt by foreign companies to penetrate the last great business frontier. It is a sentiment that goes back to the nineteenth century when Lancashire mill owners calculated how sales of their cotton would be boosted if every Chinese man could be induced to lengthen his shirt by a few inches. Vice-Premier Li Keqiang pandered to such ambitions when, in a newspaper article before visiting Spain in 2011, he wrote that 'if each of the 1,300 million Chinese people consumed a bottle of olive oil or enjoyed a few glasses of wine, all of Spain's annual production would probably not be sufficient to meet the demand'. One year at the World Economic Forum in Davos, Bill Gates asked for me to be seated next to him at lunch so that he could quiz me about how Microsoft could best get into the Chinese market: should the company operate on its own or work with the government to safeguard its intellectual property? (I told him that either way Microsoft was very likely to be pirated.)

Goizueta would have been content to learn that Coca-Cola sold more than a billion cases of its products in the PRC in the first half of 2011 – twice as many as five years earlier. It plans to invest $4 billion in the country up to 2014; PepsiCo, which is also doing well on the mainland, has a $2.5-billion, three year programme in China. According to Coke's current Chief Executive, Muhat Kent, China is a more business-friendly environment than the US: 'It's like a well-managed company. You have a one-stop shop in terms of the Chinese foreign-investment agency and local governments are fighting for investment with each other,' he told the *Financial Times*.[1]

US sales to the mainland rose by 31 per cent in 2010 to $102 billion and, as we have seen, China is the EU's biggest trading partner, with German sales trebling in five years to $71 billion in 2010. It has replaced the US as Japan's largest export market, though the figures have to be treated with some caution since they include semi-finished goods sent to be assembled on the mainland before being sold elsewhere.

China's new rich line up to buy imported luxury goods from Shenzhen to Ordos. In Chengdu the avenue leading to the giant statue of Mao is lined with outlets for Gucci, Vuitton and other European brands. Cosmopolitans have a thirst for fine French clarets, but the PRC also buys vodka from Lithuania, sparkling wine from Italy, Cheddar cheese from England and beef from Scotland. Vuitton made a splash with a mock-up of its emblematic bag the size of a wall in Shanghai (photograph at the start of this chapter). China accounts for 29 per cent of Swiss watch sales. Porsche saw business in the PRC rise by 47 per cent in the first half of 2011; it sold 10,000 of its top-of-the-range Cayenne model there in 2010, with a waiting list of fifteen months (one special touch on offer was bodywork painted pink to match a young lady's lipstick).

But the real lure for many foreign firms is to set up manufacturing operations in the mainland, to sell there or to use it as a base for exports. Ambitious Westerners now head for China just as they would have gone to make their fortunes in Europe's colonies during the nineteenth century. As Tim Clissold wrote in his excellent account of his experience, *Mr China*: 'There is a kind of an entrepreneurial Western who just can't resist it [...] the largest untapped market on earth. What more could they want?'[2]

For big foreign firms the application of their know-how to the reserve of cheap labour, tax breaks and land granted on favourable terms by local governments offers a way to reap large profits if they can sell to tens or hundreds of millions of consumers in a retail market worth $1.7 trillion – well below the US with $3 trillion but growing at 18 per cent a year. Retailers with good logistics systems, such as Carrefour and Walmart, and consumer-goods firms like Colgate-Palmolive have benefited from applying their supply-chain expertise to the PRC to get over regional fragmentation. Dan Akerson, Chairman and Chief Executive Officer of General Motors, which has 6.5 per cent of the Chinese market, calls the PRC the 'crown jewel' in his company's universe; in 2010 Chinese bought 550,000 Buicks, perpetuating a love affair that dates back to Sun Yat-sen, the Last Emperor and Zhou Enlai, all of whom used the marque. Volkswagen, which has China at the core of its global plans, sold 1.9 million cars there in 2010, a 37 per cent increase over the previous year. Ford intends to build four new plants in the PRC by 2015 and Japanese and South Korea auto companies have made major inroads.

Makers of advanced machinery in Europe, Japan and the United States tap into China's move up the value chain and the need for increased productivity as the mainland buys equipment it cannot (yet) manufacture itself. The PRC is the biggest market for ABB, the big Swiss-Swedish energy-and-technology group. Following the government's policy of opening up Western China, Siemens is building its biggest digital factory in the country in Chengdu to make industrial automation products, its first such plant outside Germany and the US. Apple's sales have overtaken those of China's Lenovo group, jumping fourfold in the year to mid-2011 in Greater China, including Hong Kong and Taiwan. The Californian company now accepts payment in yuan on its on-line App Store to boost sales further.

Foreign chemicals groups invest billions of dollars in new plants. Global pharmaceutical giants such as Pfizer, GlaxoSmithKline, Roche and Sanofi have research-and-development centres in the mainland and medical-equipment manufacturers supplying hospitals are homing in, too: a 20 per cent annual growth in medicine consumption and an explosion of demand for both medicines and machines is expected under a 900-billion-yuan programme to build hospitals and clinics across the country by 2020.

As Louis Chênevert, Chairman and CEO of the big US group United Technologies, which makes Otis lifts, remarks: 'You can't be an elevator company and not be in China.' Its Finnish competitor, Kone, won orders for 226 escalators and 178 lifts for 46 mainland railway stations in the spring of 2011. Caterpillar earth-movers are part of the China development story, with revenue in the PRC rising from $1.9 billion in 2009 to $3.3 billion in 2010. The company and its dealers have almost 20,000 staff at 16 manufacturing facilities on the mainland and is planning half-a-dozen more, but it faces growing competition from domestic rivals.

Toyota is to start producing motors and batteries for its hybrid vehicles in China in 2013. For makers of information-technology equipment the mainland has become the key to the global supply chain and is now the biggest exporter of IT hardware. More than 80 per cent of the PRC's IT goods sales come from companies with foreign investment (including Taiwan). China's place in the chain is backed by the logistics network that has grown up round firms like Foxconn, with the huge automated conveyor-belt system (bought from Siemens) at its Shenzhen headquarters. A product ordered on the Internet by a consumer in Birmingham, England, or Birmingham, Alabama, is taken off the assembly line in Shenzhen, tested, packaged, placed with other orders on a pallet, loaded into a FedEx or DHL truck, taken to the airport, flown across the world, sorted by destination and delivered to the consumer's home. No other developing nation enjoys the combination of manufacturing prowess and logistics that has been built up in China.

Consumer-goods companies and firms offering services are pushing their brands inland, choosing Chinese names that vaunt their products – Reebok's *Rvi bu* means 'quick steps' and Lay's snacks are sold as *Le shi*, or 'happy things'. Unilever held 1,500 roadshows across China in 2010. Yum Brands, which owns KFC and Pizza Hut has more than 4,000 outlets in China and adapts its menus to local tastes. David Novak, its Chief Executive, says consumer demand in the PRC is 'exploding' contributing 40 per cent of the firm's global profits. In 2011, it bought the Little Sheep chain of hotpot restaurants. But in 2012 it warned of falling same-store sales in the PRC and state television alleged improper use of antibiotics in chicken KFC got from Chinese suppliers. Starbucks has more than 800 outlets in the PRC and McDonald's 1,100. Nestlé, which has doubled sales of its Crispy Shark chocolate-wafer bar in China in five years, has bought a majority stake in a food group that makes peanut-flavoured drinks and tinned rice-pudding, and is bidding for a big confectionery maker.

Adidas intends to open more than 2,500 new outlets across China in the coming years. Walmart's floor space in China has quintupled since 2006, by far its fastest expansion in any country; the chain has 350 stores in 130 cities on the mainland and 100,000 'associates'. Japan's largest spa operator, Gokurakuyu, wants to open 100 sites in the PRC in the next five years – more than it has at home. The Chairman of the Club Med holiday firm reckons that attracting just 0.2 per cent of the Chinese would mean 2.6 million customers.[3]

Foreign financial institutions that bought into the IPOs of Chinese banks have generally earned good profits. Morgan Stanley made $1 billion and Bank of America $3.3 billion from investments in China Construction Bank. Western private-equity firms have reaped profits from backing mainland firms involved in anything from car dealerships to insurance and fish processing. British and American schools and universities have cashed in on the desire to learn English: the Disney Company offers language courses featuring Mickey Mouse, the Little Mermaid and other characters.

In a Chamber of Commerce survey in 2011, nearly 80 per cent of European firms operating in the People's Republic said that they enjoyed a 50 per cent increase in sales in 2009 and another 'significant rise' in 2010 with average profits jumping by more than 40 per cent. Seventy-eight per cent of member companies surveyed by the American Chamber of Commerce the same year said their China operations were profitable or very profitable, the highest proportion since surveys started in 2002. Other surveys by Western chambers of commerce show firms reporting bigger margins in China than globally. Eighty-three per cent of US firms planned to increase their investment in the mainland, which totalled $65 billion by the end of 2010. Though financial investment in the PRC is tricky, more than 400 mutual funds round the world have the word 'China' in their names. A survey by *China Daily* reported that 90 per cent of 69 multinational firms that responded planned to increase their investments in the PRC by 2015. Most saw their main competition coming from one another rather than from Chinese companies.[4]

So far, so good. But other sides to the China business story are less positive or downright negative. The road to profitability can be long. As Tim Clissold concluded about hopeful entrepreneurs, drawing on his own experiences in the PRC: 'After a string of negative experiences, the chastened pioneer usually concludes: "In the end it's an illusion."' The French environment-services group Veolia took fourteen years to make money in China after investing 2 billion euros in twenty projects. Despite opening a flagship store in the China World Shopping Mall in Beijing, Lego reaps only 1 per cent of its global sales in the PRC and Walmart's $7.5 billion in sales on the mainland bring just 2 per cent of the firm's annual revenues.

Having misjudged the taste of Chinese girls for dolls, the world's biggest toymaker, Mattel, closed its 3,502-square-metre, six-storey Barbie store in Shanghai; this had included a restaurant and spa, beauty treatments, cocktails, pink lights at night and outfits for the dolls by the *Sex and the City* costume designer Patricia Field. Nor do the Chinese go for do-it-yourself – thus the big US chain Home Depot had to cut back on plans to expand in the mainland and Britain's Kingfisher group closed a third of its B&Q outlets before changing strategy to sell interiors for whole apartments to be installed by workmen. Best Buy, the world's largest consumer-electronics retailer, shut nine stores in China after making the mistake of trying to impose US-style staffing and store organization. Foreign Internet companies have had a hard time on the mainland. Yahoo fell into a dispute with its Chinese partner. eBay lost market share and the online coupon firm Groupon had to readjust its strategy, while Google was hit by domestic sites better attuned to how the Chinese use the Internet.

Retailers and consumer-goods companies can find themselves unexpectedly exposed, sometimes because the authorities suddenly decide to take an interest or because of freelance business-boosting action by local managers. Unilever was fined 2 million yuan for warning that rising raw material costs might lead it to increase prices – this was held to have created disorder in the market and added to inflationary pressures since buyers were likely to rush out to buy its products. Carrefour and Walmart were fined 9.5 million yuan between them for deceptive pricing and the French group suffered its boycott when stories spread that its director backed the Dalai Lama. Walmart's thirteen stores in Chongqing were closed by the authorities in the autumn of 2011 after being accused of selling ordinary pork as organic meat at premium prices – the chain's Chinese boss resigned 'for personal reasons'. In Changsha, the American store group and Carrefour were fined for changing the sell-by dates on products to keep them on the shelves for longer.

Both the US and EU Chambers say the biggest challenge their members face in doing business in China is their concern that the regulatory environment is increasingly arrayed against them in favour of state-owned companies. The more profitable American firms have grown, the greater their pessimism about the government's commitment to improving their market access. The proportion of European companies expecting discriminatory measures against them rose from 36 per cent in 2010 to 46 per cent the following year. In one example of the delays that can occur in getting permission to import into or operate in China, it took growers of Belgian pears eight years to be allowed to sell on the mainland. The document required for a small company to set up a representative office runs to more than 400 pages.

The American Vice President of the US–China Business Council says that a fifth of its members report that China's regulations on mergers and acquisitions discourage them from seeking deals or complicate ongoing discussions. Google ran into trouble when it refused to apply censorship rules – reportedly this came after a member of the Politburo did a search for his own name and came up with links to material that would never have got round official controls. At his summit with Hu Jintao in Washington in early 2011, President Obama stressed the need for equal treatment for US companies on the mainland and Vice President Joe Biden repeated the message on a visit to Beijing in August that year. The following month, Gary Locke, the new US ambassador to China, told a business meeting that lack of openness in the Chinese economy was the 'single largest barrier' to improving Sino-American cooperation and called for 'an acceleration and expansion of the economic reforms China has undertaken'.[5]

The power of the state means that decisions taken behind closed doors can exclude those firms not favoured politically. A survey of twenty-nine countries by the Organization for Economic Cooperation and Development (OECD) found that the PRC had the least competition – a trend that has been amplified as, in a popular phrase, 'the state advances, the private sector retreats'. The weak legal system is a constant problem; so is the preference given to entrenched domestic interests. Rules about how and where firms from abroad can invest in China are opaque. Undefined 'important' sections of infrastructure, transport, agriculture and equipment manufacturing are officially listed as 'sensitive' areas. National security can be invoked, along with the need for state and commercial secrecy. In his speech in September 2011 Locke complained about 'substantial restrictions' on imports and 'expansive government interference' that shut out foreign competition in many fields and led them to wonder if they were really welcome.[6]

Apparently straightforward regulations can slot in with one another to produce a brick wall. For instance, to get a licence to trade in wholesale petroleum products a company has to own a refinery. But refineries are classed as a strategic national asset and foreign ownership is forbidden. So no foreign firm can trade in wholesale petroleum. Companies that seek safety by allying with a big Chinese state firm may find that their priorities are different and that senior Chinese appointments are decided with reference to hidden, politically motivated reasons or because of the influence of a well-connected princeling from the PRC business aristocracy. Despite holding a 20 per cent stake in a major Chinese state-controlled bank, it was reportedly only after the event that HSBC was told that the chairman was moving to another of the big four banks. Representatives of foreign investors tell of being faced with important decisions taken in their absence by local partners, or of the Chinese directors going outside the board room for a smoke and coming back to announce what is going to be done. It was after an initial bid was submitted by CNOOC for the takeover of the US oil firm Unocal that the company's four foreign directors were advised of its plans. Both HSBC and the International Finance Corporation were told that their stakes in the Bank of Shanghai could be sold only to a PRC buyer.[7]

Foreign firms may be invited in for the technology they bring but refused operational controls on its application. Their managers who perform well elsewhere may not be the right people for the PRC. Corporate structures that work in the West or Japan may not be able to cope with the vagaries of China. Ownership can turn out to be not quite what it appeared to be. Yahoo found that the online-payment unit of the largest e-commerce company, Alibaba, in which it had a big stake, had been transferred to a separate entity controlled by the Chairman; China's rules stipulate that such third-party services could be held only by companies without foreign shareholders. The state regulator has used anti-monopoly legislation to force foreign companies involved in acquisitions outside China to divest themselves of part of their operations in the PRC to the benefit of local rivals. Coca-Cola's bid for a big domestic soft-drinks manufacturer, Huiyuan Juice, was blocked by the anti-trust regulator. The private-equity group Carlyle gave up an attempt to buy a majority stake in the construction-machinery firm, Xugong, after three years of official obstruction that steadily whittled down its proposed holding. Bain, another US investment firm, found itself engaged in a complex and lengthy board battle at the electrical retailer Gome, in which it has a stake, after the company's chairman went to jail for insider dealing and corruption.[8]

The business world operates in a legally opaque context into which foreign firms can find it hard to fit. Accounting standards have improved but the books are not always transparent. Succession planning is poor. Every company of any size has a CCP cell with the power to veto major decisions. China's Company Law sets 'maintaining the socialist economic order' as its first priority. Forty per cent of chief executives and senior managers at private firms belong to the CCP. Top executive posts in the state companies that dominate major sectors are parcelled out by the authorities to trusted figures who may be rotated between corporate and Communist or provincial posts – Guo Shuqing, the Chairman of China Construction Bank, was formerly Deputy Governor of Guizhou, while the head of one of the big energy generators was appointed Vice-Governor of Shanxi and the Chairman of Sinopec became Governor of Fujian.

Personnel moves are often shrouded in mystery. The army, which had major business interests ranging from night clubs to a big mobile-telephone operator, was officially ordered by Jiang Zemin to divest itself of such concerns in 1998. In the following two years the PLA transferred 6,000 companies to the state, receiving no compensation though its budget rose substantially. But some officers simply moved with the enterprises and went on running former military commercial assets in civilian guise.

To take an example of the vagaries of business, look at China Mobile – the world's largest operator, with 600 million subscribers. The firm's Vice-President was removed in 2009 after being found to have accepted bribes, despite having spoken out in favour of greater accountability by boards of state-owned firms. Several other executives were subsequently also punished for graft. The Vice President was also sacked as head of the Party cell. Two years later his successor, the firm's Chairman, was abruptly replaced in the CCP post by the Vice-Minister of Industry and Information Technology, who called the shots thereafter. A new corruption investigation was launched, with up to ten arrests. All executives above mid-level ranking were told to hand in their passports so that they could not flee abroad. State media said the other two telecommunications groups, China Unicom and China Telecom, were also probed.

The government and Party leadership would like to breed national champions, particularly in modern technology, but this has not been overly successful and has involved preferential treatment for favoured public-sector players. The overarching question, as a Chinese economist puts it, is whether the state is a predatory protector or a protective predator, and what that means for private enterprises.

Business is further complicated by lack of clarity as to ownership rights. Due diligence for investors is very necessary but often difficult. Agricultural land, for instance, belongs to and is leased out by the state, but farmers can find their plots suddenly requisitioned by the authorities with low compensation. In 2010, 428,000 hectares of agricultural land was taken over for construction, 18 per cent more than the previous year. A boom in Chinese timber companies quoted on the Nasdaq exchange in the US came to abrupt halt in 2011 when investors belatedly realized that there was no central land registry of ownership of forests they thought were the property of the firms in which they had put their money and that they were, in fact, likely to be in the hands of collectives controlled by local governments or by the state. On top of that, usage rights were often acquired after cash had changed hands under the table, and the trees were likely to be traded out of sight by companies out for a quick return. (Among those who took a bath was John Paulson, the celebrated hedge-fund manager who made a killing by going against the sub-prime market but who dropped much of his $500 million investment in a mainland forestry enterprise listed in Canada that refused to disclose to whom it was selling its trees though an investigation cleared it of running a Ponzi scheme fraud.)

Abuse of intellectual-property rights and 'indigenous re-innovation' by joint-venture partners is a constant problem as Chinese companies go from depending on foreign technology to competing with European and Japanese manufacturers in export markets. The history of the high-speed train described in Chapter Three provides one case study; in late 2011, the chief executive of the French rail group, Alstom, said his company had chosen not to share key technology with Chinese partners but that Japanese and German suppliers had done so and suggested to a reporter that he should ask them if they were satisfied with the outcome.

The PRC's programme to launch a 220-seat airliner in the mid-decade follows years of learning from cooperation with Airbus, Boeing and other foreign firms. Beijing is putting pressure on foreign vehicle makers to share more production secrets with mainland car companies in what some of those concerned see as a 'technology shakedown' – technology transfer in return for market access. The reaction has been cautious: though its boss sees China as the jewel in the crown, General Motors is leery of sharing electric-car technology, while other firms hold back their latest know-how. It is not simply the extent of the copying but also the speed with which China moves that has surprised Western and Japanese companies. Franz Fehrenbach, Chief Executive of the big German car-parts maker Bosch, which employs 30,000 people at forty-six sites on the mainland, foresees a massive attack in the machinery sector from the PRC in the next few years as Chinese firms improve the quality of their products but keep prices low. The legal system can also throw up some unpleasant surprises: a court ruled in December, 2011, that the name of its tablet belonged to a Taiwanese firm which had earlier registered a product under the name of IPAD. China made major changes to its practices at the time of its adhesion to the World Trade organization in 2001 but, as foreign firms find all the time, that momentum has not been kept up.[9]

Chinese companies have shown considerable ability to adapt foreign techniques to the tastes of their domestic market. For instance, main-land Internet companies have strengthened their lock on the enormous user-base in the People's Republic by developing services that accord with its requirements rather than seeking – as do foreign players – to impose global styles. To help them, and to keep foreign competition at bay, technological requirements are applied to exclude firms using global-standard equipment that does not conform to PRC require-ments. Despite all its home-grown-food scandals, China periodically bans agricultural imports on health grounds. Suits brought against the PRC under WTO rules have had some success, for instance in liber-alizing distribution of imported films and books, implementing intellectual-property rules or removing restrictions on foreign car parts. But such cases are lengthy and the business situation may have moved on by the time they are settled. Beijing has dragged its feet over the global agreement on government tendering and tolerates preferential procurement policies by provincial authorities.

For China, this is the fulfilment of the dream of the late-nineteenth-century Self-Strengtheners, who aimed to develop China by using the methods of the 'barbarians' and to get the better of them. In this process, China gives away nothing fundamental but absorbs what it needs. 'We should seize the opportunity, at a time when [...] foreigners are delighted to show their superior techniques, to make a substantial study of all kinds of foreign machines and weapons in order to learn their secret completely,' as an official report to the throne proposed. Or, as the scholar Zhang Zhidong put it in a celebrated formulation at the time, 'Chinese learning for fundamental principles; Western learning for practical application'. Though Zhang and his peers did not get very far, the model was set more than a century ago and now serves as the chosen avenue for national advancement in a globalized world.[10]

Such difficulties in cracking the China market lead to occasional outbursts by Western business chieftains. Jeffrey Immelt, Chief Executive of the giant American group General Electric, which employs 16,000 people on the mainland, was quoted as telling a dinner in Rome in 2010: 'I really worry about China [...] I am not sure that in the end they want any of us to win, or any of us to be successful.' That same year, the EU Chamber of Commerce drew up a list of Chinese obstructionism that included regulatory problems, obstacles to market access and discriminatory procurement policies. At a meeting in Beijing the heads of two big German companies, Siemens and BASF, complained directly to the Prime Minister about restrictions, enforced technology transfers and the business climate in China. Chinese practices, they said, did 'not exactly correspond to our views of a partnership'; they grew so heated on the subject that Wen Jiabao advised them to calm down.[11]

But the lure of the mainland market and the attractions of the PRC as a manufacturing and assembly centre invariably win out. As Vice-Premier Wang Qishan responded when European business leaders complained to him about restrictions in China, 'I know you have complaints but the charm of the Chinese market is irresistible.'[12]

Foreign direct investment (FDI) continues to rise, topping $100 billion in 2010. Not long after Immelt's criticism, GE announced a partnership with China's main aerospace group to work on avionics for a new regional jet being built by the Chinese; it also said it was moving the global headquarters of its unit making X-ray machines from Wisconsin to China 'to help make the business more nimble and responsive while continuing to strengthen our local focus and grow our global footprint'. Within a few months of complaining to Wen Jiabao, BASF and Siemens unveiled substantial investment programmes in the mainland. Three years after Carlyle gave up on Xugong, David Rubenstein, the firm's co-founder and Managing Director, told a journalist, 'I would say that today when I go to China, I find more people in government who are interested in learning about the things that private equity can do to help an economy and help companies than you often do in Washington.'[13]

When it comes to its own involvement in foreign markets, China faces justified criticism that it scores not only through the cheapness of its products but also by the way in which the authorities have bolstered mainland companies with an array of subsidies and protective measures to shield them at home. The China Development Bank, which has teams in 114 countries, and other state financial institutions provide cheap, long-term financing arrangements that can cut the overall cost to foreign buyers by up to half of what they would pay for the equivalent goods from Western manufacturers. Large-scale business planning to move into foreign markets is supervised by the government, which dictates industrial policy and provides assistance to help achieve its aims. For instance, the Ministry of Industry and Information Technology (MIIT) has drawn up a programme to develop the white-goods household-appliance sector through expansion overseas, encouraging the three big companies in the sector, Haier (washing machines, refrigerators and other domestic durables), GD Midea and Gree (air conditioners) to develop production plants in the Americas, North Africa, and Asia.

Other countries have used a mixture of state protection, technological transfers (whether legal or not), subsidies and preferential policies
for domestic companies to spur growth. What makes China different is
its scale, its importance on the balance sheets of multinationals and the
combination of its reliance on globalization and its historic belief in its
exceptionalism.

The People's Republic wants two things: a guaranteed supply of raw
materials and the acquisition of advanced technologies from more
developed economies. But it runs into repeated obstacles, particularly
from governments concerned about national security, which are fanned
by cases such as the imbroglio between Motorola and Huawei cited earlier, hacking allegations and a shadowy programme started in Beijing in
1986 and known as 863, which aims to acquire technology abroad – by
what means is not specified.

Often foreign companies find negotiating with the Chinese a trying
process. The mainlanders field a large delegation. There are banquets
filled with toasts and expressions of goodwill but the overall objectives
have been set in advance, with the involvement of government officials,
and they are followed. Cutting an impromptu deal is not the Chinese
style. Rough tactics are often in order. In 2011 Cosco, the PRC's biggest
shipping group, withheld payment for a while on vessels leased from foreign companies after rates declined. 'A contract is not an unchangeable
bible for Chinese companies,' as a Beijing lawyer told the *Wall Street
Journal.*

The corporate hierarchy provides the framework, but what is often
unclear is where the initial go-ahead originated or where final decisions
are being made. Is it in the room or by reference back to ministries or
Party offices? Will the career of the chief Chinese negotiator be set back
if he or she deviates from the brief in return for concessions from the
other side? Will they suffer if they fail to clinch the agreement or, on the
contrary, will they benefit because they stuck loyally to their instructions?
Are different interests within the power structure competing, adding
another level of complexity to reaching agreement?

China's overseas acquisitions produce recurrent headlines about it
buying the world, and surveys show that 90 per cent of mainland companies with international exposure plan to increase their investments

overseas. But there is a lot of hype in this. On many occasions Chinese companies have not helped themselves. After the collapse of its Unocal bid, Fu Chengyu, the CNOOC Chairman, reflected: 'We learned to be more prudent in terms of public relations and political lobbying when dealing with such a big deal.' CNOOC'S next big foray into North America, an $18 billion bid for the Canadian energy resources group, Nexen, in the summer of 2012 was carefully structured to appease regulators.

The volume of deals outside the raw-materials sector is quite small. Though Chinese acquisitions abroad totalled $57 billion in 2012, most have not been the strategic technological acquisitions the PRC would like. In Britain, Bright Foods of Shanghai paid £700 million for the makers of Weetabix breakfast cereals while the Chinese sovereign wealth fund, CIC, took 10 per cent stakes in Thames Water and Ferrovial, owner of Heathrow Airport – hardly the stuff of a Chinese takeover of the commanding heights of the economy. As we saw in Chapter Twelve, national security concerns have blocked acquisitions in the US and there has been a pushback elsewhere, as in Brazil.

The PRC's big commercial agreements have been with Africa, Latin America and Australia, not with Western or Japanese companies that have the keys to the move up the value chain laid down in the latest Five-Year Plan. Outward direct investment (ODI) from the mainland totalled $59 billion in 2010 while $105.7 billion flowed in. By 2011 the cumulative stock of foreign investment in the PRC was $1.05 trillion while the outward total was only $330 billion – a large increase on the $30 billion reached in 2002, but still just 1.6 per cent of the global total. There is no doubting how big a global player the People's Republic has become and the key role that trade and investment plays in its growth, but, at the same time, to grasp where it is heading one needs to look back inside the hotpot nation at the everyday factors that shape life below the tiger's head that so impresses the rest of the globe.

15

LACK OF TRUST

One of the many extraordinary aspects of the Mao era was how the masses put up with the horrors he visited on them, from the 'anti-rightist' repression of the 1950s through the Great Leap Forward and the accompanying famine that took some 40 million lives and so on to the ten years of the Cultural Revolution. Now, the enforced passivity of the Mao era has been replaced by a more assertive population that is increasingly ready to stand up for its rights, however ill-defined they may be, and that wants its share of the economic cake. The last official count of annual protests by a semi-official think tank in 2007 put the number at 80,000. No figures have been issued since then, but unofficial sources spoke of the total rising to 100,000 in subsequent years and an academic expert who follows the subject at Tsinghua University in Beijing estimated the number in 2010 at 180,000. The solidarity promoted by the 'red songs' in Chongqing flew in the face of a disrupted nation that gives voice to its complaints, one motivation, no doubt, for Bo Xilai's campaign.

The protests are over widely separate single issues and often occur in places that have been enjoying strong growth rather than in backward rural areas. Demolition of houses and relocation of residents is the single biggest cause of discontent, according to a survey by the Research Center for Social Contradiction. There is anger at corruption and pollution. In the autumn of 2011, property owners trashed a developer's office in Shanghai as prices fell. In August of that year, 12,000 people confronted riot police in the north-eastern city of Dalian one Sunday after a local plant that makes a toxic chemical was nearly inundated by sea water during a storm threatening local residents. Some sang the national anthem and carried banners with patriotic wording to make clear that they were not regime critics. When the city's Party Secretary tried to get them to disperse, they responded by demanding to be told when the plant would be shut.

That same weekend in Qianxi County of Guangxi province, at the other end of the country, more than 1,000 people fought with local security forces for twenty-four hours, smashing a dozen police cars and injuring ten policemen in an incident that started with a row about illegal parking. In both cases many of protestors were young adults. In Beijing, migrant workers protested in the summer of 2011 outside district offices at the closure of schools for their children; one lay on the ground shouting, 'We make our contribution to Beijing too!' Middle-class citizens fearful for the value of their property protested against a planned chemical plant in the coastal city of Xiamen that would face a choice urban area by the sea. In Shanghai, people whose upmarket flats were menaced by a proposed extension of the Maglev high-speed train from the airport got round the ban on authorized demonstrations by organizing weekend 'talk-abouts', in which they strolled the streets in groups complaining about the plan. In Guangdong, similarly

middle-class residents mobilized against a proposal to build an incinerator near a housing development.

At Wuhan University in the spring of 2011, students threw eggs at a
professor from Beijing who is described as the 'Father of the Great
China Firewall' of Internet censorship; after escaping, they celebrated
their attack with jubilant postings on websites and received offers of gifts
from admirers. The professor had already been the target of a con-
certed campaign when he opened an account on a social-network site:
he had been obliged to close it after only two hours, following the posting of thousands of irate, often expletive-laden messages accusing him
of abetting repression. In a fine irony, the flood of messages was so
great that censors had been forced to block searches for his name, 'the
blocker, blocked,' as one blogger noted. An online cartoon circulated
soon afterwards showing him sitting constipated on a toilet.

The protests affect all parts of the country and have multiple causes,
as shown above. The big riots in Tibet and Xinjiang in 2008–09, which
took hundreds of lives, and were followed by self-immolation of a dozen
Tibetan monks in 2011, are a reminder of the fragile state of ethnic relations and potential for explosion in those two territories. The marches
in Inner Mongolia in 2011 following the death of a Mongol herder hit
by a Han truck driver were the biggest for two decades; a major security
operation was launched and students were confined to their universities. In Zhejiang, workers in the tinfoil centre of Yangxunqiao grew
increasingly angry in 2011 at the alarming rise in lead levels in their
blood and that of their children; they demonstrated for better controls
and compensation, but riot police stopped them from boarding buses
to the provincial capital to complain. In another village in the province
hundreds of villagers burst into a solar-panel factory, which they said was
releasing toxins into a river, smashing windows, overturning vehicles
and raising a banner with the slogan 'Return our lives'. Riot police dispersed them after four days.[1]

That summer up to 10,000 protestors staged a three-day protest in the
Guangdong blue-jeans capital of Xintang after security guards were
alleged to have manhandled a pregnant hawker from Sichuan and
demanded money from her during a clearance of street stalls. The
demonstrators besieged a government office and burned police and fire

vehicles. The 6,000 riot police who moved in used teargas, imposed a curfew and marched through the street chanting slogans in a show of force. The authorities published notices in the local newspaper offering cash rewards of 10,000 yuan, a 'good citizen award' and an urban-registration permit to migrants who gave police information on the rioters. At the same time, hundreds of migrants clashed with police in another manufacturing centre at Chaozhou in eastern Guangdong after one of them was wounded in a knife attack, allegedly by a thug employed by the manager of their factory.

Real or suspected police misbehaviour is a recurrent cause of popular anger. In Lichuan city in Hubei province in the summer of 2011, 1,500 people throwing bottles and eggs tussled with armed security forces reinforced by armoured cars after the death of a popular city legislator who had crusaded against corruption. He had been arrested on accusations of taking bribes from construction contractors but had subsequently made graft allegations of his own against senior city cadres. Relatives said he had been beaten to death while in custody. Another city in the same province was the scene of a three-day confrontation with police after the death of a twenty-four-year-old chef at a local hotel. The authorities said he had killed himself, but his father put the corpse in the hotel lobby and demanded an investigation. When police tried to seize the body, a crowd gathered to stop them doing so – press reports said as many as 50,000 people joined in. The body was eventually taken to a funeral parlour and the suicide verdict stood, but not before demonstrators had overturned police cars, trashed a fire truck and clashed with armed security forces. The incident followed a similar protest after a girl's death at the same hotel was classified as suicide. Local people said the establishment was a drug den and that police officers and officials in the city's courts and electricity service were shareholders.

The requisitioning of land by local authorities is a major complaint. In one typical incident in Guangdong, thousands of inhabitants of a 'model village' which had been feted by local officials including the province's Party Secretary, fought with police and blocked a main road after their farmland was sold to developers in the autumn of 2011. In another case, a dozen farmers from Shaanxi went to Beijing to protest in November 2011, after local authorities forced them to hand over 8,000 hectares of land for a 31 billion yuan development but failed to get it halted. Farmers complain that compensation is too low or is not paid at all. Sometimes demonstrations escalate fast – within hours hundreds of people gathered to support the head of a village in Zhejiang in his protest about the fees paid for land on which a petrol station was to be constructed; they surrounded the site and blocked a nearby highway before being dispersed by riot police. At the end of 2011, in a dramatic challenge to the authorities, more than 10,000 residents of Wukan in Guangdong took over their village and kept armed security forces at bay. They were protesting at the requisitioning of land which had been sold on to a developer and at the death of a local leader in police custody – the authorities said he had suffered a heart attack but the villagers believed he had been tortured for opposing corruption. The demonstration quickly attracted wide support on the Internet as the villagers insisted that they were not talking of revolution but simply sought justice.

There are also protests in cities, as in two cases in Fuzhou city in Jiangxi province in 2011. In one, three members of a family set themselves alight after dousing themselves in petrol – one died and two were badly burned. The other involved Qian Minggi, a fifty-two-year-old businessman who made and rented out refrigerated coffins and who was described by neighbours to the *South China Morning Post* as a kind, timid individual. After his five-storey house was demolished to make way for a road that was never built, Qian petitioned for adequate compensation, even going to Beijing to seek satisfaction. To press his case he blogged and put up giant graffiti, one of which read: 'The prosecution department is no different from a cradle of corrupt officials.' The authorities sent round men to whitewash over his words, but he promptly wrote up a new complaint.[2]

As a result of his activity, during which he accused the district Party Discipline Chief of embezzlement, Qian was held in jail, beaten up and incarcerated in a psychiatric ward. On his release he discovered that one local official whom he had thought might give him justice had been transferred elsewhere. That day he drove a van to the car park below the eight-storey prosecutors' office in his locality and set off a timed explosion. Eleven minutes later he drove another van to a district-government office; he was intercepted by a guard but staged another explosion, which killed the security man and a colleague. Qian died fifteen minutes after that, in a third explosion near the local Food and Drug office.

He left fifty-three messages on his microblog. One read: 'I ought to expect a certain amount of punishment if I robbed somebody of 10 yuan on the street. How come they can destroy my home, which was built fully in accordance with the law, but not properly compensate me?' Another stated: 'Ten years of fruitlessly trying to seek redress have forced me to go on a path I did not wish to take.' A farmer who lived near him told the *Post*: 'You never have any choice but to let them demolish your home whenever the government asks you to make way for this or that. Without exception, we ordinary civilians will swallow the disappointment. In our whole country, he is the only one who has dared to stand up and fight back in that way.' As forced demolitions continued in the district, there were reports of women being dragged away by police. When an American reporter went to the scene and tried to talk to a woman who had known Qian, a dozen officials turned up and hustled her away.

'There is almost nothing that can be called justice or rights here – otherwise the bombings would not have happened,' another local inhabitant commented. 'Things have been getting worse and worse in the past few years. Some have suggested that Qian was actually bombing the morally degenerate. I couldn't agree more.'

These outbursts are in reaction to local events and do not bring the regime into question; they fit in with the tradition from imperial times of protesting to bring local abuses to the notice of the supposedly benign ruler in the faraway capital. They do not constitute a coherent political challenge to the system. There is no alternative to Communist rule and we are far from the mass revolts seen in the nineteenth century or indeed the grassroots opposition to the Nationalist administration marshalled by the Communist Party from the late 1920s to 1949. Still, in the absence of mechanisms to mediate and mitigate conflicts between the authorities and individuals, there is a constant undercurrent of discontent as individual incidents become widely known through the Internet and telephone messaging.

The militancy of young migrant workers in episodes like those in Guangdong raises a new challenge to the stability so prized by the leadership, but so difficult to achieve in such a disparate and evolving nation. Given the potential scale of unrest and the myriad causes behind recent protests, it is not surprising that the Politburo has been focusing on what it calls 'social management', acknowledging that 'this is a time when social contradictions are becoming conspicuous in our country'. The budget for 2011 increased spending on internal security by nearly 14 per cent to 624.4 billion yuan, more than the formal army budget (though the latter is understated).

'Protest management' policies follow several tracks. In line with Mao's teaching that there are two forms of social contradictions – 'those between ourselves and the enemy and those among the people themselves [which] must be resolved by different methods' – the central authorities crack down relentlessly on political opponents while often adopting a softer line with social protests. Thus, despite the tiny number of people who answered an online call in 2011 for a Jasmine Revolution in China similar to those in Arab nations, the regime's self-protectiveness went into overdrive as seen earlier. But as far as local protests are concerned, though local officials frequently take a heavy-handed approach, the treatment becomes more conciliatory once higher authorities get involved. This, again, reflects a tradition that pits evil, grasping, grassroots despots against the benevolent ruler in the faraway capital. Opinion polls often give the government in Beijing a high popularity rating and a very low one to local officials.

The central authorities are certainly well aware of the importance of public opinion and carry out intensive polling to try to gauge public sentiment. Though careful not to lose face or encourage dissent, they do react in due course. After a decent interval following the riots of 2009, the long-serving boss of Xinjiang was moved to Beijing and replaced by a man who unfurled a series of policies designed to boost the economy, including a massive investment programme and a call for other provinces to help the western region. Several officials were removed after the protests in the summer of 2011. Following the Inner Mongolian demonstrations, the truck driver who killed the herder was sentenced to death and a change in coalmining policy was promised. In Zhejiang, some of the tinfoil workers managed to get round the police control and present their petition in the provincial capital (they ended up with a promise of free health checks, a treatment plan and compensation of 1,600 yuan for each poisoned child). Closure of migrant schools in Beijing was partially reversed.

In Dalian, the city government reacted to the mass demonstration in August 2011 by promising to close the polluting chemical factory outside the city. The authorities in Xiamen relocated their chemical plant after Beijing sent in a team to force their hand. In Shanghai, the extension of the Maglev was cancelled. In Guangdong, the incinerator was abandoned. The regime's leaders at central and provincial level know the importance of not alienating the middle class by jeopardizing their property investments.

Yet the regime's treatment of protests deals with symptoms rather than root causes – and will do so as long as it holds back from such structural reforms as the end of the *hukou* registration system, the granting of land-ownership rights, the introduction of a more responsive independent legal system and a crackdown on the arbitrary exercise of authority by local officials and their police. As *Global Times* noted after the riot in Xintang, what is needed is the rule of law rather than the rule of the jungle exercised by local authorities. However, the reluctance to confront basic issues and an inability to enforce better conduct on those running China's villages, townships and counties leads to a growing challenge in reconciling one-party top-down control with a society in which people feel increasingly free to express their opinions and to take to the streets to demonstrate their discontent. Were the two to get seriously out of kilter the whole China picture would be altered. This would not be a sudden sweeping movement but rather an incremental process made up of resentments about a wide variety of issues. We are certainly not there yet, but it is a longer-term issue that hovers over the People's Republic.

Popular disillusion with the way China lives now is heightened by the trust deficit that stretches beyond politics to safety issues, food quality, the environment and standards of medical care. Like the protests it takes many varied forms. The success of the Taobao e-commerce site, which accounts for three-quarters of online sales, is explained in part because of the escrow function installed by its owner, Alibaba, which means that payment is made only when goods are received, as a deterrent to cyber-fraud. Even faith in the Chinese Red Cross was punctured (and donations dropped) after a woman calling herself 'Guo Meimei Baby' claimed on her blog site to be the charity's commercial general manager and then posted photographs of what she said were her Maserati cars and Hermès handbags – she later admitted that it was a spoof but the damage was done with a public that has good reason to believe that it is often being misled.

Though unquantifiable, what one young woman called the 'hollowness' of society does loom. It starts at the top. How can it be otherwise when Li Keqiang, the man set to become the next Prime Minister, has told the US ambassador over dinner that the GDP figures are 'manmade' and 'only for reference'? Or when the official property index from the National Bureau of Statistics reports a 20 per cent increase in the price of apartments in Shanghai while a private data provider shows a rise of more than 150 per cent over the same period? Or when the girl singer at the opening of the Beijing Olympics was dubbed (the real performer being regarded insufficiently good-looking to be shown to the world as an ambassador of China) and all of the fifty-six children who paraded as representatives of the country's ethnic minorities turned out to be from the majority Han?[3]

The way in which institutions, starting with the law, are subject to opaque pressures means there is no recourse. 'The worst thing about Beijing is that you can never trust the judicial system,' Ai Weiwei wrote after his release from detention in 2011. 'Without trust you cannot identify anything. It's like a sandstorm [...] everything is constantly changing, according to somebody else's will, somebody else's power.'[4]

The prominent intellectual Yan Xuetong claims that the growth of hypocrisy stems from the Cultural Revolution. 'People were obliged to say what was false,' he has written. 'It was clear that nobody wanted to go to the countryside, but every young person was required to say that he desired to stay on the farm for his whole life [...] The government forced people to tell lies. You were punished if you did not do so [...]

the spirit of telling lies left by the Cultural Revolution has had a very bad influence [...] To tell lies now not only does not result in punishment. It even wins society's approval.'[5]

But this needs to be taken much further back in time. It was not the Cultural Revolution that bred falsehood on a massive and systemic scale. Its lies followed those of the Great Leap, with its unreachable output targets when even Mao counselled against exaggeration, and then the great denial of the resulting famine. The anti-rightist campaign of the mid-1950s after the short-lived burst of free speech in the Hundred Flowers period, showed the cost of telling the truth when it annoyed those in power. Going back to pre-Communist days, the Nationalist regime advanced claims in times of both war and peace that were far from the reality people saw around them. As for the two millennia of empire, there was an evident disconnect between the quasi-divine status of the occupants of the Dragon Throne in the hermetically sealed court and the way the mass of the people lived.

That disconnect – which is perpetuated in the leadership's shut-off world in its Zhongnanhai compound in a former imperial estate beside the Forbidden City in Beijing – has come under growing strain as society has evolved. People remember how the authorities tried to cover up the outbreak of Severe Acute Respiratory Syndrome (SARS) in the early years of this century. They recall the fumbling reaction to the subsequent outbreak of Avian Flu and how officials connived at contaminated-blood collection in central China, which may have infected as many as 100,000 people with HIV/Aids.

Who knows what or whom to believe? A mother from Yunnan told investigators from Human Rights Watch: 'The doctor told us all the children in this village have lead poisoning. Then they told us a few months later that all the children were healthy.' 'We asked about medicine,' a woman from Shaanxi said as she recounted her efforts to care for her poisoned child. 'They said they wouldn't give us any because medicine for lead poisoning doesn't work.'

There are regular scandals over poor-quality or counterfeit medicines and profiteering by doctors and hospitals, sixteen of which were removed from the public medical-insurance list in 2011 for having cheated insurance companies. A member of the upper house of the legislature told its session that year of cases in which hospitals sold heart stents to patients for anywhere from six to nine times the cost. Blood-plasma-extraction posts in Guizhou and Henan had to be closed down because of worries about dirty equipment. Medical treatment can vary alarmingly. Bloggers on an anticorruption website recounted having to pay doctors cash inducements to ensure safe surgical procedures. On a visit to Shenyang in 2011, I walked over offers stencilled on the pavement to buy up unused drugs for resale. In late 2011, police busted 350 criminal rings that bought empty drug packages and bottles from hospital cleaners and filled them with phoney pills for sale. In 2007, the former head of the Food and Drug Administration was executed for having accepted cash in return for approving substandard medicines, including an antibiotic blamed for at least ten deaths. When a fire broke out at a hospital in Shanghai doctors and nurses treating a man brought in after a traffic accident fled the scene, leaving him to suffocate to death on the operating table.[6]

Hospitals sell tissues from aborted foetuses for use in experiments and treatments without the mothers' knowledge: one in Guangdong attracts a stream of high-paying patients, mainly from abroad, for its high-priced stem-cell remedies and treatments that it says can treat incurable diseases. As part of its health-reform programme the government tested generic drugs in plain containers in place of expensive branded medicines but people shunned them because they feared they were inferior. In 2007, toothpaste, including tens of thousands of tubes exported from the PRC to Latin America and Australia, was found to contain diethylene glycol, an industrial solvent used in antifreeze; some were marketed for children with bubble gum and strawberry flavours sold under the name of 'Mr. Cool Junior'.

It seems that rules about everything from loan limits to golf courses are made to be broken. The central government has difficulty imposing its will on provincial entities: when Beijing opens the purse strings, as in 2008–09, the local authorities are only too happy to take the money and expand; but, when the time came for tightening, putting the tiger back in the cage is a tough process and the interlocking of companies and provincial authorities produces a patchwork of mutual interests that makes it relatively simple to evade central control.

Government decrees frequently lack teeth. A ban on smoking in indoor public places, introduced on 1 May 2011, was accompanied by no penalties for offenders and no implementation procedures. Despite legislation banning them, fakes have become a hallmark of China both in everyday products and luxury goods. Brand names are relentlessly ripped off. An online site based in Guangdong openly offers 'designer-inspired alternatives to actual Louis Vuitton'. The Guangzhou Baiyun World Leather Market is the centre of the trade in fake handbags emblazoned with the logos of Gucci, Prada and Hermès. An animal-rights group alleges that Chinese are skinning raccoon dogs alive and selling the fur to be used in fashionable UGG boots made in Australia, which are meant to contain only sheepskin.

Eighty per cent of counterfeit goods seized by US and European Union customs originate in the PRC. Chinese car makers have copied foreign makes down to slightly different versions of their names. A chain of 160 supermarkets in Anhui adopted the Chinese name of the Carrefour group and used a logo similar to that of the French company. Five phoney Apple stores selling fake products with the American company's logo traded in Kunming, capital of Yunnan, in 2011 – one was closed down, but only because it did not have the proper business licence rather than for any copyright infringement. Another store in Kunming, 11 Furniture, copied the design, colour scheme and products of Ikea outlets. A theme park in the east of the country appropriated the *World of Warcraft* video game without any reference to the copyright holder. In 2011, reports on state television appeared to show staff at the Baidu search engine helping firms to get round regulations on online advertising. Fake university diplomas are easily bought; senior provincial officials are reported to be among those holding certificates from non-existent foreign colleges.

Films and music are copied as soon as they appear, though Baidu has reached an agreement with major record labels to provide only licensed copies of songs for users to download or stream. Pirated copies of Steve Jobs' biography, selling for a fraction of the price of the original, sold like hot cakes after his death in 2011. Dyson, the innovative British household-appliance maker, complains that its profits are being hit by the cost of fighting a wave of fake products made in China. Expert craftsmen copy anything old and valuable – a sign by the West Lake in Hangzhou reads 'Antiques made to order'. Press reports put the cash generated by new 'antiques' at more than 10 billion yuan, with an accompanying creation of jobs for 300,000 people.

The counterfeiters can be extremely skilful; replicas of 1878 Large Dragon postage stamps were perfect except for a single flaw that had the weave of the paper running vertically rather than horizontally as in the original. Wen Jiabao has lamented the way in which 'we are destroying the real and building up the fake'. He has said 'A lot of our tangible cultural heritage has been torn down and destroyed, and then a lot of money is spent on building phony things'. Suburban developments ape towns and villages in the British Home Counties, Germany and France – one outside Beijing has a Gothic château, church and village square. A replica of the Austrian village of Salzkammergut, a UNESCO heritage site, is being put up in Guangdong in a project backed by a big metals firm. Developers are building a copy of Salvador Dalí's home town in Spain, which they hope will attract 15,000 holidaymakers a year. The Da Vinci furniture brand makes its products in Guangdong, ships them to Italy, and then brings them back to the PRC complete with customs documents to show that they are Italian. With a serious point, Ai Weiwei called his company 'Beijing Fake Cultural Development'.

Counterfeiting is far from a game, however. Aside from the safety dangers of fake goods or medicine passed off as the real thing, the trade involves links with organized crime at home and abroad. One example of this is in the production of cigarettes under well-known foreign and domestic brands in China, which is estimated to run to 400 billion a year. US customs say illegal imports from the PRC account for almost all the fake smokes they seize; the profits are high and the penalties low. In Yuanxiao County in an isolated, heavily wooded part of Fujian, 200 outfits turn out counterfeit cigarettes from workshops in caves and buried underground. Some are fortified, and police have to blast their way in when they stage raids, sometimes amid gun battles. Membership of the counterfeit enterprises is limited to those whose whole family comes from the area, a local woman told a reporter from the *South China Morning Post*. Corruption lessens police activity and the bosses hold multiple identity cards to avoid being tracked down. 'It is impossible to root out this business,' a police officer told the newspaper. In one place, workers were dressed up in army uniforms and pretended to carry out military drills. There is said to be a workshop under the main temple. A Godfather figure organizes foreign distribution through fishing boats that pick up consignments on the Fujian coast. Domestic markets are divided among local families. The police offer money to informers but as another woman told the *Post*: 'If you get the money, you won't have any life left to enjoy it.'[7]

In big cities, empty bottles of fine clarets fetch a nice price as they are bought by producers of low-quality wine to be filled with plonk; the going rate in 2011 for a used bottle of Château Lafite was 2,900 yuan. In Zhejiang police uncovered a gang who had made 2 billion yuan from selling cheap liquor in flasks that had previously contained the top domestic liqueur *moutai*. 'We make fakes, we sell fakes, we trade in counterfeit currency, and we buy imitation goods. Everyone is a victim and everybody is cheating on everybody else,' a despairing official from the Consumer Protection Association in Hunan told the author Sang Ye for his book *China Candid*. Modern education has not halted the charlatans who pepper Chinese history. In one case, a prominent Daoist priest won fame and a following of rich people by appearing to possess magical powers, including the ability to sit underwater in a swimming pool for two hours without breathing (it later transpired that he was encased in a glass box with a supply of oxygen).

The government recognizes the damage that arises from all the fakery and thunders against it but implementation of laws is generally lax. In the big building that houses the 'fakes market' in Shanghai, signs hang from the ceiling proclaiming that counterfeiting is illegal and asking people to report infringements to the police. But nobody stops the bulk-order buyers below the signs filling suitcases with rip-offs of branded goods.

Safety is questionable. Building standards vary greatly; one estimate is that the life of the average construction in China is around twenty years. Six big new social-housing buildings for low-income families had to be demolished in Beijing at the end of 2010 because they had been put up with substandard cheap cement. A bridge nearing completion in Hunan collapsed in 2007, killing sixty-four people. Three others gave way in the summer of 2011 and, in Hangzhou, a bridge span over the river, built in 1999 at a cost of 1 billion yuan and repaired in 2005, developed a seven-metre crack while another, constructed forty-six years earlier, showed no signs of disrepair. In November 2011, strong winds ripped off part of the roof of Beijing's huge airport; the use of poor materials in construction was blamed. The following summer, the capital's inadequate drainage system contributed to the deaths of seventy-seven people caught by flooding following the worst storms for sixty years.

Murderous fires are frequent. In November 2010 fifty-three people died and more than ninety were hurt in a blaze at a 1990s block being renovated in Shanghai. Flames set off by fireworks lit by local residents celebrating the Lantern Festival gutted a thirty-four-storey tower of the huge futuristic headquarters of the main state broadcaster; the upper storeys of the building were beyond the reach of firefighters' hoses.[8]

Food safety is a major source of worry. In early 2011 the quality of milk was tested at 1,100 dairies: 426 failed to meet the required standards. Because supply cannot keep up with demand, farmers dilute milk with water and then increase protein content by adding the chemical melamine, which is dangerous to human health. In 2008, 300,000 babies were affected by tainted milk powder from the big Sanlu Company; six of the infants died. Farmers whose milk was refused at official testing stations simply went direct to the companies, where it was bought with no questions asked. More recently, disintegrated chicken feathers and by-products of leather tanning have been substituted for melamine because they are cheaper. Still, rising costs are squeezing cattle farmers, many of whom have only a few cows and who are at the mercy of the big milk-processing firms. 'The dairy companies and the farmers are always on the opposite side of the table,' says the Secretary-General of the Dairy Association in Hebei. 'When the market is thriving, dairy farmers will do everything they can to maximize their yields, but when it fluctuates, the dairy firms suspend collection.'[9]

To help the farmers the government has raised the ceiling for bacteria in milk fourfold and lowered the protein requirement. If the health standards applied in more advanced countries were applied in the PRC, 70 per cent of small farmers would go bust and the supply of milk would be reduced to a trickle, according to the Secretary-General of the Dairy Association in Inner Mongolia where the big Yili milk farm had to recall infant formula in the summer of 2012 after it was found to contain mercury. New Zealand farm companies can sell dairy products in China for double the price of the parallel domestic product – because they are considered trustworthy by consumers. When parents of babies travel abroad they bring back boxes of foreign milk powder.

Whether food standards have actually got worse or whether more have simply come to light recently is unclear. But the effect is to make one careful about what one eats, if one has the choice. Plastic resin has been added to rice and bean sprouts are treated with potential toxic chemicals to make them grow faster and look shinier. In Guangdong, seventeen noodle manufacturers added ink, industrial dye and paraffin wax to their products and a company working with supermarket managers mixed rotten meat and fertilizers in its sausages. Shuanghui Foods, one of the biggest meat-processing firms in the country, was found to have used pork treated with clenbuterol, a toxic additive that makes the meat leaner. Soy sauce containing non-purified industrial salt has been sold with fake labels of famous national brands; other sauces contain traces of arsenic and high levels of bacteria. In Xinjiang, eleven people died in one village in August 2011 after consuming what was suspected to be vinegar tainted with antifreeze. A man in eastern China earned 240,000 yuan by selling pork injected with borax to make it resemble beef. Hams have been treated with insecticide whose chemical effect makes the meat appear more appealing.[10]

In Chongqing, a firm used melamine-tainted milk powder in its ice cream. Inspectors who raided an unlicensed workshop in the city found five tons of contaminated pig-blood curd, a local speciality, in uncovered boxes on the muddy floor; it had been soaked in a chemical liquid containing 100 times the normal safety level of formaldehyde. In Shanghai, workers at a company operating in filthy workshops mashed up buns that had passed their sell-by date, added artificial colouring, sweeteners and preservatives, and sent 300,000 a day to be sold in supermarkets. The tainted buns were packed in bags carrying a quality-safety mark. As an Internet jest put it: 'We learned of paraffin from toxic rice, learned of dichlorvos [an insecticide] from hams, learned of Sudan Red [dye] from salted duck eggs and chilli sauce, learned of formaldehyde from hotpot, learned of sulphur from tremella [jelly fungus], and finally learned of melamine from Sanlu-brand milk.'

Concern about China's food standards spread abroad when exports of fish and honey to the US were found to be contaminated; pet food was also tainted. Inside China, a cartoon posted online showed a young couple embracing in relief as 'having survived'. The man was telling the woman: 'I'm so glad you weren't poisoned by gutter oil, Sudan Red, lean-meat essence, or toxic buns! Your house didn't catch on fire! The bridge in front of your house didn't collapse, right? You're so lucky that the escalator didn't malfunction when you went to work!' The woman's reply was: 'I was so worried you'd get run over by someone going 70kph on your way to work! Or get stabbed eight times in a row! My gravest fear was that you would be accidentally injured by *chengguan* [thugs working for local governments] who were beating up someone else! I was also worried you would need to ride the high-speed train! But I didn't dare to call you because I was afraid your cell phone would explode!'

Another posting that sped round the blogosphere had it that:

Milk powder destroyed those born in the 2000s.
Examinations destroyed those born in the 90s.
Real-estate prices destroyed those born in the 80s.
Unemployment destroyed those born in the 70s.
The *chengguan* destroyed those born in the 60s.
Stepping down from one's post destroyed those born in the 50s.
Forced demolition and removal destroyed those born in the 40s.
'Reform' of the medical system destroyed those born in the 30s.
2012 will destroy everybody else.

In some instance, cheaters prey on cheaters. In one case in the Xicheng district of Beijing, reported by *Global Times* in August 2011, an enterprising journalist and an associate intercepted a merchant who was planning to sell 4,000 kilos of unfit pork and pretended to be from the '315 anti-counterfeit office'. They got him to pay a 'fine' of 50,000 yuan before letting him go and then sold the pork on to an accomplice who put it on the market at double the price he had paid. The pair moved on to try the same scam at a pork-processing factory that was turning out substandard meat, but they were caught.[11]

At the 2011 session of the national legislature, Vice-Premier Wang Qishan said he and other leaders were 'very much embarrassed' by the PRC's poor food record. Control had been weakened a few years earlier when the Food and Drug Administration was downgraded by being absorbed into the Health Ministry after its director was involved in the corruption scandal that cost him his life. Spurred to react, the State Council established a safety committee and raised the penalty for producing unsafe food to death. A rash of scandals in the spring of 2011 produced some official action, but the rules remain unclear and the implementation at local level, where it matters most, is spotty with poorly paid inspectors being easily corrupted. In the case of the Shanghai buns, inspectors visited the plant from time to time but stayed in the management offices. As *Global Times* noted, Shuanghui Foods boasted that its products underwent eighteen tests, so how did the tainted pork get through in its sausages? The newspaper quoted a food producer who recalled how he took an inspector out to dinner and his hospitality was reciprocated by the gift of a seal with which to stamp test forms.

The elite have less cause for concern about what they eat, however. In the spring of 2011 a reporter for the courageous Guangdong publication *Southern Weekend* slipped in to a 130,000-square-metre farm outside Beijing where vegetables are grown organically but only for government officials. Another farm at the foot of the Western Hills outside the capital supplies the country's leaders with safe food grown under strict environmental protection. Carefully monitored producers of pork, fish, poultry, eggs and rice do the same in Guangdong, Hubei, Liaoning and Shandong, the magazine added. The story was removed from the weekly's website and other media were ordered not to reproduce it.

China's safety fault lines stretch from toys containing lead paint to more than fifty automobile recalls a year and the questions about high-speed trains. In 2010 nearly 2,500 workers died in coalmining accidents. A spot-check on lorries stuck in a 100-mile traffic jam outside Beijing in 2010 found that 80 per cent were overloaded. The country's nuclear programme has only a quarter of the skilled supervisory staff it needs if expansion plans are realized, and a leaked US Embassy cable warned in 2008 that the choice of cheap technology that would become outdated greatly increased the risk of accidents. In Hunan, lift inspectors are each responsible for checking more than 1,000 elevators. After a plane crash in 2010, an investigation found that airlines employ more than 200 pilots with fake qualifications; at one company sources said more than 100 had false flying certificates, but only three of them were suspended because of the need to keep operating.

In business there is a serious shortage of qualified managers – one online recruitment agency reported 30,000 management vacancies. 'The No. 1 constraint on economic development in China is the availability of management talent,' according to John Quelch, former Dean of the London Business School, who was appointed to head the China Europe International Business School in Shanghai in 2011. 'It is at one level a mile wide but only an inch deep.' While acknowledging that there are some very smart entrepreneurs in the private sector, Quelch adds that, 'There is a certain undercurrent of Chinese exceptionalism, with managers thinking themselves brilliant – "We know better and we can do everything." This can lead to risky hubris.'[12]

Outside big companies, risk management is often antiquated or non-existent since the rush to do everything as fast as possible leads to corner-cutting. As China moves up the technological chain, the complexity of supervising advanced industrial systems, lack of accountability and patchy vocational training all increase the danger of breakdowns.

Though labour legislation has been toughened, and an increasing number of workers seek to defend their rights through arbitration and the courts, employee protection is often lacking, especially for those without skills. Migrant construction workers, in particular, are sometimes not paid for months on end. A member of the upper house of the legislature and his wife were found to have sold at least 130 mentally ill people as virtual slaves to coalmines, chemical plants and construction sites. Workers supplied by middle men to staff brick kilns are notoriously badly treated. At one kiln in Shanxi, children as young as eight were found to have been kidnapped and sold by traffickers for 500 yuan each, then forced to work sixteen-hour days under the watch of guards and dogs; some of these children were mentally impaired and had been taken from a state institution by a gang in Sichuan. Workers who stand up for themselves or fall short of their production quotas have been subjected to brutal treatment: one young man was horribly burned on his feet and back by hot rods and heated bricks; a teenager who was rescued from a kiln said he had seen a fellow worker fed into a meat grinder. Asked by a British television team about the attitude of police, a father who has doggedly pursued the trail of his abducted son replied: 'They don't care. They just ignore it.'

Fly-by-night and pyramid-selling schemes abound. One man persuaded a horde of believers to buy his concoction of mung beans and eggplant, which he claimed could cure cancer, diabetes and depression and had promoted on television and through DVDs and bestselling books. He also claimed to be the son of a line of doctors and to have a degree from Beijing Medical College – in fact he had worked in a textile factory, like his father, and had taken only a correspondence course. A prescription and a brief consultation (if the fake doctor was available) cost 3,500 yuan. The scheme collapsed when the price of mung beans shot up in 2010 and the press exposed his scam.

In Liaoning province in the north-east, Wang Fengyou peddled a different kind of fake medical scheme that a million people found impossible to refuse. His Yilishen Tianxi company sold cardboard boxes containing earth, grass and what he said were rare ants, a traditional ingredient in Chinese medicines. His salesman explained to prospective buyers that the ants in the boxes would be used for medical applications that would include aphrodisiacs and kidney purifiers. Some of the medicines were to be sold in the United States.

All the people his agents approached had to do was to hand over cash in return for the boxes and then feed the ants. To inspire confidence, feeding times were specified – water, sweetened with sugar or honey, through a hole in the boxes at nine a.m. and four p.m. each day and egg yolks and cake every three to five days. The boxes must not be opened and had to be kept indoors. Every seventy-four days, a company agent called to collect the ants, which had grown sufficiently, and to hand over cash representing a premium of 30–60 per cent over the original contribution. Of course if clients wished to compound their good fortune by putting that sum into purchasing more ant farms, they were more than welcome to do so.

Wang had a factory built to produce pills and wine from the ants. The pills were sold in more than 50,000 pharmacies across China though unfortunately the Food and Drug Administration in the United States pronounced them worthless. However the company's annual revenue rose to 15 billion yuan.

Provincial cadres endorsed the operation and Wang was photographed with the Governor, the rising politician Bo Xilai. In 2007 the company received a direct-marketing licence, attesting to its good standing. Wang contributed generously to charity and to local development projects. He was listed as one of China's Top 10 Entrepreneurial Leaders. But then demand for the ant pills began to decline and Wang found fewer takers for his scheme. As cash ran short, the Ponzi pyramid collapsed.

Wang was arrested and sentenced to death. Several investors committed suicide; their number included one man who set himself on fire in Tiananmen Square. Li Keqiang, the provincial Party Secretary at the time, told the US ambassador that, while Liaoning residents were dissatisfied with education, healthcare and housing, it was corruption that most angered them, and he arranged prison tours for new officials to meet bureaucrats convicted of graft to see the consequences they had suffered. Still, several schemes similar to Wang's surfaced soon afterwards.

The rare officials who speak out about scandals are usually swiftly gagged. The local Party Secretary who made known village cancer rates in Henan was fired for 'leaking state secrets'. All too often, rather than being seen as performing a valuable public service, whistleblowers and campaigners against abuses are persecuted as troublemakers because their disclosures inevitably bring them into conflict with the authorities. Media reports that step out of line are quickly suppressed. Symptomatic of the fate of those who get on the wrong side of authority was the teacher in Sichuan who campaigned on behalf of parents of children killed in the 2008 earthquake by the collapse of their poorly built schools (from which officials had diverted construction funds) was sentenced to a year of 'reform through labour' with no trial. Or take the case of Wu Lihong, a man living in the east of the country near Lake Tai, China's third-largest expanse of fresh water, which had become heavily polluted by factory waste. When he drew attention to this the local government claimed to have cleaned up the lake and tried to bribe him into silence. After Wu showed their claim to be false he was jailed for three years for allegedly having tried to extort money from one of the polluting companies; he said he was treated brutally while in prison.

In such a climate panics spread easily. After the Japanese nuclear crisis in 2011 Zhejiang province was swept by rumours that contamination was blowing in across the sea and that salt could provide protection. Despite government denials that there was anything to fear, mass buying of salt ensued at prices jacked-up by merchants. When salt supplies ran out, people stocked up on salty products such as soy sauce and fermented bean curd. The rumours spread to Beijing and set off panic buying there. It all died down after a while and a man was arrested and fined a small amount for spreading rumours on the Internet. But several newspapers presumed to speculate that the whole affair would not have taken place if people had more trust in statements from the government. The Dalian protest in 2011 followed a blizzard of social network messages alleging increasingly dangerous effects on health from the petrochemical plants outside the city after the local authorities had banned any media coverage of the issue.

The arbitrary exercise of power by those in authority is deeply ingrained, as it has been for centuries; the local clerks who worked for imperial magistrates were notorious for extracting cash from the population – peasants in Henan in the nineteenth century complained that they were 'more ferocious than demons'. Officials often live in a cocoon cut off from ordinary citizens – the US ambassodor, Gary Locke, who is of Chinese stock, caused surprise by the way in which he mingled with people on provincial tours, bought his own coffee and carried a backpack.

For some of today's functionaries, bullying ordinary citizens comes naturally. In 2009 three officials propositioned a twenty-one-year-old waitress to give them sexual services at a bath house in Hubei province.

When she declined, the head of the local county's Investment-Promotion Office tossed a wad of cash at her. The waitress tried to leave, but they blocked her exit and threw her on a couch. She grabbed a fruit knife from a nearby table and stabbed the investment official in the neck. He died while being taken to hospital; she was arrested on a murder charge.

The following year, the drunken son of Li Gang, a deputy police chief in the northern city of Baoding, ran over two young women students, killing one of them. When police tracked him down, he told them, 'Who do you think you are? My father's Li Gang.' In a case in Shandong captured on a closed-circuit video, a visiting bureaucrat from Shenzhen was caught pinching an eleven-year-old girl in the neck as he tried to hustle her into the men's toilet of the Plum Garden Seafood Restaurant. When her parents protested, he shouted at them, 'So what? How much money do you want? Give me a price, I will pay it [...] Do you know who I am? I was sent here by the Ministry of Transportation. So what if I pinched a little child's neck? Who the fuck are you people to me? How dare you fuck with me? Just watch how I am going to deal with you.'

The Internet and social-networking websites have made it increasingly difficult for the central authorities to impose their version of events, despite the erection of the Great Firewall of China and the reported 30,000 cyber-cops trawling for critical material. The high-speed train crash led to an explosion of protests which, as we have seen, affected mainstream media as well. In another case, friends of one of the country's best-known investigative journalists, Wang Keqin, set off a storm of postings on a microblog social site when police sought to prevent him from looking into a rape case involving officials in central China, leading to a flood of telephone calls to the local police station. 'For Chinese people, Weibo [the term used for such sites] is creating an arena that is much more free than traditional media,' Wang told Reuters. 'It's also turning more Chinese people into citizen journalists. Weibo is already a massive force. It can't be shut down.'[13]

A blogger called Han-Han, who enjoys motor racing and writing bestsellers when he is not online, has become a national star for independent postings that the authorities have not seen fit to close down.

When the government tried to bring in filtering software called Green Dam, the public outcry and the technology's shortcomings forced a climb-down.

Internet trackers conducting what are known as 'Human-Flesh Searches' seek out errant officials. The authorities often feel obliged to act amid a storm of electronic protest. The charges against the bath-house waitress were dropped; Li Gang's son was sentenced to six years in jail; the man from Shenzhen in the Plum Garden incident was fired, though cleared of child molestation. In Fuzhou, the head of the district government who was accused by the 2011 bomber of embezzling more than 10 million yuan was dismissed. After the brickworks scandal in Shanxi and elsewhere attracted the attention of leaders in Beijing, the provincial Governor, Yu Youjun, resigned and was expelled from the Central Committee; but no local officials were punished and some accounts traced Yu's disgrace to allegations arising from his behaviour at a previous post elsewhere.

The dangers of witch-hunts and the pursuit of vendettas in Human-Flesh Searching are evident, as are those of online campaigns that have swelled up from time to time – for instance when a boycott of the French retail chain Carrefour was called when it was wrongly accused of being linked to pro-Tibetan demonstrations. But they represent a form of virtual civil-society action, what one analyst has called 'a vibrant, subversive subculture of oblique opposition to censorship'. A posting on a popular web portal, Netease, argued that such action was 'an embodiment of the common people's right of expression and right of supervision. One reason why this embodiment has a big impact upon some people in society is because the common people do not have better channels embodying these rights. The people have the right to know the truth.' Or, as the prominent property developer, Zhang Xin, asks 'How do you address a country where the governing power is losing the trust of the people?'

That leads to a central fault line in today's China, the weakness of the legal system as an independent recourse for citizens. The PRC has 200,000 judges, 160,000 prosecutors and as many other lawyers. The government has been seeking to professionalize the practice of law, drawing on foreign expertise, and the number of cases brought by private citizens has mushroomed in recent years. Citizens have become more aware of their rights. Still, the People's Republic, like regimes before it, generally operates under rule *by* law rather than the rule *of* law. The justice system is not seen as exercising checks and balances on the executive and legislature or of protecting citizens but, in line with the Legalist approach adopted by the First Emperor more than 2,000 years ago, as a tool of the various levels of government and the Party to keep the people in line. When the Prime Minister talked in 2010 of the need for legal change he received no support from his colleagues at the top, who insisted rather on the need to safeguard 'socialist law'. As a foreign legal expert who has advised the PRC commented: 'Four days a week there is talk of reform, but three days a week it's back to Party control.'

Suspects can be held for long periods without being properly charged – Huang Guangyu, former head of the Gome retail chain, was kept in harsh conditions in Beijing's Number One detention centre for eighteen months before being charged with corruption and insider dealing and sentenced to fourteen years in jail as well as being given a fine of 600 million yuan and having another 200 million confiscated. Decisions in sensitive cases are made by officials, not in court. Compounding the administrative control of the judicial process, at least some investigation and prosecution bureaux are subject to a quota system: they are required to take a certain number of cases they initiate to court and get a certain number of guilty verdicts whatever the evidence. Police frequently rely on confession for convictions and are not scrupulous about how they are obtained. Announcing what authorities hailed as an improvement in curbing forced confessions and other illegal means of obtaining evidence, the Vice-President of the Supreme Court said that eighty-one cases of untoward behaviour by police had been heard in 2009 and 2010 – hardly a sign of progress on anything but the most minimal scale, and there was no indication of how many had resulted in action against the police.

An independent survey of the legal situation in 2011 found that there had been improvements but that there was a need for greater judicial independence. Indicators of fundamental rights are weak, including labour rights and freedom of assembly and of speech, where the PRC ranked at or near the bottom of the countries surveyed. The lack of external accountability or controls gives officials considerable opportunities not only to have their way but also to profit from their positions. Instances of this run through the system, as we will see, but even the hardened public was taken aback by cases that came to light in Hunan in 2011 in which local functionaries profited from the one-child policy by taking additional children from parents (whom they fined) and then selling the babies on to agents who peddled them to American couples for adoption.

The Beijing municipality has introduced a new rule that would make CCP officials subject to punishment for substandard performance, but the measure is only a 'temporary regulation' and its application remains unclear. Legal reformers work to try to make the system more fair and responsive but they have not got far. The campaign of arrests and 'disappearances' aimed against human-rights lawyers in 2011 can only have a chilling effect on the readiness of the profession to undertake cases against official interests or on behalf of individuals who think they have suffered from the workings of the system. As the scholar Jerome Cohen, a long-time observer of the legal scene in China, observes: 'First, the Party sometimes prohibits courts from handling disputes. Second, it uses its influence over judges to preordain the results in many "sensitive" cases. Third, despite significant advances in legal education many Chinese judges lack professional competence. Fourth, personal relationships, political connections, corruption and the felt need to protect local interests often distort judicial decision-making. Finally, substantial litigation requires lawyers, but, in less developed areas, lawyers are few, and everywhere they have to avoid offending local authorities.'

China's Socialist Rule of Law has as a basic provision that the courts must follow the Party's leadership. Hu Jintao has instructed judges that their first priority should be to strengthen the CCP; nearly all of them belong to it, anyway, along with most lawyers. The Justice Ministry stresses the need to 'always uphold the Party's absolute leadership over judicial work'. The President of the Supreme Court appointed in 2008 was formerly a policeman and has received no known formal legal training; he has told judges they should observe the 'three supremes' – the first is to strengthen the CCP; the second is to serve the interests of the people (as defined by the authorities); and only then comes the need to apply justice. Police retain virtually absolute power to apply 're-education through labour' without trial to people who they hold to have committed non-criminal offences. House arrest can be arbitrarily imposed. Petitioners who travel to Beijing to try to put their case to the central authorities may find themselves locked up in 'black jails' run as private enterprises on behalf of provincial authorities. Petitions from local residents earn negative marks on the record cards of provincial officials so they prefer to arrange matters so that no complaints are registered. Petitioners who were held there have told of beatings, rape and food and sleep deprivation, sometimes with police present. At the end of 2011, the authorities in the capital announced a six-month crackdown of these jails – not on human rights grounds but because, as a senior policeman said, 'the security market is in complete chaos'.[14]

The legal picture is further distorted by the Party's Disciplinary Commission, which has the power to pick up members and hold them for six months without any formal charges being brought. They can then be stripped of their Party membership, given a 'demerit' or expelled – and only then handed over to the regular courts. Coming under the suspicion of the Disciplinary Commission puts one in a legal limbo. Nobody knows where you are and, if you are fortunate enough to emerge unscathed, you do not talk about the experience. Figures from the Commission for 2010 showed the extent of its independence: of the 146,000 CCP members sanctioned for corruption that year, only 5,300 were then tried by the courts.

Adding all this to the weight of political control and the nebulous context of corporate law already described results in a deeply unfair and unreliable system that operates to the benefit of the rich and powerful. It makes an evident mockery of the assertion in the constitution that 'all citizens of the People's Republic of China are equal before the law', that the courts 'shall exercise judicial power independently and are not subject to interference by administrative organs, public organizations or individuals' and that 'all state organs, the armed forces, all political parties and public organizations and all enterprises and undertakings must abide by the Constitution and the law.' One must never lose sight of the material improvement in the lives of so many people in the PRC in the past three decades, or of the social revolution which has accomplished it. These are among the most important positive developments of our time. Yet, if all states embody a degree of hypocrisy, China, once more, sets some kind of record though not of a kind it would relish. Whether or not that is tenable is a significant issue hanging over the nation's success, heightened by a set of major inbuilt challenges that risk undermining its further progress.

16

CRACKS IN THE MIRROR

China's challenges are exacerbated by three specific problems that between them have the potential to put the brake on the growth machine but that, at the same time, have become central in the nation's expansion. There is no doubt about the distorting effect of corruption on the economy as well as on morality and public life as it results in mis-allocation of capital, shoddy work and an absence of accountability, but it is integral to the way the PRC operates. There is, equally, no questioning of the cost of ecological degradation, but pollution has been a direct product of the industrial advance of the last three decades. The

TIGER HEAD, SNAKE TAILS

looming imbalance between young and old faces the mainland with a demographic timebomb but is in part (though not entirely) the result of the need to control the size of the population.

Those connections make these three issues both vital and extremely difficult to handle. Two of them – corruption and environmental damage – are not new. The graft of officials from the court down to provincial magistrates was a major source of popular anger under the empire. The Nationalist Republic of 1927–49 was shot through with corruption: Chiang Kai-shek's brothers-in-law profiteered on a massive scale; officials used their positions to extort bribes and soldiers acted like leeches on refugees fleeing the fighting with the Japanese invaders. Under Mao, there was little old-fashioned cash graft but the preferential treatment of cadres constituted a different form of rent-seeking with their access to food and goods denied to the mass of the population. The economic revolution that took shape in the 1980s spawned huge corruption rings, from the Fierce Smuggler of Xiamen to petty functionaries cashing in on their power to issue business licences.

There is a straight connection between monopoly power as exercised by the CCP and corruption. The former head of the Party's Organization Department has been quoted as saying that the trade in government posts and official titles has become as frequent as it was under previous regimes. In 2009 a former CCP Secretary in a city in Anhui was found to have accepted bribes from twenty officials who were subsequently promoted. Once in position, cadres use their bureaucratic powers to make up for their low salaries. This is not simply a matter of cash changing hands – a potentially dangerous procedure, since it may be traced. Better to find a more indirect route. So Chinese cities all have shops with packs of upmarket cigarettes and foreign liquor given to officials and then sold on to the retailers to make some cash. Businessmen buy paintings or antiques and give them to cadres who then have them auctioned; the businessmen send anonymous agents to bid up the prices and ensure that their contacts with favours on offer are well rewarded in 'clean cash'.

A city government hands a public-works contract to a front company in which the officials who made the decision have shares; the company does nothing but hand the project on to subcontractors who pay bribes in return. Police on the take range from high rollers down to traffic cops in Wuhan who stopped motorists heading into the city to tell them that their cars were not clean enough to meet municipal standards; they just happened to have a friend standing by with a pail of water and a rag who would clean the vehicles for a couple of yuan. One of Bo Xilai's initiatives in Chongqing was to appoint a corps of women traffic police because they were thought to be less corrupt than their male counterparts.

High-placed cadres use their positions to protect themselves when business goes sour. The Chairwoman of the Sanlu company (responsible for selling tainted powdered milk) held a senior position in the local Communist Party and managed to cover up the wrongdoing until a New Zealand company that had a stake in her firm blew the whistle. She was eventually brought to justice and given a life sentence after the outcry grew too great to ignore; but parents who tried to sue the company were told that the courts had to 'wait for coordinated instructions from above', which never came. A former head of the Agriculture Department in Hebei province who was found guilty of involvement in another milk-poisoning scandal in 2008 was elected Mayor of a local city the following year.

Officials use their influence to gain possession of flats nominally built to house poorer people; they then sell them at a fat profit. Lavish foreign trips are a favoured way for functionaries to spend public money on themselves – the state broadcaster CCTV puts the total spent annually at the expense of taxpayers at 400 billion yuan. In one case, an eighteen-strong inspection team sent by the Hubei provincial Communist Party to report on living conditions among people displaced by the Three Gorges Dam managed to spend 800,000 yuan during their month-long assignment, including 113,000 on gifts, 123,000 on sightseeing trips and 150,000 on alcohol and cigarettes, according to a report in *Caixin* magazine.

Alternatively, friendly companies pick up household bills of well-placed contacts while local authorities ensure that their senior employees are looked after; one estimate put spending on cars for officials at more than 150 billion yuan a year at the end of the first decade of this century. Insider financial information provides tips for quick market killings – the mayor of a southern town made 19.8 million yuan after being told that a local firm was being floated on the stock exchange. We have seen the links between underworld figures and senior local officials in such cases as the huge Xiamen smuggling operation and the crime and corruption rings in Shenyang and Chongqing.

The central bank estimates that 18,000 officials have skipped abroad in the last two decades, taking a total of more than $120 billion with them. Casino gambling in Macau has been used to launder cash out of yuan into foreign currency; more sophisticated operators employed fake trade and investment documents. Some have simply taken the money out of the country in suitcases. In early 2011 a county Finance Bureau official in Jiangsu fled to Canada with his wife, two daughters and 94 million yuan while two modest employees of a state bank in southern China made off with hundreds of millions when they absconded to the US via Hong Kong.

The leadership proclaims rolling anti-corruption campaigns; after becoming Party Secretary at the end of 2012, Xi Jinping thundered against corruption as a major threat to the regime and a senior Politburo figure, Wang Qishan, was put in charge of a new campaign against graft while officials were urged to live more frugally. Offenders arrested in the purge in 2013 included a Vice-Major linked to drug gangs, an official whose two children had up to twenty-five properties and a land director with forty-seven trustees who was accused of taking $4 million in bribes. Major scandals involving senior officials erupt from time to time as in the case of Liu Zhijun, the Railway Minister alleged to have skimmed off huge bribes, or Chen Liangyu, Party Secretary of Shanghai, who was sentenced to eighteen years in prison in 2008 for accepting bribes and abusing his powers. But the effects of the campaigns are often quite limited: when prosecutors in Hainan investigated 515 officials for excessive spending of public money, just thirty-six were sent for trial.

Frequently the high-profile punishments have a political subtext. Liu was running the railway ministry as an independent fiefdom and had links to the old group round Jiang Zemin. In Shanghai, Chen had also become far too independent for Beijing's taste, reportedly refusing to heed instructions from the Prime Minister as he strutted his stuff as prince of his city. The truth is that corruption is so embedded in the regime and the reach of the authorities is so wide that almost everybody has skeletons in the closet which can be brought to light should they fall from favour or represent a challenge to the centre.

In keeping with its control ethos, the regime insists on maintaining a strict grip on the anti-graft campaigns. It swiftly closed a website called www.bribery.com, set up by a twenty-eight-year-old public-relations consultant who reported a wide range of bribery demands, which had received 200,000 visitors in two weeks. By studying photographs of officials, a microblogger charted 100 officials who wore expensive watches they were unlikely to have been able to afford from their salaries. His list started with the Railway Minister appointed to clean up the high-speed network in 2011, whom he had spotted sporting a Rolex worth 70,000 yuan. But the portal that carried the site closed it down under pressure from the authorities after it had attracted 20,000 followers. In trials in the Fujian smuggling case at the start of this century, the names of officials that defendants were allowed to cite were restricted. Consequently there was no mention of the provincial boss of the time or of senior military figures said to be involved. Li Keqiang, the future Premier, was in charge of Henan province during the tainted-blood scandal/HIV outbreak there and a major scandal involving local functionaries occurred during Bo Xilai's time running Liaoning. The possible responsibility of the two senior figures is not mentioned publicly and, in the Liaoning case, the journalist who blew open the story was sent to jail for five years.

The top leadership appears clean, though there was some private snickering about Jia Qinglin, the former Fujian boss who was a member of the Standing Committee of the Politburo until 2012 and whose wife was Party Secretary of a major trading company in the province. The Fierce Smuggler was said to have spoken of friendship with Jia but this was not brought up at the trials. A US Embassy cable disclosed in the Wikileaks releases mentioned Jia's holdings in 'major Beijing real-estate developments'.[1]

Some of the top men's family connections are questionable. A company formerly headed by Hu Jintao's son has been sued for fraud and corruption in Namibia. Members of Wen Jiabao's immediate family 'have a reputation as people who can "get things done" at the right price', according to another US Embassy cable cited by Wikileaks. The *New York Times* reported at the end of 2012 that the outgoing Premier's relatives had built up wealth of $2.7 billion – Bloomberg chronicled similar asset accumulation by Xi Jinping's family. A joke has it that Wang Qishan was put in charge of the anti-corruption drive because he has no children to protect.

Family backgrounds count for a lot and the princeling descendants of prominent figures from the past wield special influence. Among their number are the children and grandchildren of Deng Xiaoping and the son of the economist Chen Yun, who served Mao and argued with Deng about economic freedom. The son and daughter of the former Prime Minister Li Peng ran major power-generating groups resulting from the splitting up of a giant enterprise headed by their father that at one point controlled 70 per cent of the country's energy-producing assets. Such people have done extremely well in business, some acting as high-level contact fixers for foreign firms. They may have genuine talents, but it is their backgrounds and names that count for most. Lower down the scale, power elites dating back to before the Communist victory in 1949 appear to have re-emerged at local level, according to detailed research by the Australian scholar David Goodman. There is frequent talk of the 'clans' who run China for their own benefit on the basis of a nexus of politics, economics, social position and connections with the security apparatus. Some people number them in the hundreds, while others speak of the '3,000 families'.

Graft at all levels is thus as endemic in the Marxist-market system as it was under previous regimes, with 140,000 CCP members sanctioned for corruption in 2010. The stimulus programme launched in 2008 produced a plethora of opportunities for officials to make money on the side. The Party's Central Commission for Discipline reported that 6,800 cadres were prosecuted for corruption in the first eight months of 2011 and that graft cases uncovered since September 2009 had involved 3 billion yuan. Many contractors budget the payments as 'public-relations expenses'.[2]

When he was ousted on graft charges in 1995 after a power struggle with the leadership, Chen Xitong, the boss of Beijing, said he might be blamed for wrongdoing in the capital but asked: 'Who is responsible for corruption in the entire CCP?' In his speech on the ninetieth anniversary of the foundation of the CCP, Hu Jintao observed: 'If corruption does not get solved effectively, the Party will lose the people's trust and support.' More cynically, as old Maoist Deng Liqun is said to have remarked during the 1990s: if the Party does not eradicate graft it will lose the support of the people; but if it does it will lose members.

This is, of course, not merely a matter for the CCP. Few people can afford to be too righteous if they want to get on. Litigants take judges out for banquets when their cases are being heard. Parents give expensive gifts to their children's examiners. Top soccer referees have taken bribes of hundreds of thousands of yuan to fix important matches. Contacts, known as *guanxi*, are essential to do business or move ahead. A survey by the Beijing-based Horizon consultancy found that two-thirds of urban business people thought knowing the right people, particularly in the political world, was the main factor in determining success or failure.[3]

'Red hat' business chieftains meld their corporate and Communist Party positions, often with the help of local governments. The 'squeeze' and corner-cutting that runs through this nation on speed is evident when it comes to making money under the table. Chen Tonghai, former Chairman of the second-largest oil company, Sinopec, was given a suspended death sentence in 2009 for taking 200 million yuan in bribes. At a big state steel company in central China with assets of 38 billion yuan, more than 100 managers were found to have been involved in insider transactions between the firm and enterprises in which they had an interest. Inflated invoices were paid, such as the one for 110 electric air-control valves at nearly 1 million yuan each when in fact only 10 were needed at a real cost of 15,000 yuan each.

Though he has not been accused of any wrongdoing, Zhan Xialai, founder of the big car group Chery, provides an apt example of the fusing of politics and business. As well as heading the firm after it nominally broke out of the state sector, Zhan was also CCP Secretary in its home city of Wuhu until questioning of his dual role surfaced in state media in 2004. An economist recalls asking him why he did not devote himself solely to cars since he loved the industry so much. The reply was simple: 'Only by being Secretary of the Wuhu City Party Committee can I best protect Chery.' He is reported to have continued to support it from his official positions as he rose to become Secretary General of Anhui province where Wuhu is located. The company has been visited by thirty members of the Politburo since 2004, and Zhan still drops in at weekends.

Officials find it easy to conceal their assets. Wu Yuliang, Vice-Chairman of the CCP Disciplinary Commission, has acknowledged that even if officials did declare their wealth people would not believe them; he has also said that his commission had no way of verifying the figures. One snag in introducing a national property tax is that it would require a register that would be likely to show a lot of functionaries living in accommodation they could not possibly afford on their salaries but manage to occupy thanks to munificent business contacts.

Corruption and weak regulation go hand in hand; indeed, rules that do not need to be applied if there is sufficient inducement are a gift to officials on the take. Opacity often cloaks personal and corporate business and wealth. Unless they inherited their money, the rich are assumed to have exploited official connections. Hidden 'grey' income is estimated to amount to 30 per cent of GDP. A check at the state Agricultural Bank in 2010 revealed irregularities running to tens of billions of yuan. Initial Public Offerings (IPOs) by companies on the mainland have been marked by insider trading and artificially low valuations that greatly profited those with the right connections. In the first half of 2011, twenty-five mainland firms listed in New York disclosed discrepancies or saw their auditors resign.

High-scale corruption is often spiced with a sexual element. The career of Li Wei, China's 'Queen of Mistresses', shows how the system can be gamed to great profit. A refugee at the age of seven from Vietnam, she settled with her family in Yunnan in south-west China where she began trading tobacco as a teenager and developed business and official contacts. An early lover was a married bureaucrat in the Public Security Ministry who got Li and her sisters residence papers and fake identity cards that enabled them to travel freely on the mainland and to Hong Kong. In the 1990s she married an official in the Yunnan Tobacco

Bureau who introduced her to the Provincial Governor, Li Jiating, twenty years her senior.

At a party – according to her life story as told in a 2011 media article – she saw the Governor give his mistress a pleasure boat worth 6 million yuan. Soon afterwards she took that mistress's place and her new lover gave her tobacco-export quotas; she also got big bribes from business people she helped with her contacts. But in 2001 the Governor was jailed for corruption. She was also arrested but was released. She learned one lesson from the experience: 'You can't afford to invest everything in one person. You need a huge relationship net, like an umbrella.'

Next Li hooked up with Du Shicheng, the CCP Secretary of the eastern port city of Qingdao. She set up property companies to which he granted valuable land at low prices as the city underwent a renaissance as a resort and the centre for yachting in the 2008 Olympics. Cortèges of black limousines carrying visitors seeking her help with deals drove regularly from the airport to her stately villa with manicured lawns and Renaissance-style fountains in the hilly former German concession. *Caijing* magazine, which broke the story, wrote of envelopes stuffed with cash being handed over as fine wine flowed and Li, dressed in tight-fitting clothes, flirted with important suitors. From time to time she would hand Du envelopes containing up to 1 million yuan in notes. 'Du was completely in awe of Li and would have done anything she asked him to,' an official told the magazine. 'He was very vain and self-possessed but not terribly bright. He let her do the thinking.'

Li took the head of a big oil company as a second lover; he gave her licences to run petrol stations and shares worth tens of millions of yuan, according to the magazine. Her name was linked with those of a former Deputy Head of the Supreme Court, a Deputy Director of China Development Bank and a former Vice-Mayor of Beijing. Ultimately her luck ran out and she was arrested for tax evasion. Du and other men with whom she had affairs were charged with various corruption offences and sent to prison; Li's evidence helped to convict them so she got away with a relatively light sentence of four years. On her release, in 2010, she headed for Hong Kong, apparently with most of her money – and a diary. Her mansion was confiscated but has become a place of pilgrimage for young women who would like to emulate her ascent to riches and some power.

The story was not at all to the taste of the regime. The issue of the magazine in which Li's saga was detailed was swiftly removed from shops. Other print and broadcast media did not touch it. But it sped round the Internet. A Beijing blogger called her diary 'a sword of Damocles hanging over China's corrupt officials'. As a writer in the *South China Morning Post* noted: 'Her case is widely seen as having fed just desserts to lovers who took a mistress behind the back of their wife, following a tradition of wealthy men taking concubines or "second wives" that stretches back thousands of years.'[4]

There is a school of thought which argues that, by greasing the wheels of business, corruption makes it easier to get things done. Another argument has it that graft has always been part of the way China operates. Still, there can be no doubt that corruption not only gnaws at the system but also stands in the way of the country's further evolution. If regulations are there to be bought around, there is something rotten at the core. If corruption leads to construction or engineering projects going to unqualified firms, or to companies that seek only to maximize earnings in the shortest possible time, the dangers to the public are evident and China's chances of moving up the value chain will be compromised. The impact of the high-speed train crash of 2011 was so great because of the chain of revelations that led to suspicions that the disaster had been caused not only by the Minister's lust for speed but also because of the graft surrounding contracts for vital equipment. More broadly, corruption infuses the trust deficit that envelops China and makes it a less contented place.

The same applies to the second of the three big fault lines, the environment. The PRC teeters on the brink of an ecological disaster, with pollution of every kind, desertification, land erosion and deforestation plus the loss of rare species. Mao declared war on nature; industrialization and urbanization have continued the campaign, and the connivance of local officials with polluters has played a significant role. Of the world's most polluted cities, at least half are in the PRC.

As if the air pollution figures were not bad enough, a study by foreign scientists in 2012 suggested that China under-reports its annual carbon emissions by as much as 1.4 billion tonnes, about what Japan releases in a year. Industry and urbanization produce huge amounts of waste – 3,000 tons a day in Chongqing, tipped into a huge landfill that will soon be full. The mainland has also become the main destination for garbage sent from richer countries to supply its recycling industry, which imports three-quarters of its basic materials. US exports to the PRC of recovered paper and cardboard rose more than five times in the first decade of this century to 12 million tons a year. Some villages specialize in the processing of electronic waste, which is scraped out of discarded equipment to be reused – at great health risk to those doing the work. Greenpeace warned in 2011 that the PRC was sitting on at least 1 million tons of untreated industrial waste that causes cancer. It also reported that levels of toxic chromium in Yunnan were 200 times higher than normal. A chemical factory in the province had 140,000 tons of the poisonous residue close to a tributary of the Pearl River.

The potential for toxic hazard is not limited to obscure Chinese manufacturers hidden away in inland towns. In 2009, 137 workers at an Apple supplier in Suzhou were poisoned by a chemical used to clean iPhone screens; and in 2011 a report by five Chinese non-governmental organizations (NGOs) charged that Apple was using suppliers with records of violating environmental standards and taking advantage of 'the loopholes in developing countries' environmental-management systems'. (The American company replied that it was committed to the 'highest standards of social responsibility' and launched an audit of its Chinese suppliers.) The report also highlighted complaints about air pollution from a plant run by Foxconn in Taiyuan, capital of Shanxi province. (The firm said it was installing new equipment.) At another Foxconn factory, in Chengdu, a build-up of flammable dust in the air was blamed for an explosion that killed three workers producing iPads. In Shenzhen, pollutant emissions from a treatment station that takes waste from Foxconn and seven international electronics companies were found to be well above the legal level.[5]

For decades, environmental data was hushed up or simply not collected. An experiment in producing a 'green GDP' was abandoned by the authorities when the likely negative findings became evident and local officials feared that their promotion prospects would be adversely affected if they were marked on the environmental situation in their areas of responsibility. US diplomatic cables from 2006 released by Wikileaks reported that the most dangerous types of air pollution were not measured because this would lead to 'politically difficult' revelations about the severity of the problem. Academics faced the threat of funding cuts if they told the truth, the cables added. When foreign embassies released their own readings of poor air quality in the capital, the government told them they were breaking the law.[6]

The environment has become a social and political issue and not simply a matter of trying to save China's ecology. More information has been made available and this circulates speedily on websites outside official control. The central government has encouraged the use of solar power, wind power and hydropower, clean industrial technology and greater energy efficiency. But the results have been limited. The state grid company is reluctant to hook up these new sources of power since they are more expensive than coal and have problems of their own: namely when the wind does not blow or the sun does not shine or when damming of rivers causes the discontent of local residents and threatens clashes with other countries that lie downstream. As a result China has become a big exporter of wind-farm equipment, and is the major supplier of solar panels from companies set up when these sectors seemed likely to boom domestically, provoking a trade war with the US over accusations that PRC firms, helped by government subsidies, are engaging in large-scale dumping. Electric cars are a priority item in the new Five-Year Plan, launched in 2011, but the industry is struggling, both technically and in terms of producing the vehicles consumers want.

China's energy consumption is forecast to rise from 15.6 per cent of the global total in 2006 to 20.7 per cent in 2030, when it will use 16.5 million barrels of oil a day, 80 per cent of it imported. Energy-efficiency targets have been missed or achieved only by a frantic last-minute scramble. This is the result not only of growth in household and industrial demand but also of low electricity prices held down by state controls that encourage waste. The World Bank puts use of energy per unit of output in China at anywhere from 20 to 100 per cent more than in Japan or the United States. Though the target is to reduce dependency on coal, it will still provide 63 per cent of the country's energy in 2015 and the fall from the current 70 per cent will depend on the import of large amounts of natural gas, development of shale gas and success for the nuclear-power programme after a moratorium declared following the disaster in Japan in 2011.

Water is another growing crisis issue. China has long been subject to the traditional cycles of floods and drought, but the fundamental problem today is that the country is using ever-increasing amounts of water while supply is declining. Long-term, if the Tibetan glaciers which supply much of China's water melt the outlook will be dire. Freshwater resources of 2,200 cubic metres per person are a quarter of the global average. The 60 per cent of the land area above the Yangtze contains only 20 per cent of the nation's water. The northern areas that house two-fifths of the population and provide nearly half the industrial output receive only a quarter of the nation's annual precipitation and less than a tenth of the stream run-off. Availability per hectare of farmland in the Yellow River Basin is one tenth of that in the Yangtze Basin, and the amount per inhabitant less than a quarter. The northern water table is dropping steadily and aquifers are depleted by the growth of huge cities. The number of powered wells in the North China Plain rose from 1,800 in the 1960s to 700,000 by 2000; they are being driven so deep that some of the water brought up is 30,000 years old, according to the Chinese Academy of Sciences, which says that two-thirds of use is for agriculture and livestock. As with energy, low prices under official controls encourage waste; average rates are a quarter of what the World Bank thinks they should be in a country at China's stage of development. Water from a 25 billion yuan desalination project in Tianjin using Israeli equipment costs twice as much to produce as it sells for.[7]

The city of Beijing has been taking up to 400 million cubic metres of water a year from neighbouring provinces since 2003, causing resentment among farmers in already arid Shanxi and Hebei. The capital's per capita water resources are only one-tenth of the generally accepted requirement of 1,000 cubic metres. But that has not stopped the development of more than 100 water-thirsty golf courses round the city, which the authorities are loathe to restrict supply to or to risk angering the many users of the city's 3,000 bath houses, which between them consume 5 million tons of water a year. The main reservoir serving Beijing has started to dry up. Irrigation systems are backward. One-third of China's lakes have been lost in the past half-century, both because of the declining quantity of water and as a result of reclamation for farming or construction. In the summer of 2011 China's biggest expanse of freshwater, Lake Poyang in Jiangxi, shrank to a third of its normal size, with the level dropping by seven metres. Hydropower projects have cut off the flow on some rivers and altered the course of nature.

The government says it is ready to spend 4 trillion yuan on improving water infrastructure up to 2020. Yet the signs are mixed. The amount of wastewater being treated has increased, and the sector has become a target for private-equity investors. But long-standing plans to divert supply from the wet south to the parched north of the country have been repeatedly put back – the latest target date for its central and eastern links is 2014.

It is not just a matter of diminishing supply. Sixteen per cent of China's water is in the lowest quality category. Spills of petrochemicals poison waterways. The Yellow River is so filthy it can no longer be used as a drinking source. Only a quarter of the groundwater in the North China Plain is safe to drink, according to the China Geological Survey. The booming industry that burns garbage to generate electricity produces run-offs filled with heavy metals. In rural areas, 30 million tons of fertilizers seep into rivers and lakes each year. Only 20 per cent of animal excrement, a traditional crop nutrient (Mao called pigs 'fertilizer factories on four legs'), is properly treated, according to the Nanjing Institute of Environmental Science. Cities provision themselves from rivers into which raw sewage flows; the World Health Organization puts the annual toll of those who die from drinking polluted water at 95,000.[8]

China did not have an Environment Ministry until 2008 and when it was set up the new department soon found itself on the back foot as the stimulus programme introduced at the end of that year put the accent on expansion and infrastructure projects that were not necessarily eco-friendly. Three years later, Zhou Shengxian, the Environment Minister, warned in an essay that 'in China's thousands of years of civilization, the conflict between humanity and nature has never been as serious as it is today'. Growth prospects could be hit unless higher priority was given to cleaning up the skies and rivers and limiting exploitation of mineral reserves, he added. 'The depletion, deterioration and exhaustion of resources and the deterioration of the environment have become serious bottlenecks constraining economic and social development,' he went on. 'If we are numb and apathetic in the face of the acute conflict between humankind and nature, and environmental management remains stuck in the old rut with no efforts in environmental technology, there will surely be a painful price to pay, and even irrecoverable losses.'

In June 2011, Vice-Minister Li Ganjie reported that, while some environmental indicators – mainly sulphur-dioxide emissions – were 'turning better', the 'overall environmental situation is still very grave and is facing many difficulties and challenges'. But his ministry has limited authority and, while setting out the seriousness of the challenge, its annual reports do not identify those responsible, making action that much more problematic. The main planning agency, the National Development and Reform Commission (NDRC), which backs growth, is far more powerful. China's 2,500 Environmental Offices are part of provincial, county and township governments answering to authorities that may well put continuing growth ahead of ecological concerns. The first reaction when something goes badly wrong is to cover it up, even when it reaches major proportions – as in the case of the pollution of Lake Tai or a big oil spill in Bohai Bay, which went unreported for more than a month in the summer of 2011.

So the ecological crisis continues. The faster the development boom, the greater the effect. Far from the industrial heartlands and big cities, two-thirds of the 950-mile coastline of Hainan is being turned into a strip of resorts, hotels and marinas. This puts the island's ecosystem at risk as farmland and mangrove forests are built over, reducing protection against typhoons and tsunamis, and destroying marine life; at a luxury hotel, visitors are not allowed to swim in the sea because of the danger from tides. In the autumn of 2010, floods destroyed roads and some of the remaining farmland, causing 400,000 people to be evacuated. 'Hainan is a real-life example of that film *Avatar*,' Liu Futang, a former chief of Hainan's Forest Fire Prevention Bureau, told a journalist. 'Except that in *Avatar* they could organize together to fight back.' On Hainan, he added, 'I don't have much hope – nothing can stop this change.'[9]

The health costs are escalating. The birth-defect rate in Beijing has almost doubled in the last ten years, with pollution blamed as the main cause. In the coalfields of Shanxi the rate is an unusually high 8.4 per cent: 30 per cent of babies die soon after birth and 40 per cent carry their disabilities throughout their lives. In some places uncontrolled dumping of heavy metals has led to abnormally high levels of lead in blood. The number of asbestos-related deaths is put at anywhere from 15,000 to 40,000 a year. As China's battery manufacturing and recycling industry has expanded to 3,000 plants, so have lead deposits in their waste. An investigation into battery makers in Zhejiang found that most failed to apply pollution treatment, causing dangerous blood-poisoning among local inhabitants. Similar or even worse conditions are found in Guangdong. According to a study by Janet Larsen of the Earth Policy Institute, the air in Beijing and Shanghai often contains four times as many poisonous particulates as in New York City; that and the heavy smoking rate mean that the incidence of lung cancer has increased nearly fivefold since the 1970s, making it the biggest cause of death in the PRC. International studies estimate that bad air kills between 655,600 and 750,000 Chinese people a year and caused damage equal to 4–5 per cent of the country's GDP between 1995 and 2005; a later US study put the figure at 6–9 per cent.

The health dangers are far from confined to urban areas. Liver cancer is more than three times as likely to prove fatal for a Chinese farmer as for the average global citizen and stomach-cancer deaths in the countryside are double the world rate, the Earth Policy study found. Both cancers are linked to water polluted by chemicals and sewage. There are more than 450 villages spread across nearly all China where cancer rates are abnormally high because of pollution from local industrial plants. In one in Henan, visited by the geographer Lee Liu, 80 per cent of the young people were chronically sick. Compensation, when it is forthcoming, is low. In places, children with dangerous levels of lead in their blood are refused treatment and sent home to their polluted villages, according to a report in 2011 by Human Rights Watch on the situation in four provinces. It found that the authorities had placed arbitrary limits on access to blood testing or withheld the results from sufferers while merely advising that children be fed apples, garlic, milk and eggs.

Hunan in central China is notorious for its high levels of discharges of mercury, chromium lead, cadmium and sulphur dioxide. Heavy metals from smelters sink deep into the soil or poison waterways; the province's Xiang River, a tributary of the Yangtze, had arsenic levels almost double the national safety level when tested in 2008 – 59 billion yuan are to be spent on a five year clean-up. But even when the polluting plants are shut down the danger remains – in one village where the local smelter was closed some years ago, 400 people still suffer from high levels in their blood. In another village, black and yellow smoke belches night and day from a big lead and zinc producer, coating the surrounding houses with choking fumes; the plant emits 20,000 tons of sulphur dioxide a year. As if that was not enough, a nearby chemical-fertilizer plant also poisons the atmosphere. A check on the village's water supply twenty years ago found that it was too contaminated to be drunk safely, but nothing has been done. 'People are dying here, but nobody cares,' as a local woman told a reporter from the *South China Morning Post*. Most of the young people have gone elsewhere, leaving only old people and children to live and die there.[10]

Pollution has become a significant motive for the protests described in the previous chapter. 'The prevention of heavy-metal pollution [...] concerns social harmony and stability,' as the Minister for Environmental Protection noted. China argues that it is blighted with dirty manufacturing shifted from more developed countries – a real enough conclusion, though the Communist Party and PRC governments showed little concern at the time about such a growth-enhancing transfer. Beijing adds that its pollution today is comparable only to that in Europe or the United States during their industrialization. It also points out that, when the size of its population is taken into account, its per capita emissions of CO_2 gases fall far below those in the West. It resists mandatory targets on emissions, in part because it wants to remain free to grow and in part because of its usual refusal to accept external controls.[11]

The Copenhagen Conference on Climate Change in 2009 ended with public discord after a last-minute attempt by President Obama to cut a deal with Wen Jiabao came to nothing – as might have been expected since the Chinese Prime Minister could not have given ground without approval from the Politburo Standing Committee in Beijing, which was not at that point in negotiating mode. Three months later, at his press conference after the National People's Congress, the Premier was still annoyed at the way he had been treated at the conference. Some Chinese believed that, since Obama would have known that Wen had no real room for manoeuvre, it was simply a US set-up to make China the villain of the piece. But then a diplomatic cable disclosed by Wikileaks indicated private understanding for the PRC's position by an envoy from Washington at a meeting in Beijing seven months before Copenhagen. The politics of the environment will continue to be complex both domestically and internationally as the PRC faces a tug-of-war between the growth imperative and the ecological cost.

The best-intentioned plans of the centre are liable to dislocation at local level. Local governments are advised in advance about checks on pollution levels and so have time to tip off protected factories in their areas, which clean up their act till the examination is over. Beijing carries out periodic satellite monitoring of land use, but informed sources say developers may be told by friendly officials about the surveillance and stop work accordingly; in one case in Hebei reported by *Caixin* magazine, trees were planted to mask illegal work and then removed when the satellites had gone.

Polluting factories can be major sources of local employment – along the Xiang River in Hunan, 70 per cent of economic activity involves mining and smelting. Official surveillance of pollution in the countryside is low. Fines for ecological damage are small – one power-station operator in southern China told me it was cheaper to pay the penalty than to install clean equipment. Less than 10 per cent of polluters have been held responsible for their offences, according to Wang Canfa, a

Beijing law professor. In some cases, such as that of a major petro-chemical spill in the north-east, the courts declare themselves unable to handle public complaint. Faced with reports of the extent of heavy-metal poisoning of farmland, the Environment Ministry acknowledged on its website that fourteen provinces were affected but refused to give any details of what it proposed to do on the grounds that such infor-mation was a national secret.

Some observers believe that China will make significant progress as the central government encourages environmental protection and ecologically friendly growth. But the record to date has not been encouraging. Too many interests are at work in the opposite direction, together with the huge backlog of pollution and environmental degra-dation. As a researcher at the Environment Ministry acknowledged in a comment in the ministerial journal, the PRC will remain focused on industrial expansion for many years yet and 'more patience is needed to achieve green development'. So long as the regime depends on deliv-ering crude material growth, the ecology will take second place.

China's demographic timebomb is set to explode in the next decade or so. Though the number of its inhabitants is increasing by 5 million each year, the country's share of global population has dropped from 22 to 19 per cent since the late 1970s as other nations, including India, have grown faster. The combination of increased longevity with a falling birth rate means that the number of young people joining the labour force will shrink. There are a million men who can't marry because of the lack of young women and will not produce children. The 'demo-graphic dividend' of plentiful young labour that has underpinned China's rise – with a quarter of growth attributed to the expansion of the working-age population – will thus be seriously affected as the PRC approaches the 'Lewis turning point' at which the labour supply is no longer unlimited while the number of old people, who have to be sup-ported in a nation without adequate pension or welfare systems, rises.[12]

The first big change occurred between 1950 and 1976. Infant mor-tality, which had been 138.5 per 1,000 births in 1953, fell to 33 in 1990 and 13.8 in 2010. At the same time, life expectancy has risen to an aver-age of 73.5 years; it reaches 79 in Shanghai and is at its lowest, about 69, in Yunnan, Qinghai and Tibet. The number of Chinese aged over 60 in the last ten years has increased to equal the total population of Spain.

The falling birth rate is often attributed solely to the one-child policy introduced in 1978, which has led to 104 million 'single children' in the population. In fact the policy is not as draconian as is often supposed. It is relaxed for some rural residents and ethnic minorities. If husband and wife are both single children, they are allowed to have two off-spring. Demographers put the proportion of Chinese couples restricted to one child at 63 per cent.

Wealthier citizens simply pay the fine for having more than one child, which runs at around 240,000 yuan per child and is estimated to have earned the state two trillion yuan. In Beijing, fines are levied only if the mother is aged under twenty-eight and the offspring was born within four years of the first. Media in Guangdong have reported plans to lift the ban on second children in the province. The real effect has come from the combination of the policy, fast-falling fertility and the spread of contraception that began in the 1970s. The average number of children per couple has dropped to 1.5 across the country and to 1 in the most developed regions. The rate of population growth is now a third of that in 1990 and a fifth of 1970. China's fertility rate is below that of the United States, Britain and France. Ten per cent of couples are estimated to be infertile.

There are recurrent cases of criminals kidnapping young children and selling them to couples who cannot procreate; one gang in Fujian sentenced in 2010 peddled forty-six infants for up to 40,000 yuan each while 800 people in two child trafficking gangs were arrested in mid-2012. In Guangdong, the provincial sperm bank offers up to 3,000 yuan a time to donors. Clinics providing in vitro fertilization (IVF) flourish, some unlicensed and representing a further addition to China's list of health dangers. Other factors also apply. A survey in 2010 reported couples delaying plans to have a child because of the cost of maternity in a hospital or clinic and because of lack of space at home; in Beijing some respondents waited till they earned 8,000 yuan a month.

The 5.8 per cent rise in population reported by the census taken in 2010 was half the rate of ten years earlier. A United Nations projection has even forecast that low fertility would reduce the population to below

1 billion by the end of this century. Whatever the precise numbers, the result will be a growing age imbalance – China, as the saying goes, may grow old before it gets rich. Some have forecast its full impact being felt between 2015 and 2020 but Chinese demographers working from the latest census believe it will hit ten years later. They see the labour force peaking at around 1 billion in 2016–20, staying at that level for a time and then dropping to 800–900 million.

If there is disagreement about the date, there is no doubt as to the trend bred from the cumulative effect of the fall in the birth rate since the 1970s. The number of workers aged between twenty and twenty-nine is forecast to drop by a quarter between now and 2026, while the proportion of the population aged over sixty grows from the current 12.5 per cent to 20 per cent by 2020 and then accelerates to more than 300 million by 2030. This will exacerbate the process known as '1:2:4' in which, with retirement set at sixty for men, fifty for women and fifty-five for civil servants, one working offspring has to support two parents and four grandparents. The weakening of family support will present a stark challenge to the highly insufficient pension system. If wage earners are paid only half their salary when they retire, the system in urban areas is likely to go into deficit in 2015, with the shortfall being equivalent to 95 per cent of GDP by the middle of the century.

Forty per cent of elderly people living in cities say they suffer from feelings of depression, according to a study carried out under the auspices of the Chinese Academy of Sciences. The traditional nuclear family is fraying under the impact of economic development. Though the marriage rate has risen significantly since hitting a low in 2002, the number of divorces has doubled since 2002. A report in 2009 found that nearly half of China's elderly people lived alone or with their grandchildren. In rural China one repeatedly comes across villages where nearly all the residents are either elderly or infants, those in the middle having gone to work in cities. A survey in Guangdong showed that a quarter of old people received only one visit a year from their children; 75 per cent of those questioned said they longed for more moral support from their children – one man complained that he had been ill in bed for two months and his son had not come to visit him. In Beijing, 90,000 people are on waiting lists for old folks' homes. The seriousness of the problem was shown by a draft law introduced into the national legislature in 2011 requiring children to visit their parents regularly. If they did not do so, their elders could go to court 'to claim their legal rights to be physically and mentally looked after', a ministerial official said. Filial piety enforced by law: another brick out of the Confucian wall – at a time when the Bank of China forecasts a pensions shortfall of 18 trillion yuan by 2013.

With the demographic shift, China has acquired a serious gender imbalance as parents abort female foetuses or abandon female babies. Despite the large numbers of young women migrants working in manufacturing plants, males are still regarded as being more likely to be able to support their parents. By tradition, they alone can pay the required homage to ancestors and ensure that the family lineage is preserved. The demand for males has led to trafficking of boys under five, estimated at 6,000 a year, bought by couples who have not produced a male heir or simply want to short-circuit the birth process. The male:female ratio at birth has widened from 108.5:100 in 1982 to 120:100. Professor Li Jianxin, of Peking University, estimates that there will be 26 million more men than women aged between twenty-two and thirty-four by 2020, producing an army of 'leftovers' without marriage prospects whose dissatisfaction with their situation he views as a potential source of social instability. As it is, eligible young women and their families can demand what is known as the 'bride price' in the form of a dowry – including perhaps a car but certainly possession of a flat or house. (Couples who marry without such trappings have what is known as a 'naked wedding' – a television soap opera with that title topped the ratings in 2011.) Meanwhile agents arrange marriages with women brought in from Vietnam, Burma, Thailand and Cambodia. Though there are signs of daughters being more valued, at least in big urban centres, demographers estimate that there will be a shortage of 20–30 million young women of marriage age by 2050.

Male 'youth bulges' have been linked by historians to imperial expansion by European powers after 1500 and by Japan after 1914; and, more recently, to extremism and regime-challenging revolts in the Middle East and Latin America as well as to increased crime and violence.

Perhaps the army of the elderly will opt for a quiet national life, but the prospect of a testosterone challenge makes it all the more important for China's leadership to ensure that these single men have jobs. However, there are problems with this, too.[13]

Unemployment is put officially at 4 per cent. It is, in fact, considerably higher. In addition there is serious underemployment, especially in the countryside. The drive embodied in the latest Five-Year Plan towards greater mechanization, high productivity and less reliance on labour-intensive manufacturing threatens a further contraction of the labour market as it has existed in the last three decades. Expansion of the services sector, particularly in growing cities, may produce jobs for unskilled migrants, but there is the potential for a knife-edged race between a contraction of employment and the contraction of the working population. If the first comes to pass, the result could be wide social unrest as unemployment provides the glue for protests. If it is the second, wage pressure will escalate, affecting China's competitiveness against other low-cost producers, which can best be addressed by increased mechanization – which would in turn mean fewer jobs.

When it comes to the more educated, the unemployment rate has shot up among graduates as their numbers have escalated in a sixfold expansion of higher education this century. Only 2.5 million suitable jobs are available each year for 6.5 million young people leaving university. Another 2.5 million become blue-collar or service workers or do menial jobs, living in crowded communal lodgings outside big cities where they earn the soubriquet of 'ants'. More than 1 million more remain jobless, many of them products of non-specialist courses that do not equip them to take the technical posts on offer or with an aptitude for business. Adding them and the 'ants' together suggests a graduate-unemployment rate as high as 30 per cent. The potential danger for a regime of so many educated but unemployed social young people is obvious, as is the paradox they represent: a large group of people with the wrong skills and without jobs in a nation that is going to be short of workers.

Well aware of the tensions bubbling up around it, the leadership constantly seeks to radiate an image of concerned competence and an upbeat mood. Wen Jiabao acknowledges problems but tries to promote the idea that the regime will surmount them. Censorship offices at central and provincial levels order that anti-corruption proceedings must not be 'vulgarized', and there is to be no mention of 'suicides, self-mutilation or collective action' by people who have lost their homes. Liu Changle, head of China's single private television station, Phoenix, whose transmissions are limited to Guangdong, requires his journalists to keep any comments on China's political situation positive and constructive. Major web portals accept censorship as the price of building services that have hundreds of millions of users.

In the south the provincial authorities have launched a 'Happy Guangdong' campaign: 'Happiness for the people is like flowers,' Wang Yang, the Guangdong CCP Secretary wrote, adding that the role of the Party and government was to 'create the proper environment for the flowers to grow'. The municipality of Beijing wants its inhabitants to lead 'happy and glorious lives'; people were shown delivering 'happy' testimonials on video screens in the capital for the 2011 May Day holiday, while Beijing Television ran films under the title of *Happy Blossoms*. Chongqing aspires to be the city in which 'people have the strongest feelings of happiness'. There is talk of judging local officials by the degree of happiness among those they administer as well as on their growth performance. It is all very much in line with the national contentment described in the novel *The Fat Years,* in which material progress underpins national amnesia about terrible events in the near past.

Yet the Chinese harbour distinct reservations. They take great pride in the renaissance of their nation, but polls reveal deep levels of concern over their personal situation and the flaws in the society around them. Any single survey may be questionable because of its sample or its methodology or the time at which it was taken, but there is a clear pattern of high aspirations in a materialist world breeding anxiety.

A Gallup poll conducted in 155 countries between 2005 and 2009 to measure satisfaction and happiness levels placed the PRC at 125. (Denmark came top, the US fourteenth and the UK seventeenth.) A national survey published in Party media at the end of 2010 reported that 73.5 per cent of respondents felt 'vulnerable' – nearly half the officials questioned put themselves in that category. 'The widening gap between rich and poor, the need to use *guanxi* to get ahead, and rampant unfairness are making people feel not only relatively poorer but also weaker,' as a writer in the CCP's *Global Times* put it. *The Blue Book of China's Society* for 2011, compiled by the Chinese Academy of Social Sciences, reported declining levels of job satisfaction, falling confidence in social-welfare programmes and high concern about inflation. A survey by a health magazine at the same time found half the residents of Beijing, Shanghai and Shenzhen to be unhappy with their living conditions. A poll by the *People's Tribune* in 2010 revealed that 58 per cent of white-collar workers, 55 per cent of intellectuals and 45 per cent of Party and government officials felt 'powerless'.

The White Book of Happiness of Middle-Class Families, released in 2010, which surveyed 100,000 people from 35 cities, reports that even in the most contented provinces more than half those questioned said they were not happy. 'Can't afford to be born because a Caesarean costs 50,000 yuan; can't afford to study because schools cost at least 30,000 yuan; can't afford to live anywhere because each square metre is at least 20,000 yuan; can't afford to get sick because pharmaceutical profits are at least tenfold; can't afford to die because cremation costs at least 30,000 yuan,' declared a much-read round-robin email circulated in late 2010.

A survey of more than 100 million adults, carried out between 2001 and 2005 but published only in 2010, disclosed that 17.5 per cent suffered from mental disorders. Medical organizations report high levels of sleep deprivation because people had to work extremely long hours to pay off their mortgage; 70 per cent of those who had bought apartments in Beijing felt anxious as a result, it added. In another investigation, 84 per cent of high-school pupils said they felt depressed or stressed. In 2010, the Beijing Mental Health Bureau reported a rapid increase in the number of children with mental-health problems, particularly hyperactivity and inability to concentrate.[14]

An online questionnaire in late 2009 asked academics, Communist Party cadres and the general public to name the biggest problems China would face in the coming decade. Corruption and the wealth divide headed the responses followed by clashes between the authorities and 'the masses at the grassroots', property prices, and a 'crisis of trust and loss of moral standards'. 'Students come home from school and tell their parents, "One of my classmates got run over by a car today – now I have one less person to compete against",' laments Guo Qijia, a professor at Beijing Normal University. 'We have lost our humanity, our kindness and our spirit.' There was an outcry in the autumn of 2011 when a two-year-old girl was hit by two vehicles and passersby did nothing to help her. A few days later, a five-year-old boy was run over by a lorry whose driver then reportedly reversed over him to make sure he was dead and to avoid paying hospital bills for him; the body lay under the truck for seven hours while his family and the driver argued about compensation. The mood of personal concern with the way China is evolving may seem to sit ill with the booming economy, the striking recovery of growth after the downturn of late 2008 and growing wealth. But, in fact, it connects with rising questioning of the economic model that has propelled the country since Deng Xiaoping changed its course in 1978. This lies at the heart of any analysis of where the People's Republic is headed in the coming years as it faces problems that go to the core of its success.

17

THE PRICE OF SUCCESS

Sitting in the global catbird seat at the start of this century's second decade, the People's Republic has appeared able to achieve feats that elude more developed nations. While other governments pondered how to react to the crisis caused by the financial meltdown of 2007–08, Beijing jumped in with its two-year infrastructure programme of 4 trillion yuan accompanied by massive easing of credit that saw new lending double to 10 trillion yuan in 2009, 29 per cent of the nation's GDP. By 2010, annual economic expansion was back to 10 per cent and the government was trying to tame the exuberance at a time when other countries were still engaged in a quest for growth many times smaller.

China's performance led impressed observers to conclude that the world had a new master. Yet, just as the social situation is a great deal more complex than it might appear, so a look behind the curtain shows substantial shadows in the economic story and a failure to get to grips with major structural problems that threaten to cause big challenges by the middle of the decade.

The prime cause of what Wen Jiabao identified as China's unbalanced, unstable, uncoordinated and unsustainable economic situation has been its overdependence on fixed-asset investment (FAI) in infrastructure and property together with reliance on exports. The National Bureau of Statistics (NBS) reported that FAI grew by 30 per cent in 2009 to nearly 22.5 trillion yuan after 24.5–27.2 per cent jumps in each of the previous four years. In 2010, such investment accounted for 55 per cent of growth. It has amounted to over 40 per cent of GDP for nine years running and accounted for 55 per cent of growth in 2010.

Consumption, meanwhile, has lagged. Wages represent a much smaller proportion of national income than in the West. Japan's consumer sector is twice as big as China's. Consequently the main beneficiary in this supposedly Communist state has been capital, and those who control it, rather than the workers whose spending would provide a more solid basis for growth. The authorities know this but rebalancing is a long process and the quick fix of building more big projects and opening the credit taps to buy recovery proved irresistible. It is, however, a trick that will be hard to reproduce both because of the destabilizing effects on the monetary front of throwing so much cash at problems and because there is both a limit to the number of new projects China needs and diminishing returns from them – not to mention the greater caution induced after the 2011 high-speed train crash. While the PRC required infrastructure improvements, much of the investment was fostered by immediate needs rather than rationally structured long-term planning. Continuing on that path contains obvious substantial dangers to the quality of growth.

The twelfth Five-Year Plan, approved by the National People's Congress in 2011, aims to rebalance the economy by boosting consumption to lessen dependence on fixed-asset investment and exports.

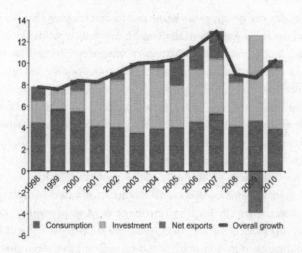

Contributions of investment, consumption and exports to China's GDP
Source: National Bureau of Statistics

The minimum wage is to double by 2015 as China counts on rising productivity to offset the risk of a drop in the expansion of exports and of losing ground to cheaper labour competitors elsewhere in Asia. Officials of the monopoly trade union were instructed to start standing up for the workers after acting for decades as a tool of management for the CCP; wage increases of 12 per cent a year were registered overall. Central and Western China were to be developed to catch up with the coastal regions that had led economic growth since the 1980s. Urbanization was to be pursued. China was to move up the technology chain by making its own airliners and advanced machinery, developing its nuclear industry and environmentally friendly energy-saving equipment, becoming a leader in biotechnology, next-generation information technology, new materials and new-power generation.

Achieving the rise in consumption China requires to rebalance its economy will not come quickly given the low starting base – a senior official for the Party School remarked to me that it would be a matter of 'two Five-Year Plans'. The time it will take to provide an adequate health

service under the programme launched in 2009 means that people will
continue to save in case they fall ill and have to seek private treatment –
individual expenditure on healthcare has risen more than twice as
much as state expenditure. State education is poor so parents save to
pay for private schooling. Secondary schools in Beijing charge entrance
fees of up to 87,000 yuan and a survey in 2011 reported parents in the
capital spending from 30,000 to 80,000 yuan a year on additional tutor-
ing. The pension system is a black hole. For all these reasons, the need
for precautionary saving will persist and restrain consumption.[1]

On the other side of the ledger, the government has had a long,
hard slog in reining in the credit boom it initiated in 2009, which
fuelled a sharp rise in local government debt as provinces, counties
and townships ratcheted up their spending on projects that enhanced
their localities and lined pockets even though they would never show a
decent return on the capital employed. The result of that was bound to
be an increase in debts held by state banks, which would never be
reimbursed.

In the summer of 2010 the State Council ordered a review of thousands of financial platforms set up by local authorities to raise funding
and escape control. Banks were instructed to restrict lending to them.
The authorities raised interest rates repeatedly and increased the
reserves the banks were required to hold. They set up audits of projects
and tightened provincial lending. But a state audit a year later showed
that 10,000 platforms still owed 10.7 billion yuan, equal to 27 per cent
of the whole economy, and considerably higher than the level of central
government debt. That was almost certainly an underestimate given
the creation of other avenues to provide back-door finance and the
way banks moved lending to unregulated trust companies off their balance sheets to disguise its true volume. The ratings agency Moody
identified an additional 3.5 trillion yuan in local debt. At the end of
2012, the bank regulator put bad loans at 478 billion yuan though this
was only 1 per cent of outstanding credit.

The headlong rush into developing transport infrastructure has suffered major casualties. Passenger numbers of high-speed trains fell by a
sixth after the crash outside Wenzhou. Work on 6,000 miles of track was
suspended. That affected labour and hit the finances of the deeply

indebted Railway Ministry. Low usage of highways by drivers means that eleven provinces or municipalities have racked up debts totalling 759 billion yuan from building toll roads – Beijing is the only one to have turned a profit. In Yunnan, the Highway Development Authority said it was defaulting after borrowing 100 billion yuan from a dozen banks to fund the construction of more than 100,000 miles of road. The southwest has relatively few cars and revenue was below expectations while borrowings dwarfed the organization's capital and broke the requirements for debt ratio of highway companies. The provincial government stepped in to avert the collapse.[2]

As state banks limited lending in 2012, local authorities turned to private trusts and the proceeds of corporate bond issues for finance from the 'shadow banking' sector, which is poorly regulated and whose legal status is cloudy. In one case, a big provincial enterprise sold 9.5 billion yuan worth of bonds and then put about half the proceeds into a trust company that invested in local-government projects, with an agreement with a local bank to buy the asset in due course. Beijing reacted to the problem by launching a trial scheme to allow four local authorities in the south and east of the country to sell bonds to raise cash that could be used to repay their bank loans.

Small and medium-sized enterprises (SMEs) found it harder to raise money and, when they did so, were faced with interest rates well into double digits (compared to the official 6 per cent) – the overnight 'gambling rate' went as high as 40–50 per cent. Some state companies had done nicely by borrowing from the big banks at 6 per cent and lending on at double that rate or more – they were told by the government to stop doing so, which clamped down on an illicit form of moneymaking but further reduced the amount of money available in the informal lending sector. The same result followed when the authorities told the banks to bring wealth-management products on to their balance sheets so that they could be accounted for rather than representing an uncontrolled source of lending. In Wenzhou, centre of the informal credit industry, scores of companies went bust in the autumn of 2011 under the effect of a combination of more expensive loans, higher wages and declining exports. A dozen bosses fled with what funds they could take with them and two plunged to their deaths from the tops of buildings – a third also jumped but survived. Wen Jiabao paid a flying visit to the city and the government adopted its usual remedy, throwing money at the problem in the form of a rescue fund.

The scale of debts led to talk of the banks being hit with an avalanche of non-performing loans (NPLs), which a Hong Kong research service, Asianomics, estimated could total 2 trillion yuan. Share prices of banks slumped, dragging down mainland stock markets of which they are the main constituent. Some analysts worry about the solvency of banks and ask whether, if some got into trouble, people would stop depositing their cash with them, particularly when they earn significantly less than the inflation rate. Still, the reality is that if things got dangerous the government would simply set up a financial vehicle to take over the bad loans as it did in 1999. This would not help with the broader policy of bringing the economy under better control but it is the way China works under a regime whose first priority is to use authoritarian capitalism to ensure CCP rule.[3]

Therein lies a central flaw in the China model. Keeping up economic expansion is not a matter of a political party seeking re-election: it is central to regime preservation, replacing the ideology of the Mao era as the CCP's prime claim to rule. But the nature of China, with its interconnecting interest groups and sheer exuberance, means that steering it is a very tricky process as the economy veers between extremes. The downside danger was shown when tough tightening to fight inflation in late 2007 and early 2008 led to factory closures, strained property developers and threatened a big jump in unemployment – all before the impact of the decline in external demand in the West sharply accentuated China's problems. Wen Jiabao spoke of a target of 7 per cent annual growth for the new Five-Year Plan instead of the 12 per cent hit in the middle of 2010, but many provinces have more ambitious plans. Wen's advice that 'we must not allow big fluctuations in economic growth' shows a desire to iron out the recent volatility but will be hard to achieve.

Beijing's task is complicated by the weakness of its administrative control over local governments in keeping with the old saying about the provinces respecting the emperor so long as he stays on the other side of the mountain. The central government employs 1 million civil servants and the provinces, counties, townships and villages 45–50 million, many of whom are more interested in pursuing local interests than in implementing the dictates from afar. To that must be added the ambitions of provincial bosses weaned on expansion and rated according to the growth they deliver. There is an underlying belief that the state will always pick up the tab in the end while the regular rotation of cadres means that they are likely to be in another job when the bills for their projects have to be paid. So, while the Prime Minister talked of a 7 per cent target for the twelfth Five-Year Plan, the municipalities of Beijing and Shanghai as well as Guangdong went for 8 per cent, Chongqing for 12.5 per cent and eleven inland provinces for a doubling of their GDP in five years – that is 14.5 per cent compound. Even top-down arithmetic cannot make 8 plus 12.5 plus 14.5 equal 7.

Beneath such immediate and recurrent issues lies a network of structural problems that leave the Deng revolution only half-achieved. Movement of labour and the urbanization the government seeks run into the restrictions of the *hukou* system. Capital markets and the currency remain under official control, though the growth of shadow banking means market interest rates are playing a greater role. The example of agriculture, which still supports the biggest proportion of the national workforce, shows how economic, political and social factors interconnected to create complications and contradictions that upset the image of China as a smoothly purring nation moving forward in a logical and irresistible fashion.

The proportion of people employed on the land has dropped from 71 per cent to 43 per cent in three decades, but this is still excessively large for a sector that contributes only 10 per cent to GDP. The fact that all farmland belongs to and is leased out by the state, usually in small plots, ensures that rural households have enough for subsistence and is thus regarded as an essential ingredient in maintaining social stability. But, although there have been some moves to consolidate individual plots into larger and more efficient farms with the opening of exchanges to trade leases in a few places, most holdings remain too small to support mechanization. Many use cheap fertilizers, which leach out the soil, or animal dung. The flow of workers to cities and lack of training of farmers in modern methods means a lack of skilled farm workforce. So agriculture has not evolved in line with industry.

Local governments have been short of money since the farming tax was abolished to help the rural economy in 2005. As a result, they often depend on transfers from the central tax take – a few places, including Beijing, Shanghai and Tibet, do well, but many other highly populated provinces and counties do not get enough. To take just one example, the local authorities in Jianli County in Hubei province, which contains 1.4 million people, draw 313 million yuan in annual revenue locally but need three times as much for spending on health, education, pensions, environmental protection and other obligations.

So the local governments raise money by taking land back from farmers, reclassifying it for commercial, residential or industrial use, and auctioning it off. Fifty million farmers have lost their homes and plots in the last three decades and 60 million are likely to be uprooted in the next twenty years, according to an estimate by the Chinese Academy of Social Sciences (CASS). When a CCP plenum considered privatizing farmland as a means of creating larger units, it backed off in the face of pressure from local authorities – and from big cities, which did not want to see country dwellers selling off their plots and migrating to add pressure on urban services (plus some ideological opposition from remnant Maoist–Marxists). The best Hu Jintao could do was to assure farmers that land contracts would 'not change for a long time'.[4]

In 2010, between 30 and 40 per cent of revenue raised by local authorities locally (as against the remittances from the centre) came from sales of leases; in Anhui and Sichuan the proportion was 70 per cent. How the process works was shown in Xianghe County in Hebei province, seventy minutes' drive from central Beijing, which is due to be linked to the capital by an urban railway line, making it an attractive development site for upmarket commuter housing. Local officials used a mixture of intimidation and actual force to make people hand over the plots on which they held leases. Men with hoes and forklift trucks were sent in to destroy crops. Relatives working in hospitals, schools and government agencies were warned that their jobs could be at risk if they did not persuade the farmers to play ball. Thugs employed by the local authorities threatened to beat up leaseholders if they did not sign away their rights; six villagers were taken to hospital with injuries.

In the end, 267 hectares were handed over without compensation. They were reclassified and 120 receptions were staged for potential investors. New leases were bought by several developers, including the big property firm Vanke and the land division of the state group China Minimetals, which paid 650 million yuan for rights to build a villa community called Lake Side. But the local cadres had gone too far, and there were suggestions that they had pocketed part of the money. The Beijing Land Bureau investigated. Xinhua ran a story. The main officials involved were sacked. The Lake Side development, where more than 300 units had been sold, was sealed off. Such outcomes are relatively rare. More often, as *Caixin* magazine put it: 'Local government officials get rich quick by ignoring property laws and grabbing land rights from hapless farmers. The shenanigans go unpunished and perhaps unnoticed beyond the borders of the village, district or county they're supposed to serve.'[5]

China has some large farms, particularly in the north-east, and there are efforts to build up large herds of livestock. The government encourages big pig breeders: those who slaughter 30,000 or more animals a year have an agreed price floor and a guaranteed market with the authorities in big cities. Still, 90 per cent of pigs are in small farms or backyards. The result of such factors is to add strain to the food-supply chain in a nation with 21 per cent of the world's population but only 7 per cent of its arable land and renewable water resources. But, for reasons of national security, the PRC cleaves to a policy of 95 per cent self-sufficiency in grain (with the exception of soya). Yet people are eating a more varied diet and in particular more meat, which requires more animal feed – which the country does not have. It has started to buy increasing volumes of corn (maize) and became a net importer of rice in 2011, quadrupling purchases in the first ten months of 2012. The economics of self-sufficiency do not make much sense for a country with a relative shortage of arable land and an abundance of labour, but national security considerations come first even if they are bound to be eroded.

As well as the plethora of small plots, agriculture is affected by urbanization – Hangzhou has lost a quarter of its land for growing vegetables and fruit in five years because of building. Then there are the effects of desertification and pollution caused by industrialization – the Environment Ministry says that 10 per cent of farmland is polluted mainly by heavy metal deposits. In all, the PRC has lost 12.4 million hectares of land since 1980. Farming is also hit by droughts and floods and the shortage of water in the northern wheat-growing plain. Irrigation is often poorly managed and wasteful, in a country that pioneered the Dujiangyan model system in Sichuan two millennia ago. Farm productivity is generally quite low; corn output per acre is only a little over half the US figure. Logistics for moving food around are weak, and there is a lack of refrigerated transport.

The net result is that the PRC faces food pressure if its run of nine good harvests this century ends, or if a switch by farmers from one activity to another results in price-boosting shortages, as has happened repeatedly with pork. The regime can alleviate pressure in the short run by releasing stocks from its food reserves, but it has to replenish these sooner or later. The basic fact is that successive governments have not modernized agriculture in line with industrial progress. Whatever caps it doffs to the countryside where Mao raised support, the Communist Party is driven by urbanites. The politics of power dictate that, to avoid antagonizing the middle class, the authorities have to maintain the flow of meat and other products which have become urban staples to boost consumption. Materialism exacts its price and rising blue-collar wages add to the pressure of demand. Relaxation of the self-sufficiency ceilings appears inevitable but the failure to develop a cheap, reliable food chain means higher inflation: this reached 6.4 per cent in June 2011, the highest for more than three years, and, after falling below 2 per cent in 2012, is set to rise again. With that goes the danger of urban unrest as well as growing dependence on foreign suppliers, which the regime would prefer to avoid in a world of volatile soft commodity prices.

Land ownership is just one aspect of the economic power of the state. China can appear to some observers as a country on market steroids and we have seen the key role played by private enterprise in the expansion of the 1980s. But it is far from a level playing field. The state sector was favoured and private enterprise penalized in the 1990s. Today the reality is that the economy is dominated by the Party and state and their acolytes in industry and finance, for whose benefit much of the system is run. A US Embassy cable in 2009 relayed the view from a contact that 'China's top leadership had carved up China's economic "pie", creating an ossified system in which "vested interests" drove decision-making and impeded reform as leaders manoeuvred to ensure that those interests were not threatened.'[6]

State-owned enterprises use market mechanisms to increase efficiency, but they are still under the orders of the government and Party. Alongside the state-owned Assets Supervision and Administration Commission of the State Council (SASAC), which supervises the 123 biggest SOEs, the state owns the four big banks, the oil companies and other major concerns that often enjoy monopolistic or oligopolistic positions. When SOEs float shares to domestic and foreign investors, the state retains a majority holding. If state companies face difficulties, the government comes to their aid – as it did when it boosted its stake in the big banks at the end of 2011. Private firms often depend on having good relations with official bodies and the SOES with which they work.

So what, it might be asked. China has enjoyed high growth rates and if that has been achieved in a state-dominated context, let that be. SOEs appear to be a bounding success story. According to their supervisory body, combined profits jumped by an average of 22 per cent a year between 2003 and 2009. But, once more, look behind the curtain. Half those profits came from the three oil and gas groups and the China Mobile communications company. The picture elsewhere is less encouraging. The Commercial Bank of China, Bank of China, China Construction Bank, and Agricultural Bank of China have done well recently but they are propped up by large spreads between the interest they charge and the rates they offer to depositors, both set by the central bank and government. Apart from their privileged market positions, SOEs rely on preferential treatment by these state banks; a study by the Hong Kong Institute for Monetary Research found that, while they contribute 25 per cent of GDP, they get 65 per cent of loans. The study, blocked on mainland websites, concluded that, if the SOEs paid a proper market interest rate rather than being given subsidized treatment, their profits would be wiped out. Bloomberg calculated in

2012 that a quarter of SOEs were unprofitable with productivity growth well below the private sector.[7]

As it is, the state's financial repression aimed at helping the banks and providing a flow of cheap investment capital acts as a tax on households, depriving them of the return they should get on their savings. Nor does private enterprise get a decent share of the cake. Most credit is decided administratively by orders to the major state banks, and entrepreneurs who want to raise money more freely have to go to the informal market where rates are much higher – the Zhejiang Bureau for Small and Medium-Sized Enterprises said in the summer of 2011 that companies were paying 25–30 per cent for one-year loans as against the 6.31 per cent laid down by the central bank, while some private businesses reported monthly rates of 5–8 per cent.

Such uncertainties feed into a more general caution about the future, which may seem at odds with the record of growth but which is in fact rooted in the country's bumpy modern history and a feeling that, while the last three decades have been good times, they may not last forever. Studies have found a growing sentiment of insecurity among the rich, who fear being nailed on corruption charges if their political connections fail them. Building a bolt-hole overseas is an increasing preoccupation of the wealthy. A report in 2011 by China Merchants Bank and the consultants Bain & Company reported that 27 per cent of 500,000 people with assets of 10 million yuan (apart from their main residence) had established a home overseas – a rise of 73 per cent in five years – and that 47 per cent were considering doing so. The main reasons given were that their wealth would be safer, that retirement would be preferable outside the PRC and that their children would be better educated abroad – half of China's yuan billionaires aged under forty went to school or college in the United States or Europe, Canada or Australia. The younger generation in China has never known a serious protracted downturn and may be more trusting in the future, but a forum in Beijing at the end of 2010 was told by experts that 30 per cent them were suffering from depression and fighting 'behavioural problems'.[8]

Inflation and negative interest rates have led to a wave of money going into stores of value given the shortage of financial instruments in which to invest. Works by China's three bestselling contemporary artists have fetched a combined $87 million. Demand for antiques and artworks has exploded to the extent of vast overbidding for minor objects – a twentieth-century pastiche of an imperial case valued at $6–8,000 fetched $1.31 million from a Chinese buyer at a sale in 2011 where a nineteenth-century jade ornament went for forty times its estimate. 'Very big, China,' as Steven P. Murphy, head of Christie's auction house, remarked in echo of Noël Coward.[9]

Buying of gold rose by 32 per cent in 2010 when residents of the city of Wuxi were reported to have bought 7.3 tons of gold bars and jewels. The following year, the central bank doubled its output of the popular gold panda coins to 6.4 million ounces. At an auction in 2010 in Hong Kong of Château Lafite, the preferred claret of China's mega-rich, the 284 lots brought $8.4 million, three times more than expected. When Chinese taste moved to Burgundy in 2011–12, prices boomed, too, while Chinese investors have bought two dozen châteaux in the Bordeaux region. Though the favoured high-price spirit is *mao tai*, a Chinese businessman paid a world-record £125,000 for a bottle of sixty-two-year-old Scotch whisky. Other stores of value have enjoyed booms, from jade and furniture to clay teapots. The index of rare postage stamps at the dealer Stanley Gibbons has been rising by an average of 44 per cent a year; a block of four stamps from the Cultural Revolution (when stamp collecting was banned as a bourgeois pastime) fetched the equivalent of £900,000 at an auction in Hong Kong. There has been a bubble in the price of fine *pu'er* tea, which trebled in a couple of years. Money also flowed into Chinese traditional medicine, doubling the index of 200 herbs in two years and pushing the value of the industry up to 350 billion yuan.

On the other hand, after a bull run in 2006–07, the Shanghai and Shenzhen stock exchanges have been lacklustre performers while other world markets raced ahead on their recovery after the 2008 crisis. In the first half of 2011, the volume of company listings in Shanghai, Shenzhen and Hong Kong dropped to one-third of the peak in 2010. The Shanghai A-share index was one of the worst global performers in 2012, with a steady downward trend; though this improved in 2013, it still remained far below peak levels. Unless they are privy to insider information or have an urge to gamble, many retail investors fight shy of the casino aspects of the exchanges. The equitation rate relating market capitalization to GDP fell to 62 per cent in 2011 from 140 per cent four years earlier while rising to more than 100 per cent in Australia, Canada, Malaysia and Chile. Public faith in the stock market was further shaken by the highly publicized case of a Guangdong investment outfit that was found to have run 'pump and dump' manipulation schemes for 562 different stocks promoted through television programmes and 'black mouth' analysts paid to boost its offerings.

The biggest magnet for disposable wealth has been property, particularly the flats and houses bought by the middle and wealthy classes since private ownership was allowed in 1998 but only with leases running for up to 70 years. In 2010, property construction accounted for more than a quarter of investment and amounted to 13 per cent of GDP, soaking up 40 per cent of the country's steel output, and making it one of the most important single sectors in the global economy. The price of residential real estate has quadrupled in Beijing and Shanghai this century to reach up to 30 times average earnings compared to a peak of five to six times in the US and UK. Developers have put up swathes of apartments that stayed empty and 'ghost cities' where new buildings stood unoccupied. In time, services build up around them and people move in, but this kind of excess capacity has become a feature of China's expansion, with side benefits in demand for building materials of all kinds. It is certainly not the most efficient way to proceed but the pace of growth has to date been able to sustain it. If that pace falls for a protracted period, the damage to this economic engine is evident.

Eighty per cent of China's urban homes are privately owned, more than in Britain, the United States, Japan and Germany. The Chinese do not go in for renting and an apartment that has been leased out loses value; this adds to the stock of empty accommodation – the dark windows that bearish analysts like to count in Pudong or Ordos as a harbinger of a property crash.

Sharp increases in the prices of houses and flats on the back of strong demand and easy credit created fears of a bubble around 2010 as the going rate for smart flats doubled in a year or two and prices ran at an average of ten times annual incomes. Polls showed property as a prime public worry. Debt to equity ratios among developers are more than 70 per cent and short-term liabilities have increased sixfold since 2006. Prices in Beijing were reckoned to have risen by 80 per cent more than average salaries. An ironic online debate about how long a poor peasant would had to have saved for in order to afford a flat in Beijing concluded that he would have had to start putting aside money under the Tang dynasty, whose rule ended in the year 907. A hit television soap opera showed the pressures on two sisters who could not afford to buy a home; in desperation, one became the mistress of a corrupt, married official to get money from him for a flat.

In reaction the government introduced cooling measures. But bears such as the hedge-fund manager Jim Chanos see a crash as inevitable. As prices and transactions fell in 2011 in Beijing, Shanghai, Tianjin, Guangzhou and Shenzhen there were comparisons with Japan, which went through a huge property boom that burst at the end of the 1980s, or with the sub-prime crisis in the US. The price of bonds issued by property firms fell by 20 per cent in two months in the autumn of 2011, and the developer Vanke said that a 'turning point' had been reached (though, as a state-controlled company, it could count on a degree of protection). While the market will undoubtedly experience recurrent dips, the extreme warnings appear to have been overplayed. Prices were more stable in smaller cities than in the big five and began to recover in the second half of 2012 as land sales picked up. Standard & Poor's estimates that most developers could withstand a 10 per cent drop in sales and that 'severe liquidity strains' would not set in till the decline reached 30 per cent.[10]

China's property market is marked by particular social and political aspects that make a full-scale crash unlikely even if deflating the bubble is one of the main challenges facing the government and some real estate firms seem bound to go bust. High savings mean people can put down a large amount of the required deposit in cash, so leverage is low by Western standards. Families club together to buy flats and homes. The PRC has a long way to go before it matches 1980s Japan, and the relatively low level of borrowing makes it very different from the US; the official regulator sounded a reassuring note in the summer of 2011 by announcing that stress tests had shown that the banks could absorb a 50 per cent drop in prices. The way in which the middle class has flocked into property means that the leadership will do everything it can to avoid a collapse that would forfeit their forbearance for the regime.

Everybody wants to get on the bandwagon. To get round official measures to control the market, couples have been known to divorce so that they can each buy property separately. Even more than elsewhere, owning a home is a sign of success. Though young people are urged not to become 'property slaves', many of them want nothing else. For those in their twenties or thirties starting out on a career, it seems the surest way of increasing wealth; they believe that regular substantial pay-rises means that mortgage payments will take a steadily diminishing share of their incomes and have never known a serious property crash. With a shortage of eligible young women, another factor also comes into play: 'So you want to marry our daughter?' say the parents of the prospective bride. 'You do have an apartment for her, don't you?' A survey published at the end of 2010 reported that 70 per cent of the women questioned would not consider marrying a man who did not own a home. 'In the 1950s [women] married heroes,' one blogger posted in response to the survey. 'In the 60s they married peasants. In the 70s they married intellectuals, and in the 80s they married businessmen. Now they are marrying houses.'

The property boom and the doubling of residential construction between 2004 and 2010 have been valuable to the leadership for the demand generated for industries such as steel, cement and glass that would otherwise be bogged down by excess capacity. Manufacturers of furniture, fabrics, household appliances and electronic goods also benefit. Local authorities rely on income from auctioning rights to reclassified agricultural land or urban areas from which the original residents have been evicted; most of them do not seem keen on the government's plan to build 34 million cheap housing units by 2015 to help poorer people, and there is considerable doubt about how the programme will fare. Developers constitute a powerful lobby in the country's politico-economic matrix. A property tax introduced on a trial basis in Shanghai and Chongqing has been pitched very low and hits only new upmarket buildings.

A property-owning dictatorship has been born and operates to its own inner logic.

In the tradition set by the First Emperor with his massive constructions, today's bureaucratic leaders retain a taste for grand projects as evidence of the material strength their regime has brought the nation and their ability to do things from which others shrink. The effect on employment, and on rural incomes through remittances sent back by migrant workers on projects, was clear in 2008–10, though one study has found that investment of 1 trillion yuan in the railways produced 6 million jobs, which is far more expensive than paying unemployment benefits.[11]

Many projects can be justified on general developmental grounds even if the financial returns are not great. Modern transport links draw China closer together. The high-speed train network, including a 1,900-kilometre track between Shanghai and Kunming, capital of traditionally isolated Yunnan, can be seen as the equivalent of the interstate highway system that revolutionized the US economy half a century ago. The world's highest-altitude railway, crossing a pass 5,000 metres above sea level, forms part of the track to the Tibetan capital of Lhasa. Though many highways are underused, China's road network needed to be vastly improved as its economy grew. In 1989 the PRC had less than 160 kilometres of motorways; now they stretch for 64,000 kilometres, the second-longest network in the world after the United States. When I first visited Beijing in 1995, the main route from the airport into the city was along a two-lane road subject to frequent jams as cars, overloaded coal trucks and carts jostled for space; now there is a multi-lane highway with a fast train running alongside.

Urban railways are being built or expanded in more than two dozen cities to overcome the paralysing gridlock that is not confined to rush hours; city governments call in the developers to bid for the land once they have decided on the routes and thus raise the cash to pay for the projects. High-speed trains represented a steep jump in passenger services, if at a price, and meant that freight and coal could move more swiftly with fewer bottlenecks on the old lines. Airlines not only cut travel times but also overcome the old barriers of mountains and rivers. Inner Mongolia is set to get eighteen airports by 2020. Developing infrastructure, ports and logistics along the Yangtze River should make China's longest waterway a key element in opening up inland China and facilitating freight transport from Chongqing all the way down to the ocean port off Shanghai capable of handling 15 million containers a year. Building power stations in the coal regions and linking them to the rest of the country by an efficient grid system makes eminent sense given the recurrent energy shortages that hit households and factories in coastal regions while the nuclear-power programme – the biggest in the world, with thirteen plants operational, twenty-seven under construction and fifty-two waiting for work to start – is a natural way to reduce use of coal.

But the results have not always been as intended by the planners, most dramatically with the scaling down of the development of the high-speed train network after the crash in 2011. There have been technical disputes and delays in modernizing the grid. The nuclear programme was suspended after the disaster in Japan. The $62 billion south–north water project to divert 6 trillion gallons a year from the Yangtze has run into repeated delays and raises concern about its effect on regions from which supply will be taken. People living along the route are unhappy at their forced relocation – one reservoir being constructed in Hubei province will entail the movement of 350,000 local residents, many of them to poor farmland far away. Water arriving in Tianjin in an early stage of the development was so filthy that more than 400 treatment plants have had to be installed.

Another huge water undertaking epitomizes China's taste for the mega and the pitfalls that this creates. The Three Gorges Dam on the Yangtze in Hubei province is the world's largest hydroelectric project. It is, by any measures, a highly impressive construction, with a length of 2,335 metres and a depth of 180 metres to the rock base. It can hold up to 39 billion cubic metres of water. Half a million tons of steel were used in its construction and 1 million cubic metres of earth were removed.

The idea of damming China's longest river both for flood control and to generate power was put forward in1919 by Sun Yat-sen, who had been the first Republican President, and preliminary work was conducted in the 1930s. A joint American-Chinese plan was drawn up after the Second World War, but had to be abandoned. Mao built dams else-where but they were hit by disaster caused by poor construction and silting. So it was not until the late twentieth century that China had the means and determination to achieve it with the enthusiastic backing of engineers who had made it to the top headed by Prime Minister Li Peng, a hydroelectric graduate from the Moscow Power Engineering University who may have felt the need for a vote of confidence after his leading role in the 1989 crackdown.

As economic growth and urbanization led to ever-rising demand for power, the dam was seen as a vital contribution, its size making it into a symbol of what China could do. Work started in 1994 and the dam began operating in 2008 with installed capacity of 18,200 megawatts, which will rise to 22,500 megawatts when further work is completed. Apart from its role in electricity generation and water regulation, it was welcomed as part of the development of western China and as a contri-bution to clean energy as China came under pressure for its emission of CO_2 gas. It also gave a major boost to China's engineering industry when hydropower was seen as the way of the future. Collateral benefits included the prospect of providing fresh water for downstream cities and facilitating river traffic to and from Chongqing. But the debit side was also long.

An early critic, Huang Wanli, who had fallen foul of Mao for rightly forecasting that a big dam on the Yellow River would silt up, warned that the same thing would happen with the Three Gorges – which, he pre-dicted, would have to be blown up. The project involved the flooding of 1,500 villages and towns and the relocation of 1.3 million people. On visiting the site Zhu Rongji thundered against substandard 'tofu' con-struction work by officials who were lining their pockets. Bridges to nowhere were built as funds flowed from Beijing. There was significant ecological damage, too, as the water backed up in a 650-kilometre-long reservoir. When the usually docile National People's Congress voted on the project in 1992, the support of 1,767 legislators was balanced by 866 who either voted against (177) or abstained (689) – for China that was quite a show of opposition, especially in the post-Tiananmen period.

Though nothing was said officially, questions rose about the dam as it went into operation. Neither Hu Jintao (himself a hydraulic engineer by training) nor Wen Jiabao attended the ceremonies to mark the formal completion of the project. Five years later, Wen admitted publicly that the dam presented 'urgent problems'. The State Council, while insisting that the project had been 'hugely beneficial overall', said that 'prompt solutions' were required over the relocation of people, environmental concerns and the 'prevention of geological disasters' as well as the impact on water supply, irrigation and navigation. When he visited the region Vice-Premier Li Keqiang promised resettled residents that 'the Party and the State will never forget the contributions you made. We're bound to help you resettle well, find jobs, and get rich step by step.'

But that seems a long way off. The dam stands in poor territory and has done no good for the local economy. Eleven localities along the reservoir were declared 'particularly poor' in 2002. Per capita GDP is 40 per cent of the national average. Above the reservoir is Zigui County, officially ranked as a 'state-level poor' and celebrated as the home of a historic figure who drowned himself in protest against corruption more than 2,500 years ago. Incomes run at the equivalent of $1.25 a day. The government offers farmers subsidies but they are small. Young people have left to work in cities. Land disputes are frequent. Resettlement 'has been marked by farmers' exchange of land for the dam', a local justice official told journalists. 'Everything had been taken away from them.'

The submersion of factories, waste dumps and mines has seriously polluted the water in the reservoir. Aquatic biodiversity is affected together with river fisheries. Forests have been chopped down or flooded. The stagnant water breeds parasites. Erosion, aggravated by farming by resettled residents on the steep gradients of the surrounding hills, provokes landslides – two such, in 2009, sent between 20,000 and 50,000 cubic metres of earth cascading into a tributary of the Yangtze, while the first four months of 2010 saw ninety-seven substantial slides. These lead to a build-up of sediment in the approaches to the dam; on the other hand, farmland downstream is being starved of nutritive silt and even the sedimentary bed under Shanghai may be affected in time. The reduced flow of water downstream has contributed to falling levels in major lakes. In the summer of 2011, central China suffered its worst drought for half a century, and then the dam was not enough to prevent subsequent flooding in the region. The geological effect remains a matter of controversy, with some critics linking it to the devastating earthquake in Sichuan in 2008; most alarming, the dam sits on a seismic fault in a region prone to earthquakes; one can imagine what a tremor combined with the weight of water pressing on the dam wall might produce.

As so often, the debate about the dam has a significant political aspect. It was the baby of the Li Peng generation of leaders. Photographs of Li hung in the steamer I took up the river as the dam was being built; in these he shed his usual dour expression to beam at managers working on his pet project. The State Council statement in 2011 contained a coded reference to the past: some of the problems that now had to be addressed had been identified during construction, it said, but had been 'difficult to resolve effectively because of limitations imposed by conditions at the time'. The *Oriental Morning Post* newspaper printed a big front-page photograph of Huang Wanli and the English-language *Shanghai Daily* referred to 'that monstrous damming project'. *China Daily* ran a frank and detailed report of the plight of resettled residents. Destroying the dam as Huang had predicted was out of the question but, with Li in his eighties and no longer a political force, at least a corner of the curtain could be lifted with the recognition that even the most Pharaonic of projects came with a cost.[12]

China has repeatedly defied forecasts that it is about to suffer a hard landing, that its high growth rate simply cannot go on. The government itself wants to slow expansion down to 7 per cent a year, a level that will sustain job creation while offering smooth, sustained progress. Some are more pessimistic – in mid-2011, as bearish sentiment towards the PRC grew in world markets, a poll of investors by Bloomberg reported that 59 per cent of those who responded saw growth dropping to 5 per cent by 2016 with 12 per cent predicting that for as soon as 2012. That looks over-bearish but there can be little doubt that growth will slow down. By mid-2012 the quarterly rate of expansion had fallen to 7.6 per cent, provoking pessimistic forecasts of an impending crash. But by the end of the year, growth was recovering and seemed set to top 8 per cent in 2013, though likely to decline again thereafter.

While lower and more sustainable growth is in line with government policy to iron out the roller-coaster pattern of previous years, the question is whether Beijing can manage a steady on-going normalization without a dangerous loss of momentum and confidence and can navigate its way through the rebalancing process. The real and ever-present danger of the fall in growth getting out of control before a new model is in place is exacerbated by the crisis on the other side of the world as exports to Europe slow and austerity policies cut into demand in the PRC's biggest trading partner. In the end, it all boils down to whether the leadership feels sufficiently determined and confident to take China away from the cheap labour, cheap capital model that powered its ascent and move off the growth high to which it has become accustomed, enduring short-term pain brought by reforms for longer-term gain in the interests of evolving a new version of the politico-economic equation forged by Deng Xiaoping three decades earlier. It will be a tricky ride with success by no means guaranteed as political factors stand in the way of needed reform and the authorities find themselves without the time needed to put things right after half-a-dozen years in which they have opted for short-term measures. [13]

As a result of the lack of structural change this century, China suffers from a string of imbalances and inefficiencies masked by the growth figures. We have seen how exposed agriculture would be if there are bad harvests. The *hukou* registration system cramps the labour market and produces social tension. The legal and accountability are weak and the trust deficit grows. Financial markets are under state control, fostering inefficiencies. State-owned enterprises are too powerful and limit competition. Low pricing means that water and energy are wasted on a major scale. Power companies have no incentive to raise production to meet increasing demand when their rates are capped but coal prices are allowed to increase; the Chairwoman of one big utility warns that one-fifth of the country's 436 coal-fired stations could go bust if they are not permitted to charge more.

As we have seen, the rapid expansion of infrastructure has involved misallocation of capital to schemes that will never earn a decent return and raised questions about the solidity of local-government finance. In 2012, new funding for infrastructure projects came mainly from money raised by corporate bond issues, financial trusts and other sources which draw on private capital. This has the beneficial effect of freeing up interest rates and giving investors a chance of a better return than they could get from the banks but it exposes them to the risk of defaults and the scale of this new and sometimes murky source of financing could set off a bubble that the government will have to bring under control before it gets out of hand. The big state banks do not act so much as regular profit-and-loss institutions as politically driven lending shops. The internationalization of the currency falls well short of the media and market hype because it is constrained by controls which the domestic authorities maintain, and which encourage speculative manoeuvres that create the idea of more activity than is really the case. Inflation is driven by a mis-match between food demand and supply which stems largely from a failure to manage agriculture more effectively. Corruption has a distorting effect both economically and morally, its importance shown by the focus which the new leadership put on launching a campaign against it at the end of 2012 when a poll in *People's Daily* showed that 91 per cent of respondents thought the new rich had benefitted from political connections. State enterprises are protected by low interest rates and monopolistic market positions, and their managers are drawn from a narrow segment of the population, the 6 per cent of Chinese who belong to the Party and may rely more on powerful connections than in competence. Meanwhile, private companies are held back although they are much bigger innovators and employment creators than the state sector. If such fault lines can be remedied and China becomes more efficient, the world will really have cause for concern but it is not clear that the political will and the necessary tools are present to achieve significant reform.

This array of problems is more than a matter of business as usual in a fast-growing economy. Fundamental issues are in play at home and abroad. These involve politics as well as the economy, and the readiness of the new leadership that took over at the end of 2012 to embrace change with all the accompanying risks in an increasingly bumpy future. Vital matters such as the environment have not been properly addressed. Nor have the overarching issues of Communist Party power and the relationship between the state and society – and the state and the market. Globally, the PRC has still not defined its world role; it remains hobbled by its control mindset and its domestic concerns in everything from the management of its currency to its dealings with foreign powers. Given its deep international involvement, how these factors play out will affect the world as a whole. So it is time to conclude by looking at the future leaders of the country and what they are likely to do – or not to do – in the coming decade.

18

THE UNFINISHED REVOLUTION

At eleven-thirty a.m. on November 14, 2012, after an unexplained delay of half an hour, China's new leader led his six colleagues in the Standing Committee of the Politburo out into one of the cavernous meeting rooms of the Great Hall of the People by Tiananmen Square at the end of the Communist Party's eighteenth Congress. Xi Jinping, who had just been named as Party General Secretary by the Central Committee, seemed utterly at ease with himself as he spoke to the domestic and foreign media.

Standing in front of a vast traditional Chinese landscape painting, he extolled the role of the Communist Party in engineering the nation's revival but then acknowledged that it suffered from corruption and 'bureaucratization'. That set up a barrier with the people who wanted to see better education, more stable jobs, more income, greater social security, better medical and health care, improved housing conditions, and a better environment. 'We have every reason to be proud – proud, but not complacent,' he added, a slight Beijing accent evident in his voice. 'To forge iron, one must be strong.' Then, with a wave and a smile at the media, he walked off at the head of the new seven-man Standing Committee of the Politburo to start his ten years at the helm of the People's Republic.

The man designated to lead China from 2012 to 2022 was the stoutly built, chubby-faced leader of the leadership princelings, children of first generation Communist chiefs. Like many of his group, Xi Jinping went through the vicissitudes of the late Mao era but survived and showed a great aptitude for playing the political system. Born in Beijing in June 1953, he grew up in the privileged surroundings of the leadership in the supposedly classless state. But as a teenager he found himself sent down to the countryside when his father, Xi Zhongxun, a guerrilla leader from the 1930s who became a Vice-Premier, fell into disfavour with the Great Helmsman and was purged in the Cultural Revolution. The son was sent to work on a farm in Shaanxi where he rose to become secretary of the production team. He lived for three years in a home in a cave, looking after pigs. One can only speculate on the psychological effect on men like Xi and Bo Xilai of the Cultural Revolution and how they remained loyal to the Party which had brought such devastation to the country and to their families' lives. Xi recalls it as an 'emotional' time in the 'illusion' of the Cultural Revolution. 'I ate a lot more bitterness than most people,' he has said, adding that much of his pragmatism 'took root back then and still exerts a constant influence on me'. It can only have strengthened his taste for order and unity and reluctance to take risks.

As the son of a renegade, he was refused Party membership ten times before it was granted in 1974. He returned to Beijing and worked as secretary to one of his father's associates, Vice-Premier Geng Biao, who was also Secretary-General of the Military Commission, giving the young man early contact with the PLA – he was said to have worn an army uniform every day at this time. According to a friend, he showed a temporary interest in Buddhism but then shed this and decided to become 'redder than red' with intense study of Marxism–Maoism. At university in Beijing, where he appears to have had an easy passage, he studied chemical engineering, Marxist theory and education. He was friendly but women found him boring, the acquaintance noted.[1]

Rehabilitated by Deng, his father was appointed to oversee economic reform in Guangdong in the early 1980s. The elder Xi told the paramount leader: 'We need to reform China and implement this economic zone even if it means that we have to pave a bloody road ahead and I am to be responsible for it.' A popular figure, he showed sprouts of political liberalism and disapproved of the crackdown of 1989. One of his protégés was Hu Jintao.

Having made the most of family connections in Beijing, the younger Xi decided that the way ahead lay in the provinces and went to Hebei as a county CCP Secretary in 1982. He then gravitated to the high-growth eastern coastal provinces of Fujian and Zhejiang, where he moved steadily up the state and Party ladder. He made a name for encouraging economic expansion as he courted Taiwanese and foreign investors and became known for fighting corruption. In 1987 he visited the United States but was reportedly not particularly impressed, though he had nothing bad to say either.

On his way to the top he worked with a wide variety of officials and state-sector bankers in the coastal provinces. Prominent among them are Li Lihui and Wang Yongli, President and Vice-President of the Bank of China, Liu Mingkang, the chief bank regulator, and Tianjin city Mayor Huang Xingguo. In Zhejiang he got to know the bosses of the Geely car company and Jack Ma, head of the e-commerce giant Alibaba, as well as bringing local entrepreneurs into provincial bodies. Politically, he presided over small reforms at grassroots level to let villagers keep tabs on their local leaders but within a strict Party framework. He also won points with poor inland provinces by leading delegations that pledged investment and assistance.

During his spell in Zhejiang, starting in 2002, the province's annual growth hit 14 per cent; the private sector manufacturing hub of

Wenzhou boomed and the trading centre of Yiwu grew hugely. Xi was marked out as a high-flyer but made sure he kept his ambition hidden. He suffered from hostility in the Party to the emerging princelings and finished last in voting for the Central Committee in 1997 – but his protectors got him in as an alternate member. Jiang Zemin and his powerful associate, Zeng Qinghong, were looking out for the younger man.

When the Shanghai boss, Chen Liangyu, was ousted in a power struggle with the centre in 2007, Beijing is reported to have had a problem finding somebody ready to take the job given the political sensitivities involved. But Xi stepped forward, calmed things down and, after only seven months, was elevated to the Standing Committee of the Politburo, subsequently amassing an array of posts as State Vice-President, Vice-Chair of the CMC, Chairman of the CCP Leading Group on Party Building, Executive Secretary of the Party Secretariat, Vice-Chairman of the Leading Group on Foreign Affairs and Taiwan Affairs, and Head of the Party School.

He was given responsibility for the 2008 Beijing Olympics and for relations with Hong Kong and Macau as well as for the PRC's sixtieth-anniversary celebrations in 2009. He travelled widely abroad on state visits and spent four days with Vice President Joe Biden when the American went to the PRC in 2011 to shore up relations between the United States and its biggest creditor – Xi smiled frequently but seemed bored at times when they visited Sichuan, where protestors trying to publicize complaints about requisitioning of their farmland were detained for the occasion. The following year, he visited the US, making a good impression and visiting the mid-Western town where he had stayed a quarter of a century earlier.

The dramatic fall of his fellow princeling, Bo Xilai, did nothing to impede the culmination of Xi's rise to the top. Despite having made a much-publicized visit in 2010 to laud the Chongqing model, Xi plainly did nothing to protect Bo two years later – reports of the visit have been removed from public records and photographs deleted from Chinese websites. In September 2012, when Xi abruptly disappeared from view for two weeks without any explanation, the rumour mill went into overdrive with stories of ailments ranging from back trouble to liver cancer and a heart attack – or that he had been attacked by Bo's military supporters. It seemed probable that the explanation was that he was busy settling the last pieces of the Bo case which had to be resolved before the five-yearly Congress could be held – the head of the Party Discipline Commission also dropped out of sight at the same time. There would have been complex discussions involving serving Politburo members and incoming figures as well as Jiang Zemin and other elders, not so much about expelling Bo from the Party, which was a foregone conclusion, but rather as to whether he should be put quietly under house arrest or paraded in a public trial – as was finally decided.

As the most prominent of the princelings in the leadership, Xi established himself as a conciliator and consensus figure who forges agreement, rather than as a politician with an agenda of change, a man who keeps on good terms with all around him and prizes Party unity above everything else. His record ties him to the high-growth coastal model but, in his initial remarks at the end of the 2012 Congress, he stressed popular concerns about livelihood, jobs, social conditions and the environment, showing an awareness of the challenges the regime faces.

His political position is strong. He has developed good links with younger generals moving to the top of the PLA including those he met during his time in the eastern coastal provinces across from Taiwan. He retains the support of the Jiang Zemin Shanghai group but, despite moving ahead of Li Keqiang, does not appear to have burned bridges with Hu Jintao, who did not seek to emulate Jiang Zemin by holding on to the Chairmanship of the Central Military Commission, but ceded it to Xi in November, 2012.

A cable from the US ambassador Jon Huntsman in 2009 gave a comprehensive portrait of the coming leader based on a conversation with an embassy contact who had known him from an early age. Xi was, this man (a professor) said, 'exceptionally ambitious' but also 'supremely pragmatic and a realist', somebody who never showed his hand and who had a genuine sense of entitlement as the son of his father and therefore one of the legitimate heirs to rule China. He does not care about money but 'could be corrupted by power', according to the cable, which was released by Wikileaks.[2]

Xi may not have gone in for personal enrichment. But an in-depth investigation by Bloomberg in the summer of 2012 showed that he had been singularly unsuccessful in applying to his own family a warning he issued to officials eight years earlier to 'rein in your spouses, children, relatives, friends and staff, and vow not to use power for personal gain'. According to this report, his extended family had investments in firms with assets of $376 million. None of these holdings were in the hands of Xi, his wife or their daughter but his older sister, her husband and daughter held substantial corporate stakes including an 18 per cent share in a rare earths company with assets of $1.73 billion. Other investments by relatives ranged through a telecommunications firm that received contracts of hundreds of millions of yuan from state-owned China Mobile, real estate in Hong Kong and Beijing, and a stake in a $1 billion US investment fund. When the story, which was based on painstaking examination of documents, ran at the end of June the Bloomberg site was blocked in China.

For his part, Xi is failingly orthodox, but there are inevitable questions in his conduct starting with the way in which he preaches an anti-graft mantra and urges officials to live more frugally while his relatives have done so very nicely out of business. He insists on the need for the Party to dominate the education of Chinese students who, he said in a speech in 2012, should 'grasp the Marxist worldview and methodology and build up confidence for socialism with Chinese characteristics'. But his daughter is studying at Harvard under an assumed name. In other speeches Xi stresses the importance of 'Marxist morality' but the system that has raised him to its top is notable for the way in which such Puritanism is regularly flouted.

Still, Xi is a more open personality than Hu. (It would be difficult to be more constrained.) At New Year in 2010 he sent an SMS with his greetings to a million officials across the country, stipulating that this was a 'personal' text. Some details of his private life have become known. His siblings live abroad: he has a sister in Canada and a brother in Hong Kong, who is said to have become fat and rich with designer clothes and expensive jewellery.

His first marriage, to the daughter of a diplomat, broke down; the couple were said by one source to have been constantly at one another's throats and she went to live in England. He then wed Peng Liyuan, a celebrated folk singer who performed with the PLA and holds the rank of major-general – though she has stopped her appearances since her husband's rise to the top. Peng has an uncle living in Taiwan and this is the first time a leading CCP figure has admitted to having a relative on the island. She says she picked Xi as a husband for his 'inner qualities' as 'the most qualified type of husband'. She describes him as frugal, hardworking and down to earth – in other words the very model of a CCP cadre.[3]

Foreign diplomats who have travelled with Xi on his trips abroad say he has a genuine sense of humour. He told the US ambassador in 2007 that he particularly likes Hollywood movies about the Second World War, singling out *Saving Private Ryan* and *Flags of Our Fathers*. 'Such Hollywood movies are grand and truthful,' he added. 'Americans have a clear outlook on values and clearly demarcate between good and evil,' the cable went on. 'In American movies, good usually prevails. In contrast … some Chinese moviemakers neglect values they should promote.'[4]

Singapore's Lee Kuan Yew calls Xi 'a thoughtful man who has gone through many trials and tribulations. I would put him in the Nelson Mandela class of persons. A person with enormous emotional stability who does not allow his personal misfortunes or sufferings to affect his judgement. In other words, he is impressive.' Henry Paulson, the former US Treasury Secretary, describes him as 'the kind of guy who knows how to get things over the goal line'. Like the well-trained bureaucrat he is, Xi usually keeps himself to himself and adopts a low profile; but on one occasion, talking to overseas Chinese during a visit to Mexico in 2009, he launched into a forthright attack on 'some bored foreigners, with full stomachs, who have nothing better to do than point fingers at us. First, China doesn't export revolution; second, China doesn't export hunger and poverty; third, China doesn't come and cause you headaches. What more is there to be said?'

In Western terms, the princelings might be expected to sympathize with calls for political and legal reform. Some have been quoted as calling at private meetings for democracy, the rule of law and controls on CCP power; according to a report in the autumn of 2011, the daughter of a former head of the Party school and boss of Shaanxi told a gathering at the Hall of Many Sages in Beijing, attended by Xi Jinping's sister, that the Communist movement was now 'like a surgeon who has cancer. It can't remove the tumour by itself; it needs help from others; but without help it cannot survive for long.'[5]

But such sentiments come from people with little real power and there is no evidence that they have any purchase on the new leaders. Indeed, a desire to preserve the privileges they have gained from growth may keep the elite and the middle class faithful to the self-defensive conservativism that has served them well in the past decade. If Xi is the main spokesperson for this group, there is no sign of a readiness to loosen the reins. As part of his post supervising the 2009 anniversary, he was charged with maintaining stability on CCP terms. He has told officials and students that they should study Party theory and avoid 'empty words' since 'unhealthy' writing could harm efficiency. If there was a strong lobby in favour of reform, both political and to the economic structure, Xi would, no doubt, take note and feed it into his calculus of the political power balance. But, as it is, he looks like an incremental operator. A meeting of 400 leading figures convened in April 2007 to give views on the succession beyond 2012 is reported to have plumped for Xi over Li because of the princeling's record and good network links as well as to prevent the emergence of a Hu Jintao–Youth League faction after the leadership transition. Asked the secret of his rise, well-placed sources reply on the lines of 'the different groups are comfortable with him'.

That argues against the new leadership undertaking the kind of reforms China needs if it is maintain its progress. Political reform has been ruled out in favour of continuing monopoly control by the CCP. Legal reform has gone backwards since the early part of this century with the law still regarded as an essential tool in maintaining that monopoly authority. So this leaves two possible areas for progress – the economy and society. The membership of the Standing Committee appointed at the 2012 Congress offers little prospect of significant advance on either front. The main voice for change was Li Keqiang, ranked second in the Politburo and set to succeed Wen Jiabao as Prime Minister at the annual plenary session of the National People's Congress in March 2013. In a series of speeches and reports, he has stressed the need to move forward. 'Reform and opening is essential to allowing people to enjoy a better life,' he said in an address after the Congress. 'If we don't do it, then we will bear historic responsibility.' The danger is that, like his predecessor, he is a voice for change with inadequate political clout to deliver against the strength of vested interests and the caution of his colleagues.

Born into a humble family in Anhui province in July 1955, Li Keqiang rose to the top through the Party Youth League as a Hu Jintao protégé. He has degrees in economics and law and devoted much time to learning English as a young man. He leans towards social measures such as the building of millions of low-cost residential units and the development of the health service. As a student at Peking University he had friends who went on to challenge the regime in the 1989 protests. 'I thought his views were very liberal,' one acquaintance from that era told Chris Buckley of Reuters. But he is not a forceful character, and his former friend noted that 'he's been an official for over two decades, and so that's also a factor'. His failure to emerge at the head of the Fifth Generation group at the 2007 Party Congress is testament to both his own limitations and those of his patron at the head of what some scornful princelings have been said to call the 'sons of shopkeepers' – presumably minding the shop till the CCP aristocrats took the reins.[6]

Li became China's youngest Governor in Henan in 1998. He set a modest tone by refusing to take part in banquets or lavish events usually laid on for provincial dignitaries, and made a point of moving round the province to get a feeling for grassroots problems. Henan's growth rose but Li was dogged by a series of problems. There was a crime wave in the capital of Zhengzhou. Then came a series of major fires, one of which claimed 309 lives in a shopping mall in the city of Luoyang. The province's cotton industry was hit by a scam in which farmers sold poor-quality goods to the local state offices. Finally, Li inherited the major HIV/Aids scandal involving tainted blood bought from poor rural inhabitants.

He was not directly responsible for any of this but was criticized for his slow reaction: the blood scandal was hushed up for years and, after Li launched an investigation into the cotton scam, Zhu Rongji showed a lack of confidence by dispatching a team of his own to look into the affair. In 2004 Li moved to Liaoning, developing Dalian and presiding over industrial and port modernization there – but, again, there was a scandal on his watch, this time over the big pyramid ant scam which burst into the open after being tolerated for eight years.

Li has not worked in the coastal fast-growth provinces and comes across as an earnest figure in the Hu mould. He is one of only two members of Hu Jintao's *Tuanpai* Youth League faction in the Standing Committee surrounded by princelings and protégés of Jiang Zemin. He lacks the appeal and experience of Wen Jiabao; when he was in charge of energy policy as Vice Premier, I asked an executive from a major oil company about him and the reply was 'his in-tray is usually full' – which could be a tribute to his industriousness but could also suggest that he does not expedite business very effectively. All of which raises the question of how effective Li will be as Premier and if he will be able to dominate interest groups, big corporate players and provincial administrations. Given Wen Jiabao's failure to deliver on his repeated calls for reform, China may find itself in a pattern of having a well-meaning prime minister overshadowed by the power of the Party machine, a natural enough situation for a Leninist state.

The other five men who joined Xi and Li on the Standing Committee in mid-November, 2012, as representatives of the Fifth Generation PRC leaders are experienced administrators who have shown their loyalty to the Party Centre. The third ranking member of the Standing Committee, Zhang Dejiang, who was set to become President of the NPC in March 2013, was provincial Party Secretary in the business centres of Guangdong and Zhejiang before becoming the Vice-Premier responsible for energy, transport and telecommunications. He was deputed to ensure stability in Chongqing after Bo Xilai's fall. A princeling, he has patron-protégé ties with Jiang dating back more than a quarter of a century, but is generally trusted as a safe pair of hands.

In fourth position, Yu Zhengsheng, the oldest member of the Standing Committee, became President of the China People's Political Consultative Congress, the toothless upper house of the legislature, a post that usually goes to the fourth-ranking Committee member. Yu, who took over from Xi as Party Secretary of Shanghai in 2007, is seen as a supporter of private enterprise. He is a princeling with a complex family background (his brother defected to the US). Fifth-ranking Liu Yunshan, the head of the Party Propaganda Department, had spent the past twelve years in such work in Beijing after rising through the ranks in Inner Mongolia. He has been at the heart of the regime's efforts to impose conformity and control. A member of Hu's *Tuanpai* faction, he has pushed China's 'soft power' efforts.

The sixth-ranking Politburo member, Wang Qishan, formerly Vice-Premier in charge of financial affairs, was named as Secretary of the Central Commission for Discipline Inspection. That made him the implementer of the new leadership's campaign against corruption. A princeling by marriage, he was previously economic point man with the US and has hands-on experience running a big bank, as Mayor of Beijing and as the man who cleaned up the first big financial crash, in Guangdong in 1999. That would have suited him for the number two post in the new government in charge of economic policy, but this could have meant that he overshadowed Li Keqiang. So a post was found outside his core competence, even though some observers see him as a man able to implement an effective campaign – the joke in Beijing was that he was appointed because he has no children and so no profiteering offspring to protect. It was also noted as the new seven-man Standing Committee filed on top the stage of the Great Hall of the People that he was the only one not to wear a red coloured tie – he chose blue neckwear. (He is also the only top leader with a receding hairline.)

Instead of Wang, Zhang Gaoli, another Jiang protégé who moved from running the big port city of Tianjin to become the seventh member of the Standing Committee, was lined up to become Vice-Premier with responsibility for the economy. His motto 'Do more, speak less' had been seen as implicit criticism of Bo Xilai. He presided over the growth of Shenzhen in the 1990s before becoming Party Secretary of Shandong. Under Hu Jintao, he moved to Tianjin which, with its 13 million inhabitants, is a major development zone intended to reinvigorate the Bohai Bay area.

The reduction in the size of the Committee from nine to seven seats could lead to more cohesive decision-making. But the selection process underlined the fluidity of elite politics in China where personal relationships and loyalties count for a great deal and the influence of old patrons can be significant. The resulting complexity impedes change which could adversely affect one or more sections of the power structure ranging from the Party bureaucracy and the state-owned enterprises to the armed forces and individuals who are doing very nicely out of the present system.

As a result, the new line-up was notable for the way in which two voices for reform were not admitted despite a real debate during 2012 about the need for change. Wang Yang, who became Party Secretary of Guangdong, China's richest province, in 2007, and Li Yuanchao, the head of the Party's Organization Department (which oversees the job performance of members), had appeared as strong contenders at the start of 2012. Wang, the only leadership figure to have worked on a factory floor, set out an agenda of change in 2011–12 including accepting lower growth, strengthening citizen's rights, stepping up the fight against pollution and moving industry up the value chain. Li had a reformist record while running Jiangsu province before moving to Beijing. But both faded as the final decision point approached.

An important factor in stopping their ascent was opposition from figures who officially stepped down ten or more years ago, led by Hu's predecessor as Party Secretary and State President. Jiang Zemin enjoyed the position of 'General Consultant for personnel matters' in this year's leadership transition. He and all other former Standing Committee members were consulted in the process.

Reuters reported that Jiang and Li Peng, the conservative prime minister from 1987 to 1998, came out against Li and Wang in informal polls held among the twenty-four Politburo members and ten Party elders before the Congress in the name of increased intra-Party democracy. Honoured guests at this year's Congress included the ninety-six-year-old hard-liner Song Ping, who initially promoted both Hu Jintao and Wen Jiabao and who apparently participated in the polls for the new Standing Committee and would hardly have welcomed reform.

According to this account, Wang was rejected in the first of these soundings in the summer because his enmity towards Bo meant that his elevation would have angered those who sympathized with the promotion of 'red culture' by the former Chongqing boss and would thus have been a source of instability. Wang's backing of private business was seen as disruptive. Li was blocked for favouring Hu Jintao's Youth League faction in promotions made by the Organization Department. In another sign of the continuing influence of the elders, Jiang was also reported to have used a fatal car crash in Beijing involving the son of one of Hu's closest aides to weaken the outgoing leader. That done, he stepped back in early 2013.

All the new five members of the Committee were in their mid-sixties when selected, meaning that they will have to retire on age grounds at the next Party Congress in 2017; Xi and Li are young enough to stay on until 2022. This means that the new group is, in the long-term span of Chinese politics, a transitory group – Generation 4.5 as one observer put it, rather than representing a fully fledged generational shift. Both the reformers, Wang Yang and Li Yuanchao, are young enough to be eligible to join the top table in 2017 after serving time in the central government or legislative posts. But attention then will be concentrated, rather, on Sixth Generation figures born in the 1960s who have begun to move into the upper reaches of the Party's power escalator. Prominent among them already are two Hu Jintao protégés who joined the wider Politburo in 2012 – Sun Zhengcai, who succeeded Zhang Dejian in Chongqing, and Hu Chunhua, who was in charge in Inner Mongolia but became Party Secretary of Guangdong when Wang Yang moved to a central government vice-premiership.

Xi's first initiative as China's leader was to home in on corruption, with Wang Qishan's appointment as an earnest to his intentions. It was an obvious target since, as we saw in Chapter Sixteen, graft constitutes a major fault line in today's China, with a history stretching back through the imperial and Kuomintang eras and now exacerbated by the sheer volume of money in the country and the growth of materialism as the main 'ism' in the PRC of the twenty-first century. In his first big address to the new Politburo eight days after taking the top job, Xi warned that 'If corruption is allowed to run wild, the ultimate outcome will be the end of the Party and the end of the state. We must be alert.' He reached back a thousand years to quote from a sage of the Northern Song Dynasty who noted that 'worms come only after matter decays' and referred to the role of corruption in the Arab Spring overthrow of regimes in the Middle East. Cadres were told to adopt more frugal lifestyles and police in some cities were given courses so that they could recognize luxury goods displayed by officials who cannot afford them on their salary.

But this campaign, like similar attacks on graft in the past stretching back well before the present regime, faces the core problem that graft is an important element in cementing the loyalty of officials. As a saying variously attributed to Mao Zedong and Chiang Kai-shek has it, if the Party does not get rid of corruption, it will lose the trust of the people, but if it does, it will have no members.

The trial of Bo Xilai, whose conduct Xi referred to as 'despicable' and having 'had a bad political effect and shocked people', provided an ideal platform to launch the crusade against corruption with the hearing into the graft of the former Railways Minister, Liu Zhijun, as a useful second act. But there is a catch. The list of Bo's crimes detailed by the Politburo when he was expelled from the Party in September, 2012, dated back fifteen years to his time in charge of the port city of Dalian, raising the inevitable question of why his nefarious conduct was tolerated for so long. Equally, Liu was allowed to go on heading the high-speed train project for years. Such campaigns have only limited impact and credibility as long as they hit only a few high-profile political targets such as Bo and Liu, who fell into disfavour for going their own way. The litmus test will be whether the campaign encompasses the families of top leaders – some commentators suggested that they might be required to declare their assets. This would have to include relatives of Xi and outgoing Premier Wen Jiabao, whose wealth was highlighted by Bloomberg and the *New York Times*.

More broadly, there was the question of whether, despite the real depths of the graft problem, the campaign – along with a rise in nationalistic rhetoric in China's disputes with its East Asia neighbours – would prove to be essentially a diversion from the structural reform that is needed but may be put off owing to the short-term cost, especially coming in a year when the economy was showing signs of a mild recovery to greet the new leaders.

Therein lies the greatest danger for China – not of economic collapse as such or of a political revolt but of being run by a regime too strong to be reversed but too intent on maintaining its position of power to be able to adapt to rapidly changing circumstances. The consensus style of rule under Hu and taken up by Xi is a great improvement on the wild, individualistic adventurism of the Mao era but it militates against change and bold decision-making, let alone risk-taking.

Nobody at the top has any interest in being seen to rock the boat, to champion liberalizing reforms or to bring the regime into question in any way. As regards the economy, everybody has signed up for the roadmap of the Five-Year Plan, which went into effect in 2011 and lasts until 2015. All share a fundamental aim: to preserve the Communist Party's monopoly of power using the mixture of growth and political control set in place by Deng Xiaoping.

In achieving this and in sustaining economic expansion, the leadership faces probably the most complex large-scale job of any ruling group on earth, complicated by all the snake tail factors explored in this book and headed by the need to maintain growth, the nature of that growth and the huge social changes the country is undergoing. There is no alternative to the CCP, the Party having made sure that no opposition exists ready to take over if it were to falter. But the innate conservatism of the twenty-first century regime means that any significant changes can only be seen as a threat to the system, even if an objective observer would see them as necessary to preserve that regime. This is the fundamental trap into which the PRC has worked itself as the policies that brought such success from the 1980s on are starting to outlive their usefulness and produce steadily less impressive results with attendant negative effects that are becoming ever more serious.

The first three decades of economic change are likely, in retrospect, to turn out to have been the relatively easy time given the headwinds behind China both domestically and globally. Now comes the biggest task. Admirers of the Chinese model present the country as being run by a superior meritocracy winnowed out by a rigorous selection process that replicates the old imperial examination system for the mandarinate. As we have seen, this is not the case; if any further proof was needed of the less than impartial criteria for promotion, it was provided by the politicking that led to the selection of the Standing Committee in 2012 and the exclusion of those who threatened to press for change. There is nothing surprising in that. Indeed, the imperial system was far from an objective system since only rich parents could generally afford the education of their sons, and, at various time, merchant families were excluded and degrees were sold as dynasties sunk into short-term self-preservation and showed a reluctance to embrace the change and innovation needed for survival.

The PRC is not going to go the way of the Qing but change is always difficult, especially for regimes which cannot question their own mythology and become trapped by orthodoxy. In China's case, structural economic reform would cut growth and increase inflation by several points in the short run, as well as threatening the privileges of entrenched and politically powerful vested interest groups and risking the alienation of a middle class whose younger members have known nothing but strong material advancement. Some commentators believe that reform will be forced on China if annual economic expansion drops to, say, 3 per cent. In fact, the very reverse could happen if the leaders see the country on a seriously downward trajectory and the regime's self-preservation urge leads them to batten down the hatches in the knowledge that change could make things even worse, and more perilous for them.

Reform of the legal system to make it more independent would bring into question the monopoly power of the Party – even a proposal to end the arbitrary 'reform through labour' system at the beginning of 2013 was quickly watered down. Relaxing social controls would bring the threat of instability. Political change to allow for competition to the CCP or the strengthening of civic society to provide a counter-balance to the Party would bring into question the very foundation of the regime. Adopting a foreign policy in keeping with China's economic weight would involve global responsibilities and a readiness to compromise which the PRC has not shown itself willing to embrace. A more liberal approach to Tibet and Xinjiang would run counter to the dogma of national unity which the PRC holds so dear. Such reconsideration of the system is needed but the example of the Soviet Union is held up as a dire warning – remove one brick from the wall and the whole edifice may come tumbling down, if only because the post-1949 system connects all the moving parts around the ruling centre.

This is true on the broad political front but also as regards specific areas where change is needed. The China model contains so many interlocking parts that a comprehensive blueprint would be required which would simply be too complex to undertake. To take one down-to-earth example, relaxing the *hukou* registration system or giving land ownership rights to farmers would mean overhauling the fiscal system by empowering local governments to raise more funding from taxation in order to pay for welfare for migrants workers and reduce dependence on sales of requisitioned land. That would reduce the fiscal grip Beijing enjoys as disburser of central tax revenues to provinces which, as things stand, are short of money to meet their spending commitments. Thus the seemingly simple issue of allowing migrant workers to enjoy rights to health care and education for their children leads to a change in a national political equation that underpins the system.

The Party Congress of 2012 pointed towards a preservation of the status quo in its political, social, economic and legal forms, with attacks on corruption as a means of avoiding more basic structural issues. Xi Jinping's concern in his first remarks as leader was to strengthen the Party; corruption and the increasing gulf between Communist cadres and the people are seen by the leadership not so much as ills in themselves as sources of peril for the ruling group. As Xi took over, 'Party strengthening' became the new watchword with all the buttressing of control and self-absorption by the CCP that this implied.

So we come back to the core issue of control and the retention of power, which has been at the heart of China's history since the First Emperor sought to standardize everything from the currency to the width of the wheel tracks on China's roads and to eradicate any challenge to his authority. Far more than the Confucian heritage, keeping as tight a grip as possible on the nation has been the hallmark of China's rulers for more than 2,000 years, with the Legalist philosophy embraced by Qin Shihuangdi as its underpinning. In the last three decades, the evolution of the economy and society and the deep involvement with the wider world complicate that task greatly. China will not implode. It has the resources and dynamism to go on growing and to continue to amaze the rest of the globe. Its presence will be felt more widely than that of any other powers except for the United States. But nor will it rule the world; it does not want to and, even if it did, could not do so since no single state can dominate the globe any more, whatever the relative decline of the West.

China's main concerns will be domestic, above all in the key question of whether the jealously guarded domestic system that has evolved since 1978 can cope with the multiplicity and scale of the tests ahead. To that there can be no clear answer except from those who do not take into account the extreme complexity of the People's Republic and prefer to pluck facile conclusions from extrapolation of the past into the future, or base themselves on the temporary trends of the present. As this book has argued on many levels, this uncertainty is compounded by the reluctance to address the need to take significant steps forward to broaden and deepen the Dengist revolution that remains only half-accomplished. That applies to the economy, for sure, but, even more fundamentally, to the political and legal systems and to a society which is evolving in ways that escape the Party's grip.

The refusal to share power more widely is in keeping with China's tradition of state authoritarianism stretching back to Qin. This is seen as a source of strength by those who believe that the country's long tradition and reluctance to change make it superior to the messy West, its meritocracy inherently superior to elected politicians. That is a fundamental misrepresentation which ignores present truths in favour of a romanticized version of the past that relates less and less to the China of today, and of the years to come. Rather than pointing to a future in which the PRC dominates the world, the reality of China in the second decade of the twenty-first century is that its regime is locked into a pressure cooker with the risk that, in the absence of safety valves, an end to high growth could bring an explosion that would rock its society. If basic economic, political, social and legal reforms left undone since the 1980s are not addressed, China's onward march will be hobbled, and the world as a whole will feel the consequences as the snake tails wrap themselves round its tiger head.

NOTES

CHAPTER ONE

1 Income, urban population, illiteracy, mortality, birth rate, ageing, NBS *Science*, London, 29 July 2011.
2 Copper forecast, Commodities Research Unit (CRU), London, November 2010.
3 Hu, Xinhua, 1 July 2011; Wen, press briefing after NPC, 14 March 2011; Li, *Qishi*, April 2010; Wang, private information.
4 Bridge information from Andrew Batson interview with officials; Xi, *Qishi*, April 2011; Transparency International Bribe Index, 2011.
5 Museum, *Caixin*, 10 August 2011; *China News Watch*, 22 August 2011; *Guardian*, 25 August 2011; *People's Daily*, 3 November, 2011.
6 *Financial Times*, 7 July 2011.
7 *People's Forum*, 1 April 2010.
8 Ferguson, *Wall Street Journal*, 22 November 2010; Munk debate, Toronto, 2011; http://www.thedailybeast.com/newsweek/2011/08/14/china-faces-its-own-fiscal-problems; Zakaria, Kissinger; Munk debate, Toronto, 2011; Bloomberg, 27 January, 26 September 2011.
9 Contractors, Engineering News Record listing for 2010.

CHAPTER TWO

1 Plan, NDRC Report to Fourth Session of the Eleventh National People's Congress, Beijing, 5 March 2011.
2 Drinking, Li Yichong, *Addiction*, July 2011; Versailles, Harbin Pharmaceutical website.
3 *Hunrun Rich List* 2010–11.
4 Deaths, New Culture News, *South China Morning Post*, 23 July 2011.
5 Wenzhou wedding photographs, *Lower Tier Times*, August 2011.
6 Advertisement, *Guardian*, 23 August 2011.
7 French to author, 2011. See also French, *Fat China*.
8 Agence France-Presse, 4 September 2009.
9 Belong, Third Survey of Social Status of Women in China, 2010; Survey, Grant Thornton, March 2012; *South China Morning Post*, 2 October 2011; *Financial Times*, Women at the Top, November, 2011.

10 Dong Did Kirsten Tatlow, *New York Times*, 26 January 2011; *Financial Times*, Women at the Top, November 2011.
11 World Bank, *Economist*, 23 April 2011; Top 10 per cent study, China's Hidden Income, Credit Suisse, 6 August 2010; Wang Xiaolu, China Reform Foundation, The Distribution of Grey Income and National Income; Merchants Bank report 2010; Victor Shih, Presentation to INET Conference, Bretton Woods, 10 April 2011; Gini study, http://blogs.wsj.com/2012/12/10/perception-vs-reality-charting-chinas-family-value.
12 Health, World Health Organization; http://www.nationmaster.com/graph/hea_tot_exp_on_hea_as_of_gdp-health-total-expenditure-gdp;   Tickets, Dodson, p. 137.

CHAPTER THREE

1 This account of the high-speed train projects draws on work done by my colleague Dian Qu for Trusted Sources, which also provided the map and earlier research by Justine Moxham. I am grateful, once again, to Bo Zhuang for arranging the visit to the tunnelling project in Hunan. Other sources include excellent reporting by *Caixin* magazine – see http://english.caing.com/2011/high_speed_train_collision/; http://english.caixin.cn/2011-09-01/100297517.html; http://blog.english.caixin.cn/article/360/.
2 State Information Office, 25 July 2011; *Beijing News*, 27 July 2011; *Economic Observer*, 31 July 2011; *People's Daily*, 1 August 2011; State Council, *China Digital Times*, 21 October 2011.
3 http://english.caixin.cn/2011-08-23/100293979.html.

CHAPTER FOUR

1 OECD, PISA Study, December 2010.
2 Mass-transit systems, McKinsey, *What Matters*, 7 January 2011.
3 Army, *China Supply Chains*, July–August 2010.
4 Gou, carpet, bed, *Financial Times*, 6–7 August 2011.
5 Report, *Observer*, 28 August 2011.
6 Survey, Federation of Hong Kong Industries, 2010.
7 Deutsche Welle, BBC, 22 October, 2011.

CHAPTER FIVE

Accounts of Yiwu and other cities and villages in this chapter are drawn from the author's visits.
1 SOEs, China Leadership Monitor (no. 34); Rare earths, *Financial Times*, 26 September and 21 October 2011.

2   Fenby, *Modern China*, p. 11.

3   'The Shanxi Banks' by Randall Morck and Fan Yang, draft paper, October 2009; 400,000 companies, UBS estimate.

4   *China Daily*, 13 and 15 October 2011; Christians, *China Quarterly*, June 2011.

CHAPTER SIX

1   Central Committee, CLM, No. 32 point to surface; Sebastian Hellmann and Elizabeth Perry, *Mao's Invisible Hand*, Harvard University Asia Center, 2011.

2   Kahn, *New York Times*, 26 November 2006.

3   Kissinger, *On China*, chapter 3.

4   Slapping, http://www.danwei.org/front_page_of_the_day/proqing_dynasty_scholar_was_sl.php.

5   Ishiwara, Fenby, *Generalissimo*, pp. 201–2.

6   Can you imagine? Li Zhisui, *Private Life of Chairman Mao*, p. 150.

7   Yu, *South China Morning Post*, 29 August 2011.

8   I'll just go, *China Daily*, 10 June 2011.

9   There are many fine books on Tibet. Among them, see Robert Barnett, *Resistance and Reform in Tibet* (Indiana University Press, 1994), Isabel Hilton, *The Search for the Panchen Lama* (Viking, 1999) and for a picture of life in Tibet today Sun Shuyin, *A Year in Tibet* (Harper, 2009). Dalai Lama, *Washington Post*, 14 July 2011; Zhang, Xinhua, 7 March 2011.

10 Sangay, http://www.bbc.co.uk/news/world-asia-pacific-14440846; *Financial Times* magazine, 6–7 August 2011.

11 Chen, *Global Times*, 25 August 2011.

12 Beijing, Dalai Lama statements, *New York Times*, 5 October 2011.

13 Xinjiang, *New York Times*, 4 September 2010; *South China Morning Post*, 28 October 2010. For different analyses of China in Xinjiang see, Dru Gladney, *Dislocating China* (Hurst, 2005) and Barry Sautman, 'Is Xinjiang an Internal Colony?' *Inner Asia* (vol. 2, no. 2), 2000. O'Neill, *South China Morning Post*, 9 May 2010.

CHAPTER SEVEN

1   Philip Snow (see bibliography) is particularly illuminating on this period of Hong Kong's history. Steven Tsang (see bibliography) gives an excellent overall account.

2   The Patten era is covered supportively in Jonathan Dimbleby, *The Last Governor* (Little, Brown, 1997), and critically by one of the Governor's fiercest critics, the diplomat Percy Craddock, in his book *In Pursuit of British Interests* (AC Black).

3   Truman. Merle Miller, *Plainly Speaking* (Putnam, 1973), pp. 426–7.

4 The Nixon–Mao meetings and the diplomatic negotiations are best described in Margaret MacMillan, *Seize the Hour* (John Murray, 2006). Henry Kissinger's *On China* provides his account but adds little.

CHAPTER EIGHT

1 Among many works on the Communist Party, I would point particularly to the books by Richard McGregor and David Shambaugh cited in the bibliography. Hu, speech, 1 July 2011.
2 *The New York Times*, 10 August 2012.
3 Mao Yishi, *Caixin*, June 2011.
4 Hu and Wen; see Lam, Hu, Nathan and Gilley.
5 Ambassador, Wikileaks, 13 June 2011.
6 80 per cent, Chen Zhiwu at London School of Economics, 23 January 2010; *People's Daily*, 26 October 2011.
7 Graduates, Education Ministry website, June 2011.
8 Hu, Xinhua, Full Text of Hu Jintao's Speech at CCP Anniversary, 1 July 2011.
9 *Financial Times*, 18 September 2011; *China Digital Times*, 21 October 2011.
10 Freedom House report, April 2011; Wang, press conference, 29 December 2010; Official, *Xi'an Daily*, 10 August 2011; Hu Shuli, Reuters Oxford lecture, 2011.
11 *South China Morning Post*, 22 August 2011.
12 *New York Times*, 16 July 2011.
13 *China Digital Times*, September–October 2011.
14 Lawyers, White Paper, *China Daily*, 27 September 2010; Hu, press conference, Washington, 19 January 2011; full account of 2011 disappearance, Paul Mooney, *South China Morning Post*, 4 July 2011; He, *Media Works*, 24 January 2011; Chen, *South China Morning Post*, 24 January 2011; Deng, *Guardian*, 13 January 2011; Gao, reporter, Associated Press, 10 January 2011; daughter, *Wall Street Journal*, 28 October 2010; Liu, http://www.siweiluozi.net/2011/08/ive-only-begun-to-scratch-surface-liu.htm, http://twitter.com/#!/liushihui; Teng, *Wall Street Journal*, 28 December 2010; NI, http://www.scmp.com/portal/site/SCMP/menuitem.2af62ecb329d3d7733492d9253a0a0a0/?vgnextoid=d8e85f3c312dd210VgnVCM100000360a0a0aRCRD&ss=China&s=News#Top; Mooney, *South China Morning Post*, 30 January, 30 June, 4 July 2011.
15 CHRD, 23 March 2011; http://bl154w.blu154.mail.live.com/default.aspx?wa=wsignin1.0; http://chrdnet.org; Ai, *Global Times*, 9–10 August 2011.
16 *Global Times*, 9 August 2011.
17 Bodyguards, *China Daily* (European edition), 29 April–5 May 2011; Propaganda Bureau, March 2011.
18 *People's Daily*, 9 June 2011; propaganda instruction, 8 June 2011; village elections and fate of independents covered in Kerry Brown, *Ballot Box China* (see bibliography).
19 Liu Shulin, *Global Times*, 20 May 2011.

20 McGregor, p.1; Li Zhongjie, http://www.reuters.com/article/2011/06/09/
    us-china-party-idUSL3E7H90CI20110609.
21 Wu, NPC Speech, 10 March 2011; Xinhua, 1 July 2011.

                        CHAPTER NINE

1 Frederick Teiwes and Warren Sun, *China Journal* (Issue 66), 2011;
   http://ips.cap.anu.edu.au/chinajournal/issues/abstracts/.
2 The fullest biography of Deng is that published by Ezra Vogel in 2011 – this
   contains a wealth of new material. The end of the Mao era is expertly covered in Richard Baum, *Burying Mao*. See also Fang Lizhi, 'The Real Deng',
   New York Review of Books, 10 November 2011.
3 Praise, Vogel, p. 37; Lushan, Fenby, *Modern China*, 409; violence, Fenby,
   Modern China, p. 515.
4 MacLaine, Vogel, p.4.
5 Kent Deng gives details of the state of China in pp. 136–145.
6 Yashen Huang's book is the best guide to this period, containing a wealth of
   statistical material to support his central argument.
7 Zhao, p. 252; Chen Yun, differences, pp. 91–4.
8 Fok, Zhao, p. 198.
9 Lijia Zhang to author, 2011.
10 Rather, CBS, Fenby, *Modern China*, pp. 606, 614.
11 There are many books about the Beijing spring from which I would mention
    the inside account given by Nathan and Link in *The Tiananmen Papers*, the
    excellent book by Black and Munro and Jonathan Mirksy's reports in the
    Observer. Zhao Zhiyang gives his account in *Prisoner* (Part One).
12 Zhao's account of the struggle with Li is in *Prisoner*, pp. 10–22.
13 Mirksy, *Observer*, 30 April. As well as the account in *The Tiananmen Papers*,
    Deng's activities at this period are covered in detail in Vogel, chs 20–21; Li,
    South China Morning Post, 4 June 2010.
14 Elders, Wang, Nathan and Link, pp. 354–62.
15 Zhao, p. 27.
16 Zhao, p. 33.
17 Jiang, Sullivan, Lawrence, *China Since Tiananmen* (ME Sharpe, 1995), pp.
    21–22.
18 Li, *Der Spiegel*, 29 November 1989.
19 Major, John, *The Autobiography* (Harper Collins, 1999), p. 120.
20 Adviser, private information.
21 August, Oliver, *Inside the Red Mansion: On the Trail of China's Most Wanted Man*
    (John Murray, 2007) gives an English-language account of the affair.
22 For Jiang era see Lam, Jiang.

CHAPTER TEN

1   Mao has been the subject of numerous biographies, the main ones mentioned in the bibliography. The bestselling work by Jung Chang and Jon Halliday is all black and white with little shading or context. It contains some questionable accounts, for instance of an understanding between the Kremlin and Chiang Kai-shek to allow the Red Army to escape on the Long March, which bears little relation to the course of events. It has been heavily criticized on academic grounds (see the book edited by Gregor Bernton and Lin Chin). But it served a salutary purpose in lifting the curtain that had cloaked the Great Helmsman in too many previous works, a process that has continued with further digging into the reality of Maoist China. Philip Short's biography is probably the best general work while Pierre Ryckman's writing under his pen name of Simon Leys has produced first-rate essays – see Simon Leys, *Broken Images* (Alison & Busby, 1979).

2   The famine has been recorded in two outstanding books – Yang Jisheng's *Tombstone*, which is being translated, and Frank Dikötter's account based on provincial archives.

3   Lin, Li Zhisui, p. 453.

4   Perry Link, *Washington Post*, 17 May 2009.

5   Chan Koonchung, p. 297.

CHAPTER ELEVEN

1   The best account of the Opium Wars and its many twists and turns is the 2011 book by Julia Lovell.

2   Xiong Yuezhi in Liu Tao and David Faure, *Unity and Diversity* (Hong Kong University Press, 1966), pp. 100, 110.

3   Fenby, *Modern China*, p.10.

4   Roger Pelissier, *The Awakening of China* (Secker and Warburg, 1967), p. 97; Fenby *Modern China*, pp. 19–22.

5   Immanuel Hsü, *Rise of Modern China* (Oxford University Press, 2000), pp. 282–91 deals with the Self-Strengtheners. See also Albert Feuerwerker, *China: Early Industrialization and Mandarin Enterprise* (Harvard University Press, 1958), and Ann Arbor, *The Chinese Economy (Part 1, 1870–1911)* (University of Michigan Press, 1981).

6   Scheme, Hallet Abend, *My Life in China* (Harcourt Brace, 1943), p. 24.

7   Poem, Alexander Monro (ed), *China: City & Exile* (Eland, 2011), p. 63.

8   Steven Pinker, *Better Angels of Our Nature* (Allen Lane, 2011), p. 195. On this scale, Pinker puts the Taiping as the tenth-most-deadly episode in world history, and the Mao era as eleventh – though he understates the number who died then.

9   Undergroud, Randall Morck and Fan Yang, 'The Shanxi Banks', draft paper, 2009, p. 15.

10 For Ricci, see Mary Laven, *Mission to China* (Faber, 2011).
11 5,000 cases, St Petersburg, Randall Morck and Fan Yang, p. 17.
12 See Frank Dikötter, *The Age of Openness* (Hong Kong University Press, 2008); Bickers, *History Today*, October 2011.

CHAPTER TWELVE

1 Xinhua, 2 September 2011.
2 Ambassador, Wikileaks, 13 June 2011, of cable 9 January 2009.
3 Clinton, *The Atlantic*, 10 May 2011.
4 Clinton, speech, Hong Kong, 26 July 2011; Wu, Gates, Singapore Shangri-La Forum, 2011; http://www.iiss.org/conferences/the-shangri-la-dialogue/shangri-la-dialogue-2011; Wang, *China Daily*, 16 July 2011.
5 Japan, http:/ / www.bbc.co.uk/ news/ business -12631357;*Global Times*, http://www.thehindu.com/news/international/article2459736.ece.
6 Author visit, March 2011; *Financial Times*, 1 February 2011.
7 CNOOC, Competing, McGregor, pp. 54, 62.
8 Tianjin Pipe, Bloomberg, 9 December 2010.
9 60 per cent, Council on Foreign Relations, New York, 2011; *Financial Times*, 29 August, 2011.
10 *Financial Times*, 8 August 2011.
11 Xinhua, 6 August 2011.
12 Trade war, Xinhua, 11 October 2011; Clinton, speech to Economic Club of New York, 14 October 2011; Bernanke, Congressional testimony, 4 October 2011; Romney, *Washington Post* op-ed, 13 October 2011; Krugman, *New York Times*, 20 January 2011.
13 Big Mac, *Economist*, 30 July 2011.
14 US companies, AmCham survey, Beijing, March 2011; ADB study, September 2011; Lamy, *Financial Times*, 25 January 2011.
15 Ambassador, *China Daily*, 27 June 2011.
16 Iceland, *Financial Times*, 2 September 2011.
17 Chinese Direct Investment in the European Union, University of Leeds, July 2011; Tianjin case, *Wall Street Journal*, 9 June 2011.
18 Godemont, 'A Global China Policy', European Council on Foreign Relations, June 2010.
19 Poll, Yomiuri Shimbun, 8 November 2010.
20 Yomiuri, 3 August 2011; Xinhua, 29 August 2011.
21 Singh, *Economist*, 18 December 2010; Fragile, *Financial Times*, 13 December 2010.
22 Raghav Bahl, *Superpower: The Amazing Race Between China's Hare and India's Tortoise* (Portfolio Penguin, 2010); for literacy, see *Financial Times*, 26 August 2011.
23 Scientist, Michael Wesley, Lowry Institute, *Financial Times*, 26 April 2011.
24 Afghanistan, Robert Fox, *Evening Standard*, 27 May 2011.
25 NYR, 20 November 2010.

26 *Economist*, 13 August 2011; Deborah Brautigam's book (see bibliography) gives a comprehensive account of China's involvement in Africa.

27 Carson, Wikileaks, *Financial Times*, 10 December 2010; *Der Spiegel*, Wikileaks, 9 December 2010; Zuma, *Guardian*, 24 December 2010.

28 Zimbabwe, *Guardian*, 2 February 2011; Traders, South Africa, banks, Angola, *Economist*, 23 April 2011.

29 http://news.bbc.co.uk/1/hi/programmes/from our own correspondent/ 9386678.stim; *New York Times* in *Observer*, 28 November 2010; *Der Spiegel*, 9 December 2010; *South China Morning Post*, 24 October 2010; Outcome, *New York Times*, 4 April 2011.

30 http://www.rnw.nl/africa/article/zambia-china-must-obey-our-rules-says-president; http://blogs.ft.com/beyond-brics/2011/10/24/zambia-striking-the-dragon/#axzz1bmCaxq7E; http://online.wsj.com/article/ SB10001424052970204644504576650374119213568.html; http://english. caixin.cn/2011-10-23/100316622.html.

CHAPTER THIRTEEN

1 Kitchen, *Economist*, 11 June 2011.

2 http://tribune.com.pk/story/262148/pakistan-our-only-all-weather-friend-china/http://pakobserver.net/detailnews.asp?id=112595.

3 Yan, p.100.

4 Boycott, quote from organizer, Zhao Bandi, to press, Beijing, June 2011.

5 Obama, press conference, Washington, 19 January 2011.

6 'Realist' view is best expressed in Aaron Friedberg, *A Contest for Superiority* (Norton, 2011).

7 Levine, Harry Harding (ed.), *China in Asia in China's Foreign Relations in the 1980s* (Yale University Press, 1984), p.107; Pei, *Foreign Policy*, March 2012.

8 Wang, Foreign Affairs, March 2011; ISPI op cit; conference, other quotes, François Godemont, China debates its global strategy, European Council on Foreign Relations, 2011; see also A. I. Johnston, *Is China a Status Quo Power?*; international security, spring 2003; Joshua Kurlantzick's book (see bibliography) covers China's soft diplomacy.

9 Shambaugh, *Washington Quarterly*, winter 2011.

10 Hu, interview with *Wall Street Journal* and *Washington Post*, 17 January 2011; Trap, Suisheng Zhao, China's New Foreign Policy, ISPI, May 2011.

11 Generals, Xi, author private information.

12 Xinhua, Reuters, 25 August 2011. For military build-up, see Ronald O'Rourke, China Naval Modernization, Congressional Research Service, 1 October 2010; Wikileaks, *The Age*, Melbourne, 28 February 2011; Jeremy Bernstein, Nukes for Sale, *New York Review of Books*, 1 May 2010.

13 Mullen, Associated Press, 15 July 2011.

14 Zhang, Foster the Core Values of Contemporary Revolutionary Soldiers, *Xuexi*, 2008.

15 Attacks, Nigel Inkster, World Without Secrets, *Montrose Journal*, winter 2010; special report on China's role in the world, *Economist*, 4 December 2010; Richard Clarke, *Wall Street Journal*, 15 June 2011; Google blog posting, 2 June 2011; *People's Daily*, 6 June, 5 August 2011; 50,000, Associated Press, 9 August 2011; McAfee, Reuters, 3 August 2011; http://www.reuters.com/article/2011/08/03/cyberattacks-idUSN1E76R26720110803); Units, Rogers, *Financial Times*, 13 October 2011.

CHAPTER FOURTEEN

1 Important day, Gerth, p.15; Ice box, author conversation; Li, *El País*, 4 January 2011; Gates, author conversation; Pulpy, *Financial Times*, 7 January 2011; Kent, *Financial Times*, 26 September 2011; Invest, Bloomberg, 20 August 2011.

2 Clissold, p. xi.

3 GM, Yum, Club Med, *Financial Times*, 29 January, 2 February, 16 February 2011, 4 June, 2012; *Bloomberg Markets*, March 2011; Chênevert, *Wall Street Journal*, 7 March 2011; Hotels, *South China Morning Post*, 29 March 2011.

4 European firms, European Chamber of Commerce survey, May 2011; US firms, American Chamber of Commerce report, March 2011; *China Daily* (European edition), 11–17 March 2011.

5 Council, *China Daily* (European Weekly) 27 May–2 June 2011; Locke, speech of American Chamber of Commerce and US-China Business Council, Beijing, 20 September 2011.

6 OECD, *Wall Street Journal*, 16 November 2011.

7 'Petroleum, European Chamber of Commerce in China', position paper, 2010.

8 Joint ventures are well analysed in *McKinsey Quarterly*, December 2010, Past lessons for China's new joint ventures.

9 Alstom, *Financial Times* 1 November, 2011; Bosch, *Financial Times*, 19 January 2011.

10 Self-Strengtheners, Fenby, *Modern China*, p. 37; Jonathan Spence, *To Change China* (Penguin Books, 1980).

11 Immelt, *Financial Times*, 14 July 2010; 'European Union Chamber of Commerce in China', position paper 2010/2011.

12 Author's private information.

13 X-ray, *China Daily*, 27 July 2011; BASF Siemens, *Financial Times*, 19 January, 28 November 2010; *South China Morning Post*, 2 March 2011; Rubenstein, Buyouts conference, New York, 26 April 2011.

CHAPTER FIFTEEN

1 *Guardian*, 19 September 2011.
2 *South China Morning Post.*
3 Li, Wikileaks, 6 December 2010; Property, Tom Orlik, *Understanding China's Economic Indicators* (FT Press, 2011), chapter 3.
4 The City: Beijing, *The Daily Beast*, 28 August 2011; 2011 http://www.thedaily beast.com/newsweek/2011/08/28/ai-weiwei-on-beijing-s-nightmare-city.html.
5 Yan, pp. 250–51.
6 Suffocate, Agence France-Presse, 26 August 2011.
7 *South China Morning Post*, 26 July 2009.
8 20 years, McKinsey, *What Matters*, 7 January 2011.
9 Hebei, *China Daily* (European edition), 8–14 July 2011.
10 Xinjiang, Associated Press, 22 August 2011.
11 *Global Times*, 19 August 2011.
12 Quelch, *China Daily* (European Weekly), 19–25 August 2011.
13 Reuters, 11 August 2011.
14 Human Rights Watch report, November 2009.

CHAPTER SIXTEEN

1 Wikileaks, *Daily Telegraph*, 6 December 2010.
2 Commission, *China Daily* (European edition), 21–27 October 2011.
3 Horizon survey, Beijing, 2010.
4 Caijin, *South China Morning Post.*
5 Report, Institute of Public and Environmental Affairs, Beijing, 31 August 2011.
6 Wikileaks, *Guardian*, 28 August 2011; see also Rachel Stern in *China Quarterly*, June, 2011.
7 Academy, *Science*, 3 March 2011.
8 *South China Morning Post.*
9 World Health Organization.
10 *Washington Post.*
11 *South China Morning Post.*
12 Environment Ministry.
13 A quarter, *Science*, 29 July 2011.
14 Polls.

CHAPTER SEVENTEEN

1 School costs, *Caixin*, 30 August 2011.
2 Train, *Financial Times*, 28 October 2011; *Wall Street Journal*, 20 October 2011; Toll Roads, *South China Morning Post*, 18 October 2011.

3   Local-government debts, Shih, http://blogs.wsj.com/chinarealtime/
    2010/03/17/victor-shih-sees-bank-bailout-redux/; Fitch, Asianomics,
    http://www.bloomberg.com/news/2011-03-08/china-faces-60-risk-of-bank-
    crisis-by-2013-fitch-gauge-shows.html; Walter, Howie, *Wall Street Journal*, 21 June
    2011; Bank of China, http://www.ft.com/cms/s/0/e2aa6306-4a78-11e0-82ab-
    00144feab49a.html#axzz1SSKyjNks. Roubini, http://www.project-syndicate.org
    /commentary/roubini37/English; See Michael Pettis, http://
    www.carnegieendowment.org/2011/06/01/quick-guide-to-china-s-latest-big-
    bailout/2qt, http://ftalphaville.ft.com/blog/2011/04/04/535101/michael-
    pettis-on-chinas-useless-banks/; The Bailout that Busted China's Banks, *Wall
    Street Journal*, 24 October 2011.
4   CASS, Bloomberg, 24 October 2011.
5   *Caixin*, 14–15 July 2011, http://english.caixin.cn/2011-07-14/100279565.html,
    http://english.caixin.cn/2011-07-26/100284174.html.
6   Wikileaks, *Daily Telegraph*, 6 December 2010.
7   HKMI, April 2009. http://www.hkimr.org/cms/upload/publication_app/
    pub_sum_0_2_210_wp200916_summary.pdf.
8   Merchants' Bank, *Global Times*, 22 April 2011; Young, *People's Daily*, 14
    December 2010, http://english.peopledaily.com.cn/90001/90776/90882/
    7230135.html.
9   Murphy, *Financial Times*, 24 June 2011.
10 S&P, *Financial Times*, 30 September 2011.
11 Deutsche Bank, Macro Strategy, 29 June 2009.
12 *China Daily*, 19, 24, 28 May, 6 June 2010, 3 June 2011; *Oriental*, 1 June 2011;
    Shanghai Daily, 2 June 2011.
13 Poll, http://mobile.bloomberg.com/news/2011-09-28/china-economy-
    slowing-to-5-annual-growth-by-2016-in-global-investors-poll.

CHAPTER EIGHTEEN

1   Wikileaks, *Der Spiegel*, 10 May 2010, http://www.spiegel.de/international/
    world/0,1518,732972,00.html.
2   Ditto.
3   Xi family, Bloomberg, June 29, 2012; Just My Husband, Reuters, 18 August
    2011.
4   Wikileaks, *Guardian*, 4 December 2010, http://www.guardian.co.uk/world/
    us-embassy-cables-documents/100934.
5   John Garnaut, *Sydney Morning Herald*, 17 October 2011.
6   Buckley, Reuters, 28 October 2011, http://uk.reuters.com/intromessagegeo?
    origLocation=/article/2011/10/28/uk-china-politcs-li-id
    UKTRE79R0WJ20111028&dartZone=/news/uk/article. See also Nathan and
    Gilley, McGregor, pp. 23–24.

ACKNOWLEDGEMENTS

During the past seventeen years of involvement with China, I have been hugely helped by a wide array of friends, acquaintances and sources in the People's Republic and observers elsewhere. I will not name them individually here since the list would be too long and might contain some who would prefer not to be cited, but my debt is enormous and reflects, I think, the strides made by journalists, academics, business people, commentators and other observers towards understanding a country that, while still puzzling in many ways, is now being seen for what it is in its many dimensions.

I would, however, like to single out for special thanks Bo Zhuang, Dian Qu and Chieh-Ju Liao, my long-standing colleagues in the China team at the research service Trusted Sources, as well as Fergus Naughton for his help and Larry Brainard for his perceptive guidance on economic matters, Andrea Giunti for his charts and Nicholas Mather for agreeing that I should write this book while continuing to head the China team. Among journalists whose work I have drawn on, I am particularly grateful to the correspondents of my principal daily sources of information – the *Financial Times*, the *Wall Street Journal*, the *Guardian*, the *South China Morning Post*, the *Economist* and the *New York Times* – though I have drawn on the work of many more correspondents, which I am sure they will recognize. I am deeply thankful to them all. Once again, Robert Ash and Willy Wo-Lap Lam provided wisdom and perspective while Paul French sparked off ideas. The postings and discussions on ChinaPol, the site run by the late Rick Baum, were invaluable as a guide to events and thinking. Xiao Qiang, Chief Editor of *China Digital Times*, and his team at the School of Journalism at UC Berkeley provided information on censorship orders I have cited in the book. David Shambaugh came up with useful textual points.

I am equally grateful to the friends who put me up and put up with me during visits while I was writing the book and disappeared for unsociable bouts of work at country homes from Exmoor to Bali via the Marais and Touraine. From near and far, Sara and Alexander provided family support and my overwhelming debt to my wife is recorded in the dedication.

At Simon & Schuster in Britain, Mike Jones took responsibility for commissioning and publishing the book, displaying his habitual calm and professionalism in overseeing a project that (given its up-to-the-present nature) was always going to present production problems. Monica Hope was a dream copy editor, combining speed of execution, good humour and a seemingly endless capacity to absorb last-minute changes while Martin Bryant did a fine proof-reading job. Rory Scarfe and Emily Husain kept things on track to the bitter end, Jo Whitford expertly helped update this paperback edition, and Hannah Corbett and Florence Partridge weighed in early on the promotional front. In the US I am grateful for Peter Mayer's enthusiasm for the book and flexibility in agreeing to the many changes required to keep up with China's development, for Dan Crissman's expert, speedy and companionable editing and for Jack Lamplough's work in spreading the word. As always, I owe a considerable debt to Christopher Sinclair-Stevenson for setting up the arrangements and for his enthusiasm for the book.

SELECT BIBLIOGRAPHY

Adshead, S.A.M., *Material Culture in Europe and China, 1400–1800* (MacMillan, 1997)

Baum, Richard, *Burying Mao* (Princeton University Press, 1994)

— *China Watcher, Confessions of a Peking Tom* (University of Washington Press, 2010)

Becker, Jasper, *City of Heavenly Tranquillity* (Penguin Books, 2008)

— *The Chinese* (John Murray, 2000)

Benedict, Carol, *Golden-Silk Smoke* (University of California Press, 2011)

Benton, Gregor and Lin Chun (eds), *Was Mao Really a Monster?* (Routledge, 2010)

Bergère, Marie-Claire, *Sun Yat-sen* (Stanford University Press, 1998)

Bickers, Robert, *The Scramble for China* (Allen Lane, 2011)

Black, George and Munro, Robin, *Black Hands of Beijing* (Diane Publishing, 1993)

Brautigam, Deborah, *The Dragon's Gift* (Oxford University Press, 2009)

Brown, Jeremy, and Pickowicz, Paul (eds), *Dilemmas of Victory* (Harvard University Press, 2010)

Brown, Kerry, *Ballot Box China* (Zed Books Ltd, 2011)

— *Friends and Enemies* (Anthem Press, 2009)

Buruma, Ian, *Bad Elements* (Weidenfeld & Nicolson 2001)

Chan, Koonchung, *The Fat Years* (Transworld, 2011)

Chang, Gordon, *The Coming Collapse of China* (revised edition) (Arrow Books, 2003)

Chang, Jung, and Halliday, Jon, *Mao* (Cape, 2005)

Chang, Leslie, *Factory Girls* (Picador, 2009)

Chen Guidi and Wu Chuntao, *Will the Boat Sink the Water?* (Public Affairs, 2006)

Cheng Li (ed.), *China's Changing Political Landscape* (Brookings Institution Press, 2008)

Clissold, Tim, *Mr. China* (Constable & Robinson Ltd, 2004)

Crossley, Pamela, *The Manchus* (Blackwell, 1997)

— *The Wobbly Pivot* (Wiley-Blackwell, 2010)

Dikötter, Frank, *Mao's Great Famine* (Bloomsbury Publishing Plc, 2010)

Dodson, Bill, *China Inside Out* (John Wiley & Sons, 2011)

Dumas, Charles, *China and America: A Time of Reckoning* (Profile Books Ltd, 2008)

Fenby, Jonathan, *Modern China* (Penguin, 2009; updated paperback 2010)

— *The Dragon Throne* (Quercus, 2008)

— *Generalissimo: Chiang Kai-shek and the China He Lost* (Simon & Schuster, 2003)

— *Dealing with the Dragon* (Little, Brown, 2000)

Fewsmith, Joseph, *China after Tiananmen* (Cambridge University Press, 2008)

Fingleton, Eamonn, *In the Jaws of the Dragon* (Griffin Books, 2009)

Fox, John and Godement, François, *A Power Audit of EU-China Relations* (European Council on Foreign Relations, 2009)

Friedberg, Aaron, *A Contest for Supremacy: China, America and the Struggle for Mastery in Asia* (Norton, 2011)

Friedman, Edward, *Backwards Towards Revolution: The Chinese Revolutionary Party* (University of California Press, 1974)

— Pickowicz, Paul and Selden, Mark, *Chinese Village, Soviet State* (Yale University Press, 1991)

— *Revolution, Resistance and Reform in Village China* (Yale University Press, 2005)

Halper, Stefan, *The Beijing Consensus* (Basic Books, 2010)

Hutton, Will, *The Writing on the Wall: China and the West in the 21st Century* (Little, Brown, 2007)

Gerth, Karl, *As China Goes, so Goes the World* (Hill and Wang, 2010)

Gilley, Bruce, *China's Democratic Future* (Columbia University Press, 2005)

Gittings, John, *The Changing Face of China* (Oxford University Press, 2005)

Giustozzi, Antonio, *The Art of Coercion* (Hurst, 2011)

Gladney, Dru, *Dislocating China* (Hurst, 2004)

Goldman, Merle and Leo Ou-Fan Lee (eds), *An Intellectual History of Modern China* (Cambridge University Press, 2001)

— and Roderick MacFarquhar (eds), *The Paradox of China's Post-Mao Reforms* (Harvard University Press, 1999)

Goodman, David, *The New Rich in China* (Routledge, 2008)

Gu Zhibin, *China Beyond Deng* (MacFarland, 1991)

Guo Sujian (ed), *China's 'Peaceful Rise' in the 21st Century* (Ashgate, 2006)

Jacques, Martin, *When China Rules the World* (Penguin Books, 2009)

Kissinger, Henry, *On China* (London: Penguin Books, 2011)

Kurlantzick, Joshua, *Charm Offensive* (Yale University Press, 2007)

Kynge, James, *China Shakes the World* (Weidenfeld & Nicolson, 2006)

Lieberthal, Kenneth, *Governing China* (Norton, 2004)

Leonard, Mark, *What Does China Think?* (HarperCollins, 2008)

Li Lanqing, *Breaking Through* (Oxford University Press, 2009)

Long, Simon, *Taiwan: China's Last Frontier* (Macmillan, 1991)

Lovell, Julia, *The Opium Wars* (Picador, 2011)

Mann, James, *The China Fantasy* (Penguin Books, 2008)

MacFarquhar, Roderick (ed), *The Origins of the Cultural Revolution* (3 vols) (Oxford University Press, 1974, 1994, 1999)

— *The Politics of China* (Cambridge University Press, 2011)

— *The Politics of China: The Eras of Mao and Deng* (Cambridge University Press, 2007)

— and Schoenhals, Michael, *Mao's Last Revolution* (Harvard University Press, 2008)

McGregor, Richard, *The Party, The Secret World of China's Communist Rulers* (Penguin Books, 2010)

Mackinnon, Alex and Powell, Barnaby, *China Counting* (Palgrave Macmillan, 2010)

Mann, James, *The China Fantasy* (Penguin Books, 2008)

Meisner, Maurice, *The Deng Xiaoping Era* (Hill and Wang, 1996)

Meredith, Robyn, *The Elephant and the Dragon* (W.W. Norton & Company Ltd, 2007)

Mitter Rana, *A Bitter Revolution* (Oxford University Press, 2004)

Monro, Alexander (ed.), *China, Ciry and Exile* (Eland Publishing Ltd, 2010)

Morris, Ian, *Why the West Rules – for Now* (Farrar, Straus and Giroux, 2010)

Mow, Shirley, Tao Jie and Zheng Bijun (eds), *Holding Up Half the Sky* (City University of New York: The Feminist Press, 2004)

Nathan, Andrew, and Gilley, Bruce, *China's New Rulers* (New York Review of Books Press, 2005)

— Link, Perry, and Zhang Liang, *The Tiananmen Papers* (Little, Brown, 2001)

Nolan, Peter, *State and Market in the Chinese Economy* (Macmillan, 1993)

Oi, Jean, Rozelle, Scott and Zhou Xuenguang (eds), *Growing Pains: Tensions and Opportunities in China's Transformation* (Asia-Pacific Research Center, 2009)

Orlik, Tom, *Understanding China's Economic Indicators* (FT Press Science, 2011)

Peerenboom, Randall, *China Modernizes* (Oxford University Press, 2007)

Perry, Elizabeth J. and Selden, Marl (eds), *Chinese Society* (Routledge, 2003)

Rawski, Evelyn, *The Last Emperors* (University of California Press, 1998)

Schell, Orville, *Mandate of Heaven* (Little, Brown, 1995)

Schram, Stuart, *Mao Tse-tung* (Pelican, 1970)

Selle, Earl Albert, *Donald of China* (Harper, 1948)

Shambaugh, David (ed), *Charting China's Future* (Routledge 2011)

— *China's Communist Party* (University of California, 2008)

— *The Modern Chinese State* (Cambridge, 2000)

Shirk, Susan, *Fragile Superpower* (Oxford University Press, 2008)

Short, Philip, *Mao: A Life* (Hodder and Stoughton, 1999)

Smil, Vaclav, *China's Past, China's Future* (Routledge Curzon 2004)

Solinger, Dorothy, *From Lathes to Looms* (Stanford University Press, 1991)

Snow, Philip, *The Fall of Hong Kong* (Yale, 2003)

Spence, Jonathan, *The Search for Modern China* (W.W. Norton, 1990)

— *The Gate of Heavenly Peace* (Pengun Books, 1982)

Steinfeld, Edward, *Playing Our Game: Why China's Rise Doesn't Threaten the West* (Oxford University Press, 2010)

Taylor, Jay, *The Generalissimo* (Harvard University Press, 2009)

Thaxton, Ralph, *Catastrophe and Contention in Rural China* (Cambridge University Press, 2008)

Tong, James, *Revenge of the Forbidden City: The Suppression of the Falun Gong* (Oxford University Press, 2009)

Tsang, Steve, *Yui-sang: A Modern History of Hong Kong* (I. B. Taurus, 2003)

Twitchett, Denis, Loewe, Michael, Smith, Paul Jakov, MacFarquhar, Roderick, Fairbank, John, Mote, Frederick, Franke, Herbert, Peterson, Willard, Liu Kwang-Ching and Feuerwerker, Albert, *Cambridge History of China* (Vols, 1, 3, 5, 7–15) (Cambridge University Press, 1978–2009)

Vogel, Ezra F., *Deng Xiaoping and the Transformation of China* (Harvard University Press, 2011)

Wakeman, Frederic, *Spy Master* (University of California Press, 2003)

— *Strangers at the Gate* (University of California Press, 1966)

Walter, Carl, and Howie, Fraser, *Red Capitalism* (John Wiley, 2011)

Wasserstrom, Jeffrey N., *China's Brave New World* (Indiana University Press, 2007)

— *China in the 21st Century* (Oxford University Press, 2010)

Watts, Jonathan, *When a Billion Chinese Jump* (Faber and Faber Limited, 2010)

Wo-Lap Lam, Willy, *China after Deng Xiaoping* (P. A. Professional Consultants Ltd., 1995)

— *The Era of Jiang Zemin* (Simon & Schuster, 1999)

Wood, Frances, *The Lure of China* (Yale University Press, 2009)

Yan Xuetong, *Ancient Chinese Thought, Modern Chinese Power* (Princeton University Press, 2011)

Ye Zuicheng, *Inside China's Grand Strategy* (University of Kentucky Press, 2001)

Zhao Ziyang, *Prisoner of the State* (Simon & Schuster, 2009)

Zhu Rongji, *Zhu Rongji meets the Press* (Oxford University Press, 2011)

INDEX

currency xiv, 7, 13, 241–2,
243–5, 265, 268, 369, 370

Da Vinci furniture 305
Dadong city 99
Dagong agency 242
Dai Bingguo 263
Dairy Association 307–8
Dalai Lama 102, 103, 104,
105, 106, 107, 149, 252,
267, 283
Dali 212, 213
Dalian city 55, 99, 294, 300,
314, 379, 384
Danone 174
Daoism 148, 149, 221, 306
Daoist temple 24, 89
Daokui Li, David 14
de Tocqueville, Alexis 163
death penalty 34, 79
deaths in custody 9
deaths on roads 33
democracy 377
Democracy Party of China
189
Democratic Progress Party
(DPP) 127, 128, 131
Deng Liqun 327
Deng Xiaoping 2, 18, 19, 22,
29, 42, 53, 57, 59, 60, 86,
97, 114, 115, 117, 131,
138, 139, 164–71, 174–6,
177, 178–80, 181–3, 189,
190, 197, 206, 208, 233,
234, 385, 388
biography 165–8
family 326
Southern Tour 182
in US 232
Diaoyu Islands 251
diet 21, 24, 33, 87, 169–70,
355
Dixie Mission 230
do-it-yourself 283
Donald, W. H. 228
Dong Jiqin 158
Dong Mingzhu 27–8
Dongbao village 37
Dongfeng missile 271
Dongguan 68, 174
dossiers 146
Drogba, Didier 50
drugs 303, 324
see also opium
Du Shicheng 329
Dui Hua Human Rights
Foundation 154
Dujiangyan system 356
Dunhuang 225
Dutch colonies 123–4

Dyson 304

Earth Policy Institute 336
earthquakes 10, 34, 35, 159,
192, 196, 313, 367
East Turkestan Islamic
Movement 109
Eastern Lightning 90–1
eBay 283
e-commerce 57, 281, 285,
301
Economic Observer 45
Economist 13, 246, 257
education 26, 27, 30, 343,
350, 376
see also schools
eggs 229, 257, 309
Elder Brothers 89
elections 138, 146, 161, 163,
215
electronic-manufacturing
services (EMS) 60–1,
63–7
Emergency Shelter 158
energy 2, 7, 100, 143–4, 238,
256–7, 262, 332–3, 365,
368
hydropower 365
see also coal; gas; nuclear
power; oil
environment 5, 7–8, 49,
330–9, 365–6
Environment Ministry 334–5,
337, 339, 356
Environmental Offices 7, 335
Epoch Times 150–1
Ericsson 66
Ethiopia 256
ethnic minorities 87
eunuchs 199, 201, 221,
224–5, 226
European Union (EU) 13,
183, 246–9, 262, 267, 283
Chamber of Commerce
246
euro-zone 2, 83
Ever Victorious Army 212
executions 34, 79
exports 2, 4, 5, 6, 7, 16, 32,
39, 68, 80–1, 119, 130,
142, 182, 192–3, 227–8,
229, 241, 243, 244, 368
from Hong Kong 119
oil 168

Facebook 24, 147
fakes 304–6, 312
Falun Gong 90, 150–1, 158
protest demonstrations
150

families 325–6, 340–2
famine 24, 83, 167, 203, 204,
205, 218, 293, 302
farmers 30, 37, 77, 82–3,
170–1, 174, 205, 257,
307–8, 310, 354–5, 356,
369, 374, 379
farmland 353–4, 366, 374
Fat Years, The novel 208,
344
Federal Reserve 242, 244
Fehrenbach, Franz 288
Feng shui 90
Feng Yuxiang 166
Fenshui town 81
Ferguson, Niall 14
Ferrovial 292
films 33, 161, 177, 263, 304,
336, 344
war 377
financial system 76, 368–9,
387
Financial Times 11, 27, 65, 79,
106, 242, 274, 278
fires 307
Five Dynasties and Ten
Kingdoms 223–4
Five-Year Plan, *2011–15* 41,
42, 343, 348–9, 352, 353,
385
fixed-asset investment (FAI)
135–6, 348
Flexitronics 65, 68
Flying Tigers force 230
food 244
demand 21
diet 24, 33, 87, 169–70,
355, 369
eggs 229, 257, 309
rice 87, 308, 355
safety 8, 281, 307–10, 323
transport 356
see also famine; pork
Food and Drug
Administration 303,
310
Forbes magazine 18
Forbidden City, Beijing 10,
48, 92, 96, 179, 202, 204,
215, 220, 224, 302
Ford, Henry 229
foreign direct investment
(FDI) 290
Foreign Ministry 268
forests 31, 287
Fortune 500 list 144
Foshan 68
Foxconn 31–2, 64–5, 68, 69,
71, 128, 193, 254, 280–1,
331

Jonathan Fenby has edited the *Observer* and the *South China Morning Post* and is a former bureau chief in France for the *Economist* and Reuters. He is the author of eleven books including the acclaimed *Genralissimo, The Penguin History of Modern China* and *The General*, a biography of Charles de Gaulle. He lives in London but is often in China, where he heads the team for the research service Trusted Sources, and writes for publications in Britain, the US and Asia, and broadcasts frequently.

Praise for *Tiger Head, Snake Tails,* shortlisted for International Affairs Book of the Year by The Political Book Awards 2013:

'A bestselling examination of modern China by an experienced and fluent commentator.' *Financial Times*

'An engrossing and highly informative dissection of the complexities of China today – Fenby's analysis also exhibits appropriate skepticism about the stability of China's regime and its uncertain place in the world.' David Shambaugh, professor of political science and international affairs, George Washington University, and author of *China Goes Global: The Partial Power*

'This is a one-stop account of where the fastest-growing major nation stands, and what it means for both China and the world.' *Total Politics*

'Jonathan Fenby's latest book provides an excellent introduction to the problems confronting its people as they embark on the transition to the fifth generation of leadership since the Communist takeover in 1949.' Lord Patten

'Fenby, a shrewd and experienced journalist, keeps a sober head and argues that although no economic collapse is imminent, the story does have plenty of negative.' Francis Wheen, *Mail on Sunday*

'Fenby . . . gives us a compelling, rich and readable account . . . [T]his entertaining and authoritative book is one that everyone involved with China will want to read.' Ian Morris, author of *Why the West Rules*